Die Bedeutung der Religion
für Gesellschaften
in Vergangenheit und Gegenwart

Akten
des Fünften Gemeinsamen Symposiums der
EVANGELISCH-THEOLOGISCHEN FAKULTÄT DER UNIVERSITÄT TARTU, der
ESTNISCHEN STUDIENGESELLSCHAFT FÜR MORGENLANDKUNDE und der
DEUTSCHEN RELIGIONSGESCHICHTLICHEN STUDIENGESELLSCHAFT
am 2. und 3. November 2001 zu Tartu/Estland

herausgegeben von
Manfried L.G. Dietrich und Tarmo Kulmar

Forschungen zur Anthropologie und Religionsgeschichte
(FARG)
Band 36

begründet von
Alfred RUPP†

herausgegeben von
Manfried L.G. Dietrich — Oswald Loretz

2003
Ugarit-Verlag
Münster

Die Bedeutung der Religion
für Gesellschaften
in Vergangenheit und Gegenwart

Akten
des Fünften Gemeinsamen Symposiums der
EVANGELISCH-THEOLOGISCHEN FAKULTÄT DER UNIVERSITÄT TARTU, der
ESTNISCHEN STUDIENGESELLSCHAFT FÜR MORGENLANDKUNDE und der
DEUTSCHEN RELIGIONSGESCHICHTLICHEN STUDIENGESELLSCHAFT
am 2. und 3. November 2001 zu Tartu/Estland

herausgegeben von
Manfried L.G. Dietrich und Tarmo Kulmar

2003
Ugarit-Verlag
Münster

Die Bedeutung der Religion für Gesellschaften in Vergangenheit und Gegenwart
hrsg. von Manfried L.G. Dietrich und Tarmo Kulmar
Akten des Fünften Gemeinsamen Symposiums der
    Evangelisch-Theologischen Fakultät der Universität Tartu, der
    Estnischen Studiengesellschaft für Morgenlandkunde und der
    Deutschen Religionsgeschichtlichen Studiengesellschaft
    am 2. und 3. November 2001 zu Tartu/Estland
FARG Bd. 36

© 2003 Ugarit-Verlag, Münster

Alle Rechte vorbehalten

All rights preserved. No part of this publication may be reproduced,
stored in a retrieval system, or transmitted, in any form or by any means,
electronic, mechanical, photo-copying, recording, or otherwise,
without the prior permission of the publisher.

Herstellung: Hanf Buch und Mediendruck GmbH, Darmstadt

Printed in Germany

ISBN 3-934628-15-X

ISSN 0341-8367

Printed on acid-free paper

Inhalt

Einführung vii

Lea Altnurme
Letters to the Medium or Looking to New Age for Answers 1

Riho Altnurme
The Church in Soviet Estonia.
Overt Collaboration and Covert Resistance 15

Manfried Dietrich
"Ich lehrte mein Land, die Ordnungen Gottes zu halten"
Zur Bedeutung der Religion für die antiken Gesellschaften
Mesopotamiens 25

Alar Helstein
The Heritage of an Abandoned Mistress.
The Influence of Christianity on Modern Science 47

Andres Herkel
Einige Argumente wider die Gegensätzlichkeit
von Religion und Wissenschaft 57

Henn Käärik
Einige Bemerkungen zur Max Webers Protestantismus-These 67

Thomas R. Kämmerer
man-nu ana šá ta-kil-ú lu ta-kil
"Einem jeden möge (erlaubt sein) zu glauben, woran er glaubt"-
Zur religiösen Toleranz und ihrer Auswirkung
auf die Gesellschaften des Alten Vorderen Orients 73

Tarmo Kulmar
Die Institution der Sonnenjungfrauen bei den Inkas.
Ihre Rolle in der Religion und der Gesellschaft 89

Märt Läänemets
The Way to the Bodhisattvahood in *Gaṇḍavyūhasūtra*
with Special Reference to the Term *dharmadhātu* 99

Alar Laats
An Attempt at Christological Understanding of Humanity especially in the Eastern Orthodox and the Lutheran Traditions 119

Tõnu Lehtsaar
The Psychological Consequences of Secularization 131

Linnart Mäll
The Concept of Humanistic Base Texts 137

Einike Pilli
Young Adulthood: Search for a Dream and Need of Mentoring 155

Ain Riistan
Living with the Sermon of the Mount. An Uncomfortable Presence of Transcendence 163

Peeter Roosimaa
"Wastne Testament" das erste estnischsprachige neue Testament 171

Andres Saumets
Auf dem Wege zu neuzeitlicher Toleranz und Gewissensfreiheit. Randbemerkungen zur Frage der (Nicht)tolerierung der Täufer in der Reformationszeit 187

Sergei Stadnikov
Heilige Geschichte als Paradigma am Beispiel von Jerusalem 205

Tiina Vähi
Hexenprozesse und der Werwolfglaube in Estland 215

Pille Valk
Religious Education through the Eyes of Pupils, Teachers and Headmasters 239

Indizes 253
    1. Sachen 253
    2. Namen 258
    3. Stellen 260
    4. Wörter 262

Einführung

Manfried Dietrich, Münster - Tarmo Kulmar, Tartu

Ein Jahr nach der Wiedereröffnung der EVANGELISCH-THEOLOGISCHEN FAKULTÄT DER UNIVERSITÄT TARTU 1991 trafen sich Anfang November 1992 Kolleginnen und Kollegen der jungen Fakultät unter Leitung des Gründungsdekans, Kalle KASEMAA, und der Vorsitzende der DEUTSCHEN RELIGIONSGESCHICHTLICHEN STUDIENGESELLSCHAFT, Saarbrücken, Alfred RUPP mitsamt einigen Mitgliedern der Studiengesellschaft zur Kontaktnahme und zu wissenschaftlichem Austausch in Tartu. Unterstrichen wurde der Wille zu weiterer Zusammenarbeit zwischen beiden Institutionen durch die Veranstaltung eines Symposiums am 5. und 7. November 1992, am Ende der Konsultationswoche, das dem Thema *Mensch und Religion* gewidmet war. Da das Symposium einen befriedigenden Verlauf nahm, wurde beschlossen, Kooperationen zwischen den theologisch und religionswissenschaftlich forschenden Einrichtungen von Tartu und Saarbrücken-Münster auf dem eingeschlagenen Weg weiterzuführen und auszubauen. Dies sollte, so irgend möglich, in einem Rhythmus von zwei Jahren geschehen.

Das 2. Symposium mußte wegen des Todes von Alfred Rupp, dem Vorsitzenden der Studiengesellschaft, im Januar 1993 etwas hinausgeschoben werden und fand unter der Leitung von Kalle KASEMAA am 7. und 8. April 1995 statt. Das Thema dieses Symposiums war: *Engel und Dämonen – theologische, anthropologische und religionsgeschichtliche Aspekte des Guten und Bösen.*

Das 3. Symposium mit dem Thema *Religionen in einer sich ändernden Welt* und das 4. mit dem Thema *Endzeiterwartungen und Endzeitvorstellungen in den verschiedenen Religionen* konnten jeweils im Abstand von zwei Jahren abgehalten werden: Zum 3. am 14. und 15. November 1997 lud Peeter ROOSIMAA als Dekan der Fakultät ein und zum 4. am 5. und 6. November 1999 Tarmo KULMAR.

Das 5. Symposium, das am 2. und 3. November 2001 unter der Leitung des Dekans Tõnu LEHTSAAR und unter dem Thema *Die Bedeutung der Religion für Gesellschaften in der Vergangenheit und Gegenwart* stand, fand zu Ehren der EVANGELISCH-THEOLOGISCHEN FAKULTÄT DER UNIVERSITÄT TARTU statt, die den 10. Jahrestag ihrer Wiedereröffnung 1991 feierte.

Zu dem Symposium haben 2001 nicht nur die EVANGELISCH-THEOLOGISCHEN FAKULTÄT DER UNIVERSITÄT TARTU und die DEUTSCHEN RELIGIONSGESCHICHTLICHEN STUDIENGESELLSCHAFT eingeladen, sondern auch die ESTNISCHEN STUDIENGESELLSCHAFT FÜR MORGENLANDKUNDE. Dies bedeutete eine bemerkenswerte Erweiterung nicht nur hinsichtlich der veranstaltenden Institutionen, sondern, wegen der hinzukommenden Mitwirkenden, auch hinsichtlich der behandelten Inhalte. Der damit verbundene Ausbau des interdisziplinären Gesprächs ist für die Tartuer theologischen und religionsgeschichtlichen Symposien zehn Jahre nach ihrer Einführung sehr wichtig und verhilft ihnen im Einklang mit den heute gültigen Kriterien für eine geisteswissenschaftliche Kompetenz zu einer breiteren Anerkennung. Das Programm, das die Tartuer Veranstalter für die Entfaltung des Tagungsthemas zusammengestellt haben, bietet ein entsprechend breites interdisziplinäres Spektrum an Themen, die nicht nur Disziplinen der Theologie, sondern auch der Philosophie, Folklore, Soziologie, Buddhologie, Altorientalistik und Altamerikanistik umfassen.

Das Programm, das die beiden Tagen Freitag, den 2. November 2001, und Samstag, den 3. November 2001, gefüllt hat, hatte folgende Abfolge:

Freitag, 02.11.2001
    Vormittag: Vorsitz Th.R. Kämmerer (9.15-13.15 Uhr)

Dekan Tõnu LEHTSAAR: *Eröffnung des Symposiums*
Manfried DIETRICH: *Grußwort*

Ain RIISTAN: *Living with the Sermon of the Mount. Uncomfortable Presence of Transcendence*
Peeter ROOSIMAA: *"Wastne Testament": das erste estnischsprachige Neue Testament*
Andres SAUMETS: *Auf dem Wege zu neuzeitlicher Toleranz und Gewissensfreiheit: Randbemerkungen zur Frage der (Nicht)tolerierung der Täufer in der Reformationszeit*

Tiina VÄHI: *Hexenprozesse und der Werwolfglaube in Estland*
Riho ALTNURME: *Church in Soviet Estonia: Overt Collaboration and Covert Resistance*

Nachmittag: Vorsitz Dekan Prof.Dr. Tõnu Lehtsaar (15.15-18.30 Uhr)

Manfried DIETRICH: *"Ich lehrte mein Land, die Ordnungen Gottes zu halten". Zur Bedeutung der Religion für die antiken Gesellschaften Mesopotamiens*
Thomas KÄMMERER: *man-nu ana šá ta-kil-ú lu ta-kil "Einem jeden möge (erlaubt sein) zu glauben, woran er glaubt" - Zur religiösen Toleranz und ihrer Auswirkung auf die Gesellschaften des Alten Vorderen Orients*

Sergei STADNIKOV: *Heilige Geschichte als Paradigma am Beispiel von Jerusalem*

Tarmo KULMAR: *Die Institution der Sonnenjungfrauen bei den Inkas: Ihre Rolle in der Religion und der Gesellschaft*

Samstag, 03.11.2001

Vormittag: Vorsitz Manfried Dietrich (9.15-13.15 Uhr)

Alar HELSTEIN: *The Heritage of an Abandoned Mistress: The Influence of Christianity on Modern Science*

Märt LÄÄNEMETS: *The Way to the Bodhisattvahood in Gaṇḍavyūha-sūtra with Special Reference to the Term dharmadhātu*

Linnart MÄLL: *The Concept of Humanistic Base Texts*

Andres HERKEL: *Einige Argumente wider die Gegensätzlichkeit von Religion und Wissenschaft*

Henn KÄÄRIK: *Einige Bemerkungen zur Max Webers Protestantismus-These*

Nachmittag: Vorsitz Tarmo Kulmar (15.15-17.30 Uhr)

Lea ALTNURME: *Letters to the Medium or Looking to New Age for Answers*

Einike PILLI: *Young Adulthood: Search for a Dream and Need of Mentoring*

Pille VALK: *Religious Education through the Eyes of Pupils, Teachers and Headmasters*

Tõnu LEHTSAAR: *The Psychological Consequences of Secularization*

Manfried DIETRICH: *Abschluß des 5. Symposiums und Ausblick auf das 6. Symposium Anfang Oktober 2003 mit dem Thema "Die Bedeutung von Grundtexten für die religiöse Identität"*

Im vorliegenden 36. Band der FORSCHUNGEN ZUR ANTHROPOLOGIE UND RELIGIONSGESCHICHTE kommen die aufgeführten Vorträge in zumeist überarbeiteter Form zum Abdruck – es kommt hier allerdings ein Beitrag hinzu: Dankenswerterweise hat Alar LAATS, der am Symposium nicht teilnehmen konnte, seinen dafür vorgesehenen Vortrag mit dem Titel *An Attempt at Christological Understanding of Humanity especially in the Eastern Orthodox and the Lutheran Traditions* zur Veröffentlichung im Sammelband zur Verfügung gestellt. Die Herausgeber der Akten des Symposiums danken den Referentinnen und Referenten herzlich für die Bereitschaft, ihre Vorträge für die Veröffentlichung bereitzustellen und für die Drucklegung aufzubereiten.

Die Vorträge werden nicht in der Reihenfolge wiedergegeben, wie sie, grob systematisch geordnet, während des Ablaufs des Symposiums zu Gehör gekommen sind, sondern in der alphabetischen Abfolge der Autorennamen.

Letters to the Medium
or
Looking to New Age for Answers

Lea Altnurme, Tartu

Religion as one of the ways of coping has recently attracted fairly close attention. Numerous studies have been conducted on its role in overcoming stress, depression, traumas and diseases.

Coping in general represents an ongoing transactional process between a person and its environment. Schematically, it may be regarded as a complex problem-solving process, which contains different stages of activity: the definition of the problem, the generation of different solution options, the selection of a solution, the implementation of the solution, the redefinition of the problem and the meaning of the problem to the person after it has been solved. In addition, it involves one's coping with the associated feelings (Pargament, Kennell, Hathaway, Grevengoed, Newman, Jones 1988:90). Two dimensions can therefore be observed in coping: the need to cope with the problem itself and the need to cope with the associated feelings and behaviour. Religion may be effective in either case, helping to both find the solution and to express the feelings (Pargament, Hahn 1986:196). For these purposes, religion offers a number of coping methods. Unlike the common stereotype, these methods are not necessarily defensive, passive, emotion-focused and denial-oriented (Pargament, Tarakeshwar, Ellison, Wulff 2001:498). Religion provides a frame of reference for understanding, predicting and controlling events and preserving self-esteem. In addition, it provides emotional support (Pargament, Kennell, Hathaway, Grevengoed, Newman, Jones 1988:91). Religious values may help reduce the threat perceived in a critical situation, which, when seen through one's beliefs, may turn into a challenge or opportunity. Redefinition may also offer problem-solving strategies that initially were not apparent (Ellison, Sherkat 1995:1259).

It has been observed that while in crisis, many people indeed turn to religion for support, trying to preserve what they consider important in their lives, or, if this is no longer possible, to introduce changes with the help of religion. Christopher Ellison and Darren Sherkat have identified situations which more often than others may call for religious coping: 1) "boundary experiences", which are a challenge to the entire human existence; 2) situations that destroy the concept of the world as one that is just and predictable; 3) situations that cannot be explained in a non-religious way (Ellison, Sherkat 1995:1259).

On the one hand, religion may be a positive factor in solving physical, psychical as well as mental problems. On the other hand, however, it may also have a negative impact, for instance in cases where emphasizing sin and guilt or fear of judgement may exacerbate the problems and complicate one's coping with them (Pargament, Tarakeshwar, Ellison, Wulff 2001:498; Ellison, Sherkat 1995:1260; Schnittker 2001:405).

Not everyone includes religion in the process of coping. This will more frequently be done when religious beliefs and practices are part of the person's worldview and religion is seen as a source of solving the problem (Pargament, Tarakeshwar, Ellison, Wulff 2001:509). Crucial in this respect are the influence of and support from spiritual authorities, church members or sympathisers (Maynard, Gorsuch, Bjorck 2001:72; Krause, Ellison, Shaw, Marcum, Boardman 2001:652). For instance, church members are more likely to seek religious solace than non-affiliates (Ferraro, Kelley-Moore 2001:244). This shows that the role of spiritual and emotional help as forms of social support is very important in this regard.

Religious coping has so far been researched primarily from Christian perspective, with the researchers trying to discover relationships between coping with stress, health problems or depression on the one hand and the perception of God and the frequency of service attendance and praying on the other. An example of that may be the three models of religious coping style created by Kenneth Pargament *et al.* The models have a person's relationship with God at their core. The relationship determines the different styles of problem solving: the self-directing, the deferring or the collaborative one. The self-directing style presupposes activity on the part of man, who is responsible for solving his problems. God has not been directly involved into the process. The deferring style, however, presupposes that the active role is left with God, who is expected to do the problem solving. The collaborative style is characterised by both parties - man and God - being active and collaborating (Pargament, Kennell, Hathaway, Grevengoed, Newman, Jones 1988: 91-92). This example demonstrates the importance in Christianity of the perception of God, who is often credited with activity and agency in the spiritual domain and who can be influenced by prayer. God is the one to look to for comfort, miracles, help, care and support. Such a mechanism, however, is not at all functional in New Age, where God has been replaced by Self, and activity in the spiritual world is expected from man himself. Nevertheless, New Age may be considered one of the most powerful agents, apart from Christianity, that tries to offer various means of coping in difficult situations. Christopher Ellison and Darren Sherkat have pointed out that it would also be necessary to study the potential of New Age as a coping-facilitating factor (Ellison, Sherkat 1995:1259). This article is an attempt to shed some light on the question of what opportunities for coping in difficult situations are sought from New Age.

Subjects and Method

This study is based on a fairly unusual collection of letters given to me by a medium after she terminated her activity in 1998. The medium was known as a "channeller" mediating esoteric information by means of automatic writing. Her primary means of helping people was by letter, which accounts for the existence of such a unique collection. Additionally, she operated as an artist of mediation and performed at exhibitions. Phenomena like mediation, channelling, healing, etc., have traditionally been part of New Age spirituality. It is not surprising therefore that the medium in question was clearly displaying New Age orientation.

The letters, dating from 1993-1995, were mainly written to her by those seeking help. The collection contains letters from 353 people. Some only wrote to her once while others wrote a number of times. Most of the correspondents were women (85%). This was no surprise, since women are, as a rule, more religious than men. In addition, it must be mentioned that due to cultural traditions, dependency has been valued and bred in women rather than men (Maynard, Gorsuch, Bjorck 2001:67). Therefore women, as opposed to men, are not ashamed to seek help.

It was possible to identify the places of residence of 76% of the correspondents. Twenty per cent of them lived in Tallinn, 40% in another city and 40% in a village or small town. The letters were sent from all over Estonia, without any region being unrepresented.

The age could be established with 33% of the correspondents. Fifty one per cent of them were aged 25-45 years. Twenty six per cent were younger than 25 years and 23% older than 45 years. However, 33% is too small a percentage to allow any age-related generalizations.

Analysis of the subject matter of the letters, primarily by the problems, pleas and questions presented in them, revealed four groups of letters. The first and largest was authored by those pleading for help in the field of physical or mental health or interpersonal relationships. These problems were often intertwined and further complicated by the father's or spouse's alcohol addiction. The explanations provided suggest that the problems involved a high stress load. Part of the letter writers described their situation using the word "suffering" and asked why they suffered or should suffer. Often, they expressed feelings of fear, guilt and being punished. This group of people constituted 44% of the correspondents.

The second group was composed of people who had lost a close relative or friend. They, too, often expressed feelings of guilt and being punished. However, their questions were different: "Why did it happen?", "How is the deceased doing on the other side?" and "How should I go on living now?" This group of mourners constituted 4% of the correspondents.

The third group was made up of people expressing dissatisfaction with their daily life and its routine. They wrote that their life was empty and lacking something and that they needed mental support. Such states of mind were probably occasioned by depression; however, it could not be clearly confirmed from the letters. These people turned to the medium for help in finding the purpose and meaning of their lives. The common questions asked were: "Why do I live?" and "What is my task in this life?" The group of the dissatisfied constituted 12% of the correspondents.

While the letter writers belonging to the three previous groups were mostly characterised by a predominantly secular way of thinking or a slight New Age orientation, those belonging to the fourth group were characterised by mystical experiences and magical thinking along the lines of New Age spirituality. Their problem was lack of sympathisers and the need to express themselves and share their experiences to those who would understand and accept them. Observable in them was the pursuit to get into the inner circle of the so-called spiritual people. This group of people constituted 20% of the correspondents.

A fifth group could also be observed. This comprised people familiar to each other, who shared information about camps, lectures, courses, exhibitions, etc. This group also comprised 20% of the correspondents.

This study focuses on the first group of correspondents, whose problems were related to physical or psychical complaints and complicated or failed interpersonal relationships. The reason for the focus is that this group is the largest and has to do with problems that are the likeliest to motivate one to turn to a New Age healer. Furthermore, the limited scope of the article does not permit analysis of the other groups and their problems.

It seems that turning to a medium is a fairly common form of seeking help in Estonia. At the same time, we do not know much about the people who visit a sorcerer or their problems. Further, we do not know much about the kind of help they hope to find and the basis for their hopes. Therefore, the letters to the medium are a very helpful source permitting to study all this. The letters shed light on the segment of population who would turn to a medium as well as on the problems leading to that. The letters are utterly sincere, since the writers have presumed that the medium they seek help from is a so-called "seer" from whom it is senseless to hide anything. Insofar as the process of coping is concerned, the said letters enable us to follow just a part of it. They give us a glimpse of how people perceived, defined and sought solutions to their problems, which is one of the principal issues of this study. At the same time, the letters contain no information on how help was rendered and received and how efficient it was in terms of coping. Considering the New Age context in which help was sought, the second principal question is this: What were the most popular beliefs involved in the problem-solving process, and how were they implemented?

This study makes use of the grounded theory approach, which prefers the data and the field to theoretical assumptions. This means that the subject is not studied in the traditional sense but "discovered" and defined during the study of the field. The data obtained are interpreted taking account of the context and then placed into the theoretical frame (Flick 1998:41). The reason for the selection of the grounded theory approach was that when I became the owner of the letters and started to study them, I had not much of an idea about their content. It was reasonable therefore to let the letters "speak for themselves".

Findings

The letters clearly reveal the stressful circumstances in which the people of the first group lived. Most of the problems highlighted by the authors were, according to their own explanations, of an emotional and spiritual nature, even in case of physical complaints. The problems had to do either with the writers themselves or with their close ones (mostly children or spouses). The letter writers acutely felt the need to find out the meaning of their sufferings. It seems that lack of meaning is indeed an extremely frightening experience. As evident from the letters, people are ready to suffer or even sacrifice themselves if they only had an answer to the question "why"? In their study, Giora Keinan and Dalia Sivan have described this phenomenon. In general, people tend to present their experiences in causal relationships. This tendency manifests itself in different ways and, depending on the circumstances, is also expressed in different ways. A thing that particularly vividly highlights the said tendency, however, is psychological stress. It produces a sense of losing control. As a general coping response, people commit themselves to seeking reasons in order to regain control. Consequently, stress increases people's need for identifying the reasons for their problems (Keinan and Sivan 2001:127). The causal linking of phenomena or events, regardless of its adequacy, helps a person to cope with the cognitive load that produces stress (Giora Keinan and Dalia Sivan 2001:133). It is therefore no surprise that if the finding out of reasons and meaning in a traditional way has failed, people turn to religion, here to New Age, for help. The spiritual environment for most of today's Estonians, which is characterised by a materialistic and utilitarian mentality, offers little help or even complicates coping in situations like a crisis, a loss or a severe disease. For instance, the letter writers often noted that before turning to the medium, they had tried therapeutic or psychiatric treatment, which, however, had left them disappointed. Meredith McGuire, who has studied alternative medicine in today's Western society, has said that medical approach exacerbates suffering. Formal medicine reduces a human to a clinical case instead of treating him or her as a personality. It leaves no room for his or her story, experiences of fear or suffering and thoughts or feelings (1994:241). Therefore, emotional and spiritual needs are not being met in the first place.

The correspondents of the first group can broadly be divided into two subgroups based on what solution the people themselves suggested to their problems. Those belonging to the first subgroup, who in this paper are called "waiters for a miracle", expressed the intolerability of their situation and their irreconcilability with it. The tried to restore the previous situation and expected the medium to work miracles. Those belonging to the second subgroup, who might be called "fighters with the powers of darkness", were primarily preoccupied with trying to find the causes and meaning of their miseries and, if possible, eliminating these causes. Why they are called "fighters with the powers of darkness" is discussed below.

"Waiters for a Miracle"

Despite their designation, the "waiters for a miracle" may still be regarded as people who are fairly actively seeking solution to their problem, who have not yet lost hope and who try to find help in order to escape from the intolerable situation, which they can neither render meaning nor be reconciled to, and to restore the *status quo*. This contingent of help-seekers seemed to have no religious orientation. They briefly described their problem, occasionally inquiring about its possible causes, and pleaded for help, clearly hoping for a miracle. This hope was based on the medium's reputation as a seer or oracle capable of communicating with the other world and obtaining information from there. The people hoped that there was a possibility of accessing the source of all knowledge and that there was a person capable of doing that. They hoped that somewhere there was a ready-made solution and that they only needed to get it and everything would be remedied or transformed in an instant. By this they admitted the bankruptcy of their spiritual world and survival skills. Catherine Garrett has stated that disease and misery damage a person's self and lead to suffering (Garrett 2001:338). Further developing the statement, it may be assumed that any event that is psychically shocking, including that involving loss of control over one's life, damages a person's self-understanding and ruins his or her self-image. Consequently, the desire to restore the previous situation at any cost also encompasses the desire to restore one's personal identity. This, however, is not always possible.

Investigating traumatised people, Marcia Webb and Otto Whitmer have pointed out that coping with trauma must include cognitive appraisal of the traumatic event, which implies the necessity to render meaning to the traumatic event and integrate it into a broader and more understandable scheme of reality (Webb, Whitmer :445). The same applies to the "waiters for a miracle". What they were not able to cope with was exactly the incorporation of the stress-causing event into their self-image, since they obviously lacked a suitable frame of reference to help them render meaning to it. Such a situation also forced them to turn to a medium for help. Different studies have shown that religion might be of help in this regard, since it facilitates adjustment and offers new explanations to replace the old ones, which are no longer relevant owing to the crisis of meaning and values caused by the traumatic situation. However, one means of religious coping may prove more effective than the other. For instance, seeking support from a religious group may prove more effective than bargaining with God and pleading for a miracle (Webb, Whitmer 2001:446).

Reviewing the situation of the "waiters for a miracle", two points may be emphasized: on the one hand, an experience that caused stress and shook the person's identity and world view, which in the long run forced even the "waiters for a miracle" to search for the causes and meaning of their situation (even though they themselves tried to avoid it and restore the *status quo*) in order to regain control over their life; on the other hand, their inability to deal with the experience, since their spiritual world and survival skills were inadequate for that. Such a situation certainly put them under pressure to undergo conversion, that is, to radically change their worldview, identity and basic values. Although the situation was highly favourable, it is unfortunately impossible, in most cases, to ascertain from the letters whether the conversion really took place or to establish how these cases were resolved. However, the collection also contains an occasional letter in which people thank the medium and describe the changes that had taken place in their lives after getting help. Considering the medium's role of mediating "the other side", one conceivable solution in this regard could be an experience of how the objectified world, which previously was perceived as mute matter, acquires meaning during the communication and starts to speak.

"Fighters with the powers of darkness"

This group was clearly aware of New Age literature, and their letters suggested a degree of New Age orientation. They often mentioned that they learned about the medium from an esoteric magazine. They described their difficult situation, expressed feelings of guilt, fear, suffering and being punished and searched for the cause and meaning of the misfortune that had befallen them. The feeling of being punished calls for finding out the guilt and remedying it, fear calls for regaining control and balance and suffering calls for finding out the cause and eliminating it. All these feelings expressed by the letter writers, particularly those of being punished and suffering, also represented an assessment of one's situation, and help from the medium was expected to solve the problem in its entirety. Often, these people presented their reasons for the misfortune that had befallen them, of which the commonest were bad karma, a curse and the forces of darkness. The medium's help was also sought for coping with these. Judging by this collection of letters, bad karma, a curse and the powers of darkness seemed to be the most "workable" beliefs in New Age, as they were believed to be a key to providing explanation and rendering meaning to the above mentioned feelings.

Some of the letter writers in this subgroup blamed their afflictions on crimes committed or mistakes made in their previous lives and the resulting bad karma. They believed that these crimes and mistakes caused sufferings in this life, which meant that they considered themselves responsible for their sufferings. They sought the medium's help for finding out who they had been in their previous lives and what mistakes they had made to serve punishment for. The meaning found in this manner amounted not only to an intellectual explanation but also to a search for possibilities of remedying the mistakes they assumed to have made in their previous lives. They expressed a desire to learn and receive new guidelines and hope for the future. Two examples:

> *I tend to think that it has to do with the implementation of the karma law in my case. If I knew the reason and the way I should behave, could I then remedy my life?*

and

> *Did I meet my close ones in my previous lives already? This would perhaps help me understand and organise the current [complicated] relationships?*

According to popular religion in Estonia, karma also means fate. For instance, a middle-aged woman wrote:

> *I have not protested against my fate. I am happy to be able to pay back my debt.*

Some of them believed that their sufferings were caused by a curse somebody had put on them out of revenge or envy. They described a curse as an action of the powers of darkness or an infection that may be transmitted from one person to another. From the medium, these people sought release from the curse through purification or the so-called "breaking of the curse". They hoped to renew their lives and become successful.

It may be assumed that believing in a curse and believing in karma are mutually exclusive or at least separated from each other, since one regards the misery as originating from within the person and the other from outside forces. However, this is not always the case. For instance, a young woman wrote:

> *I was told that a great curse had been put on me. If this is cosmic karma, it comes from some distant quarters and I have no fear for myself. I have fear for my child, that the karma or curse may be transmitted to it. Please find out what the curse is and what I must do to break it. I do not want my child to die due to the severity of the karma.*

Another example:

> *My husband got help indeed; however, after that the other family members started to do badly. Did my husband's karma or curse fall upon us or was it something else?*

The above examples demonstrate that in some cases a curse and karma, and even fate, are perceived as one phenomenon, like a disease that can be transmitted from one person to another and be remedied using the same means as used against a disease, by combating it and strengthening oneself. Closely related to a curse is also faith in bad energy or in the action of the powers of darkness. For instance, a mother described her son's alcohol addiction with the following words:

> *I am convinced that negative energy, or some powers of darkness, seize control of him and inspire this mindless activity, even hooligan behaviour.*

It is clear that on these occasions, too, opportunities were sought to thwart and eliminate the bad energy or the powers of darkness.

It is noteworthy that astrology, which otherwise is popular, was generally not invoked in trying to render meaning to one's problems. When introducing themselves, people indeed mentioned the sign of zodiac under which they were born, sometimes indicating their birth time to the minute. However, failed or complicated interpersonal relationships, for instance, were never blamed on the adversity of the signs of zodiac or accidents on the so-called "unfavourable configuration of stars". They never even wondered whether these might be the cause of the problems, even though astrology would lend some credence to such assumptions and, moreover, would agree well with faith in fate (which was also expressed). Obviously, the reason is that an explanation to the effect that "the stars have not been favourable to you" was an insufficient help for the people in their efforts to cope with their feelings of guilt, fear and being punished. Nevertheless, there is a connecting link between the concepts of karma and astrological predestination. In a few cases, the people assumed that under the influence of one's karma, one chooses the moment of one's birth, that is, plans one's fate, oneself. In addition, astrology could play a role in overcoming fear, for instance, since fear is always related to the future events, and astrology is invoked for predicting and planning the future in the first place (it also takes the form of "psychological counselling"). Therefore, astrology may produce a feeling of control and have a certain pacifying effect. Although there were no direct references to the applicability of this scheme in the letters (and rightly so, since the medium the letter writers turned to was not engaged in astrology), some of them contained a request to the medium to "look up" the best solution for the problem taking account of the future.

Undoubtedly, the beliefs and examples referred to above represent a magic way of thinking. It is particularly evident when the people try to help or influence another person who is seen as the source of their problem(s), such as the son with alcohol addiction. Galina Lindquist, who has investigated the proliferation of sorcery in Russia, asserts that people resort to magic when trying to restore their agency, that is, their ability to deliberately and intentionally exert an influence on the world where it has been severely reduced, in order to regain control over their life under extremely uncertain circumstances (Lindquist 2000:249). While Christians often believe that the agency originates from outside the person (from God), those having a magic mindset think it originates from the person himself. Magic vests one with power (Lindquist 2000:251). With that, a person tries to re-establish order and re-seize the initiative. During magical rites, he reconstructs himself as a sovereign agency. Such a concept, according to which people themselves are the causal agents of the cosmic forces functioning through them rather than through an institution (church), is highly typical of New Age mentality (Lindquist 2000:270). Data on magic devices and deeds aimed at exerting influence on the spiritual world in order to solve one's problem (which were performed either on the medium's advice or by the medium herself) are contained in just a few letters of thanks. Therefore, while it is possible to get a glimpse of the way people viewed their situation or even interpreted it in the spirit of New Age, the way they attempted to solve their problems and the results of these attempts can only be guessed.

Healing in New Age

The letters to the medium represent a fragment of a larger phenomenon called New Age, which in this article is viewed as both a cultic environment and a way of thinking characteristic of it. In order to understand their place in the broader community, the New Age concepts of man, his problems and their solutions are examined.

Paul Heelas has noted that there is a tendency in New Age to perceive man as one inevitably ill, whose spirit has been perverted by the patterns of upbringing, traditions, norms, etc. established in society. It is believed that materialism, competition and social demand for acting out certain roles destroy the genuinely human nature. To live by such traditions, which have been inculcated by the home, school or other institutions, is to be victimized by an unnatural, deterministic and misleading routine (Heelas 1996:18). It is generally believed that such a person is himself a source of his own problems, including illnesses. However, New Age also accepts faith in harmful agents originating from outside, such as a curse and demon-possession as well as environmental pollution. What, in this context, is illness as defined in New Age? Wouter Hanegraaff has pointed to the fact that in alternative medicine, distinction is made between the concepts *illness* and *disease*. *Disease* only denotes a biophysical condition whereas *illness* may additionally include a person's social, psychological and mental condition. *Illness* encompasses *disease* (Hanegraaff 1996:43) but may also denote different kinds of misfortune, such as poverty, unemployment, housing problems, complicated human relationships and obsessive thoughts.

The examples from the letters presented above confirm that. A curse, bad karma, and in some cases even fate were regarded as illnesses, which should recede in a way similar to healing. According to the New Age concepts of man and illness, where illness is seen as encompassing all the aspects of human life, the healing process is meant to include the entire person. Therefore, it requires paying attention to the physical, emotional and spiritual aspects of the patient's experiences. In New Age, problems, misfortunes, diseases, etc. are expected to point to the mistakes made (either in this or in some previous life); however, instead of promoting guilt, punishment and fear, attempts are made to interpret them in a more positive manner, for instance, as challenges, opportunities, experiences and, first and foremost, lessons, which should guide people on the path of spiritual development. Therefore, the different forms of therapy used in New Age pursue the goal of personal growth in addition to that of healing. This means that most of the spiritual practices found in New Age are healing practices, and vice versa. Marion Bowman has even said that the characteristic feature of the 20th century is the need for healing. Healing has turned into a new soteriology. The question, "What can I do to be saved?" has been replaced with the question, "What can I do to be healed?", and "What can I do to save the world?" with "What can I do to heal the world". The answer options are many (Bowman 1999:181).

This is a brief and schematic description of the New Age understanding of man, illness and healing. On this basis, a multitude of different forms of healing and counselling have been built. However, despite the abundance of forms, the process of problem solving and the responsibility for that is left with the afflicted party himself. Ultimately, healing, as well as spiritual growth in the process, is one's own business; no one else can accomplish that for him (that is, can heal and save him). All the mediums, healers, coaches, teachers, gurus and masters should, according to New Age teaching, be just counsellors, assistants and guides. In reality, however, they wield more power than that.

Coming back to the "waiters for a miracle" and "fighters with the powers of darkness", it may be maintained that they based the solving of their problems, fully or partly, on help from the medium, who certainly was an authority and a great hope for them. Considering the New Age context, in which help was rendered, it may be assumed that in he case of the waiters for a miracle, for instance, success in solving their problems depended on whether they were able to abandon their claims on the medium as a miracle-worker and accept her as the preacher of the New Age message instead. In the case of the "fighters with the powers of darkness", however, success in solving their problems was apparently contingent on the extent to which they were able to concentrate on coping with their own feelings rather than influencing other people, since New Age ideology (as opposed to practice) has little to offer in the last respect.

Finally, a brief account may be given of the possible positive and negative consequences of the New Age-based coping methods. Studying the religious life stories of Estonians, I noticed that bitter and antagonistic interpersonal relationships could improve when they were interpreted on the basis of the karma idea. At the same time, active search for energy vampires in one's surroundings, for instance, is highly likely to result in a deterioration of the relationships. Thus, one can probably see both positive and negative coping in New Age, as is the case with Christianity.

Conclusions

In conclusion, it may be said that the letters, which serve as a basis for this study, permit us to partially follow New Age as a way of coping. The first group (which amounted to 44% of the 353 letter writers) sought the medium's help for problems that constituted a serious stress source and had to do with themselves or their close ones. The overwhelming majority of the help-seekers were women (85%). In many cases, they were motivated to turn to the medium following a failed therapeutic or psychiatric treatment. Their primary problem was the inability to render meaning to the traumatic experience or the difficulties in rendering it. This testifies to the weakness of the materialistic and utilitarian mentality, which is widespread among the Estonians. Some of the letter writers saw the solution to their problems in a miraculous restoration of their previous situation, which they expected from the medium. Others, who were characterised by a degree of New Age orientation, leaned on different beliefs common in New Age to render meaning to their problem. The most popular among these beliefs were, karma, a curse and the powers of darkness. The beliefs lent themselves primarily to explaining the feelings of guilt, suffering and being punished associated to the problem. The letter writers saw the solution to their problem in influencing the spiritual world by the magical way of thinking they seemed to practice.

References

Bowman, Marion "Healing in the Spiritual Marketplace: Consumers, Courses and Credentialism" *Social Compass*, Vol.46, No.2, 1999

Ellison, Christopher G. and Sherkat Darren E. "Is Sociology the Core Discipline for the Scientific Study of Religion?" *Social Forces* Vol.73, No.4, 1995

Ferraro, Kenneth F. and Kelley-Moore, Jessica A. "Religious Seeking Among Affiliates and Non-affiliates:Do Mental and Physical Health Problems Spur Religious Coping?" *Review of Religious Research* Vol. 42, No.3, 2001

Flick, Uwe *An Introduction to Qualitative Research*, London: SAGE Publication, 1998

Garrett, Catherine "Transcendental Meditation, Reiki and Yoga: Suffering, Ritual and Self-Transforamation", *Journal of Contemporary Religion*, Vol.16, No.3, 2001

Hanegraaff, Wouter *New Age and Western Culture. Esotericism in the Mirror of Secular Thought*, Leiden, New York, Köln: E.J.Brill, 1996

Heelas, Paul *The New Age Movement: The Celebration of the Self and the Sacralization of Modernity*, Oxford:Blackwell, 1996

Keinan, Giora and Sivan, Dalia "The Effects of Stress and Desire for Control on the Formation of Causal Attributions", *Journal of Research in Personality*, Vol. 35, 2001

Krause, Neal; Ellison, Christopher G; Shaw, Benjamin A; Marcum, John P; Boardman, Jason D. "Church-Based Social Support and Religious Coping", *Journal for the Scientific Study of Religion*, Vol.40, No.4, 2001

Lindquist, Galina "Not my will but thine be done: church versus magic in contemporary Russia", *Scottish Journal of Religious Studies*, Vol.1. No.2, 2000

Maynard, Elizabeth A.; Gorsuch, Richard L; Bjorck Jeffrey P. "Religious Coping Style, Concept of God, and Personal Religious Variables in Threat, Loss, and Challenge Situations", *Journal for the Scientific Study of Religion*, Vol.40, No.1, 2001

McGuire, Meredith B. *Ritual Healing in Suburban America*, New Brunswick, New Jersey:Rutgers University Press, 1994

Pargament, Kenneth I. and Hahn, June "God and the Just World: Causal and Coping Attributions to God in Health Situations", *Journal for the Scientific Study of Religion*, Vol. 25, No.2, 1986

Pargament, Kenneth I; Kennell, Joseph; Hatahaway, William; Grevengoed, Nancy; Newman, Jon; Jones, Wendy "Religion and the Problem Solving Process: Three Syles of Coping" *Journal for the Scientific Study of Religion*, Vol. 27, No.1, 1988

Pargament, Kenneth I; Tarakeshwar, Nalini; Ellison, Christopher G; Wulff, Keith M. "Religious Coping Among The Religious: The Relationship Between Religious Coping and Well-Being in a National Sample of Presbyterian Clergy, Elders, and Members" *Journal for the Scientific Study of Religion*, Vol. 40, No.3, 2001

Schnittker, Jason "When is Faith Enough? The Effects of Religious Involvement on Depression" *Journal for the Scientific Study of Religion*, Vol.40, No.3, 2001

Webb, Marcia; Whitmer, Kara J. Otto "Abuse History, World Assumptions, and Religious Problem Solving, *Journal for the Scientific Study of Religion*, Vol.40, No.3, 2001

The Church in Soviet Estonia
Overt Collaboration and Covert Resistance

Riho Altnurme, Tartu

The Estonian historian Indrek Jürjo has claimed that during the Soviet period the position of the Estonian Evangelical Lutheran Church (EELC) in society was "a combination of collaboration, survival and cautious resistance". [1] In general, one can agree with this claim. Below I will attempt to characterise two facets of church activity: collaboration and resistance. Examples are provided from the period 1944-1949, when the relations and co-operation between church and state developed into the form they retained for the remainder of the Soviet period. [2]

1. Co-operation in the Sovietisation of society
1.1. Theological justifications – a connection with Marxist ideology

It is often impossible to discern where the border between Christian theology and Marxist ideology runs in church documents that called on people to support the existing order. This is partly a relatively ordinary desire to "render unto Caesar the things that are Caesar's" (Matthew 22:21), which is overshadowed by an understanding of the state as an instrument of God's (retributive) will. The desire for peace – both worldly and eternal peace – appears in the pastoral letters from the very beginning. Towards the end of the period there appears a stronger penchant towards "Christian socialism", an attempt to find a justification for the peaceful and fruitful co-existence of church and state. One may say that by that time the church was beginning to move from a passive, wait-and-see position to actively supporting the state. The elimination of the separation between church and state also appears to have been intentional. One must, of course, take into consideration the fact that almost all of these documents were

---

[1] Jürjo, Indrek. *Pagulus ja Nõukogude Eesti. Vaateid KGB, EKP ja VEKSA arhiividokumentide põhjal* [Exile and Soviet Estonia. Views based on the KGB, EKP and VEKSA archival documents], Tallinn, Umara, 1996. P. 179.

[2] The article is based on the author's PhD thesis *Eesti Evangeeliumi Luteriusu Kirik ja Nõukogude riik 1944-1949* [The Estonian Evangelical Lutheran Church and the Soviet State 1944-1949]. Dissertationes Theologiae Universitatis Tartuensis 5. Tartu, Tartu University Press, 2000 [Supplemented and corrected edition 2001].

censored by the Commissioner of the Council of Religious Affairs.[3] In the calls for loyalty made by Bishop's *locum tenens* Pähn, one can also see a desire to survive an expectedly brief period of Soviet rule without conflicts with the regime.

In a telegram sent to Stalin in November 1947, the "peoples' leader" was thanked above all for religious freedom, but also for victory over the fascist conquerors, in whose ideology there was, as the telegram stated, nothing in common with Christian teachings. "With victory over fascism, opportunities arose to implement principles important to Christians, such as equality, fraternity and friendship between peoples" – it was thus that the consistory formulated the points of contact between Christianity and Marxism. The Christian church was not tied to a specific form of government, it always had to support the state and people, "especially in a time of Socialist rule, the ideology of which has much in common with Christian ideology". It was confirmed that the consistory would call upon believers to pray for the state and its leaders, based on 1 Tim. 2; 1, 2.[4]

Submission to the Soviet regime and the will of God was required, and God wished to punish men. Penance was to lead people to repentance, which would also help God to forgive man. Bishop's *locum tenens* A. Pähn wrote in his last pastoral letter in February 1949 that God was judging his people, calling them to repentance (Rev. 2:5) and piety (5 Ms. 10; 12).[5]

By 1949-1950 a certain change had taken place in the church's description of the present situation. The language used in church documents became similar to that prevalent in the newspapers of the time. Morals became the common interest of the church and the new social order. Capitalistic morals had to disappear along with capitalism, and were replaced by Soviet morals, which was characterised by frankness and caring for one's fellow man.

> It is clear to believers that Communism offers great opportunities to implement to an unprecedented extent the humble trust and tolerant dedication affirmed by the Gospel of the early Christian congregation and Jesus Christ.[6]

---

[3] Lotman, Piret. *Tsensuur kui usuvastase võitluse meetod Nõukogude okupatsiooni algul Eestis.* – Uurimusi tsensuurist. [Censorship as a method in the battle against religion at the beginning of the Soviet occupation in Estonia] Publications of the Estonian National Library IV. Compiled by Piret Lotman. Tallinn, 1995. P. 133.

[4] Eesti Riigiarhiiv (ERA) [Estonian State Archive], fund (f.) R-1989, inventory (i.) 1, archival dossier (d.) 4, page (p.) 157, 158.

[5] Eesti Evangeelse Luterliku Kiriku Konsistooriumi arhiiv (EELKKA) [Archive of the Consistory of the Estonian Evangelical Lutheran Church], Konsistooriumi ringkirjad, peapiiskopi läkitused ja karjasekirjad (Kr, pp, kk) [Consistory Circulars, Archbishops' Missives and Pastoral Letters], EELK Piiskopi karjasekiri palvepäevaks 02.1949 [EELC Bishops' Pastoral Letter for the 02.1949 day of prayer].

[6] Ibid, EELK Konsistooriumi ringkiri [EELC Consistory Circular] No. 261, 28.04.1949.

At the same time, the denigration of the secularised churches of the Western world could not be avoided – these were "the slaves of capitalism and in the service of imperialism, under the name of cosmopolitism". On the basis of the Gospel, the suffering of millions of people in the Western world was decried. In conclusion, the desire to join "in prayers and creative work with those who seek peace and a progressive society" [7] was expressed.

It was sought to define the relations between church and state in a declaration that was to be passed by the 13th extraordinary church council (the address to members of the church was based on the above-mentioned declaration, albeit more modestly phrased). The main author of the declaration was Pastor Evald Saag, who was assisted by Jaan Kiivit Senior. Relations between church and state were defined from the point of view of the church.

> The EELC considers the Soviet regime to be a government that is compatible with the will of God, considers normal relations between church and state in conditions of the complete separation to be most appropriate, and admits that it [the government] is, due to the deep conflict between creative work and violent imperialism, on the side of creative work and in defence of peace. [8]

Co-operation with the state was also imminent in social matters:

> The EELC is raising new people in faith, the purity of customs, love of work, justice, love for one's fellow man and mercy; combating mistrust, languor, crime, hypocrisy, inanity, superstition that calls itself religion and various other mindsets that are dangerous to society; thereby working towards the victory of socialism. [9]

1.2. Participation in state campaigns and the celebration of state holidays

"Patriotic work", as it was called by the governmental bodies, was not initially very popular. The bishop's *locum tenens* told the commissioner frankly that they could not do as the Orthodox Church in Estonia had done – actively supporting the Soviet regime – since that would quite simply have appeared hypocritical. Time was required for re-orientation. [10] The church did not initially understand what the state wanted of them, and there was not a common understanding among government representatives as to what could be demanded from the church. Some patriotic activities seemed to the regime to excessively popularise the church. The church's support for the Red Army in the years 1945-46 can

---

[7] Ibid.

[8] Gosudarstvennyi Arhiv Rossijskoi Federacij (GARF) [State Archive of the Russian Federation], f. R-6991, i. 3, d. 1340, pp. 257–259.

[9] Ibid, p. 259.

[10] ERA, f. R-1989, i. 2, d. 3, p. 47.

also to a certain extent be seen as an act of compassion, and the church could not have acted otherwise. Support was mainly provided to families of war dead and war invalids.

Dates of important state events, including the October Revolution, were celebrated. In 1946 only a few services [11] dedicated to the anniversary were held, and in future these took place more often, and the consistory reminded churchgoers of the anniversary in its circulars. [12] On 17.12.1949 the consistory decided to send a congratulatory telegram to J. Stalin on the occasion of his 70th birthday. In Tallinn and county centres celebratory services were to be held, and in other congregations "the 70th birthday of Comrade Stalin was to be celebrated in dignified prayer" [13] at the service to be held on 18.12.

The clergymen of congregations attempted to help people adjust to the situation and fulfil their everyday tasks. In the Soviet state this also meant support for the Soviet system of government. In treating the issue of collectivisation, the consistory advised people in its circular to accept the situation.

> Especially now, when a thorough reorganisation is taking place in rural life in this country – individual farms being transformed into collective farms – congregation functionaries must help people make the transition to the new situation with understanding and inner peace. This path would be easier and more beneficial for them. [14]

In the 4th quarter of 1948 the commissioner noted the participation of the clergy in social reconstruction work. In several congregations confirmands also took part in this work. In Tallinn a separate working group led by the bishop's *locum tenens* was formed on the basis of congregations. The largest number of people from this group working at one time was 108. Bishop's *locum tenens* Pähn himself had worked 30 hours during 1948, pastors Kiivit and Leib each worked 54 hours, etc. The consistory expressed dissatisfaction that these were not included in the general schedule of work, which seemed to imply that their effort was not needed. [15] This is quite a good example of the state's split attitude to the church's participation in social campaigns – they were as if forced to do it, but when they began to become conspicuous in their enthusiasm, it was attempted to restrain them again, in the fear that the church would begin to acquire too much influence on people among whom the clergy worked.

At the request of the Soviet information bureau, the commissioner had A. Pähn prepare an article in which he recalled to Estonia compatriots who had fled

---

[11] Ibid, p. 97.

[12] EELKKA, Kr, pp, kk, EELK Konsistooriumi ringkiri No. 556, 01.07.1947.

[13] EELKKA, Konsistooriumi protokollid (Kprot) [Minutes of Consistory] 1949, Minutes 12, p. 1, 17.12.1949.

[14] EELKKA, Kr, pp, kk, EELK Konsistooriumi ringkiri No. 629, 02.11.1948.

[15] ERA, f. R-1989, i. 2, d. 7, p. 284.

into exile. Thus the church also had to participate in the repatriation process, [16] during which two clergymen, Paul Saar and Herbert Stillverk, returned to Estonia. Since the article gave the impression that only clergymen were being called upon to return, it was late and was written not by a repatriated pastor but by the bishop's *locum tenens*, it was not published.

On 05.07.1949 the consistory decided to declare the 4th of September a day of prayer for peace. [17] The decision was, however, amended, and the day of prayer was first held on 28.08.1949. [18] Hence the active "struggle for peace", which became the main form of expression for the church in social life, had begun. [19]

1.3. Co-operation with state security agencies

One of the most unpleasant facets of life in Soviet society was the system, created by the state security agencies, of monitoring and informing on one another, which had a significant influence on the social atmosphere of the time. For the church it has been quite unpleasant to admit that collaborators were recruited even from among the clergy, and from the very highest level down. The extent to which the promises made by agents were fulfilled is another matter.

In recruiting clergy for collaboration, the Ministry of Intelligence mainly used previous anti-Soviet activities to blackmail the recruits. Later, when an agent proved untrustworthy, the previous deeds were added to the charge(s) against him. Initially agents generally informed others that they had been recruited. In about 1949 the Ministry of Intelligence began to carry out purges among its agents and attempted to determine who could be considered a "vetted" agent. Agents were recruited among the clergy, the managing bodies of congregations and also among the ordinary members of congregations who may have access to information of interest to the state security agency, especially concerning the attitudes of the leadership of the church.

All of the members of the consistory (apart from one exception – Joosep Liiv) were in different periods collaborators. The level of co-operation differed,

---

[16] A total of 20,575 people were repatriated to the ESSR between 1945 and 1950, of whom 9450 were prisoners of war who had been forcibly returned. The remaining 11,125 had not all returned voluntarily. By 1949 repatriation had more or less come to an end. — Jürjo, I. Pagulus [Exile]. P. 17.

[17] EELKKA, Kprot 1949, Protokoll [Minutes] 7, p. 3, 05.07.1949.

[18] EELKKA, Kr, pp, kk, EELK Konsistooriumi ringkiri No. 549, 17.08.1949.

[19] A book summing up the church's struggle for peace, entitled *Eesti Evangeelne Luterlik Kirik ja rahuliiikumine* [The Estonian Evangelical Lutheran Church and the peace movement] was published in as late as 1986. Compiled by Tiit Salumäe. Publication of EELC Consistory, Tallinn, 1986.

insofar as this can be determined from the extant materials. Members of the consistory arrested during this period were all characterised as double agents who provided no useful information. The few surviving references to their reports are exceptions to the rule. In reorganising the consistory, the Soviet regime attempted to find more effective agents to staff the new church leadership. On the basis of the reports, it appears that, of the new members of the consistory, Lembit Tedder, Georg Klaus and Julius Voolaid were the most active collaborators. Less information is available about the other new members. In the case of Jaan Kiivit Senior, one may specifically speak of reports about Paul Voldemar Koppel, and Edgar Hark is mentioned as an agent in connection with the reorganisation of the consistory, [20] as is Albert Roosvalt.

The main task of agents of the state security agency was the gathering of information about the attitudes of others (and one another). One of the most important operations was the replacement of the membership of the consistory with more loyal individuals, which took place with the assistance of freshly recruited agents. In the second half of 1949 repatriates Paul Saar and Herbert Stillverk were quite actively monitored.

There are at least indirect data that all later Soviet-era archbishops co-operated with the internal security apparatus. The real extent of the work of each collaborator with the state security agency cannot be fully determined on the basis of the sources presently available. There are few comments that anyone directly refused recruitment. There is even less source material concerning co-operation with the state security agency in the later period.

2. Anti-Soviet opposition in the church
2.1. Participation in underground resistance

In the period directly after the war, part of the clergy participated quite actively in the underground resistance (including the activities of the "forest brothers"), especially in the area of "anti-Soviet agitation", as the bodies of state authority referred to the exchange of views. In the war many clergymen had fought against the Soviet regime. This also led the Religious Affairs Council, which co-ordinated religious affairs across the Soviet Union, to characterise Lutherans as supporters of fascism. [21]

In the first wave of arrests, in 1944-1945, the authorities mainly punished clergymen for anti-Soviet activities during the German occupation. Of 13 arrested Lutheran pastors, only two were accused of anti-Soviet activities during the new Soviet occupation. Others were accused of earlier co-operation with the German occupation regime, which had generally been of a rather innocent

---

[20] I. Jürjo also refers to his activity as a so-called route agent. — Jürjo, I. Pagulus. P. 161.

[21] According to report by UN [Council of Religious Affairs] Chairman Poljanski on 25.07.1945. — GARF, f. R-6991, i. 3, d. 12, p. 25.

nature, although there were exceptions, such as voluntarily joining the German army or police. [22]

In connection with one arrestee, one must recount an extraordinary story from earlier times. Pastor Johann Ekbaum had taken part in a "counter-revolutionary uprising" in the southern part of Pärnu County in 1941. From the 3rd to the 8th of July power in the vicinity of Kilingi-Nõmme was held by Estonian freedom fighters. According to the indictment, Ekbaum, who was then pastor of the Saarde congregation, was one of the main organisers, was also in contact with the German Army Command and acquired weapons from them. [23]

Only one of the clergymen arrested in that period was accused of having concealed "forest brothers" [members of the underground resistance]. Thus it may appear that initially support for the underground resistance was not great among the clergy. In the context of future developments, however, one may argue that the state security apparatus simply did not yet possess enough information. It was not yet possible to monitor the content of sermons, and there is only one case in which a complaint was lodged for precisely that reason. [24] In later periods state security reports frequently contain excerpts from sermons, and in the 1960s, within the framework of the atheism campaign, special social action groups were created for the monitoring of sermons.

A second wave of arrests took place between 1948 and 1951, when more than 10 clergymen were arrested. [25] Now the reasons for arrest no longer lay in the past, but in the period under discussion in this paper. The main accusation was "anti-Soviet agitation", which referred to the free expression of one's (anti-Soviet) political views. Often the punishment appears to have fallen on more religiously active clergymen such as Harri Haamer for instance. More surveillance data were gathered about him than about any other clergyman. Elmar Kull may be considered a typical example of a pastor accused of anti-Soviet agitation. Among other things, he apparently referred to the five-pointed Soviet star as the symbol of the antichrist. [26] There were clergymen whose participation in anti-Soviet activities was known, but who were monitored in the hope of gathering data about their connections.

In conclusion, it may be said that a great number of clergymen participated in underground resistance as abettors/agitators. In their public statements they most often expressed the hope, widespread among the people, that the Soviet regime would soon fall. Some also had connections with the underground

---

[22] E.g. Valter Rõude (Vaher, Ülo. Eesti Evangeelse Luterliku kiriku represseeritud õpetajad. EELK UI diplomitöö [Repressed pastors of the Estonian Evangelical Lutheran Church]. Voka, 1997. P. 86) and Mihkel Laid (Ostrov) (Branch of Estonian State Archive (former Party Archive) (ERAF), f. 129, i. 1, d. 23752, pp. 47, 74).

[23] ERAF, f. 130, i. 1, d. 13136, pp. 2-4.

[24] ERA, f. R-1989, i. 2, d. 4, pp. 4, 5.

[25] In the years 1948-1949 10, data for later years have not been checked.

[26] ERAF, f. 131, n. 1, s. 211, l. 204.

movement (the forest brothers). The conviction that clergymen would not be arrested for propagandistic reasons, since this could harm the Soviet Union's relations with other countries gave the clergymen added courage. [27] It was for this reason that the second wave of arrests was so unexpected. It is possible that since the clergy did not hide their views (public speeches, sermons, etc.), they were more vulnerable than others. Known anti-Soviet activities were used by the state security apparatus for blackmailing people into becoming agents.

In later periods the relations between clergy and resistance were relatively cold. Both the structure of the Lutheran church under state control and Estonians' (and resistance fighters') alienation from the church have been noted as reasons for this. In the years 1955-1985 only one Lutheran clergyman, Harri Mõtsnik, was arrested. He was also not sent to a prison camp, but was released after a "sincere confession". At the end of the 1970s clergymen were, however, forced to change congregations as punishment for the active propagation of youth work (Villu Jürjo) and were held at psychiatric hospitals due to their nationalist views (Vello Salum). [28] The church nevertheless maintained a certain anti-Soviet image, and during the Soviet period people also joined the church for political reasons. Thus many clergymen were active in politics during and after the restoration of Estonia's independence.

2.2. Protests against state interference in church work

Initially the church leadership did not restrain itself, and protested when the authorities interfered with the work of the church. The consistory very frequently complained about the take-over of a congregations' rooms.

In 1945, for instance, a letter from the Elva congregation requesting that rooms be guaranteed to the congregation instead of permitting these to be transferred to a tractor station was forwarded to the commissioner. [29] Complaints were also made against the illegal prohibition of church choirs and Holy Communion at Tallinn Central Hospital, and a plea was made for a more flexible approach to the duration of confirmation.

One letter of support written by the consistory for an arrested clergyman – Bernhard Talvar, pastor of the Haljala congregation – has been preserved. In a letter sent in 1945 the People's Commissar for State Security of the ESSR was requested to release Pastor Talvar from arrest and into the custody of members

---

[27] E. Paldra apparently expressed himself thus. — ERAF, f. 131, i. 1, d. 114, p. 90.

[28] Niitsoo, Viktor. *Vastupanu 1955-1985* [Resistance 1955-1985]. Tartu, Tartu University Press, 1997. Pp. 112-116.

[29] EELKKA, Kirjavahetus usuasjade volinikuga (Kuv) [Correspondence with Commissioner of Council of Religious Affairs] 1945, Usuasjade Nõukogu NSVL RKN juures ENSV volinikule [Council of Religious Affairs under the aegis of the USSR Council of People's Commissars], No. 289, 14.03.1945.

of the consistory. The justification given for this was the great shortage of pastors and the poor health of the arrestee. [30] The consistory also disputed the entry of pastors in the list of *kulaks* – in 1947 a letter of protest was sent to the commissioner in support of Uustal, Dean of Viljandi and Laurson, pastor of Sangaste congregation, in which it was stated that "pastors are only the servants of their people and do not own land, but the land they use belongs instead to the congregations". [31] Thus they could not be considered *kulaks*.

In 1947 it was sought to suspend the agreements for the use of the churches, since these did not provide for the use of land and pastorates by the churches. [32] At the same time, the consistory protested against the closure of the university church in Tartu. The justification provided for this was that not closing the church would mean acting in accordance with the example of the rest of the Soviet Union, where churches were being returned to religious societies. [33] Although such protests did not generally bear tangible results (perhaps the letter about confirmation had some effect, and as a result permission was granted to make the duration of confirmation more flexible), these gave evidence of the church's dissatisfaction with the existing order and of the courage to express that dissatisfaction.

The consistory's protest against the speech by Minister of Education Arnold Raud at the Estonia-wide meeting of educational workers in 1947 was quite extraordinary. The speech was also published in the press. [34] The Minister of Education demanded the intensification of ideological education among young people, justifying this with the widespread attendance of confirmation classes. According to the minister, in schools a battle was to be launched against "the opium of the people". Anti-religious articles were to appear in the press. The presentation was discussed at the 09.09.1947 meeting of the consistory, and it was decided to change the schedule for the celebration of the 30th Anniversary of the October Revolution – "the address to the people should be cancelled, because the senders of the address have, due to the authoritative speech by Minister Raud, been belittled in the eyes of the people". [35] Instead it was decided to send a greeting to J. Stalin. [36] At the same session the consistory took an official position concerning A. Raud's speech, primarily disparaging the offensive remarks contained therein about the clergy and the faithful. In ad-

---

[30] EELKKA, Kuv 1945, NSVL RKN juures asuvale Usuasjade nõukogu volinikule ENSV-s [To Commissioner of Council of Religious Affairs in ESSR under the aegis of USSR Council of People's Commissars], 02.1945.

[31] EELKKA, Kuv 1947, Usukultusasjade Nõukogu Volinikule Eesti NSV-s, No. 587 [To the Commissioner of the Council of Religious Affairs in the Estonian SSR], 23.10.1947.

[32] Ibid, No. 323, 28.05.1947.

[33] Ibid, No. 601, 22.10.1947.

[34] "Nõukogude Õpetaja" [Soviet teacher] No. 35 (177), 23.08.1947. P. 3.

[35] EELKKA, Kprot 1947, Protokoll [Minutes] 7, p. 2, 09.09.1947.

[36] ERA, f. R-1989, i. 1, d. 4, pp. 157, 158.

dition, the consistory submitted a complaint to A. Veimer, Chairman of the Council of Ministers of the ESSR, in which reference was made to the constitutional right to "freedom to perform religious practices". Both the state security apparatus and the Commissioner of the Council of Religious Affairs devoted great attention to the incident (the consistory's actions constituted refusal to do patriotic work, which was considered a priority). The above-mentioned incident was of great significance in the subsequent summary of charges presented upon the arrest of Pähn. [37] The state security agency responded sharply to the protest, and the replacement of members of the consistory began from this point. The consistory's protest signalled to the Soviet authorities the actual attitudes of church leaders who had been considered loyal. Protests became henceforth much less frequent.

Conclusion

The role of the church in Soviet society was to continue to hold an intermediary position – as a tolerated organisation, overtly pro-Soviet, but at the same time covertly in opposition to the existing regime. The role of the clergy as pastors was thus endangered due to their inability to serve as an example by achieving harmony between words and deeds, yet had to follow the same patterns of behaviour as did other Soviet citizens, doing one thing and thinking something else. The beginning of the Soviet period also offers examples of active resistance, but these are nevertheless exceptions. It was only towards the end of the period that members of the resistance arose from the ranks of the church.

---

[37] Cf. Paul, T. Leeri. P. 505.

"Ich lehrte mein Land, die Ordnungen Gottes zu halten"
Zur Bedeutung der Religion für die antiken Gesellschaften Mesopotamiens

Manfried Dietrich, Münster

1. Einleitende Bemerkungen

Für das Symposiums-Thema *"Die Bedeutung der Religion für Gesellschaften in der Vergangenheit und Gegenwart"* sei im folgenden die Welt des a n t i k e n M e s o p o t a m i e n s unter dem Thema *Zur Bedeutung der Religion für die antiken Gesellschaften Mesopotamiens* zum Sprechen gebracht. Dabei sollen sumerische, babylonische und assyrische Texte nach der Relevanz der Religion in der Gesellschaft befragt werden.

Der Behandlung des Themas seien einige Überlegungen zur Definition der beiden zentralen Begriffe "Religion" und "Gesellschaft" vorgeschaltet. Dabei soll der Frage nachgegangen werden, inwieweit diese Begriffe bei der Betrachtung mesopotamischer Texte angewendet werden können. Schließlich sind beide unserem abendländischem Denken entsprungen und dem Vorderen Orient, zumal dem antiken, fremd.

1.1. "Religion"

Die Definition des Begriffs "Religion" ist in der modernen Diskussion stark umstritten, wie beispielsweise R. ALBERTZ (1999, 10-11) feststellt:

Theologie, Altertumswissenschaften, Religionsgeschichte, Ethnologie bzw. Kulturgeographie, Religionssoziologie und Religionspsychologie haben je eigene Konzepte zum Religionsbegriff entwickelt, die sich teils ergänzen und befruchten, teils aber auch stark divergieren.

Eine informative Auswahl von Zitaten für das Verständnis des Religionsbegriffs führt John BOWKER, der Herausgeber DES OXFORD-LEXIKON DER WELTRELIGIONEN, im Einleitungskapitel *Religion* an — dort findet sich beispielsweise auch die des Herausgebers John BOWKER, eines Soziobiologen (J. Bowker 1999, xvii):

Religionen sind die frühesten kulturellen Systeme zum Schutz der Genvervielfältigung und der Aufzucht von Kindern. . .

Moderne Religionswissenschaftler vertreten ähnlich John BOWKER die These, daß Religion und Kultur ineinandergriffen. In Anlehnung an ein Denkmodell von Dario SABBATUCCI, der von der *Auflösung des Religionsbegriffs im Kulturbegriff* spricht (D. Sabbatucci 1988, 57-58), formuliert etwa Günter KEHRER (1998, 419):

> *Religion war christliche Religion, unterscheidbar von Kultur, die von dieser Religion geprägt wurde und die diese Religion prägte. DAVIO SABBATUCCI hat diese Dialektik von Kultur und Religion in ihrer historischen Singularität eindrücklich herausgearbeitet bis zu der Konsequenz, den Religionsbegriff in den Kulturbegriff aufzulösen und damit den Gegenstand "Religion" verschwinden zu lassen.*

Dieses Verständnis des Begriffs "Religion" ist verzerrend einseitig und kann eine latente Angst vor deren transzendenten Kraft nicht verbergen. Alfred RUPP hat dieses Verständnis vor einem Jahrzehnt mit folgender Begründung zurückgewiesen (A. Rupp 1991, 161):

> *Es wird verkannt, daß "Religion" sowohl als Ganzes als auch in Gestalt der einzelnen Gegebenheiten immer in komplexen Zusammenhängen steht, worunter "Kultur" und "Gesellschaft" allerdings nichts anderes als einzelne Aspekte neben anderen sind. Wenn sie ... übersystematisierende Funktion erhalten, führen sie zur Verfehlung des Gegenstandes der [Religions-]Forschung.*

Nach Alfred RUPP (1984, 18) ist Religion aus der Sichtweise des Menschen e i n e *transzendente Norm*, die einerseits,

> *im Hinblick auf die "Transzendenz", das unmittelbare Einsichtsvermögen des Menschen überschreitet,*

und andererseits,

> *im Sinne des "Normativen", das entscheidende Zentrum für das gesamte menschliche Handeln, für die gesamte menschliche Existenz ist.*

Die Kultur beschreibt nach Alfred RUPP (1984, 18-19), anders als die Religion,

> *die Gestaltung von Umwelt als Möglichkeit personaler Existenz und als konkrete Selbstdarstellung des Menschen. In diesem Sinne durchdringt Kultur alle drei Umweltbereiche: die "naturhafte Umwelt", die "personhafte Umwelt" und ... die "kulturelle Umwelt". Grundlage für die kulturelle Wirksamkeit des Menschen ist vor allem die naturhafte Umwelt. Aber auch die personhafte Umwelt wird in menschliches Kulturschaffen einbezogen, z.B. indem der Mensch Gemeinschaftssysteme erschafft und für ihren Fortbestand sorgt.*

Die von Alfred RUPP vertretene Gegenüberstellung von Kultur und Religion baut also darauf auf, daß Kultur dem Bereich menschlichen Wirkens zugehört und Religion ihren **Ausgangspunkt außerhalb** dessen hat und auf einer transzendenten Ebene liegt, die sich dem unmittelbaren Einsichtsvermögen des Menschen entzieht — eine vergleichbare Einstellung gegenüber der Religion vertritt beispielsweise auch Alfred Bertholet, der im WÖRTERBUCH DER RELIGIONEN folgende Definition wiedergibt (A. Bertholet 1985, 504 l.):

Formal ist R. eine unbedingte Sinngebung des Lebens f. Individuum u. Gemeinschaft in Beziehung auf eine überindividuelle u. überkollektive sinnsetzende "transzendente" Macht, material entfaltet sie sich in Kultus, Mythus u. Ethos.

Über diese Tatsache ist m.E. Rechenschaft abzulegen, wenn man sich mit dem Symposiumsthema *"Die Bedeutung der Religion für Gesellschaften in der Vergangenheit und Gegenwart"* beschäftigt. Schließlich setzt allein diese Formulierung eine Differenzierung zwischen den Begriffen "Religion" und "Kultur" voraus und nimmt damit eine Stellung ein, die der entgegensteht, die sich in der modernen Religionswissenschaft immer weiter ausbreitet.

Eines ist klar: Wenn man sich mit der Relevanz von Religion im altmesopotamischen Denken und deren Widerhall in der Literatur beschäftigt, dann gilt die Forderung, sich Rechenschaft über den Begriff "Religion" abzulegen, in erhöhtem Maße. Nur wenn der Begriff "Religion" als "transzendente Norm" und nicht als eine Facette der "Kultur" verstanden wird, kann man ihn auf die betrachteten Texte anwenden. Denn hier zeigt es sich auf Schritt und Tritt, daß die Religion als "transzendente Norm" gilt.

Als "transzendente Norm" strahlt die Religion auf alle Bereiche der Kultur (wie etwa Kunstschaffen, Architektur, Wissenschaft, Literatur) aus, steht aber nicht auf ihrer Ebene.

1.2. Gesellschaft

Der Begriff "Gesellschaft" bezeichnet das jeweils umfassendste System menschlichen Zusammenlebens und bezieht sich auf eine nicht bestimmte Summe von Individuen, die durch ein Netzwerk sozialer Beziehungen miteinander in Kontakt stehen (vgl. N. Luhmann und H. Wienold 1995, 235-236). Man verwendet diesen Begriff deswegen nur in Verbindung mit spezifizierenden Beiwörtern wie etwa "bürgerliche", "entwickelte", "tribale", etc.

In der Religionswissenschaft spielt der Begriff "Gesellschaft" als übergeordnete, von Soziologen substanziierte Größe nur eine untergeordnete Rolle. Hier ist eher der teilweise deckungsgleiche Begriff "Gemeinschaft" angesiedelt, die

auf instinktivem Gefallen oder auf gewohnheitsbedingter Anpassung oder auf ideenbezogenem gemeinsamen Gedächtnis der beteiligten Personen beruht (F. Hegner 1995, 228). Für die Gemeinschaft ist das Individuum konstitutiv: Ohne Individuen gibt es keine Gemeinschaft, die einerseits die personhafte Umwelt des Individuums ist und andererseits durch das Individuum repräsentiert wird (vgl. A. Rupp 1984, 19-20).

Der Begriff "Gesellschaft" ist wegen seiner abstrakten Konnotation durchaus problemlos auf die Aussage mesopotamischer Texte anwendbar, wenn diese von der *awīlūtu* "Menschheit, Menschen" [1] sprechen, die ein Netzwerk sozialer Beziehungen verbindet. Es ist aber zu überlegen, ob nicht auch hier der Begriff "Gemeinschaft" passender wäre; denn die Texte haben dann, wenn sie von *awīlūtu* "Menschheit, Menschen" sprechen, weniger anonyme Zeitgenossen einer grenzenlosen Gesellschaft als vielmehr eine überschaubare Interessen- und Lebensgemeinschaft im Blick, wie sie sich beispielsweise aus einer Nachbarschaft ergibt.

1.3. Zusammenwirken von Religion und Gesellschaft

Da für die "Gemeinschaft" — das gilt letztlich auch für die Gesellschaft — das Individuum konstitutiv ist und die von ihm ausgeübte Religion als transzendente Norm verstanden wird, ist bei der Betrachtung des Zusammenwirkens von Religion und Gemeinschaft aufgrund der Aussagen einschlägiger Texte zuerst die Frage nach dem Einwirken der Religion auf das Individuum zu stellen. Sobald von diesem gesagt wird, daß es auf welchem Wege auch immer — beispielsweise über die Magie oder die selbstauftretende oder herbeigeführte Mantik — eine direkte Verbindung mit der transzendenten Ebene bekommen hat, kann sich die Frage anschließen, in welcher Weise und in welchem Umfang das Individuum seine Erfahrung an die Gemeinschaft weitergegeben hat. Daß sich das "angesprochene Individuum" in seiner Beschreibung des Ereignisses an Formen gehalten hat, die ihm von der transzendenten Norm vorgegeben waren, versteht sich — die Prophetinnen und Propheten der antiken Welt Altsyriens, Assyriens und des Alten Testaments illustrieren dies aufs beste. Als Beispiel sei das Traumgesicht der Addu-dūrī von Māri genannt, das auf eine politische Katastrophe zur Zeit des Königs Zimrī-Līm am Anfang des 17. Jh.s v.Chr. weist und für den König eine ernste Warnung ausspricht — ARM 10,50 (siehe M. Dietrich 1986, 89-90):

> (3) Seit dem Untergang des Hauses deines Vaters (Jaḫdun-Līm) (4) habe ich nie wieder einen derartigen Traum (5) gesehen — mein Erlebnis war (6) — wie auch schon früher — (7) ein doppeltes: (8) In meinem Traum trat ich in den Tempel der Bēlet-ekallim (9) ein, und (— siehe da! —) Bēlet-

---

[1] Wolfram vom Soden, *Akkadisches Handwörterbuch* (Wiesbaden 1958-1981), S. 91 a: "Menschheit, Menschlichkeit"; *The Assyrian Dictionary of the Oriental Institute of the University of Chicago* A/2 (1968), S. 57-63: "mankind, etc.".

ekallim (10) war nicht an ihrem Ort! Auch die Statuetten, (11) die (gewöhnlich) vor ihr (stehen,) waren nicht vorhanden! (12) Ich sah es und weinte unaufhörlich. (13) Dieser mein Traum geschah während der ersten Nachtwache (: nach Anbruch der Dunkelheit zwischen 18 und 21 Uhr). (14) Ich wandte mich um, und da steht Dādā, ein Priester (15) der Ištar von Qabra, (16) im Tor (zur Nische) der Bēlet-ekallim (17) und libiert Bier. (18) (Dabei) ruft er ständig folgendes (19) aus: "Kehre zurück Dagān! (20) Kehre zurück Dagān!" Solches (21) ruft er ständig aus.

Das zweite (meiner Erlebnisse): (22) Eine Ekstatikerin hat sich im Tempel der Anunnītum (23) erhoben und gesagt: "Zimrī-Līm, (24) ziehe nicht zu einem Ausmarsch aus, (25) bleibe in Māri!" (26) Ich selbst bitte nun inständig: (27) "Mein Herr sei nicht nachlässig, (28) sich selbst in Schutz zu nehmen!" . . .

Neben der Betrachtungsweise des Zusammenwirkens von Religion und Gesellschaft aus der Sicht des Individuums steht gleichberechtigt die aus der Sicht der Gesellschaft in Gestalt einer Interessen- und Lebensgemeinschaft. Sie bietet als Größe, die von der Religion als transzendenter Norm geprägt ist, den Raum für das aktive Individuum. Dieses kann sich auf der einen Seite innerhalb der Grenzen der Gemeinschaft frei bewegen und entwickeln, wird auf der anderen Seite aber auch durch deren Grenzen in Schranken gehalten und geschützt. Damit stehen wir — weniger im Blick auf die Einstufung der Religion als Bestandteil der Kultur als vielmehr im Blick auf die Funktion der Religion innerhalb der Gesellschaft — der Sentenz des Soziobiologen J. BOWKER nahe, die oben schon hervorgehoben worden ist:

Religionen sind die frühesten kulturellen Systeme zum Schutz der Genvervielfältigung und der Aufzucht von Kindern...

2. Zur Bedeutung der Religion für die antiken Gesellschaften Mesopotamiens

2.1. Vorbemerkung

Im Blick auf die antiken Gesellschaften Mesopotamiens — das gilt auch für die anderer Regionen der Alten Welt — wird gerne etwas mitleidig festgestellt, daß sie sich noch auf der Stufe jener befänden, die 'voll von der Religion durchdrungen' seien. Wenn man Texte betrachtet, die sich mit religiösen Themen beschäftigen, dann kann dies nur bestätigt werden: Sie geben zu verstehen, daß das Leben religiös orientiert ist und sich innerhalb der Formen abspielt, die die Religion als transzendente Norm vorgegeben hat. In den folgenden Ausführungen soll anhand von Sprüchen, Abschnitten aus Briefen, Gebeten und Liedern, Königsinschriften und epischen Werken die allgemeine Gültigkeit dieser Beobachtung aufgezeigt werden — Mythen, in denen Götter handeln, seien zunächst unberücksichtigt.

Vorneweg ist noch zu festzuhalten, daß sich die meisten Texte Aussagen über das religiöse Leben eines *Individuums* machen. Ob es sich bei diesem um einen König oder eine andere Person handelt, ist weniger von Belang.

Auswirkungen der Religion auf das Verhalten der *Gesellschaft* als mehr oder weniger weit gefaßte Lebensgemeinschaft kommen verhältnismäßig selten zur Sprache. Das bestätigt die Tatsache, daß das Individuum für die Gesellschaft konstitutiv ist.

Folgende Themenbereiche sollen im Mittelpunkt der Betrachtungen stehen:
1. *Persönliches Glück, Gesundheit und öffentliche Anerkennung als Zeichen für die Religionsgebundenheit eines Individuums* (Punkt 2.2) und
2. *Ordnung und sozialer Friede im Lande als Zeichen für die Religionsgebundenheit der Gesellschaft* (Punkt 2.3).

Im abschließenden Punkt (3) wird eine Zusammenfassung geboten.

Die Texte, die nebeneinandergestellt und damit auch in einem thematischen Zusammenhang gesehen werden, stammen aus unterschiedlichen Literaturgattungen und wurden in einem Zeitraum von über 1.000 Jahren niedergeschrieben. Dieses Vorgehen mag aufs erste unübersichtlich erscheinen, gibt aber gleichzeitig auch zu verstehen, daß Literaturgattungen keine Grenzen für den behandelten Stoff darstellen und daß die Einstellung eines Bewohners von Mesopotamien gegenüber der Religion als lebensbestimmender transzendenter Norm über den langen Zeitraum von mehr als Tausend Jahren mehr oder weniger unverändert geblieben ist.

In der folgenden Darstellung kommen zuerst Sprüche aus sumerischen und babylonischen Sammlungen zu Wort. Daran anschließend werden Gebete und Lieder vorgestellt, die geeignet sind aufzuzeigen, daß die Sinnsprüche aus der Lebenserfahrung von Individuen abgeleitet worden sind — je ein Zitat aus einem Brief an den König und aus einer Königsinschrift werden ergänzend dazugenommen.

2.2. *Persönliches Glück, Gesundheit und öffentliche Anerkennung als Zeichen für die Religionsgebundenheit eines Individuums*

2.2.1. *Sumerische und babylonische Sprüche*

In sumerischen und babylonischen Spruchsammlungen sind Maximen überliefert, die als Voraussetzung für ein erfolgreiches und glückliches Leben die innere Verbindung mit der Gottheit nennen, die nach außen in gottbezogene Aktivitäten einmündet. Als Beispiel seien folgende beiden Sprüche angeführt, von denen der erste sumerisch abgefaßt ist und vom Anfang des 2. Jt.s stammt und der zweite babylonisch aus dem 1. Jt. v.Chr.; auch wenn deren Abfassungszeit um etwa 1.000 Jahre auseinanderliegt, geben beide dieselbe Einstellung wieder. Also kann man davon ausgehen, daß sie ein gleichbleibendes mesopotamisches

Denken spiegeln, das für die Akzeptanz der transzendenten Norm im täglichen Leben symptomatisch war.

— Der sumerische Spruch ist in der Sammlung 26 A 12 überliefert (B. Alster 1997, 279):
Gottesfurcht schafft Wohlergehen,
   Klagelieder lösen Sünde,
   Opfer verlängern Leben.

— Der babylonische Spruch stammt aus der Sammlung "Ratschläge und Ermahnungen" (W. von Soden 1990, 168):
(143) (Gottes-)Furcht erschafft Gutes,
   (144) das Opfer bewirkt Leben über alle Erwartung,
   (145) auch (erreicht) das Gebet die Sündenvergebung.
(146) Den Gottesfürchtigen mißachtet nie[mand],
   (147) wer die Anunnaku fürchtet, verlängert [seine Tage]!

Beide Sprüche gehen davon aus, daß das gottgefällige, religiöse Leben nicht nur das eigene Leben positiv gestaltet, sondern auch, wie der babylonische Spruch verdeutlicht, zu einer Anerkennung in der Gesellschaft führt:

(146) Den Gottesfürchtigen mißachtet nie[mand].

Diese Sprüche formulieren positive Auswirkungen eines gottgefälligen Lebens, andere nennen negative: Das persönliche Unglück ist ein Zeichen dafür, daß sich das Individuum von seiner Gottheit entfernt hat, so daß die Gottheit ihm nicht mehr helfend zur Seite stehen kann. Das drücken folgende beiden sumerischen Sprüche aus:

— Spruch aus der Sammlung UET 6/2 299 (B. Alster 1997, 316):
Ein Mann, der seinen Gott nicht verehrt,
   wird in die Wüste geworfen,
   sein Leichnam wird nicht beerdigt werden,
   sein Sohn wird seinem Totengeist kein Wasser durch das Rohr libieren.

— Spruch aus der Sammlung 28.9 (B. Alster 1997, 285):
Wenn ein Mann seinem Gott keine Ehre erweist,
   dann wird er nicht beerdigt werden,
   sein Erbe wird ihm keine Totenopfer spenden.

Beide Sprüche stellen die negativen Auswirkungen des gottlosen Individuums insbesondere nach seinem Ableben heraus, das nicht nur seine Familie, sondern auch die gesamte Gemeinschaft trifft: Der, dessen Totengeist nicht zur Ruhe kommt, bleibt für alle Lebendigen eine ernste Bedrohung.

Diesen Gedankengang bietet der Fluch ein gutes Beispiel, den Ḫammurapi, der König von Babylon im 18./17. Jh. v.Chr., in den Epilog seiner Gesetzessammlung aufgenommen hat. Der Fluch soll einen Gottlosen zur Rechenschaft ziehen: Er wird vor seinem Gott keine Gnade und in seiner Familie und seinem Volk keine Achtung mehr finden, weil er gegen die Regeln der Religion und der Gesellschaft verstoßen hat.

Der vernichtende Fluch des Ḫammurapi richtet sich gegen einen möglichen Gegner, der sich irgendwann dem Initiator der Stele widersetzen könnte, indem der seinen eigenen Namen an die Stelle des seines Vorgängers in die Stele meißeln läßt. Denn eine solche Tat stünde gegen den Willen des Gottes Enlil, der Ḫammurapi zum König gemacht hat, und käme einer mutwilligen Mißachtung der Ordnung dieses Gottes gleich. Die Folge wäre, daß Enlil dem Frevler seine Gunst entziehen und ihn dem Untergang zuführen müßte. Im Fluch wird ihm aber nicht nur sein persönlicher Untergang angedroht, sondern auch der Verlust seiner möglicherweise wohl verdienten Herrschaft — Codex Ḫammurapi, Kol. XLIX 53-80:

> (53) Enlil, der Herr, (54) der die Geschicke bestimmt, (55) dessen Befehl (56) nicht geändert werden kann, (58) der mein Königtum (57) groß gemacht hat, (59) möge ununterdrückbare Wirren, (60) Verzweiflung, (61) die zu seinem Untergang führt, (62) in seinem Wohnsitz (63) ihm (bescheren), (64) eine leidvolle Regierungszeit, (65) wenige Tage, (66) Jahre (67) der Hungersnot, (69) unerhellbare (68) Finsternis, (70) Tod des *Augenlichts* (71) zum Schicksal (72) ihm bestimmen; (73) Untergang seiner Stadt, (74) Zerstreuung seiner Leute, (75) Thronwechsel, (78) Tilgung (76) seines Namens und seines Gedenkens (77) aus dem Lande (79) möge er mit seinem gewichtigen Ausspruch (80) befehlen!

Den kausalen Zusammenhang zwischen Gottesferne und Unglück drückt folgender sumerischer Spruch aus — Spruchsammlung UET 6/2 252 (B. Alster 1997, 309):

> Wenn ein Mann ohne seinen Gott lebt,
>   erzeugt er nicht viel Speise, erzeugt er nicht wenig Speise;
>   geht er auf den Fluß zum Fischen, dann wird er keinen Fisch fangen,
>   geht er in die Steppe, dann wird er keine Gazelle fangen ...
> Wenn ihm sich hingegen sein Gott wieder zuwendet,
>   dann wird er mit allem versorgt, das er erwähnt.

Ein vielsagendes Beispiel für das Zusammenspiel von Gesellschaft und Religion bietet der folgende sumerische Spruch — 14.39 (B. Alster 1997, 219; W.H.Ph. Römer 1990, 33):

> Ehefrauen zu heiraten, ist Sache des Menschen,
>   aber Kinder zu bekommen, ist Sache Gottes.

2.2.2. Auszug aus einem Propheten-Brief aus Māri

Die Bedeutung der Ehrerbietung Gottes für den Erfolg von Aktionen gilt in besonderer Weise für den König als dessen "Vertreter" auf Erden. Zur Illustration dessen sei auf einen vielbeachteten Abschnitt aus einem Propheten-Brief aus Māri verwiesen: Anläßlich einer drohenden kriegerischen Auseinandersetzung zwischen Jasmaḫ-Addu und seinem verfeindeten Bruder Išme-Dagān hat die Gattin des Jasmaḫ-Addu, Šibtu, ca. 1720 v.Chr. eine Seherin und einen Seher gefragt, was angesichts eines Waffengangs passieren werde. Die Lage sei ernst, stellten die beiden Befragten fest, weil die Truppen des Bruders sehr groß und stark seien. Da sich unter ihnen aber auch Söldner befänden, seien sie letztlich aber unzuverlässig — aus ARM 10,4:

> ... (28) Das Heer des Išme-Dagān (29) ist (zwar) groß! Auch wenn sein Heer groß ist, (30) werden seine Hilfstruppen doch zersprengt werden! (31) Sind (denn) nicht m e i n e Hilfstruppe Dagān, (32) Addu, Itūr-Mēr und Bēlet-ekallim (33) — dazu ist Addu auch noch der Herr über die Fortune —, (34) die an der Seite meines Herrn marschieren?!" ...

2.2.3. Gebete und Lieder

In Gebeten und Liedern treten Beter an ihre Gottheiten heran, um sie zur Gewährung von Heil und Gesundheit zu bitten. Nachfolgend seien drei Beispiele auszugsweise vorgestellt: Der Dialog zwischen König Assurbanipal und dem Gott Nabû, der Anūna-Hymnus und das Gedicht des *Ludlul bēl nēmeqi*.

2.2.3.1. Der erste und letzte Redeabschnitt aus dem Zwiegespräch zwischen König Assurbanipal und dem Gott Nabû (siehe A. Livingstone 1989, 33-35):

Selbstvorstellung Assurbanipals mit Frömmigkeitsnachweis und Bitte
  (1) Ich verkündige stets deinen Ruhm, Nabû, vor den versammelten großen Göttern:
     (2) Öffentlich dürfen meine Neider nicht Macht über meine Atemzüge gewinnen!
  (3) Im Tempel der Königin von Ninive wende ich mich stets an dich, Siegreicher unter den Göttern, seinen Brüdern:
     (4) Du bist die Hilfe Assurbanipals in Zukunft, auf immer!
  (5) Seit meiner Jugend habe ich stets zu Füßen des Nabû gelegen:
     (6) Laß mich nicht im Stich vor meinen versammelten Neidern!

Selbstvorstellung Nabûs und Aufmunterung zu anhaltender Frömmigkeit
  (7) Hör', Assurbanipal, ich bin Nabû:
     In zukünftigen Tagen (8) werden deine Füße niemals schwanken, niemals zittern deine Hände!

(9) Angesichts dessen sollen deine Lippen nicht ermüden, sich an mich zu wenden,
(10) deine Zunge soll nicht abgeblockt werden durch deine Lippen!
(11) Ich, der ich dir stets, Gutes zu reden, gebe,
(12) erhebe dein Haupt, richte deine Gestalt im Emašmaš auf...

Zuspruch Nabûs mit Hinweis auf die Treue seit der Geburt
(6) Klein warst du, Assurbanipal, der ich dich überließ der Königin von Ninive,
(7) schwach (wie ein Baby) warst du, Assurbanipal, der ich dich festsetzte auf dem Schoß der Königin von Ninive:
(8) Vier Brüste waren an deinen Mund gelegt: 2 sogst du, 2 melktest du vor dir.

Dieses Zwiegespräch zeigt, wie sehr ein assyrischer Weltenherrscher darum bemüht war, sich der Gunst seines Gottes zu vergewissern — aufschlußreich wäre es zu wissen, welche konkrete Situation zu diesem Zwiegespräch geführt haben könnte.

2.2.3.2. Aus dem Anūna-Hymnus aus Nippur (17. Jh.)

Der altbabylonische Anūna-Hymnus aus Nippur, den W.G. Lambert 1989 neu bearbeitet hat, gehört in die Gruppe von "Hiob-Texten" und schildert in mehr als 200 Zeilen die verzweifelte Lage und das Schuldbekenntnis eines Leidenden. In poetischer, teilweise nur noch mit Mühe erschließbarer Sprache malt der Leidende seine mißliche Lage aus, die ihn zur gesellschaftlichen Isolation und an den Rand des Grabes geführt habe. Schließlich kommt er zur Einsicht, daß er an seinem Unglück selbst Schuld sei, weil er einen Lebensweg gewählt habe, der von seiner Schutzgöttin Anūna-Ištar immer weiter weggeführt habe. Als er dies erkannt und seinen Lebenswandel dementsprechend korrigiert hat, wandte sich ihm die Göttin wieder zu und verhalf ihm wieder zu Glück und Gesundheit.

Der im Hymnus wiedergegebene Gedankengang ist ein aus dem Leben gegriffenes Beispiel für den oben zitierten Spruch der sumerischen Sammlung 26 A 12:

Gottesfurcht schafft Wohlergehen,
   Klagelieder lösen Sünde,
   Opfer verlängern Leben.

Gleichzeitig ist der Hymnus, wie der nachfolgend zitierte Abschnitt (siehe M. Dietrich 2001a, 81-82) zeigt, ein Beleg für das Bemühen eines Bewohners von Mesopotamien, den von der Religion als transzendenter Norm vorgegebenen Rahmen zu beachten und einzuhalten:

Klage (55-66)
Abwendung der Ahnen
>(55) Nicht steht sein Gott ihm mehr zur Seite,
>>(56) der Schutzgeist, sein Glück, hat sich entfernt.
>(57) Die Väter, die Lichten (= Verstorbene), hassen ihn, diffamieren ihn,
>>(58) sie blicken böse auf ihn wie auf einen Feind, zür[nen ihm.]

>(59) Seine beiden Familienoberhäupter haben die Öl(zufuhr) unterbrochen, haben ein Tabu (daraus) gemacht,
>>(60) täglich ist sein Leben, als ob es [. . .] wäre.
>(61) Die Mutter, seine Lebensspenderin, hat ihre Gunst zu ihm aufgegeben,
>>(62) nachdem sie ihre Abwendung ausgesprochen hatte, konnte sie eine Zuwendung nicht mehr [durchführen.]

Abwendung der Familie und Freunde
>(63) Die Brüder und Freunde sind sehr wütend auf ihn,
>>(64) er ist für sie für die Niederungen der Unterwelt bestimmt.
>(65) Der Diener war ermüdet am Tragkorb der Göttin,
>>(66) er wandelte einher bei Tag(eshitze) und bei Nacht.

Göttliche Zuwendung (67-68)
>(67) Sie spricht ihn an: "Erkannt ist deine Last:
>>(68) Sie ist (aber) gewiß kein zu schweres Gericht einer zürnenden Göttin!"

Aus dem Abschnitt Reue und Sündenbekenntnis (73-100)
>(69) "Ištar, du bist es, die [das Leben] wahrt,
>>(70) Sachwalterin des Lebens - es ist das zu ihr Gehörige!
>(71) Fürwahr, was wäre einer ohne dich [. . .?]
>>(72) Siehe, sein Silo wäre [. . .!]

Realisierung der transzendenten Norm
>(73) Wer kann ohne dich seinen Weg [recht gehen?]
>>(74) Sie kann sein Gebet erhören[, sich seiner erbarmen.]
>(75) Ištar, wer kann ohne dich seinen Weg [recht gehen?]
>>(76) Sie kann sein Gebet erhören, sich [seiner erbarmen.]

>(77) Es seufzt zu dir und sucht deinen Schrein auf
>>(78) der Weinende, der nachlässig war: Bewirke ihm Er[barmen!]
>(79) Er hat sich niedergebeugt und angesichts seiner Schuld gestöhnt,
>>(80) angesichts der Sünde, die er begangen hat, ruft er zu dir.

>(81) Er zählt auf alles, was seit frühester Zeit [besteht . . .,]
>>(82) dessen er erinnerlich war und was er vergessen hatte [. . .]
>(83) Während er seinen Wandel überprüft, weint er [zu ihr,]
>>(84) mit Seufzen, das er ausstößt, wiederholt er [vor ihr:"]

(85) "Ich habe begangen eine Freveltat, [eine Sünde,]
(86) Ištar, die mir (trotzdem) Gutes getan hat, zu dir seufze ich, Iš[tar, . . .!]
(87) Kein schlechtes Gewissen hatte ich, (obwohl) ich nicht (mehr) auf das Tor der Göttin zuging,
(88) nicht (mehr) ihr zurief 'Es ist genug!' wie ein Greis!"

Zuwendung der Gottheit (121-124)
(121) Nachdem ich (all dies) aufgezeigt, mich auf dem beschwerlichen Weg (der Gottheit) genähert hatte,
(122) hat mein Gott mich anerkannt, ein Gewinn in [. . .:]
(123) "Ein Diener ist er! Vor seinen Herrn hat er seine Sünde gebracht!
(124) Nicht soll sich verkürzen sein Leben!"

Anschließend das Gelöbnis (125-132)
(125) Es lasse sich freundlich stimmen Ištar, der Zorn komme zur Ruhe!
(126) Meine Rechte möge sie ergreifen und sie [an meiner Seite] halten!

(127) Nicht darf ich durchbohrt werden durch den Stachel [der Ištar -]
(128) leben will ich, wo auch immer mein Ende liegen mag!
(129) Durch das Wüten der Anūna darf ich nicht getötet werden -
(130) leben will ich, wo auch immer mein Ende liegen mag!

(131) Unsere Herrin, dein Diener hat sich dir vollends zugewandt!
(132) Erhebe ihn! Erhalte ihn am Leben, damit er zur Ruhe komme!

2.2.3.3. *Aus dem Marduk-Hymnus Ludlul bēl nēmeqi (1. Jt.)*:

Die Textzeugen des Klagelieds *Ludlul bēl nēmeqi* ("Ich will preisen den Herrn der Weisheit") stammen zwar aus dem 1. Jt. v.Chr., haben aber ältere Traditionen aufgegriffen (siehe W. von Soden 1990, 140-143): Wie im Anūna-Hymnus beklagt sich ein Sänger, dessen Namen als Šubši-mešrê-Šakan bekannt ist, daß er vor seinem persönlichen Niedergang ein einflußreicher Babylonier gewesen, dann aber von seiner Umwelt verschmäht und verachtet worden sei, so daß er sich nirgendwo mehr habe sehen lassen können. Die Ursache für seinen Leidensweg, eine Gelbsucht-Erkrankung (siehe Th. Kämmerer 2001, 79), hat dieser Herr als Strafe seines Gottes Marduk gedeutet, der sie ihm wegen seines offenbar nicht immer geglückten gottgefälligen Lebens auferlegt hätte. Wollte er bei dieser Ursachenfindung seine Hoffnung auf Genesung nicht verlieren, dann galt es, die Versöhnung mit Marduk herbeizuführen, die allein das Ende der Krankheit mit sich bringen konnte.

I *Schilderung des desolaten Zustands des Leidenden*
 (43) Es verwarf mich mein Gott, er suchte das [Weite,]
   (44) es hörte auf meine Göttin, entgernte [sich *von mir*.]
 (45) Voll war der gute Schutzgenius an meiner Seite [des Zorns] gegen mich,
   (46) es erschrak mein (weiblicher) Schutzgeist; sie sah sich nach einem anderen um.

 (47) Fortgenommen wurde meine Würde, meine Männlichkeit wurde verdunkelt;
   (48) was mein Wesen ausmachte, flog davon, übersprang mein 'Schutzdach'.
 (49) Bewirkt wurden für mich Omenbefunde, die erschreckten;
   (50) aus meinem Hause wurde ich ausgewiesen (und) lief draußen herum.
   . . .

 (82) Meine Stadt sieht mich wie einen Feind böse an;
   (83) gleich als ob es eine Feindin wäre, (verhält sich) mein aggressives Land.

 (84) Zu einem Fremden wurde für mich mein Bruder;
   (85) zu einem Bösen und einem Teufel wurde für mich mein Freund.
 (86) Mein wütender Genosse denunziert mich;
   (87) mein Kollege macht ständig die Waffen schmutzig;
   (88) der gute Gefährte bringt mein Leben in Gefahr.

 (89) Offen in der Öffentlichkeit verfluchte mich mein Sklave;
   (90) meine Sklavin vor der Menschenmenge sprach Schmähung(en) gegen mich aus.
 (91) Es sah mich der Bekannte und drückte sich zur Seite;
   (92) wie einen nicht Blutsverwandten behandelte mich meine Familie.

II
 (1) In diesem wie dem folgenden Jahr ging der Termin vorüber;
   (2) ich wende mich um, aber es sieht böse, sehr böse aus.
   (3) Schlimmes für mich kommt noch dazu, mein Recht finde ich nicht.
 (4) Den Gott rief ich an, aber er wandte mir sein Antlitz nicht zu;
   (5) ich betete zu meiner Göttin, aber sie erhob ihr Haupt nicht zu mir hin. . .

Selbstrechtfertigung
 (23) Dabei dachte ich doch selbst an Beten (und) Gebet,
   (24) Gebet war (für mich) Einsicht, Opfer meine Gewohnheit.
 (25) Der Tag der Gottesverehrung war Herzensfreude für mich,
   (26) der Prozessionstag der Göttin Ertrag (und) Gewinn.

(27) Die Fürbitte für den König war Freude für mich,
   (28) und Freudenmusik für ihn geriet (mir) zum Guten (noch) obendrein.
   (29) **Ich lehrte mein Land, die Ordnungen des Gottes zu halten;**
   (30) den Namen der Göttin wertzuhalten, wies ich meine Leute an. . .

IV *Einkehr und Wende: Dankopfer*
   (48) [Ich, der ich] ins Grab (fast) hinabgestiegen war, kam zurück zum [Sonnenaufgangs-]Tor;
   (49) [im] Überfluß-Tor wurde mir Überfluß [gegeben] . . .

2.2.3. *Zwischenergebnis*

Maximen der sumero-babylonischen Spruchliteratur, die das Glück des mesopotamischen Individuums von seiner Bereitschaft abhängig machen, daß er seinen Lebensweg auf seinen Gott ausrichte, wurden anhand des königlichen Dialogs zwischen Assurbanipal und Nabû und anhand von zwei Klageliedern, des altbabylonischen Anūna-Hymnus und des Marduk-Hymnus aus dem 1. Jt. v.Chr., beleuchtet.

Hinsichtlich der beiden Klagelieder ist bemerkenswert, daß die Dichter den Grund für das Leid, das sie in allen Farben beklagen, nicht irgendwo, sondern im eigenen Lebenswandel suchen, der sich für sie keineswegs immer durchschaubar darstellte. Sie zweifeln bei ihren Recherchen nach der Ursache für die Entzweiung mit ihren Gottheiten bekanntlich weniger an einer ihnen widerfahrenden göttlichen Gerechtigkeit als daran, daß sie ihren Wandel vor der Gottheit stets richtig eingeschätzt haben. Von daher sind sie aufschlußreiche literarische Belege für das Bemühen eines antiken Mesopotamiers, den von ihren Gottheiten vorgegebenen Rahmen unbedingt einzuhalten, d.h. der transzendenten Norm zu entsprechen. Sollten sie versagen, dann stürzten sie sich ins Unglück.

Damit läßt sich der erste Punkt der Ausführungen zum Unterthema *Persönliches Glück, Gesundheit und öffentliche Anerkennung als Zeichen für die Religionsgebundenheit eines Individuums* mit folgender Feststellung abschließen: Die Religion war für den Mesopotamier gleichbedeutend mit Leben und Tod; die Tatsache des Lebens sah er als Zeichen der inneren Harmonie zwischen seinem Schöpfer und sich an.

2.3. *Ordnung und sozialer Friede im Lande als Zeichen für die Religionsgebundenheit der Gesellschaft*

Wie einleitend hervorgehoben, ist das Individuum für die Gesellschaft als mehr oder weniger weit gefaßte Gemeinschaft konstitutiv. Daraus läßt sich im Vorgriff ableiten, daß das Ergebnis, das für das Individuum formuliert worden ist, auch für die Gesellschaft gilt.

Da die Texte Mesopotamiens verhältnismäßig selten von Auswirkungen der Religion auf das Verhalten der *Gesellschaft* im allgemeinen handeln, kann die Darstellung dieses Punktes auch kürzer ausfallen als die über das Individuum.

Nachfolgend seien nun drei Texte zur Sprache gebracht, die jeweils aus unterschiedlichen Literaturgattungen und Zeiten stammen und den Vorwurf des Fehlverhaltens gegenüber einer Gottheit jeweils gegen eine andere Gruppe von Menschen richten: die Klage um die Zerstörung Urs als Stadtklage (Anfang 2. Jt.), die Ḥarrān-Inschrift des Nabonid als Königsinschrift (6. Jh.) und das Erra-Epos als Epos (8. Jh.).

2.3.1. *Die Klage um die Zerstörung von Ur (Anfang 2. Jt.)*

Eine Literaturgattung, in der ausgeführt wird, daß das religiöse Verhalten einer Menschengruppe ihr zum Glück oder zum Unglück geworden sei, sind die *Städteklagen* vom Anfang des 2. Jt.s v.Chr. In diesen Klageliedern beweint der Dichter jeweils wortreich die Zerstörung seiner Heimatstadt durch Feindeshand und stellt fest, daß das Unglück nur deswegen möglich war, weil sich ihre Gottheit im Zorn von ihr abgewandt und sie verlassen hatte. Der Grund für dieses Verhalten der Gottheit wird bei der Einstellung der Einwohner zu ihr gesucht, die sie durch ihr gottloses Leben vertrieben hätten. Die Städteklagen drücken das altorientalische Denkschema aus, wie wir es bei den Individualklage kennengelernt haben: Ein gottgefälliges religiöses Leben führt zum Wohlstand der Stadt, ein gottfernes dagegen zu deren Untergang.

Als Beispiel kann die *Klage um die Zerstörung von Ur* gelten, in der in poetischer Breite der Untergang von Ur am Persischen Golf geschildert wird, als sich zu Beginn des 2. Jt.s Elamer und Subaräer (Bewohner des Osttigrislandes) ihrer bemächtigten und sie dem Erdboden gleich machten. Die Stadt und ihre erfolgreichen Herrscher hatten ihren Reichtum aus dem Überseehandel geschöpft.

Bei den Städteklagen bezieht sich der Vorwurf des Fehlverhaltens von Menschen, denen der Untergang ihrer Stadt zur Last gelegt wird, auf die Stadtbevölkerung. Diese war in zweierlei Hinsicht gemischt: Zum einen lebten hier Gemeinden unterschiedlicher Kulte nebeneinander, wie die Aufzählung der Gottheiten zu erkennen gibt, die ihre Heiligtümer verlassen haben, zum anderen dürften hier angesichts dessen, daß Ur der Sitz eines Königs und zugleich eine blühende Hafenstadt war, Einheimische und Auswärtige dicht beieinander gelebt haben. Der Dichter macht in seiner Klage jedoch allem Anschein nach keinen Unterschied zwischen den einzelnen Gruppen, sondern sieht die Stadt als Ganzheit – A. Falkeinstein 1953, 194-213:

> (38) O Stadt, bitter ist die Klage um dich geworden,
> (39) bitter ist, o Stadt, die Klage um dich geworden.

Bemerkenswert ist es allerdings, daß der Dichter den Hauptgott von Ur, Nanna,

um den Erhalt seiner Stadt beim kosmischen Hochgott An und seiner Gattin
Mullil Einspruch erheben läßt. Er beschreibt den letzten Versuch des Hauptgottes Nanna, als das Unheil beginnt hereinzubrechen, folgendermaßen:

> (143) Da verließ ich (Nanna) meine Stadt nicht,
>> (144) gab ich mein Land nicht auf.
>
> (145) Vor An vergoß ich meine Tränen,
>> (146) vor Mullil bat ich selbst flehentlich:
>
> (147) 'Meine Stadt soll nicht vernichtet werden,
>> (148) Ur soll nicht vernichtet werden,
>> (149) seine Bewohner sollen nicht nicht zugrunde gehen!', sagte ich zu ihnen.
>
> (150) Aber An kehrte sich nicht an dieses Wort,
>> (151) (und) Mullil erfreute mein Herz nicht mit (der Antwort): 'So ist es gut, so sei es!'   ...

Dieser Vorgang macht ersichtlich, daß Nanna bis zuletzt in seinem Heiligtum geblieben und um die Verschonung der Stadt bemüht war. Nachdem er als letzter die untergangsgeweihte Stadt verlassen habe, sei die Vernichtung über seine Heimat hereingebrochen:

> (208) An diesem Tag schwand der Stadt das Licht, wurde die Stadt zur Ruine;
>> (209) Vater Nanna: wurde die Stadt zur Ruine gemacht — das Volk klagt,
>
> (210) an diesem Tag schwand dem Land das Licht — das Volk klagt.

Das Ende der umfangreichen Klage geht davon aus, daß sich die Lage wieder beruhigt hat und Nanna nach dem Wiederaufbau von Stadt und Heiligtum wieder in seine Heimat eingezogen ist. *Ex eventu* heißt es mit Blick auf die Rückkehr der Stadtbevölkerung zum bewährten religiösen Verhalten und den Beginn besserer Zeiten:

> (432) Auf den, der die Opfer bringt, der (damit vor dich) tritt, schaue freundlich,
>> (433) dann werden, Nanna, dessen scharfer Blick die Eingeweide durchdringt,
>> (434) die Menschen damit ihren trüben Sinn wieder aufheitern.
>
> (435) Denen, die im Lande leben, wird es dann (wieder) wohlergehen.
>> (436) Nanna, wenn du die Stadt wieder hergestellt hast, wird sie dich immerdar preisen.

Demnach wird die Bevölkerung, die für ihr Fehlverhalten gegenüber Nanna und seinen Mitgöttern mit der Vernichtung ihrer Stadt bestraft worden war, wieder mit dem Segen Nannas bedacht, sobald sie zu ihrem gottgefälligen Verhalten von ehedem zurückgefunden hat.

2.3.2. Die Ḥarrān-Inschrift des Nabonid (6. Jh.)

Nabonid, der 559 als letzter Herrscher den babylonischen Thron bestiegen hat, legte als Usurpator in einer umfangreichen Inschrift Rechenschaft über seinen Weg auf den Thron von Babylonien ab — da diese in Ḥarrān gefunden worden ist, wird sie nach diesem Ort benannt. Nabonid war Verehrer des Mondgottes Nannar-Sîn, stand also abseits des in Babylonien vorherrschenden Marduk-Kults, den auch seine Vorgänger im Neubabylonischen Reich, beispielsweise Nabopolassar oder Nebukadnezar II. vertraten. Es versteht sich, daß es Nabonid deswegen schwer hatte, bei seinen Untertanen, die landauf, landab von Marduk-Priestern angeführt wurden, Anerkennung zu finden.

Um eine Wende herbeizuführen, verkündeten die Theologen am Hof Nabonids: Die Ursache für den Bankrott des Landes und die damit verbundenen gesellschaftlichen Turbulenzen sei, daß die gesamte Bevölkerung des Reichs dem Marduk-Glauben anhingen. Da dies gegen den erklärten Willen des nun herrschenden Mondgottes Nannar-Sîn sei, habe das Land abgewirtschaftet und sei die Geslleschaft moralisch verkommen – H. Schaudig 2001, 497:

(14). . . Die Menschen, die Söhne Bābils, Barsipas, (15) Nippurs, Urs, Uruks (und) Larsas, die Tempelverwalter (und) (16) Menschen der Kultstädte des Landes Akkad (Babylonien) verfehlten sich gegen seine (Sîn) große Gottheit und (17) mißachteten (sie) und frevelten (gegen sie), (18) nicht kannten sie das <tobende> Zürnen des Königs der Götter, des Nannār, (19) ihrer Kultordnungen vergaßen sie und sprachen dauernd Lügen (20) und Unwahrheiten, verbissen sich wie Hunde immerzu (21) ineinander, (Kopf)krankheit und Hungersnot ließen sie (selbst?) in ihrer Mitte (22) entstehen, er verminderte die Menschen des Landes. . .

Die Gesellschaft, die hier kritisiert wird, wird durch die Reichsbevölkerung Babyloniens vertreten, die auf Marduk ausgerichtet ist. Ihr schweres Los des wirtschaftlichen Niedergangs und moralischen Verfalls erklärt sich aus der historisch prekären Lage, in der sich das späte Neubabylonische Reich unter seinen schwachen Herrschern befand: Aus dem Osten drängten mit unbändigem Siegeswillen die Perser, Anhänger des Ahuramazda, herein und führten den Babyloniern schonungslos ihre Dekadenz vor Augen. Diese Situation nützte Nabonid, der der taumelnden babylonischen Gesellschaft klarzumachen versuchte, daß an ihrer Unzulänglichkeit die abgewirtschaftete Marduk-Ideologie Schuld sei. Sie brauchte sich nur der durch ihn propagierten des Nannar-Sîn zuzuwenden, um den Weg in eine bessere Zukunft zu finden.

An dem Abschnitt aus der Königsinschrift Nabonids ist im Zusammenhang mit unserem Thema *Zur Bedeutung der Religion für die antiken Gesellschaften Mesopotamiens* zweierlei besonders bemerkenswert: Zum einen führt er zur Beschreibung des Niedergangs keine wirtschaftlichen oder kriegerischen Gründe auf, sondern ethisch-moralische für gesellschaftliches Verhalten. Also sieht er den eigentlichen Grund für den Niedergang Babyloniens im Verfall der Moral.

Diesen malt er mit einprägsamen Bildern aus.

Zum anderen begründet dieser Abschnitt den Niedergang damit, daß die Reichsbevölkerung nicht etwa gottlos gewesen wäre, sondern daß sie einem falschen Glauben anhingen. Er ist also ein beredtes Beispiel dafür, daß im Alten Orient eine absolut gottlose Gesellschaft undenkbar ist; das Problem der Gesellschaft kann nur darin liegen, daß sie einer Religionsform nachgeht, die ihr nicht zu Erfolg verhilft und darum nicht mehr aktuell ist. Mit anderen Worten legt dieser Text den Gedanken nahe, daß die Bedeutung der Religion für eine Gesellschaft auch negativ sein kann, wenn ihre Vertreter unfähig geworden sind, auf aktuelle Gegebenheiten die richtigen Antworten zu geben.

2.3.3. *Das Erra-Epos (8. Jh.)*

Ein Abschnitt aus dem Erra-Epos, dessen Text der Dichter Kabti-ilāni-Marduk gegen Mitte des 8. Jh.s v.Chr. in einer Vision diktiert bekommen haben will, beschreibt wie die Ḫarrān-Inschrift Nabonids den gesellschaftlichen Verfall im Lande — hier allerdings nicht auf eine bestimmte Bevölkerungsgruppe bezogen, sondern allgemein — II C 11-37 (siehe M. Dietrich 2001b, 32-35):

(11) Er (:Erra-Išum) fragt sich:
Wozu bleibst du (noch untätig) sitzen?

Erras Entschluß, die Naturgesetze außer Kraft zu setzen
(12) Öffne den Weg, damit ich auf den Kriegspfad ziehen kann!
(13) Die Tage sind beendet, die Zeit ist verstrichen!
(14) Ich gebe Befehl, die Strahlen des Šamaš niederzumachen,
(15) des Sin Antlitz während der Nacht zu bedecken!
(16) Zu Adad sage ich: "Verschließe deine Brunnen,
(17) entferne die Wolke, stoppe Schnee und Regen!" ...

Drohung, die Gesellschaftsordnung aufzulösen
(32) Stadt für Stadt werde ich einem Verfolger in die Hand geben,
(33) der Sohn wird nicht fragen nach dem Wohl des Vaters, der Erzeuger nicht nach dem des Sohnes,
(34) die Mutter wird gegen die Tochter lachend Böses planen!

Um die Aussage dieses Abschnitts besser einordnen zu können, sei sein historischer Kontext und sein Kontext im Epos knapp umrissen: Das Werk des Kabti-ilāni-Marduk ist aller Wahrscheinlichkeit nach etwa in die Mitte des 8. Jh.s v.Chr. zu datieren, als starke politische und wirtschaftliche Unruhen Babylonien erschüttert haben. Der Dichter erkannte den Grund für die Turbulenzen im gottlosen Verhalten der Bevölkerung, die im Kosmos einen Störfaktor darstellte. Mit ihrer Vernichtung sollte der heile Zustand, wie er in der Zeit vor der Erschaffung des Menschen herrschte, wieder hergstellt werden. Für dieses Vernichtungswerk waren der Todes- und Pestgott Erra und sein Adjutant Išum zuständig. Diese konnten mit ihren Helfershelfern allerdings nur tätig werden, wenn Marduk, der Herrscher im Kosmos und Wahrer der Natur, zu der auch der Mensch gehört, vorübergehend von seiner Regentschaft durch Erra abgelöst werde.

Dies zu erreichen, schildert der Dichter als ein schwieriges und umständliches Unterfangen: Zuerst müsse Marduk davon überzeugt werden, daß im Kosmos wieder Ruhe einkehren müsse, dann müßten alle anderen Göttinnen und Götter dem Unternehmen zustimmen. Zunächst weigert sich Marduk, weil er befürchte, daß sich die "Ordnungen von Himmel und Erde" auflösten, wenn er den Thron verlasse. Als er schließlich zustimmte, konnte Erra die Macht ergreifen und die Vernichtung der Menschheit einleiten (vgl. M. Dietrich 2001b, 27-31).

Wie der oben zitierte Abschnitt zeigt, ging es dem Dichter bei dem Machtwechsel von dem erhaltenden Gott Marduk zu seinem zerstörerischen Kontrahenten Erra nicht alleine um die Auflösung der Naturgesetze, sondern auch um die Zerstörung der kulturellen Einrichtungen und der Gesetze der Moral, die die Gesellschaft zusammenhalten.

2.3.4. *Zwischenergebnis*

Das Unterthema *Ordnung und sozialer Friede im Lande als Zeichen für die Religionsgebundenheit der Gesellschaft* wurde hinsichtlich betroffener Personengruppen aus drei Blickwinkeln behandelt: aus dem der Stadtbevölkerung nach den Stadtklagen, aus dem der Reichsbevölkerung nach der Ḥarrān-Inschrift Nabonids und aus dem der Menschheit im allgemeinen nach dem Erra-Epos. Dabei wurde bestätigt, daß es in allen drei Bereichen das Individuum ist, das als konstitutiver Bestandteil der Gesellschaft in der Gestalt einer mehr oder weniger weit gefaßten Gemeinschaft, die die Religion als transzendente Norm vertritt. Also steht dem nichts im Wege, die für das Individuum gewonnene Erkenntnis von der Bedeutung der Religion auf die Gesellschaft und Gemeinschaft zu übertragen: Ordnung und sozialer Friede sind das Zeichen für die innere Harmonie zwischen der Gottheit und ihrer Kultgemeinde auch dann, wenn sie eine Stadt- oder Reichsbevölkerung ist.

3. Schlußbemerkung

Ausgehend von einer Definition der Begriffe "Religion" und "Gesellschaft" mit Bezug auf die Aussagen mesopotamischer Texte ließ sich das Thema *Zur Bedeutung der Religion für die antiken Gesellschaften Mesopotamiens* in zwei Unterthemen gliedern, von denen sich das erste mit der Einwirkung der Religion als transzendente Norm auf das Individuum und das zweite mit der auf die Gesellschaft als eine mehr oder weniger weit gefaßte Gemeinschaft bezog. Das Ergebnis ist in einem Satz zusammenzufassen: Individuum und Gesellschaft waren nach dem antiken mesopotamischen Verständnis durchdrungen von der Religion. Ihr Leben und Denken waren von einer Größe bestimmt, die jenseits des unmittelbaren Einsichtsvermögens eines Menschen liegt (A. Rupp 1984, 18).

Nur dann, wenn der Mensch und seine Lebensgemeinschaft innerhalb des Rahmens der transzendenten Norm blieben, waren sie durch die Zuwendung ihres Gottes von Glück, Erfolg, Anerkennung und Wohlstand begünstigt. Wenn sie allerdings die Grenzen der Norm verließen, dann entzog die Gottheit ihnen ihren Segen, wandte sich von ihnen ab und ließ sie in Not, Krankheit, wirtschaftlichen, sozialen und kulturellen Untergang sinken.

Eine Wende zum Guten war stets möglich und erwünscht: Hat ein Individuum oder eine Gemeinschaft wieder den Weg zu ihrem Gott gefunden, dann hat sich dieser finden lassen und seinen Segen erneuert.

Literatur

Rainer Albertz 1999: *Allgemeine Angaben zum Sonderforschungsbereich 1776 "Funktionen von Religion in antiken Gesellschaften des Vorderen Orients"*, in: *Antrag auf Einrichtung eines Sonderforschungsbereichs 1776* (Münster), S. 1-62.

Bendt Alster 1997: *Proverbs of Ancient Sumer. The World's Earliest Proverb Collections*. Vol. I, II (Bethesda, Maryland).

ARM Archives royales de Māri (Paris).

Alfred Bertholet 1985: *Wörterbuch der Religionen*. Vierte Auflage . . . von Kurt Goldammer (Stuttgart).

John Bowker 1999: *Das Oxford-Lexikon der Weltreligionen*. Für die deutschsprachige Ausgabe übersetzt und bearbeitet von Karl-Heinz Golzio. Lizenzausgabe für die Wissenschaftliche Buchgesellschaft (Darmstadt) [Originaltitel: *The Oxford Dictionary of World Religions* (Oxford University Press 1997)].

Manfried Dietrich 1986: *Prophetenbriefe aus Mari*, in: O. Kaiser, Hrsg., *Texte aus der Umwelt des Alten Testaments* II/1 (Gütersloh), S. 83-93.

Manfried Dietrich 2001a: *"(Nur) einer, der von Sünde nichts weiß, eilt zu seinen Göttern". Der altorientalische Mensch vor seiner Gottheit*, in: A. Albertz, Hrsg., *Kult Konflikt und Versöhnung*. Alter Orient und Altes Testament 285 (Münster), S. 73-97.

Manfried Dietrich 2001b: *"Ich habe die Ordnungen von Himmel und Erde aufgelöst". Eschatologische Vorstellungen in der babylonischen Mythologie*, in: M. Dietrich, Hrsg., *Endzeiterwartungen und Endzeitvorstellungen in den verschiedenen Religionen*. Forschungen zur Anthropologie und Religionsgeschichte 34 (Münster), S. 15-41.

Adam Falkenstein 1953: *Sumerische und akkadische Hymnen und Gebete*. (Zürich).

Friedhart Hegner 1995: *Gemeinschaft - Gesellschaft*, in: W. Fuchs-Heinritz, u.a., Hrsg., *Lexikon zur Soziologie* (^{3}Opladen), S. 235-237.

Günter Kehrer 1998: *Religion, Definitionen der*, in: H. Cancik, B. Gladigow, M. Laubscher, Hrsg., *Handbuch religionswissenschaftlicher Grundbegriffe* III (Stuttgart), S. 418-425.

W.G. Lambert 1989: *A Babylonian Prayer to Anūna*, in: H. Behrens, u.a., DUMU-E$_2$-DUB-BA-A. Studies in Honor of Åke W. Sjöberg (Philadelphia), S. 321-336.

Thomas R. Kämmerer 2000: *Pathologische Veränderungen an Leber und Galle. Das Krankheitsbild der Gelbsucht.* RA 94, S. 57-93.

Alasdair Livingstone 1989: *Dialogue Between Assurbanipal and Nabû*, State Archives of Assyria III, *Court Poetry and Literary Miscellanea* (Helsinki), S. 33-35.

Niklas Luhmann 1995: *Gesellschaft*, in: W. Fuchs-Heinritz, u.a., Hrsg., *Lexikon zur Soziologie* (^{3}Opladen), S. 235-237.

RA Revue d'Assyriologie (Paris).

Willem H.Ph. Römer 1990: *Ausgewählte Beispiele aus einigen anderen "Sprichwörter"-Sammlungen*, in: in: O. Kaiser, Hrsg., *Texte aus der Umwelt des Alten Testaments* III/1, *Weisheitstexte I* (Gütersloh), S. 31-40.

Alfred Rupp 1984: *Religion, Kultur und Gemeinschaft*, in: A. Rupp, Hrsg., *Religion, Kultur und Gesellschaft. Vorträge auf dem 1. Symposion der Deutsch-Ostasiatischen Vereinigung für Forschung über Religion, Anthropologie und Kultur, Korea 1983* (Saarbrücken), S. 13-36.

Alfred Rupp 1991: *Religion als normativer Horizont und die legitimierende Evidenz des Vordergründigen.* Mitteilungen für Anthropologie und Religionsgeschichte 6 (Saarbrücken), S. 149-184.

Dario Sabbatucci 1988: *Kultur und Religion*, in: H. Cancik, B. Gladigow, M. Laubscher, Hrsg., *Handbuch religionswissenschaftlicher Grundbegriffe* I (Stuttgart), S. 43-58.

Hanspeter Schaudig 2001: *Die Inschriften Nabonids von Babylon und Kyros' des Großen samt den in ihrem Umfeld entstandenen Tendenzschriften. Textausgabe und Grammatik.* Alter Orient und Altes Testament 256 (Münster).

Wolfram von Soden 1990: *"Weisheitstexte" in akkadischer Sprache*, in: O. Kaiser, Hrsg., *Texte aus der Umwelt des Alten Testaments* III/1, *Weisheitstexte I* (Gütersloh), 110-188.

UET Ur Excavation Texts (London).

Hanns Wienold 1995: *Gesellschaft*, in: W. Fuchs-Heinritz, u.a., Hrsg., *Lexikon zur Soziologie* (^{3}Opladen), S. 235-237.

The Heritage of an Abandoned Mistress
The Influence of Christianity on Modern Science

Alar Helstein, Tartu

It is common knowledge that the influence of Christian religion on Western culture is enormous. Christianity has shaped art, music, literature, world-views, social structures, people's sense of identity, and so on. What is not so commonly accepted, is the recognition that Christianity has also made a contribution to the birth of modern natural sciences.

Most people who are not themselves studying the history of sciences or medieval thought have usually heard only stories about conflicts between Church and scientists, the cases of Giordano Bruno and Galileo Galilei, for example. However, a deeper reflection on the history of Europe would, in my opinion, make it quite reasonable not to assume that the relationship between natural sciences and theology consisted of conflicts only. It would be a very unusual assumption, since it would set one realm of Western thought, the natural sciences completely apart from every other field of intellectual, cultural, and social activity. All these other fields would be influenced by the Christian religion, but only the natural sciences would be immune to this influence and develop purely on the grounds of scientific reasoning. Clearly, this is not a view that one could accept without any questions. From this initial reflection it would, rather, seem more promising to reject such a view and suggest that, initially, theology and natural sciences were both parts of a single, unified Christian world-view.

However, if we state that Christianity played a positive role at the foundations of modern science, we are immediately confronted with two sets of questions. The first set of questions concerns the clarification of this statement. We would need an historical account that would demonstrate some positive relation between the medieval theology and the thought of the first modern scientists. There would have to be some sound historical evidence that medieval theology somehow inspired or anticipated the scientific ideas. The second, and probably even more important set of questions would compel us to find out, why did this positive relationship, if it ever existed, change? Why did theologians and scientists suddenly jump at each other's throats? Were there any theological arguments that made impossible the adherence to the unified world-view?

In the following essay I will try to reflect on both sets of problems. First, I will review some theories according to which Christianity exerted a major, if not crucial, influence on the rise of modern science. I will try to evaluate these theories and correct some of their overly exaggerated statements. However, I will also advocate the view that, for the first modern scientists, Christian theology was a major source of inspiration and that their scientific and religious beliefs were, without any problems, unified in a single world-view. After that I will direct my attention to the collapse of this unified world-view and suggest that this collapse was, to a great extent, caused by an over-enthusiastic reception of the Newtonian physics by the 18th century theologians.

Clarification of the Term "Modern Science"

Before we can go to the proper subject of this essay, one clarifying comment still needs to be made. It concerns the term "modern science". In my opinion, modern science is a specific phenomenon that cannot be equated with science in general. And in the discussions about the relationship between Christianity and modern science this distinction is of crucial importance. Clearly, there can be no talk of Christian influences in the case of Greek mathematics or Chinese technological achievements, for example. These topics belong to the science in general and they certainly also played an important part in the development of specifically modern science. But modern science, as we now know it, has some distinctive features and it is precisely those specific features that have something to do with Christian religion.

The first special characteristic of modern science is rather formal. It is based on geographic and chronological margins and its content is that modern science was born in Europe in the 16th and 17th centuries. The birth of modern science is generally associated with the names of Copernicus, Kepler, Galilei, and Newton.

These four "fathers" of modern science laid a foundation of the process we could now call a "scientific revolution". This scientific revolution consisted, generally speaking, of two major changes. First, it stressed that the proper methods for studying nature are empirical observation and experiment. Second, it started to use mathematics for associating observations and experiments with each other, thus creating a coherent scientific theory. These developments led to a new understanding of reality where every physical object, be it a stone, a planet, or a star, was subject to the same set of physical laws. This understanding of reality has often been called the "mechanistic" view of nature.

The mechanistic view of nature was something completely new compared to previous physics that had been based mainly on Aristotle. Aristotle had explained physical interactions metaphysically, using categories of potentiality and actuality. We know that Aristotle was a systematic observer of nature, but the idea of experiment in the modern sense apparently never occurred to him. This becomes clear from his treatment of falling bodies. He says that the speed of the body falling towards the earth depends on its weight. A very simple experiment would have been enough to show that this is not the case – when two bodies with differing weight are dropped simultaneously they reach the ground at the same time. The fact that Aristotle never thought of conducting this experiment indicates a profound difference between his thinking and that of modern scientists. [1]

Christian Preconditions of Modern Science

This difference between Aristotle and modern scientists may, at a first glance, suggest that medieval Christianity could not in any way aid the development of science, because of its philosophical background which was very much Aristotelian. However, there are historians of science who claim that this is not the case, since medieval theologians did not accept Aristotle's views uncritically, but corrected them at many points according to their own theological beliefs. And the resulting image of the world was, according to these theorists, extremely favorable for developing science in a modern sense. One of the most prominent of such theorists is Stanley Jaki. [2]

Jaki's argument is based on comparison of Christianity with other great cultures of the world. He suggests that Christian doctrine of creation out of nothing, combined with Greek philosophy and the use of Arabic numerals, produced a unique understanding of the world and only in the context of this understanding was it possible to develop modern scientific concepts. This new understanding of the world can be summarized in seven points [3]:

(1) A linear conception of time, developed from the idea that God has a plan, a goal for his creation. The idea that history is a development towards the fulfilment of God's plan clearly distinguishes past, present, and future providing a context for understanding cause-effect relationships. It is much easier to postulate causal (mechanical) relations within a single timeline, where physical interactions follow each other, than it would be to do so in the universe, where everything is in cyclical motion and where future can affect the present.

(2) The absence or weakness of pseudo-scientific explanations of natural phenomena, such as astrology. Astrology has been a very powerful phenomenon in every great culture, including European. But the church fathers and theologians also repeatedly condemned it, so at least the idea that astrology might not be valid was present in 16th and 17th centuries. At the root of astrology, especially the Greek astrology lies the view that heavenly objects

---

[1] Michael Bumbulis, "Christianity and the Birth of Science" (1996), *www.ldolphin.org/bumbulis*.

[2] Stanley Jaki, *The Road of Science and the Ways to God* (Edinburgh: Scottish Academic Press, 1978).

[3] Eric V. Snow, "Christianity: A Cause of Modern Science?" (1998), *www.icr.org/pubs/imp/imp-298.htm*.

are somehow more "perfect" than the earthly ones. Therefore, the behavior of planets and stars influences the non-perfect existence of beings on earth. Clearly such view prevents scientists from looking for causal relations only between earthly objects themselves.

(3) The distinction between animate and inanimate objects in the world. If there is no such distinction and every plant and stone is considered to have its own soul or will, then it would be hard to picture purely mechanical interactions between these objects. Christian doctrine of creation provides exactly this distinction by categorizing created objects and beings according to the day of their creation.

(4) The concept of the universe as having a fixed structure and being orderly. This conception is very closely connected to the idea that God himself is rational. A rational God would not create an irrational universe. But if God created a rational universe and created human beings in his image, so that they also are rational, then the study of nature is enabled and justified. Moreover, this study is a valuable theological activity, because it is the study of "God's mind".

(5) The absence of the concept of heavens as being alive or divine. Many non-Christian cultures have associated heavenly bodies with some deities. This would prevent their study, because you cannot explain the behavior of a deity with physical interactions and mechanical laws. Christian theology, on the other hand, could never make such claims, because one God is the sole creator of the whole universe including the planets and stars. God is transcendent and cannot be directly present in any of the created objects, except for the unique event of his incarnation in Jesus Christ.

(6) The general acceptability of scientific investigation. As we already have seen, the scientific activity could not be considered theologically as something heretical or non-Christian. The world is God's creation and its study helps theologians understand its authors mind.

(7) Anthropological view that human person is somehow qualitatively different from the animals. This view is, again, rooted in belief that human beings are created in the likeness of God and this likeness is expressed in human ability to think rationally. Human beings are also created to "rule over the world" and clearly, the knowledge about the world is useful for exercising this rule.

These seven points can also be interpreted as margins that separate Aristotle's thinking from the medieval Christian theology. In many of its aspects medieval theology is more a synthesis of Aristotle and Augustine, rather than pure Aristotelianism.

The main problem for theologians with Aristotle was that his universe was not created. The world was necessary and given. There was no place for God's freedom to create the world or not to create. In 1277 the Bishop of Paris condemned 219 propositions drawn from Aristoteles' works. Among these propositions were the idea of eternal cycles (proposition no. 92) and the concept of eternal existence of the universe (propositions no. 83-91). [4]

But even more important was probably the rejection of the Aristotelian distinction between "essence" and "form" by some theologians. In the Aristotelian framework the source of knowledge would be the "essence" – the common (metaphysical) nature of all objects of the same kind. In the new philosophy, however, the knowledge was based only on the singular. There would be no essences of Aristotelian kind at all. It may be argued that this "nominalist" stress on the singular led to the conception of inductive science. [5]

Inheritance of the Medieval Thinkers

But this modification of the Aristotelian framework was not all that happened during that time. It may be even called only the first precondition of modern science. The other precondition was the theology of the thinkers of that time itself. This theology was not only about "adjusting" Aristotle so that he would fit the Christian understanding. This theology also provided some insights that may well be interpreted as anticipating some principles and discoveries of the future science. In this way it seems plausible that Christianity did not only create a favorable intellectual atmosphere for the modern science, but may even have given a direct inspiration for some concepts and models of the new science.

One such figure of great importance is a Franciscan monk, Roger Bacon (1210-1292). He was among the first to stress the scientific importance of the empirical and experimental studies. Bacon's observations in the field of optics were probably the main sources behind the idea of the telescope. Bacon is also important for emphasizing the role of mathematics for sciences. This was one aspect that lacked in the Aristotle's physics. Aristotle could observe the nature, but he apparently did not think that mathematics would be useful in the study of nature, because nature does not display anything close to the harmony in mathematics. Here's where Bacon's ideas turn the tables. Bacon realizes that behind the seeming ambiguity of the natural phenomena there may still be hidden a strict mathematical order. Later, Galilei took up this idea and develop-

---

[4] Ernan McMullin, *Construction and Constraint: The Shaping of Scientific Rationality* (Notre Dame: Univeristy of Notre Dame Press, 1988), 60. Edward Grant, *The Foundations of Modern Science in the Middle Ages* (Cambridge: Cambridge University Press, 1996), 70-74.

[5] McMullin, *op. cit.*, 60.

ed the modern notion of experiment, where nature must be put into an artificial situation, so that its hidden orderliness would be revealed. [6]

The next major thinker on the road from medieval Christianity to modern science is William Ockham. He criticized Aristotelian metaphysics, claiming that this metaphysics limits God's freedom and omnipotence by forcing God to act according to certain rules and by stating that the world had no beginning. In Ockham's view, God is completely free to create the world however he chooses. Ockham is also a nominalist and therefore he, like Bacon, stresses that knowledge is based on experience of individual things. From this he develops his famous principle, "Ockham's razor" stating that there is no need to postulate a greater number of entities or factors when fewer will be enough to explain certain phenomena (*non est ponenda pluritas sine necessitate*). This principle has become one of the classic characteristics of good science. [7]

The third figure whose inheritance has found its way to modern science is Jean Buridan, the Rector of the University of Paris around 1340. Buridan is credited mainly for his theory of impetus. This theory had a long history [8] and it may have provided an alternative to Aristotelian understanding of motion and maybe it even anticipated Newton's First Law of Motion. According to Buridan, moving bodies can acquire impetus that helps them to speed up and remain in motion (Aristotle had explained the same phenomena with the conception of the air pushing the object from behind). Buridan makes even a more daring move. He applies his theory of impetus on heavenly bodies. That would be inconceivable for Aristotle, since celestial and terrestrial spheres are completely different from each other. The celestial sphere was orderly and eternal, the terrestrial on the other hand was constantly changing and short-lived. [9] But Buridan claims that there is a similarity in the movement of earthly and heavenly objects. His theological argument that he uses to explain this clearly shows how closely physical science and theology were related. Buridan writes:

> "Also, since it does not appear from the Bible that there are intelligences to whom it pertains to move the heavenly bodies, one could say that there seems no need to posit such intelligences. For it might be said that when God created the world He moved each of the celestial orbs however He pleased; and in moving them He impressed an impetus which moves them without His moving them any more, except in the way of general influence, just as He concurs on co-acting in everything which is done. ... And those

---

[6] Bumbulis, *op. cit.*

[7] Grant, *op. cit.*, 142-146. David Luscombe, *Medieval Thought* (Oxford, New York: Oxford University Press, 1997), 155-157.

[8] Frederick Copleston, *A History of Medieval Philosophy* (London: Methuen & Co, 1972), 272-273.

[9] Bumbulis, *op. cit.* Grant, *op. cit.*, 95-98.

> impetuses impressed upon the heavenly bodies were not afterwards lessened or corrupted because there was no inclination of the heavenly bodies to other motions nor was there the resistance which would corrupt or restrain that impetus." [10]

Buridan's work was very popular among Christian scholars in the 15th century. There may well be a relatively direct link from Bacon, Ockham, and Buridan to Copernicus, Galilei, and Newton. Especially Copernicus and Galilei worked precisely in this late-medieval mindset that was influenced by these pioneers of scientific thought.

At this point, however, some critical remarks must be made. It seems that sometimes the advocates of Christian influences on modern science seem to overlook the negative reactions that the theories of Bacon and others encountered in the Church leadership. Bacon, for example, was held in prison in the Paris convent, because of the alleged "novelty" of his teachings. His fellow brothers did not think of him as a scientist, but as a "wizard" who probably even knew the secret of how to turn lead into gold. [11] This shows that the overall medieval mindset, although it was Christian, was not overwhelmingly favorable to the development of sciences.

More importantly, the interpretation of Aristotle by the leading medieval theologian, *doctor angelicus*, Thomas Aquinas (1125-1274) did not have this "nominalist" tendency to look with special interest at singular and particular entities. For that reason it would seem that his doctrine of God as the "unmoved mover" or the first cause of every motion could not effectively provoke a scientific interest for the study of nature. His theology had already explained how nature works. There is a series of causes that reaches back to God from every particular appearance. In this view, with its rather pantheistic tendencies, a scientist could, of course, study these causal relations between different levels of reality, but it would be ultimately uninteresting for him to do that, because Aquinas has already told him, what he will find at the end of his inquiry – he will find God. And this is not even an interesting God with certain patterns of rationality, with intentions and personality. This is only a God who is the absolute principle of the movement, nothing more and nothing less. This result practically cancels out the effect of Aquinas' theory that the study of nature is in principle a good and valuable activity that helps to show the power of God even to a non-Christian mind. And since Aquinas was extremely influential, it is necessary to bear in mind that his thought probably rather hindered than promoted the development of modern science.

---

[10] John Buridan, "Questions on Aristotle's Metaphysics", in *Philosophy in the Middle Ages: The Christian, Islamic, and Jewish Traditions*, edited by Arthur Hyman and James J. Walsh (Indianapolis/Cambridge: Hackett Publishing Company, 1973).

[11] Dianna L. Dodson, "Fryar Roger Called Bachon", (1999), *www.thehistorynet.com/ BritishHeritage/articles/1999/05992_text.htm*.

To conclude this brief discussion of the medieval thought we should note that it would be an overstatement to suppose that this period was nothing but the preparation for the birth of modern natural sciences. In fact, a great deal of intellectual and political activity of that time was directed towards the opposite goal, i.e. safeguarding commonly accepted beliefs.

However, there seem to be some aspects of medieval thought that indicate some ways in which Christianity actually may have paved the way for today's natural sciences. The first aspect is that medieval theologians rarely considered the world of nature as something irrational or not worthy of studying. It was firmly believed that this world was created by a rational God and the rationality of this God manifests itself in the nature. The second aspect is that, at the side of the mainline Aristotelian understanding, there was within this general theological context an alternative, more nominalist and experimental approach to the nature and this was something that the first modern scientists could make use of. And finally, there apparently were at least some theories like Buridan's theory of impetus, that were based on theological ideas and later turned out to be anticipations of some modern astronomical of physical theories.

Newton's Mechanics and Theology – an Unhappy Marriage

This close connection between theology and physics not only characterizes the medieval thinkers, but it is also an important feature in the thinking of the representatives of the modern scientific revolution. Let us consider Sir Isaac Newton (1642-1727) himself as an example.

Throughout his life Newton was interested in Bible and theology, although he was not an orthodox theologian. His theological beliefs were, rather, Arian, i.e. he denied the divinity of Christ and had difficulties accepting the doctrine of Trinity, but he was certainly as much interested in establishing Christianity on a sound and authentic foundation, as were the great theologians of Reformation. [12]

Newton's science was closely related to his theology. For him, the order and beauty of nature, the skillfully constructed bodies of animals, and other such phenomena indicated the presence of an intelligent, incorporeal, and omnipresent being in the universe. He writes:

> "Whence arises this uniformity in all their outward shapes but from the counsel and contrivance of an Author? Whence is it that all the eyes of all sorts of living creatures are transparent to the very bottom and the only transparent members in the body, having on the outside a hard transparent skin and within transparent layers

---

[12] H. McLachlan, ed., *Sir Isaac Newton, Theological Manuscripts*, selected and edited by H. McLachlan (Liverpool: The University Press, 1950).

with a crystalline lens in the middle and a pupil before the lens – all of them so truly shaped and fitted for vision that no Artist can mend them? Did blind chance know that there was light and what was its refraction, and fit the eyes of all creatures after the most curious manner to make use of it?" [13]

More specifically, the absoluteness and universality of the laws of motion seemed to be in direct connection with omnipotent and omnipresent God. God was somehow directly present to every event and entity throughout the physical space. This view was sometimes even interpreted in a way that for Newton, space was the actual sensory organ of God. However, Newton himself probably would not have agreed with such statement. [14]

In any case, Newton's philosophy of nature became very popular among theologians, especially through the works of Samuel Clarke. [15] During the 17th century it had become a common understanding among educated people that Christian religion and its revelation could not be proved without some help from philosophy. It was thought that theology is limited by faith and, therefore, remains foreign to those who do not believe. Theology, once a mistress of every human intellectual activity, had now itself grown to be dependent on philosophy, including natural sciences.

In this atmosphere theologians received Newton's theories with extraordinary enthusiasm. There appeared a phenomenon, called "physico-theology" which pointed out some features of the natural world that could not have been brought to existence by natural causes alone. Newton himself said that the stability of the planetary system around the Sun is such that it can only be explained with God's direct intervention that keeps the system from collapsing. [16] But this was a development that turned out to be the crucial factor in the final separation of theology from modern science.

Newton and physico-theologians had created a "God of the gaps", a God who would be used as an explanation of such natural phenomena that the science itself cannot explain. But it is easy to see how this view of God can be discredited, if scientific discoveries show that the gaps can be explained purely through natural causes. As soon as it turned out that the stability of planetary systems is nothing unnatural, considering the interplay of the movement of the planets and the forces of gravity, Newton's physico-theology started to look very primitive, even foolish.

---

[13] *Ibid.*, 48-49.

[14] H. G. Alexander, ed., *The Leibniz-Clarke Correspondence* (Manchester, New York: Manchester University Press, 1956).

[15] John Hedley Brooke, *Science and Religion: Some Historical Perspectives* (Cambridge: Cambridge University Press, 1991), 157.

[16] Sir Isaac Newton, *Mathematical Principles of Natural Philosophy* (Berkeley: University of California Press, 1947), 544. Brooke, *op. cit.*, 144-151.

On the other side, many theologians were also unhappy with the new mechanistic picture of the world. Among other problems, it posed a threat to traditional catholic interpretation of Eucharist. According to Thomas Aquinas, the accidents of color, odor, and taste of bread and wine could remain unchanged, while their substance would be turned into the body and blood of Christ. But in the new philosophy there was no longer such distinction between accidents and substance. Every change in substance would be detectable by the senses. This and similar problems led to a situation where theology had no effective strategies for dealing with the new questions and challenges posed by the ever faster developing sciences.

Thus it is no wonder that a completely new understanding of the relationship between science and theology started to develop in the 19th century. According to this understanding, theology has nothing to offer to natural sciences. Physics needs nothing beyond physical principles to explain nature. This is the common view until our times. Sometimes it has even been extrapolated backwards to suggest that Christianity or theology have never contributed anything to the development of science. This, however, as we have seen, is an overstatement. Christianity has had its specific and unique role in the history of modern science.

We will never know what would have happened if Newton had not interpreted the relationship between science and theology in this particular way. In a sense, Newton remained in the tradition of Aristotle and Aquinas, stressing the existence of unbroken causal chain from this world to God. Therefore, the rejection of Newton's physico-theology may also be interpreted as the ultimate rejection of Aristotelian physics and metaphysics. At the end of this process theology and physics now stand as completely separated areas of human thought. The open question is: Will they remain separated forever? Or is there a way to re-introduce the ideas of God's freedom and love into the discussions between physicists and their audience? The answer will be given by history, but I would not completely rule out the possibility that theology, the abandoned mistress will return and claim her heritage.

Einige Argumente wider die Gegensätzlichkeit von Religion und Wissenschaft

Andres Herkel, Tallinn

Für das in der Überschrift genannte Gegensatzpaar gibt es nähere und entferntere Analogien: Mythos und Logos, Mythologie und Logik, Intuition und Rationalität, kosmologisches und historisches Bewußtsein usw. Der vorliegende Aufsatz betrachtet nicht die Beziehung oder Gegensätze zwischen Religion und Wissenschaft in der modernen Welt, sondern im Blickpunkt unseres Interesses sollen die alten Hochkulturen (Altindien, antikes-Griechenland) und die Entstehung einer solchen Denkweise stehen, die man mit dem modernen wissenschaftlichen Denken vergleichen kann. Konkret betrachten wir hier zwei hervorragende Denkrichtungen - den *Mahāyāna*-Buddhismus und die Schule der Pythagoräer. Verläuft der Weg der Entstehung des wissenschaftlichen Denkens auf einer Einbahnstraße, auf der man Glaube und Mythos, Intuition und kosmologisches Bewußtsein lieblos beiseite wirft? Oder herrschen zwischen Religion und Wissenschaft, zwischen Mythos und Logos irgendwelche anderen, friedlicheren Verbindungen?

Ein charakteristischer Zug des menschlichen Denkens ist jedoch die Kategorisierung der Welt mittels gegensätzlicher Paare und damit verbundener einseitiger Wertschätzung: Dem Guten steht das Böse gegenüber, dem Erhabenen das Niedere, dem Schönen das Häßliche. Wie schon gesagt, werden diese einfachen Muster dazu benutzt auch für die Entwicklung des Denkens selber und für die Unterscheidung verschiedener Denktypen. Eines der bekanntesten Beispiele ist Lucien Lévi-Bruhls Hypothese des vorlogischen Denkens.[1] Diese Theorie stellt die auf mystische Zusammenhänge basierenden Denkweisen sogenannter primitiver Völker der westlichen Denkweise gegenüber, die sich auf die Gesetze der Logik stützt.

Obwohl Lévi-Bruhls Hypothese wegen ihrer diskriminierenden und vereinfachten Haltung heutzutage stark an Einfluß verloren hat, so lebt doch ihr Geist der Gegensätzlichkeit beharrlich weiter. Nach der allgemein verbreiteten Auffassung entstand das logische und wissenschaftliche Denken erstmalig in Griechenland. Gegen diese Behauptung ist von sich aus schwierig etwas entgegenzusetzen. Sicher aber muß man nicht mit alledem übereinstimmen, wenn in diesem Zusammenhang in gleicher Weise vereinfachte Gegensatzpaare schlichtweg wiederholt werden: unlogisch *contra* logisch, mythologisch *contra* wissen-

---

[1] L. Lévy-Bruhl, Les fonctions mentales dans le sociétés inférieures. Paris, 1910.

schaftlich oder gar religiös *contra* philosophisch.

Manchmal ist es nicht einmal nötig, ganze Bücher zu lesen, um etwas über diese Gegensätze zu erfahren, da schon die Titel für sich sprechen. Zum Beispiel Wilhelm Nestles Werk *Vom Mythos zum Logos* (1942) [2] und genauso wiederholt es im russischsprachigem Kulturraum Feohari Kessidis "Ot mifa k logosu" (1972). In der französischen Fachliteratur begünstigt jene Gegensatzpaare ein so berühmter Forscher wie Jean-Pierre Vernant, der für einen Artikel die Überschrift *Du mythe à la raison* (1957) [3] wählte. Der Vernant-Schüler Marcel Detienne nimmt ebenfalls für die Überschrift seiner Forschung den Gegensatz zwischen religiösen und philosophischem Denken zum Anlaß – *De la pensée religieuse à la pensée philosophique* (1963) [4]. Um diese Aufzählung noch repräsentativer zu machen, ergänzen wir hier noch die Monographie des Engländers Francis Cornford *From Religion to Philosophy* (1912) [5]. Dies sind bei weitem keine schlechten Arbeiten. Gleichsam liegt aber das Problem derartiger, in der Überschrift verwendeter Ideologeme, darin, daß die Entwicklung vom Logos zum Mythos als eine Einbahnstraße betrachtet wird, bei der die Aufgabe moderner Forscher ist, Wegweiser und Kilometersteine sorgfältig zu lesen und zu kartieren. Besonders willkürlich wird eine solche Herangehensweise, wenn versucht wird, diesen als unumstößlich dargestellten Entwicklungspfad nach antikgriechischem Vorbild auch anderen antiken Hochkulturen aufzudrücken.

Meiner Meinung nach ist es aber auch möglich, entgegengesetzte Beispiele zu finden, die eine solche einseitige Entwicklung *ad absurdum* führen lassen. Besonders treffend dafür ist der *Mahāyāna*-Buddhismus, welcher sich in den ersten Jahrhunderten nach Christus in Indien entwickelte. Bekannterweise hat der *Mahāyāna*-Buddhismus, und besonders die zur *Mādyamika*-Schule gehörenden Gelehrten, viele rein theoretische Erkenntnisse gewonnen: unter anderem mehrwertige Logik, eine *Prasaṅgika* genannte rhetorische Technik, mit der der Opponent jegliche Behauptungen ins Absurde führen kann; die Verwendung der Begriffe Null und Unendlich und die Unterscheidung zwischen dem Zeichen und dem, was das Zeichen bedeutet. [6]

---

[2] W. Nestle, Vom Mythos zum Logos. Stuttgart, 1942; F. Kessidi, Ot mifa k logosu (stanovlenije gretšeskoi filosofii). Moskva, 1972.

[3] J.-P. Vernant, Du mythe à la raison : la formation de la pensée positive dans la Grèce archaïque. – *Annales*, 1957, p. 183 – 206. Die gleiche Formulierung verwendet Vernant noch Jahre später als Untertitel des mit Pierre Vidal-Naquet zusammen verfaßten Sammelbandes La Grèce ancienne. 1. Du mythe à la raison. Paris, 1990. Dort erscheint auch der früher in den "Annalen" veröffentlichte Artikel.

[4] M. Detienne, De la pensée religieuse à la pensée philosophique. La notion de daîmon dans le pythagorisme ancien. Paris, 1963.

[5] F. M. Cornford, From Religion to Philosophy. London, 1912.

[6] Leider kann an dieser Stelle nicht ausführlicher auf die Errungenschaften des *mādhyamika* eingegangen werden. Siehe R. H. Robinson, Some Logical Aspects of Nāgārjuna's System. – *Philosophy East & West*, 1957, vol. 6, pp. 291 – 308; F. Streng, Emptiness: A Study in Religious Meaning. New York, 1967; L. Mäll, Une approche possible du

Vergleiche zwischen den Betrachtungen Nāgārjunas, des berühmtesten Vertreters der *Mādyamika*-Schule und modernen Denkern wurden Ende des 20. Jahrhunderts besonders populär. Vor allem betrieben derartige Studien Autoren in den Zeitschriften für vergleichende Philosophie *Philosophy of East & West* und *International Philosophical Quarterly*, betrachtend dabei die Ansichten Nāgārjunas im Vergleich mit modernen Thesen der Physik, [7] mit der Kritik der Sprache von Wittgenstein [8] und mit der Dekonstruktion von Derrida [9]. Damit hat sich die Paul Masson-Oursel´sche Vorhersagung der vergleichender Philosophie bestätigt. Er führt an, daß ein einziges Gedankensystem nicht in der Lage ist, als universeller Maßstab des menschlichen Geistes zu gelten und daß die Philosophie erst dann auf höchstes Niveau gelangt, wenn Forschungen sich nicht mehr auf die Errungenschaften nur einer Zivilisation stützten. [10] David Loy, einer der eifrigsten Entwickler der mit dem Buddhismus verbundenen Komparativismus, sagt zum Beispiel, daß kein Stilkontrast so schwer vorzustellen sei wie der zwischen Nāgārjunas lakonischem Stil und der mehrschichtigen *bricolage* von Jacques Derrida – behandeln doch beide ähnliche oder nahe beieinander liegende Probleme: Zeit und Kausalität, Leerheit (sanskr. *śūnyatā*), Differenz (frz. *différance*) und Dekonstruktion. [11]

So besteht kein Zweifel, daß Nāgārjuna – wie auch seine Schüler, Enkelschüler und andere, die diese Tradition fortsetzten (Āryadeva, Čandrakîrti, Bhāvaviveka, Šāntideva, Šāntarakšita, Kamalaśîla) denjenigen Denktyp vertreten, der einen Vergleich mit unseren modernen Wissenschaften zuläßt. Nicht genug, daß sie über viele theoretische Erkenntnisse verfügten, zu denen die westlichen

---

Śūnyavāda. – *Tel Quel*, 1968 (32), p. 54 – 62 (russ. *Terminologia Indica*. Tartu, 1967, lk. 13 – 24); D. Seyfort Ruegg, The Uses of the Four Positions of the *Catuskoti* and the Problem of Description of Reality in Mahāyāna Buddhism. – *Journal of Indian Philosophy*, 1977, Vol. 5, No. 1 / 2, pp. 1 – 71; L. Mäll, Nulli ja lõpmatuse kohal. Tartu, 1998, lk. 299 – 311.

[7] V. Mansfield, Mādhyamika Buddhism and Quantum Mechanics: Beginning a Dialogue. – *International Philosophical Quarterly*, 1989, Vol. 29, No. 4, pp. 371 – 391; V. Mansfield, Relativity in Mādhyamika Buddhism and Modern Physics. – *Philosophy East & West*, 1990, Vol. 40, No. 1, pp 59 – 72.

[8] C. Gudmunsen, Wittgenstein and Buddhism. London 1977; T. Anderson, Wittgenstein and Nāgārjuna's Paradox. – *Philosophy of East & West*, 1985, Vol. 35, No. 2, pp. 157 – 169.

[9] D. Loy, The Mahāyāna Deconstruction of Time. – *Philosophy East & West*, 1986, Vol. 34, No. 1, pp. 13 – 23; D. Loy, The Clôture of Deconstruction: A Mahāyāna Critique of Derrida. – *International Philosophical Quarterly*, 1987, Vol. 27, No. 1, pp. 59 – 80; K. Liberman, The Grammatology of Emptiness: Postmodernism, the Madhyamaka Dialectics and the Limits of the Text. – *International Philosophical Quarterly*, 1991, Vol. 31, No. 4, pp. 435 – 448; I. Mabbett, Nāgārjuna and Deconstruction. – *Philosophy East & West*, 1995, Vol. 45, No. 2, pp. 203 – 225.

[10] P. Masson-Oursel, Comparative Philosophy. New York, 1926, p. 33 – 35 .

[11] D. Loy, The Clôture of Deconstruction, p. 64 – 65.

Wissenschaften erst in den letzten Hundert Jahren gelangten. Besonders bemerkenswert ist, daß Texte auf höchstem philosophischem Niveau nicht nur von uns sicher bekannten Autoren geschrieben wurden, sondern auch mündlich weitergegeben worden sind, deren teilweise mythologische Autorenschaft man Gautama Buddha selbst oder einiger seiner herausragendsten Schüler zuschrieb.

Es gilt nun, hier zu betonen, daß buddhistische Sutren Texte mit religiösem Inhalt waren und Nāgārjuna, Čandrakîrti und andere Gelehrte zweifellos religiöse Denker waren, die Gautama Buddhas Erleuchtungsideal folgten. Also können wir hier nicht von dem Ersetzen der religiösen durch die philosophische Denkweise sprechen. Gleichfalls kann von dem Ersatz des mythologischen Denkens durch wissenschaftliches Denken nicht die Rede sein, denn wissenschaftliches Denken entstand, aber die Mythologie ging nicht verloren. Im Gegenteil, im *Mahāyāna* gestaltet sich die Galerie der mythologischen Wesen (Buddhas und Bodhisattvas) besonders reichhaltig. Das bedeutet, zur gleichen Zeit, in der die Gedankenwelt komplizierter, bzw. "wissenschaftlicher", logischer und philosophischer wird, [12] werden im Falle des Mahāyāna auch die Mythologie und Kosmologie reichhaltiger und komplizierter. Im Gegensatz zu der im *Hînayāna* beschränkten Mythologie erscheinen auf ungezählten Buddhafeldern (*buddhaksetra*) ungezählte Buddhafiguren. [13] Diese Bereicherung der Mythologie setzt sich noch später im *Vajrayāna* fort. [14]

Eine derartige Kulturtatsache läßt sich nun überhaupt nicht mehr vereinbaren mit der durch die griechische Antike beeinflußte festgefahrene Vorstellung einer Einbahnstraße vom Mythos zum Logos, bei der der ältere Denktyp einfach zurückweicht.

Die moderne Denkpsychologie hat sich weitestgehend von dem Modell des Gegenüberstellens von Mythologischem und Logischem verabschiedet und das beste Erklärungsprinzip für die Entwicklung des Denkens ist die Reflexion bzw. Fähigkeit, über das Denken als solches kritisch zu denken. Diese Herangehensweise läßt sich auch mit der *Mahāyāna*-Mythologie vereinbaren. So muß man die Bodhisattvas im *Mahāyāna* und *Dhyāni*-Buddhas im späteren *Vajrayāna* als anthropomorphe Meditationssymbole sehen. Die Technik zur Hervorrufung dieses Zustandes wird Imagination oder Visualisation (*bhāvanā*) genannt. Also

---

[12] Buddhisten unterscheiden verschiedene Denktypen längst nicht so streng, wie wir es gewöhnlich tun. Die wichtigste Trennung, die Buddhisten vornehmen, ist die Unterscheidung von gewöhnlicher Wahrheit und höherer Wahrheit. Siehe F. Streng, The Significance of Pratîtyasamutpāda for Understanding the Relationship between Samvrti and Paramārthasatya in Nāgārjuna. – The Problem of Two Truths in Buddhism and Vedanta. Dordrecht / Boston, 1973, pp. 27 – 39; gleichfalls auch in anderen Artikeln des gleichen Sammelbandes.

[13] D. L. Snellgrove, Celestial Buddhas and Bodhisattvas. – The Encyclopedia of Religion. Ed. in chief M. Eliade. Vol. 3. New York, 1987, p. 133 - 144; L. Mäll, Op. cit., lk. 183 – 185, 277 – 287; A. Sadakata, Buddhist Cosmology: Philosophy and Origins. Tokyo, 1998.

[14] J. Blofeld, The Way of Power. London, 1970; L. Mäll, Op. cit., lk. 185 – 186 jm.

kann man hier von bewußter Mythenschaffung sprechen, was sehr gut mit dem Entwicklung der Reflexion im Denken zusammenpaßt.

Eine der besten Arbeiten über die Ausbildung des reflexiven Denkens gibt der englische Ethnologe Robin Horton,[15] der darüber in Afrika geforscht hat. Zunächst findet Horton zwischen traditionellem (afrikanischen) und wissenschaftlichem Denken überraschend viele Ähnlichkeiten: beispielsweise beide verwenden Vergleiche, um komplexe Erscheinungen durch einfachere zu erklären. Und trotzdem gibt es etwas, was in Afrika fehlt, was aber in Europa zum Motor für sowohl wissenschaftliche Methodik als auch für die Herausbildung des Selbstbewußtsein war – das Vorhandensein von alternativen Denkweisen in einer Kultur. Traditionelle Kulturen aber beinhalten nicht mehr als ein einziges Denksystem. Dem Bestehen dieser Monosystemik helfen starke Schutzmechanismen und Tabus, die den Vergleich mit anderen Völkern nicht zulassen, geschweige den, mit fremden in schöpferischen Dialog zu treten oder sogar Elemente ihrer Denkweise zu übernehmen.[16] Erst wenn eine Kultur alternative Denksysteme besitzt, läßt sich darüber streiten, welches das richtigere ist oder welches die genaueste Übereinstimmung mit der Wirklichkeit hat. Nur in einer polysystemischen Kultur kann eine Methodologie entstehen, die es ermöglicht, das Denken selbst zu analysieren und verschiedene erklärende Systeme zu erforschen wie nach dem inneren Aufbau von Wissenschaft, Glaube oder Mythologie. Um es kurz zusammenzufassen: Nur in einer polysystemischen Kultur entsteht Reflexion bzw. denken über das Denken selbst.[17]

Nach Horton läßt sich das Phänomen des griechischen Altertums mit der Entstehung einer polysystemischen Kultur erklären. Er nennt als entscheidenden Faktor die Verbreitung der Schriftkunde, die Entwicklung heterogener Gemeinschaften und weitreichende Handelsbeziehungen.[18]

Meines Erachtens kann man Hortons Ansicht auch auf die altindische Kultur erweitern – besonders für die Periode der Entstehung des Buddhismus aber auch noch etwas später. Der Buddhismus entstand in einer Zeit des intensiven Gärens und Konkurrierens verschiedener Lehren. Um verschiedene Lehrer scharten sich Gruppen von wandernden Asketen, die alle eine höhere Wahrheit bzw. einen Weg der Erlösung oder Erleuchtung suchten. Dies bedeutete das Aufeinandertreffen von verschiedenen Ansichten und Weltanschauungen, wobei vielleicht der psychologische Einfluß des einen oder anderen Lehrers wichtiger war als konkrete Argumente. Dispute unter den Lehrern waren ganz gewöhnlich. Derartige Streitgespräche waren strengen Disputregeln unterworfen, wobei es praktisch ein ungeschriebenes Gesetz war, daß der im Wortgefecht unterlegene

---

[15] R. Horton, African traditional thought and Western Science. – *Africa*, 1967, Vol. 37, pp. 50 – 71, 155 – 187.

[16] R. Horton, Op. cit, pp. 175 – 176.

[17] P. Tulviste, Mõtlemise muutumisest ajaloos. Tallinn, 1984, lk. 80 – 81.

[18] R. Horton, Op. cit, pp. 180 – 185.

Lehrer seine durchgefallene Lehre nicht mehr weiter verbreiten konnte. Normale Verhaltensweise in einem solchen Falle war, daß man dann Schüler des Siegers wurde. [19] Daraus folgt, daß nicht nur der Gegensatz verschiedener Lehren und Glaubensrichtungen etwas ganz gewöhnliches waren, sondern auch das Glaubenswechseln. Eine solche Umwelt schuf alle Voraussetzungen zur Verbreitung eines polysystemischen und reflexiven Denkens unter der geistigen Elite.

Etwas ähnliches setzte sich dann später zur Blütezeit des Buddhismus fort. Der Buddhismus teilte sich rasch in viele verschiedene Schulen. Unter ihnen gab es auch solche, die der Auffassung waren, daß Buddhas Wort nicht als ewig geltende und dogmatische Wahrheit zu halten sei, sondern daß die Lehre sich jederzeit weiterentwickeln müsse. Zweck der Tradition war hierin nicht die Erhaltung des "reinen Urtextes", sondern die Entwicklung der Lehre, entsprechend der individuellen Besonderheiten der neuen Schüler. [20] (Wenn wir also den modernen Sprachgebrauch benutzen, dann war eben Offenheit und Polysystemik dies, was man von Generation zu Generation weitergab.)

Zusammenfassend kann man mit der These übereinstimmen, daß gerade das Vorhandensein alternativer Denksysteme in einer Kultur zur Triebfeder wird, die die Entwicklung des Denkens fördert. Man kann aber nicht mit jener These übereinstimmen, daß mit der Entwicklung des Denkens mythologisches Denken durch logisches Denken ersetzt wird. Gerade das Vorhandensein verschiedener Denksysteme als solches ist wesentlich, nicht aber die Frage, welches der konkurrierenden Systeme ist "richtig" oder wird von jemanden für richtig gehalten.

Derartige Schlußfolgerungen finden sich auch in vielen Gedankengängen von Claude Lévi-Strauss und Juri Lotman. Lévi-Strauss meint, daß die Entwicklung der Menschheit nicht Schritt für Schritt wie etwa auf einer Treppe vonstatten geht, sondern eher auf- und abgeht, mit unerwarteten Ritten oder wie in einem Würfelspiel, indem in einem günstigen Moment die Ergebnisse verschiedener Würfel einen kumulativen Effekt ergeben. [21] Das, was weiterführt, ist nicht eine Kultur für sich, sondern die "Koalition der Kulturen", deren produktive Verschränkung. Nach Lotman ist ein Bewußtsein, welches fähig ist, neue Texte zu schaffen, von seiner Wesensart heterogen und muß in sich verschiedene semiotische Strukturen enthalten. Er sagte: "Eine minimale denkbare Einheit muß wenigstens zwei unterschiedlich aufgebaute Systeme enthalten, die sich gegenseitig die gewonnenen Informationen austauschen." [22] Also ist es nicht in erster Linie wichtig, ob das dominierende Denksystem Religion oder Wissen-

---

[19] A. Paribok, "Voprossõ Milindõ" i ih mesto v istorii buddiiskoi mõsli. – Voprossõ Milindõ (*Bibliotheca Buddhica* XXXVI). Moskva, 1989, str. 19 – 62.

[20] L. Mäll, Op. cit., lk. 226 – 227.

[21] C. Lévi-Strauss, Anthropologie structurale deux. Paris, 1973, p. 393 – 394.

[22] J. Lotman, Kultuurisemiootika. Tallinn, 1990, lk. 218.

schaft, Mythos oder Logos ist – wesentlich ist die Entstehung einer neuen Qualität, die durch das Aufeinandertreffen verschiedener Denksysteme ermöglicht wird.

Folglich entsteht die Versuchung zu fragen, ob dieser Weg vom Mythos zum Logos, den wir aufgrund der griechischen Antike gewöhnt sind, als sicher gegeben hinzunehmen, immer ein so fließender und klarer Übergang war, wie dies in der Geschichte der Philosophie bei oberflächlicher Betrachtung scheint. In der Geschichte der antikgriechischen Philosophie sind die Beziehungen zwischen Religion und Wissenschaft bei Pythagoras und seiner Schule besonders verworren. Aber gerade deshalb wollen wir hier kurz die Lehre der Pythagoräer und deren Widerspiegelung in der modernen Wissenschaft betrachten.

Der Pythagoräismus setzte seine Priorität auf die Reinigung der Seele und Befreiung im Gange des Werden und Vergehens. Zusätzlich zu Askese und strengen Vorschriften konzentrierte die Schule ihre Bemühungen auf den Begriff der Zahl. Die Zahl war gleichsam Gottheit und Seele, ordnendes Prinzip und schaffende Macht, die das Urchaos durch eine harmonische und geordnete Welt ersetzte. Besondere Bedeutung hatte beispielsweise die Zahl Eins, die für die Pythagoräer nicht nur einfach eine Zahl wie jede andere, sondern Symbol allumfassender Einheit, die Grundlage aller anderen Zahlen war. Die Zahlen der Pythagoräer waren gleichsam Gestalten: Die Eins entsprach dem Punkt, die zwei der Linie zwischen zwei Punkten, die drei entsprach der flächigen und die vier der räumlichen Gestalt. So war das Operieren mit Zahlen – also Mathematik – den Pythagoräern eine heilige Handlung. Diese von ihrem Inhalt her religiöse Handlung führte also zu herausragenden wissenschaftlichen Leistungen wie etwa dem Satz des Pythagoras, zur Entdeckung der irrationalen Zahlen und den Grundlagen der Stereometrie.

Gewöhnlich unterscheidet man in der Entwicklung des Pythagoräismus drei oder sogar vier Etappen. Von ihnen – zwar am schlechtesten dokumentiert, aber philosophiegeschichtlich am interessantesten – ist die mit Pythagoras selbst verbundene Periode des frühen Pythagoräismus. Die hauptsächliche Quelle dafür bilden die ein wenig später aufgezeichneten Texte des Philosophen Philolaos. In den Werken Platons und Aristoteles finden sich auch noch Hinweise, doch nach ihnen läßt sich nicht die authentische Lehre rekonstruieren. Danach folgen bereits die Beschreibungen der weitaus späteren Philosophen wie Porphyrios und Iamblichos. Diese Quellen sind meines Wissens schon lange in gleicher Weise den Forschern der antikgriechischen Philosophie zugänglich und das Bild, das sich aufgrund jener über die frühen Pythagoräer ergibt, ist verschwommen.

Umso mehr Aufmerksamkeit verdient es, daß die wesentliche Errungenschaft der Pythagoräer – die Entstehung der Mathematik im Rahmen einer religiösen Lehre – sehr unterschiedlich interpretiert worden ist. Nach der Betrachtung der sogenannten alten Schule erfolgt eine klare Abgrenzung zwischen Mythos und Logos oder zwischen Glauben und Wissenschaft. Beispielsweise meinen die deutschen Gelehrten Adolf Döring und besonders Erich Frank, daß der frühe Pythagoräismus nur eine religiöse und moralische Lehre mit dem zentralen Anliegen die Reinigung der Seele war. Wissenschaftliche, darunter mathematische, Interessen konnten erst später hervortreten, als die glaubenshaft-mystische Dominante zu schwinden begann. [23] In die gleiche Richtung gehen auch die Vertreter der englischen Schule John Burnet [24] und Francis Cornford. Die Ansicht von Cornford unterscheidet sich nur gering von denen der deutschen Gelehrten – er vertritt den Standpunkt, daß in der Schule der Pythagoräer von Anfang an zwei radikal unterschiedliche, absolut nicht zusammenpassende Systeme vorhanden waren, das mystische und das wissenschaftliche. [25]

In modernen Abhandlungen ab der zweiten Hälfte des 20. Jahrhunderts nehmen die gegensätzlichen Darstellungen von glaubenshaft-mystischen und wissenschaftlichen Paradigmata schrittweise ab. Den Anfang macht Gustav Junge (1958), der in einem der Entdeckung der irrationalen Zahlen gewidmeten Artikel gleichsam die wesentliche Bedeutung mathematischer Forschungen im religiösen Suchen der frühen Pythagoräer bestätigt, denn gerade jenes Suchen war Grundlage für diese bahnbrechende Entdeckung. [26] Nach der Auffassung von William Guthrie (1962) waren die religiösen und glaubensphilosophischen Seiten in der Lehre der Pythagoräer eng miteinander verwoben, denn "Mathematik war eine religiöse Übung, und die Dekade war ein heiliges Symbol" und die Erlangung der Seelenreinheit ging über die Anstrengung des Verstandes, zum Beispiel verhalf dazu, das Universum mit Hilfe von Proportionen zu verstehen. [27] In ähnliche Auffassung betont dies noch stärker Cornelia de Vogel (1966). [28] Von da an trat eine tolerantere Sichtweise auf die Rolle des Religions bei der Entstehung von Wissenschaft in den Vordergrund, [29] obwohl nach wie vor Publikationen erscheinen, die die alten Gegensätze in Ehren halten.

Ich bin kein Spezialist auf dem Gebiet der Geschichte der griechischen Philosophie und möchte auch hier keine weitergehenden Schlußfolgerungen in bezug auf den Pythagoräismus machen. Paradigmatische Verschiebungen sind in der Geschichte der Wissenschaft natürlich, und es ist dann auch nicht verwunderlich, daß man die Denkakzente der frühen Pythagoräer umbewerten muß.

Eine Entwicklung des Denkens in der Geschichte aber kann man sicher

---

[23] A. Döring, Wandlungen in der pythagoräischen Lehre. – *Archiv für Geschichte der Philosophie*. Berlin, 1892, Bd. V, S. 503 – 531; E. Frank Plato und die sogenannten Pythagoreer. Halle, 1923.

[24] J. Burnet, Early Greek Philosophy. 3th ed. London, 1920.

[25] F. M. Cornford, Mysticism and Science in the Pythagorean Tradition. – *Classical Quarterly*, 1922, pp. 137 – 150, and 1923, 1 – 12.

[26] G. Junge, Von Hippasus bis Philolaus. Das Irrationale und die geometrischen Grundbegriffe. – *Classica et medievalia*. Copenhague, 1958, vol XIX, p. 45.

[27] W. K. C. Guthrie, A History of Greek Philosophy. Vol. I The earlier Presocratics and Pythagoreans. Cambridge, 1962, p. 152 – 153, 182 u.a.

[28] C. J. de Vogel, Pythagoras and early Pythagoreanism. An Interpretation of Neglected Evidence on the Philosopher Pythagoras. Assen, 1966, pp. 8 – 19.

[29] P. Gaidenko, Evoljutsija ponjatija nauki. Stanovlenije i razvitije pervõh naučnõh programm. Moskva, 1980, str. 23 – 26.

nicht leugnen. Zugleich lohnt es sich nicht zu bezweifeln, daß die Entstehung der Philosophie, der Logik, der Mathematik, und der systematischen Rechts- und Geschichtsbetrachtung in Griechenland durch das schrittweise Hervortreten des neuen, vom Typ her wissenschaftlichen Denkens ermöglicht wurde. Jedoch fand diese Entwicklung längst nicht nur in diese eine Richtung statt und folgte auch nicht nach solch universellen Regeln, wie man sich das gerne so vorstellte. Gewöhnlich hält man es für selbstverständlich, daß dann, wenn sich das wissenschaftliche Denken entwickelt, das ästhetische und künstlerische Denken dies ebenfalls tut. Aus irgendwelchen Gründen hält man es dann auch für selbstverständlich, daß religiöses und insbesondere mythologisches Denken in diesem Falle weichen müßte. Leider sind diese Vorurteile immer noch nicht ganz ausgeräumt. Das Beispiel des Buddhismus zeigt, daß im Zusammenhang mit der Entwicklung des wissenschaftliche Denkens gleichermaßen auch das religiöse Denken und die damit verbundene Mythologie komplizierter werden. Das Beispiel der Pythagoräer mag vielleicht nicht ganz so überzeugend sein, dennoch bestätigt es uns aber, daß die Rolle der Religion bei der Entstehung der Wissenschaft bei weiten größer gewesen sein könnte, als wir bisher angenommen haben.

Offenbar stammt die Gegensätzlichkeit von Religion und Wissenschaft aus einer viel späteren europäischen Geschichtsepoche, aus der Zeit der Renaissance, in der neue Kulturströmungen und die damit verbundene experimentelle Wissenschaft in Widerspruch zu dem bis dahin herrschenden klerikalen Weltbild stand. Diese Kluft, die dann zwischen Religion und Wissenschaft entstand, wurde später viel zu leichtfertig auf andere Zeitepochen und Kulturen übertragen.

Vernant's beeindruckende Aussage "der Logos befreit sich vom Mythos, als wenn Schuppen von den Augen eines Blinden fielen",[30] erfordert eine kritische Umbewertung. Ebenso hält auch Burnets Behauptung keiner Kritik stand, wenn er sagt, daß die Grundlage der Fortschritte der Griechen besondere intellektuelle Fähigkeiten waren, die diejenigen anderer Völker übertrafen.[31] Burnet's Aussage zeugt von unbegründeten Eurozentrismus, um nicht gar sagen zu müssen, von Rassismus.

Da wir natürlich solche naiven Erklärungen von der Auserwähltheit eines bestimmten Volkes beiseite lassen, betonen wir nochmals Horton's These, daß die Entwicklung des Denkens nur dann möglich wird, wenn in einer Kultur alternative Denksysteme verbreitet sind. In den alten Kulturen waren diese Alternativen mit glaubenshafter Suche verbunden. Schließlich gilt, daß Polysystemik in Denken und Reflexion nicht nur Anstöße für die Entwicklung des wissenschaftlichen Denkens gibt, sondern auch, daß das religiöse (und teilweise

---

[30] J.-P. Vernant, P. Vidal-Naquet, Op. cit., p. 196.
[31] J. Burnet, Op. cit., p. 10. Eine ähnliche Behauptung äußerte auch beispielsweise Ivan Rožanski, Drevnegrtšeskaja nauka. – Otšerki istorii jestestvennonautšnöh znanii v drevnosti. Moskva, 1982, str. 204.

auch mythologische) Denken neue kreative Anstöße in einer polysystemen Kultur erhält.

Deutsche Übersetzung: Hans-Gunter Lock

Einige Bemerkungen zur
Max Webers Protestantismus-These

Henn Käärik, Tartu

Die von Max Weber aufgeworfenen Fragen nach der inhaltlichen Affinität und nach dem Kausalnexus zwischen protestantischer Ethik, kapitalistischem Geist und kapitalistischem System inspirieren fortdauernd neue Fragen und neue Antworten, neue Deutungen und neue Umdeutungen, neue Ergänzungen und neue Widerlegungen. Ziel des folgenden kurzen Beitrages: nochmals über einige Aspekte von den Wechselbeziehungen zwischen den dogmatischen Gründen und der religiösen Praxis des Calvinismus nachzudenken.

Es sind *prima facie* die dogmatischen Grundlagen, vor allem die Prädestinationslehre (Lehre von der Gnadenwahl), die die Sonderstellung des Calvinismus in der Entwicklungsgeschichte des Okzidents "prädestinieren". Wenn man, so Max Weber, nach der Bedeutung, welche jenem Dogma nach seinen kulturgeschichtlichen Wirkungen zuzumessen ist, fragt, so müssen diese sicherlich hoch veranschlagt werden.[1] Ein (kleiner) Teil der Menschen ist als selig, ein anderer als verdammt von Gott vorbestimmt. Gottes Ratschluß ist vollständig heimlich und unabänderlich. Keine menschliche Tat kann an Gottes absolut freien und willkürlichen Entschlüssen etwas ändern. Ganz unzweideutig: logisch wäre nur der Fatalismus als Konsequenz der Prädestination deduzierbar.[2] Und hier führt Max Weber eine für seine religionssoziologische Gesamtkonstruktion grundlegende Idee von der Bewährung ein. Gerade infolge der Einschaltung des Bewährungsgedankens erwies es sich als möglich, die psychologische Wirkung der Prädestinationslehre völlig umzuwandeln. Nur die Kombination von Prädestinations- und Bewährungsgedanken erlaubt uns diesen enormen Einfluß zu erklären, den der Calvinismus auf die ganze soziokulturelle und wirtschaftliche Sonderentwicklung des Abendlandes ausgeübt hat.[3]

Eine zentrale Frage muß für jeden einzelnen Gläubigen entstehen und alle anderen Interessen in den Hintergrund drängen: "Bin ich erwählt? Und wie kann *ich* dieser Erwählung sicher werden?"[4] Calvin selbst konnte sich als Rüstzeug

---

[1] M. Weber, Gesammelte Aufsätze zur Religionsoziologie. Bd.1. Tübingen: J.C.B. Mohr (Paul Siebeck), 1920, S. 89.

[2] Ebd., S. 111.

[3] Vgl. W. Schluchter. Religion und Lebensführung, Bd. 2. Studien zu Max Webers Religions- und Herrschaftssoziologie. Frankfurt: Suhrkamp, 1991, S. 294–296.

[4] M. Weber, Gesammelte Aufsätze zur Religionssoziologie. Bd. 1, S. 103.

Gottes und deshalb seines Gnadenstandes sicher fühlen. Man muß sich an dem durch den wahren Glauben bewirkten beharrlichen Zutrauen auf Christus genügen lassen. [5] Für die Epigonen und Alltagsmenschen dagegen muß "die *certitudo salutis* im Sinn der *Erkenn*barkeit des Gnadenstandes zu absolut überragender Bedeutung aufsteigen ...". [6] Das widerspruchsvolle Verhältnis zwischen den dogmatischen Grundlagen und der seelsorgerlischen Praxis ist in seiner Angespanntheit für den Calvinismus einzigartig. Einerseits geht es um die dogmatische Theorie, das logische Bedürfnis des Dogmatikers, Ideenreduktionismus, andererseits um das Sicherheitsbedürfnis des Gläubigen, Bedürfnis nach der *certitudo salutis*, Interesse an Heilsgewißheit, Interessenreduktionismus. [7]

Um diese Spannung gewissermaßen zu mildern, brauchte die nachcalvinische Theologie eine Stützkonstruktion, welche wir unter dem Namen "Bewährungsgedanke" kennen.

Der Glaube muß sich in seinen Wirkungen objektiv bewähren, um den unverlierbaren Gnadenstand, um die Heilsgewißheit zu erlangen. Es handelt sich um die praktische Bewährung durch Wirken innerhalb der Welt, um die Bewährung des Glaubens im weltlichen Berufsleben, um die Bewährung vor Gott im Sinn der Versicherung des Heils, um die Bewährung vor den Menschen im Sinn der sozialen Selbstbehauptung. [8] Der Gläubige bewährt sich vor Gott zwar durch Befolgung seiner Gebote, in erster Linie aber mittels der Erfüllung der durch die *lex naturae* gegebenen Berufsaufgaben. [9] Der Bewährungsgedanke ist "psychologischer Ausgangspunkt der methodischen Sittlichkeit", "Schema der Verknüpfung von Glauben und Sittlichkeit". [10] Trotz dieser mannigfaltigen und wichtigen Erläuterungen ist der Status des Bewährungsgedankens in dem Kategoriensystem Max Weberscher Religionssoziologie nicht endgültig klar. Das berührt zuallererst die Beziehung zwischen dem Bewährungsgedanken und der protestantischen Ethik. [11]

Natürlich gestattet der Bewährungsgedanke den Gläubigen nur ihren Gnadenstand (gewissermaßen) zu erkennen und zu kontrollieren, nicht aber zu verändern. Gute Werke sind als Zeichen der Erwählung unentbehrlich. Sie sind das technische Mittel, die Angst um die Seligkeit loszuwerden, nicht jedoch, die

---

[5] Ebd.

[6] Ebd., S. 104.

[7] Vgl. W. Schluchter, Religion und Lebensführung, S. 295.

[8] M. Weber. Gesammelte Aufsätze zur Religionssoziologie, Bd. 1, S. 99–235.

[9] Ebd., S. 101.

[10] Ebd., S. 125.

[11] Der Begriff "protestantische Ethik" selbst bleibt, streng genommen, explizit unbestimmt. Zwar behauptet Weber, daß ein historischer Begriff nicht nach dem Schema "genus proximum, differentia specifica" definiert werden kann, und daß die endgültige begriffliche Erfassung nicht am Anfang stehen kann, sondern am Schluß der Untersuchung (ebd., S. 30). Später hat Weber diese Betrachtungsweise aufgegeben. Vgl. M. Weber. Wirtschaft und Gesellschaft. Grundriß der verstehenden Soziologie. 5. Aufl. Hrsg. v. J. Winckelmann. Tübingen: J.C.B. Mohr (Paul Siebeck), 1971, S. 1.

Seligkeit zu erkaufen.[12]

W. Schluchter weist auf einen möglichen wesentlichen Umbruch in der Genese des Bewährungsgedankens: Diesem wird neben der manifesten noch eine latente Bedeutung unterschoben. Die guten Werke zur Mehrung des Ruhmes Gottes müssen auch weiterhin als gottgewollt und vor allem gottgewirkt gelten, sie werden aber zugleich ins Zeichen der Erwählung uminterpretiert.[13] Immerhin ist hier zu vermuten, daß im Rahmen des Bewährungsgedankens von Anfang an jede sittliche Tätigkeit als Zeichen der göttlichen Gnade interpretiert wurde.

Stattdessen wäre es zweckmäßig, von zwei Entwicklungsstufen des Bewährungsgedankens zu reden. Für die erste ist ein sublimer Gedankengang kennzeichnend. Das Handeln des Menschen entspringt dem durch Gottes Gnade gewirkten Glauben und dieser Glaube wiederum legitimiert sich durch die Qualität jenes Handelns als von Gott gewirkt.[14] Auf dem zweiten kann der Puritaner nicht nur seinen eigenen Gnadenstand und eigenes Verhalten, sondern auch dasjenige Gottes kontrollieren.[15]

Zweifellos bedeutete der Prozeß der Angleichung der Prädestinationslehre an den Bewährungsgedanken einen schwierigen Kompromiß. Darum hat Max Weber mit Recht angemerkt, daß dabei die Gnadenwahl nicht uminterpretiert, gemildert oder im Grunde gar aufgegeben wurde.[16] Wenn nun W. Schluchter diesbezüglich die berühmte Formulierung Max Webers zitiert – Interessen, nicht Ideen, beherrschen unmittelbar das Handeln der Menschen, aber die Weltbilder, welche durch Ideen geschaffen wurden, haben sehr oft als Weichensteller die Bahnen bestimmt, in denen die Dynamik der Interessen das Handeln fortbewegte –, kann ich mit ihm nicht vollkommen einig sein. Ich vermute vielmehr, daß es im Verlaufe der obenerwähnten Angleichung bzw. bei einer "praktischen Interessenverschlingung" den praktischen Interessen gelang, sich die Weichen für die Bahnen im wesentlichen selbst zu stellen, um in ihnen sich das Handeln dann in Eigendynamik fortbewegen zu lassen – das bedeutet Transformation der dogmatischen Grundlagen des Calvinismus, eigentlich eine Umdeutung des Gottesdogmas.

Max Weber unterstellt dem Protestantismus, ein gespaltenes Verständnis über den Charakter des biblischen Gottes:

> *"Beide, Luther und Calvin, kannten eben im Grunde ... einen doppelten Gott: den geoffenbarten gnädigen und gütigen Vater des N.T., – denn dieser beherrscht die ersten Bücher der Institutio Christiana, – und dahinter den "Deus absconditus" als willkürlich*

---

[12] M. Weber. Gesammelte Aufsätze zur Religionssoziologie, Bd. 1, S.110.
[13] W. Schluchter, Religion und Lebensführung, S. 295.
[14] Ebd., S. 108.
[15] Ebd., S. 123.
[16] Ebd., S. 105.

> *schaltenden Despoten. Bei Luther behielt der Gott des Neuen Testaments ganz die Oberhand, weil er die Reflexion über das Metaphysische, als nutzlos und gefährlich, zunehmend mied, bei Calvin gewann der Gedanke an die transzendente Gottheit Macht über das Leben. In der populären Entwicklung des Calvinismus freilich konnte sie sich nicht halten, – aber nicht der himmlische Vater des Neuen Testaments, sondern der Jehova des Alten trat nunmehr an ihre Stelle."* [17]

Wolfgang Schluchter rezipiert diesen wichtigen Max Weberschen Absatz folgendermaßen:

> *"Auch Weber hat bereits in der ersten Fassung der "Protestantischen Ethik" auf die Spannung in der Gottesvorstellung des Calvinismus verwiesen. Dieser kennt den doppelten Gott, "den geoffenbarten gnädigen und gütigen Vater des N(euen) T(estaments), ... und dahinter den "Deus absconditus" als willkürlich schaltenden Despoten" des Alten Testaments."* [18]

Es ist offenkundig, daß W. Schluchter den Gedankengang Max Webers demnach gedeutet hat, als gebe es für ihn nur zwei Götter: den allgnädigen Gott des Neuen Testaments einerseits und den allmächtigen alttestamentlichen *Deus absconditus* andererseits. Gewiß, der Begriff *"Deus absconditus"* ist alttestamentlicher Herkunft (Jesaja 45.15) und bezeichnet den Gott Israels, später auch allgemein das Unoffenbarsein Gottes. Es ist anzunehmen, daß Max Weber den alttestamentlichen Jahve und den *Deus absconditus* nicht identifiziert und stattdessen letzteren als eine selbständige Gottheit betrachtet hat. Das ergibt sich schon aus dem Text, weil hier erstens Jehova an *ihre* Stelle tritt und zweitens sich der *Deus absconditus* als eine transzendente Gottheit im populären Calvinismus "nicht halten konnte" und deshalb von Jahve ersetzt wurde. Weiterhin ist Jahve inhaltlich – ungeachtet dessen, daß er den Titel *"Deus absconditus"* trägt – im Unterschied zum Calvinschen Gott nicht völlig verborgen. Denn er ist wenigstens "teilweise" erkennbar [19], seine Ratschlüsse sind – auf Grund der

---

[17] M. Weber. Gesammelte Aufsätze zur Religionssoziologie. Bd.1. S. 92.

[18] W. Schluchter. Religion und Lebensführung. S.301. Vgl. W. Schluchter. Rationalismus der Weltbeherrschung. Studien zu Max Weber. Frankfurt: Suhrkamp, 1980, S. 26; ders., Einleitung. Zwischen Welteroberung und Weltanpassung. Überlegungen zu Max Webers Sicht des frühen Islams. In: Max Webers Sicht des Islams. Hrsg. v. W. Schluchter. Frankfurt: Suhrkamp, 1987, S.38.

[19] M. Weber. Gesammelte Aufsätze zur Religionssoziologie. Bd. 3. Das antike Judentum. Tübingen: J.C.B. Mohr (Paul Siebeck), 1921, S.116: "persönlich muß man mit Jahwe verkehrt, in der "Ratsversammlung" des Gottes gewesen sein und die Stimme des Herrn selbst gehört haben, wenn das Orakel gelten soll". Vgl. auch U. Masing. The Word of Yahweh. In: *Acta et Commentationes Universitatis Tartuensis (Dorpatensis).* B XXXIX,

berith zwischen Jahve und Israel und der darauf beruhenden Reziprozitätserwartungen – im wesentlichen erkennbar und nicht endgültig unabänderlich.

Man kann aus allem schließen, daß Max Weber in der "Protestantischen Ethik" mit drei verschiedenen Gottesbegriffen operiert. Stellen wir aber nun die folgende Frage: War Jahve wirklich der Gott, der – nach Max Weber – an die Stelle des Calvinschen *Deus absconditus* trat? Wahrscheinlich nicht, weil die Ratschlüsse des nachcalvinischen Gottes einerseits zwar erkennbar, andererseits aber unabänderlich waren. Die guten Werke konnten keine Basis für die Seligkeit sein.

So ist es denkbar, noch von einer vierten Gottheit zu reden, bei der es sich eigentlich um eine äußerst wirkungsvolle Synthese von dem Gott Calvins und dem des Alten Testaments handelt.

Mehr noch, unabhängig von dem, wie man die mit der postcalvinistischen Gotteskonzeption verbundene Einzelfragen löst [20], ist folgendes klar: die Epigonen Calvins sahen sich von Anfang an gezwungen, einige der dogmatischen Grundlagen des orthodoxen Calvinismus zu revidieren.

1938, pp.1-59.

[20] Auch Jahves Wiederkehr wäre hier als eine prinzipielle Verschiebung in der Gottesvorstellung zu deuten.

Zur religiösen Toleranz
und ihrer Auswirkung auf die Gesellschaften
des Alten Vorderen Orients

Th.R. Kämmerer, Tartu

> *man-nu ana šá ta-kil-ú lu ta-kil*
> "Möge einem jeden erlaubt sein,
> an das zu glauben, woran er glaubt" [1]

1. Einleitung

Bei der Zugrundelegung des für die diesjährige Tagung gewonnenen Titels "Die Bedeutung der Religion für Gesellschaften in der Vergangenheit und Gegenwart" bedarf es, wenn wir uns auf die Kulturen des *Alten Vorderen Orients* beziehen, einer gewissen Zurückhaltung, Begriffe der heutigen *Soziologie*, wie z.B. *Gesellschaft*, unreflektiert zu übernehmen. Allzu schnell müssen wir erkennen, dass es im Weltbild antiker Kulturen, und nicht nur in denen des Alten Vorderen Orients, eben keine Trennung zwischen Gesellschaft und Religion gibt, da man die irdische Welt in allen ihren Ausprägungen als durchdrungen vom Wirken und Willen der göttlichen Mächte betrachtete. Als ein *nibūt ilim,* als ein "Ernannter durch die Gottheit" war sich der damalige Herrscher seiner Aufgabe als *pāqid būtim,* als "Betreuer des Tempels", als *zāninum na'ādum ša būtim,* als "ehrfürchtiger Versorger des Tempels" oder als *mubbib šulu' bū ilim,* als derjenige, "der den Tempel der Gottheit rein hält" durchaus bewusst. Seine Direktiven empfing der Herrscher direkt von der für ihn verantwortlichen Gottheit. So sind es eben die Gottheiten, die das Schicksal eines jeden Menschen "in der Hand halten":

> *Ištar* (EŠ₄.TÁR) ... *ši-ma-at mi-im-ma-mi qá-ti-iš-ša ta-am-'a-at*
> Ištar ... ergreift das Schicksal eines jeden mit ihrer Hand. [2]

Dieser Umstand wird auch dadurch nicht wieder relativiert, dass verschiedentlich, besonders jedoch in der Zeit der dritten Dynastie von Ur, eine zumindest

---

[1] A. Livingstone, Sate Archives of Assyria 3 (Helsinki 1989), S. 35: Nr. 14, Z. 1.

[2] F. Thureau-Dangin, Revue d'Assyriologie 22 (1925), S. 169-177, Z. 14.

die Ökonomie betreffende, zunehmende Säkularisierung zu beobachten ist. Diese war gerade dadurch bedingt, dass "die Ackerland und Werkstätten besitzenden Tempel (...) weitgehend in die königliche Ökonomie eingegliedert waren". [3] Wenn *I.M. Diakonoff* "Palast" und "Tempel" wiederum auch unter dem Terminus "state sector" zusammenfasst, so doch nur, um diesen von dem "communal private sector" abzugrenzen. [4] Auch *H. Neumann* spricht in diesem Zusammenhang verallgemeinernd von "Palast- und Tempelwirtschaft". Allerdings sei gesagt, dass es sich hierbei lediglich um eine sich neu organisierende Administration der Ökonomie handelt, die das gesellschaftliche, religiöse Leben des Einzelnen jedoch weitestgehend unberührt lässt und vom Einzelnen als solche wahrscheinlich auch nicht anders bewertet wurde als in den Jahrhunderten zuvor. Hier ist dem Umstand Rechnung zu tragen, dass eine Regulierung durch die Staatsgewalt, der "common sense" und der "individual sense" auch zu anderen Zeiten der Antike wie auch der Moderne so gut wie nie in Übereinstimmung zu bringen war bzw. ist.

Erst wenn wir uns bewusst gemacht haben, vor welchem politisch-historischen Hintergrund wir Fragen nach der "Bedeutung der Religion für Gesellschaften in der Vergangenheit und Gegenwart" erörtern müssen, wird deutlich, welchen konkreten Bezug auch die "religiöse Toleranz" für antike Gesellschaften gehabt haben mag. So stellt - für den Alten Vorderen Orient gesprochen - "religiöse Toleranz" zugleich stets auch "politische Toleranz" dar.

Religion verlangte vom Einzelnen ebenso wie vom Herrscher, stets nach dem Willen der Götter zu forschen und den Einklang der menschlichen Sphäre mit dem Göttlichen zu erhalten oder diesen wiederherzustellen, um irdisches Wohlergehen dauerhaft zu sichern. Hierzu bediente man sich einer verschiedenartig ausgeprägten Methodik, die durch Kommunikation mit den Göttern durch Divination, Ritualen, Festen usw. gegenwärtiges oder zukünftiges Übel für den Einzelnen und für das Gemeinwesen abzuwehren suchte.

Wenn auch die Methodik einer erfolgreichen Kommunikation zwischen Mensch und Gottheit in keilschriftlichen Weisheitstexten vielfach beschrieben und erläutert wurde, so war bereits dem damaligen Menschen die damit verbundene grundlegende Problematik des Misslingens deutlich vor Augen:

a-a-ú ṭè-em ilī (DINGIR.MEŠ) *qé-reb šamê* (AN-*e*) *i-lam-mad*
"Wer erfährt (schon) den Willen der Götter inmitten des Himmels?" [5]

---

[3] H. Neumann, Handwerk in Mesopotamien (2. Auflage, Berlin 1993), S. 20.

[4] I.M. Diakonoff, Acta Antiqua Academiae Scientiarum Hungaricae 22 (Budapest 1974), S. 52.

[5] W.G. Lambert, Babylonian Wisdom Literature (Oxford 1960), S. 40: *ludlul bēl nēmeqi* II 36.

Von dem damit verbundenen, ethischen Dilemma, naturgemäß gezwungen zu sein, den Willen der Götter zu achten, zugleich aber nicht in der Lage zu sein, diesen überhaupt zu erkennen, berichtet uns schon der Klagende in *ludlul bēl nēmeqi*. Jede Aussage, sei sie *theologisch* oder *soziologisch* intendiert, wirkt bei dieser Erkenntnis besonders stark. Es stellt sich zunehmend die Frage, worin gerade eine bestimmte Aussage oder die sie verursachende Idee schließlich *theologisch* begründet ist:

Ḫa-am-mu-ra-pí-mi be-lum ša ki-ma a-bi-im wa-li-di-im a-na ni-ši i-ba-aš-šu-ú ...

Ḫammurapi, der Herr, der wie ein leiblicher Vater zu den Menschen ist, ...[6]

Es ist nur verständlich, wenn sich im Laufe der Geschichte der altorientalischen Kulturen *religiöse* Vorstellungen vor dem Hintergrund dann auch *politischer* Veränderungen gewandelt haben.

Derartige Veränderungen stellen sich dem Religionshistoriker in doppelter Hinsicht dar. Einmal *synchron* als dasjenige Gotteskonzept der Zeitgenossen, als auch *diachron* in bezug auf den Glauben der Vorfahren. Ziel einer derartigen Forschung ist die wissenschaftliche Betrachtung, wie ein im Altertum lebender Mensch z. T. rein subjektiv solche Veränderungen abwog, Veränderungen, deren *sozio-religiöser* Bestandteil wiederum er selbst war. Und tatsächlich besitzen wir aus dem Alten Vorderen Orient überlieferte Dokumente in *sumerischer, babylonischer* und *assyrischer* Sprache, die uns Aufschluss geben darüber, wie der damalige Mensch *theologische Veränderungen* wahrgenommen und verarbeitet hat, von seiner *eigenen religiösen Erfahrung* ganz zu schweigen, befindet sich diese doch weit außerhalb unseres heutigen Erkenntnisstandes.

2. Religiöse Toleranz im Zeichen eines multikulturellen Europas und eines zunehmenden Islamismus

Betrachten wir vergleichend die *islamische* Welt des Vorderen Orients und das gerade zu einer Zeit, die uns allen als die "Zeit nach dem 11. September 2001" noch lange im Bewusstsein bleiben und in die Geschichte eingehen wird, - insofern "Religion und Gesellschaft" einmal ganz aktuell verstanden - so müssen wir erneut die Frage nach religiöser Toleranz in engem Zusammenhang mit der jeweiligen Staatsstruktur erörtern. Denn gerade das klassische Rechtssystem des Islams geht von einer einheitlichen Gesellschaft aus, der Gesellschaft der Muslime: *al-Islam din wa daula* "Islam ist Religion und politische Macht". So gehören zum islamischen Fundamentalismus, der *usuliya*, a. der *Universalanspruch*, wonach den Herrschenden Autorität und Vollmacht zukommt, die Gottesherr-

---

[6] Codex Hammurapi XLVIII 20-24.

schaft, die *Hakimiyyat Allah*, und damit staatsübergreifend das islamische Gesetz der *Scharia* weltweit zur Geltung zu bringen und b. der *Totalitätsanspruch*, der es dem Islam gestattet, *sämtliche* Lebensbereiche des Menschen zu erfassen.

Dieses führte schließlich zu der Herausbildung eines Zweiklassensystems, das die in einem islamischen Staat lebenden Bürger in *Muslime* und *Schutzbefohlene* aufteilt und diesen rechtlich eine nur untergeordnete Rolle zukommen lässt. Insofern können wir auch hier genauso wenig wie in den altorientalischen Kulturen religiöse Phänomene nicht von der sozio-politischen Sphäre trennen. Und dennoch liegt gerade der Unterschied zu den antiken Kulturen darin, dass dort eben nicht eine einheitliche Gesellschaft gebildet bzw. angestrebt wurde.

Es fällt schwer, in den islamischen Staaten Phänomene wie "religiöse Toleranz", "Glaubensfreiheit", aber auch "politische Toleranz" wiederzufinden. Zumindest werden sie überdeckt und unsichtbar gemacht durch jene islamistischen Bewegungen, die meinen, einen heiligen Krieg, einen Krieg im Namen Gottes, gegen den *Westen*, gegen *Andersgläubige* beginnen zu müssen. Doch sogar gegen *Anhänger des Islams* kann durch den Vorwurf der *Zandaqa*, der Abweichung von der Offenbarung, rechtmäßig vorgegangen werden.

Diesen Westen beschreibend zitiert am 21.09.01 der Rheinische Merkur, eine Deutsche Tageszeitung, den *Göttinger* Islamwissenschaftler *B. Tibi*, den Begründer der *Islamologie,* einer sozialwissenschaftlich ausgerichteten Islam-Forschung, dass "die liberalen Multikulti-Europäer in postmoderner Manier im Namen einer Religionsfreiheit unter Toleranz Selbstaufgabe und Zulassung einer logistischen Basis für den Fundamentalismus auf seinem Territorium versteht." Und so *B. Tibi* weiter: "Das, was (die Europäer) unter Toleranz versteh(en) ist, dass man praktisch alles gelten lässt! Und sie denken, dass sie auf der anderen Seite dafür Anerkennung bekommen. Dieses Verhalten der Selbstverleugnung bis hin zur Aufgabe der Identität der eigenen Zivilisation wird nicht gewürdigt. Und zwar mit recht! Wer so etwas mit seinen Wurzeln, seinen Normen und seiner Kultur tut, hat dem anderen nichts mehr zu bieten, oder keine Identität!"

Eine derart *falsch* verstandene Toleranz kann per se gar nicht die Ausmaße des *Dilemmas* und dessen Folgerungen begreifen, in dem auch heute noch der *Islam* schlechthin steckt. Für eine derartige Toleranz findet sich im *fundamentalistischen* Islam, dem Objekt dieser Toleranz, nur sehr schwer eine auf sie selbst gerichtete gleichwertige Akzeptanz. Dies gilt keineswegs nur für *fundamentalistisch* orientierte Gruppierungen, die sich übrigens gleichermaßen, wenn auch mit geringerem, *militärischen* Potential in *anderen* als religiös klassifizierte Gemeinschaften wiederfinden. Dieses wird deutlich, wenn man sich z. B. *Sure 2* (al-Baqarah), *Vers 256,* vor Augen hält, wo es zwar *einleitend* heißt:

وَلَا يَئُودُهُ حِفْظُهُمَا وَهُوَ الْعَلِيُّ الْعَظِيمُ

"*Es soll kein Zwang sein im Glauben*",

dies jedoch im Koran so nicht stehen bleibt und relativiert wird mit den Worten:

اَللّٰهُ وَلِىُّ الَّذِيْنَ اٰمَنُوْا يُخْرِجُهُمْ مِنَ الظُّلُمٰتِ اِلَى

"Gewiss, Wahrheit ist nunmehr deutlich unterscheidbar von Irrtum!"

somit ausschließlich die *muslimische* Wahrheit für alle Menschen als *allein gültig* anzuerkennen ist. Wie dieses praktisch auszusehen hat, erfahren wir von *Abu Sa'id al-Khudri,* von dem überliefert wurde, dass er *Mohammed,* den Stifter des moslemischen Glaubens, sagen hörte: "Wer von euch etwas Übles sieht, soll es mit eigener Hand ändern, und wenn er dies nicht vermag, so soll er es mit seiner Zunge verändern, und wenn er dies nicht kann, dann mit seinem Herzen, und dies ist die schwächste Form des Glaubens."

Abdul Aziz Ibn Saud überträgt diesen Grundsatz auf die Moderne: "Wir wollen Europas Gaben, aber nicht seinen Geist", wobei dies nach *B. Tibi* ein "Traum von der halben Moderne" ist, der die technischen Errungenschaften von den Prämissen ihrer Herkunft isoliert.

3. Religiöse Toleranz im antiken und mittelalterlichen Europa

Ganz anders dagegen z.B. die Ergebnisse des *Augsburger* Religionsfriedens vom 25.09.1555:

"Man schlägt den anderen nicht tot, weil er den falschen Glauben, das falsche ‚Wesen' hat."

Sein Grundsatz *"cuius regio, eius religio"* konnte aber schon damals nicht befriedigen und setzte immerhin die Gegenreformation in Gang.

Der Begriff *Toleranz,* abgeleitet von lat. *tolerare,* bezieht sich im ursprünglichen Sinn - und das soll besonders betont werden - auf die *religiöse Duldsamkeit* und umfasst damit die Bereitschaft und das Gebot, andere Glaubensbekenntnisse zu dulden und anzuerkennen. Dieses Gebot zur Duldsamkeit hat naturgemäß eine sehr lange Entwicklungsgeschichte hinter sich. So lässt sich die *philosophische* Ausformung dieses Toleranzbegriffes vornehmlich auf die *Stoa* zurückführen. 308 v. Chr. hat *Zeno von Kition* in Athen sein Lehrsystem begründet und im wesentlichen schon abgeschlossen, obschon es bis in die römische Kaiserzeit hineinwirkte. Neben *Cicero* sei hier nur *Seneca* und natürlich auch *Sokrates* genannt. Die Religion der *Stoa* war *pantheistisch* geprägt vom Humanitätsideal: "Wir alle sind Brüder und haben in der gleichen Weise Gott zum Vater", so der griechische Philosoph *Epiktet* (50 – 138).

Für uns nachhaltig greifbar wurde Toleranz im Verhältnis von römischer Staatsreligion und Christentum. Im Toleranzedikt von Mailand wurde 313 n. Chr. durch die Kaiser *Konstantin I.* und *Licinius* den Christen wie auch allen anderen Kulten der damaligen Zeit freie Religionsausübung gewährt. So hatte das römische Reich Fremdreligionen geduldet, solange sie nicht den Kaiserkult als

Bindeglied des Reiches ablehnten, kein Wunder also, dass Juden und Christen lange verfolgt worden waren.

Wirkten die Stoiker in Griechenland und Rom, gelangen wir mit *Kyros II.*, dem Großen (559 – 530 v. Chr.), in den Alten Orient. Sehr oft wird er als derjenige Herrscher zitiert, der bereits im orientalischen Altertum eine *Kultur der Toleranz* schuf. So respektierten die persischen Eroberer, die in der Mitte des sechsten vorchristlichen Jahrhunderts unter dem Begründer der Achämeniden-Dynastie, *Kyros II.*, dem Großen, das erste *Weltreich* der Geschichte errichteten, die Kulturen und Religionen der unterworfenen Völker, also noch deutlich vor *Zeno* in Athen.

Dem Prinzip der religiösen *Toleranz* folgten schließlich auch Alexander der Große (336 – 323) und seine Nachfolger. Allerdings mag bei ihm auch das politisch begründete Anliegen eine Rolle gespielt haben, eine Verschmelzung der *mazedonisch-griechischen* und *iranischen* Bevölkerung herbeizuführen. Seine Politik des Ausgleiches blieb nicht ohne Widerstand, wenn auch die Griechen seine *Apotheose* akzeptiert haben mögen.

Dieser Toleranz setzte schließlich *Antiochos Epiphanes* IV. von Syrien ein jähes Ende, indem er versuchte, seine eigene Religion auch seinen Untertanen aufzudrängen. Dadurch, dass er 167 den Jahwekult verbot und statt dessen den Opferkult für Zeus und den König einführte, provozierte er 166 einen Aufstand unter Führung des Priestergeschlechts der *Hasmonäer*, bzw. *Makkabäer,* denen es unter ihrem Anführer Jonathan (160-143 v. Chr.) gelang, die Juden von der *syrisch-römischen* Vormundschaft zu befreien.

4. Religiöse Toleranz im Alten Vorderen Orient

Kyros II. trat in *Ägypten* sogar als *Pharao* auf, in *Babylonien* ließ er sich als *Nachfolger Ḫammurapis* verehren. Das Leben in den eroberten Ländern verlief weiter in den gewohnten Bahnen. Nur die Abgaben hatten pünktlich an die Beamten in den königlichen Residenzen zu fließen. So garantierten die *Achämeniden* die Freiheit der Religion in den von ihnen besetzten Gebieten:

> "... und als ich (Kyros), wohlwollend, Babylon betrat, errichtete ich unter Jubel und Freude den Regierungssitz im königlichen Palast ... Ich erlaubte niemanden, das Land von Sumer und Akkad zu unterdrücken. Ich behielt vor Augen die Nöte Babylons und all seiner Heiligtümer, um ihr Wohlsein zu fördern. Die Einwohner von Babylon ... ihr unziemendes Joch hob ich weg. Ihre verfallenen Wohnstätten stellte ich wieder her. Ich bereitete ihrem Unglück ein Ende." [7]

---

[7] Kyros-Zylinder 22-26.

Wenn dieses für die *Achämeniden* im besonderen gilt, ist eine derartige *Toleranz* im Alten Vorderen Orient durchaus nichts ungewöhnliches, da die vorchristlichen Religionen einschließlich des Judentums vor *Ezra* (4. Jahrh. ?) und *Nehemiah* (5. Jahrh.) nicht dogmatisch ausgerichtet und zu anderem Glauben intolerant waren. So fehlt in den alten *polytheistisch* geprägten Religionen des Vorderen Orients der Begriff eines Konzeptes vom "falschen Glauben", somit einer *Häresie* um des reinen Glaubens willen fast völlig.

Soweit ein kurzer *historischer* Überblick.

Die *Religionsgeschichte* kennt eine *formale* und eine *inhaltliche Toleranz*, wie sie in dem ebenfalls in dieser Publikation erschienen Artikel von A. Saumets beschrieben wird. Der *inhaltlichen Toleranz* liegt der Gedanke zu Grunde, dass alle Religionen eigentlich *eins* seien, ähnlich wie dies von dem Schweizer Theologen *H. Küng* u.a. mit der Vorstellung einer einheitlichen *Weltreligion* vertreten wird. Von der Anerkennung der Menschenrechte ist die Toleranz nicht zu trennen. Toleranz reicht aber immer nur soweit, wie die zu tolerierende Meinung die Rechte anderer Menschen nicht verletzt bzw. beeinträchtigt.

In der Neuzeit hat die Toleranz im Hinblick auf Glauben und seine Ausübung mit *F.M. Voltaire,*[8] *G.E. Lessing*[9] und *Friedrich II. von Preußen*[10] ihre Höhepunkte gefunden. Die Aufklärung hat Toleranz als soziale Tugend aus der Achtung vor dem Recht der eigenen Gewissensentscheidungen anderer abgeleitet. Dies lässt sich damit begründen, dass ohnedies niemand die volle Wahrheit für sich beanspruchen kann. Selbst dann, wenn man der Überzeugung ist, die reine Wahrheit zu besitzen, kann Toleranz die Achtung vor den irrenden Wahrheiten des anderen begründen.

Im Abendland waren staatliche und kirchliche Interessen bis in das vergangene Jahrhundert oftmals so eng miteinander verflochten, dass heftige Konflikte ausgetragen werden mussten. Dies schien im Hinblick auf unsere Kultur und das Christentum überwunden, doch bekommen Probleme dieser Art durch den *Islam* in einer ganz neuen und ungeahnten Größenordnung eine äußerst gefährliche Aktualität.

Bei den wiederholten Verweisen durch arabische Führer auf vorislamische Traditionen – so lässt sich der Diktator des heutigen *Iraks* gerne im Habitus *Nebukadnezars* II. (603-560) abbilden – ist es angebracht zu fragen, wie es sich mit dem Toleranzbegriff in den Kulturen des *Alten Vorderen Orients,* somit den *vorislamischen* Kulturen, verhält. Kannten diese Kulturen überhaupt das Institut eines *Dschihads,* eines "heiligen Krieges gegen Ungläubige"?

---

[8] Vgl. F.M. Voltaire, Traité sur la tolérance (Genf 1763).

[9] Vgl. das dramatische Gedicht "Nathan der Weise" von G.E. Lessing.

[10] "Die Religionen müssen alle toleriert werden und muss der Fiskal nur das Auge darauf haben, dass keine der anderen Abbruch tue, dahier muss ein jeder nach seiner Fasson selig werden."

Zum Verständnis dieses Sachverhaltes sind einige erklärende Worte zum Wesen des *Polytheismus* vorauszuschicken:

Gerade in den späten Formen dieses sich vom *Monotheismus* unterscheidenden Gotteskonzeptes, wie wir sie aus dem 2. und 1. vorchristl. Jahrtausend kennen, sieht sich der Gläubige jeweils einer einzigen Gottheit, seinem persönlichen Gott, gegenüber und betet ausschließlich zu ihm, normalerweise also nicht auch zu anderen Gottheiten. Dieses bedeutet jedoch keineswegs, dass er die Existenz anderer Gottheiten verneint: Er nimmt diese sogar in seine Gebete mit auf, auch solche, deren Namen er gar nicht zu nennen vermag:

"Möge der Gott, den ich kenne oder nicht kenne, sich mir gegenüber beruhigen,
möge die Göttin, die ich kenne oder nicht kenne, sich mir gegenüber beruhigen." [11]

Ausdrücklich gibt er zu verstehen, dass das Verständnis göttlichen Seins und göttlichen Planens außerhalb seiner Vorstellungskraft liegt:

a-a-ú tè-em ilī (DINGIR.MEŠ) *qé-reb šamê* (AN-*e*) *i-lam-mad*

"Wer erfährt (schon) den Willen der Götter inmitten des Himmels?" [12]

Damit *bestätigt* er *andere* Gottheiten – nicht nur der hier verwendete Plural, auch die theologische Abgrenzung *Marduks* Größe in seiner Hierarchie zu anderen ihm unterlegenen Gottheiten zeugt dafür. So ist dem Gläubigen aber auch in gleicher Weise bewusst, dass er das Göttliche in seiner allumfassenden Gestalt keineswegs adäquat verehren und anbeten kann.

So erscheint es dem Babylonier durchaus als gerechtfertigt, in einer Fürbitte gleich mehrere Gottheiten zu bemühen:

Vs. ² *bu-luṭ be-li ūmū* (UD.MEŠ)-*kà li-ri-ku*
⁴ *šanātu* (MU.MEŠ)-*ka li-te-ed-di-ša*
⁶ ᵈ*Ellil* (EN.LÍL) *la muš-pe-lu-ú ši-im-ka li-ši-im*
⁸ ᵈ*Mullil* (NIN.LÍL) *i-na pí-ša tà-a-bi li-ik-ru-bu-ka*
¹⁰ *ilū* (DINGIR.MEŠ) (KALAM.MA) (:) *ša ma-ti li-ik-ru-ba-ak-ku*₈
¹² ᵈ*Be-le-et ili* (DINGIR.MEŠ) *be-el-tu*₄ *ra-bi-tù ku-uz-ba li-‰oe-en-kà*
¹⁴ ᵈ*Marduk* (AMAR.UTU) *be-el na-ag-bi na-ga*₁₄-*ab-šu lip-te-ku*

---

[11] A. Falkenstein - W. von Soden, Sumerische Hymnen und Gebete (Zürich 1953), S. 225, Nr. 45.

[12] W.G. Lambert, Babylonian Wisdom Literature (Oxford 1960), S. 40: *ludlul bēl nēmeqi* II 36.

Vs. ² Lebe Mein Herr!
⁴ Deine Tage mögen sich erneuern.
⁶ Enlil, der nicht Wankelmütige, möge Dein Schicksal bestimmen.
⁸ Mullil, (seine Gemahlin), möge Dich durch ihren guten Ausspruch segnen.
¹⁰ Die Götter des Landes mögen Dich segnen.
¹² Die Herrin der Götter, die große Herrin, möge Dich mit Anmut erfüllen,
¹⁴ Marduk, der Herr der Gesamtheit, möge Dir seine Gesamtheit öffnen." ¹³

Er geht sogar noch weiter, indem er formuliert:

II ³⁴ *šá dam-qat ra-ma-nu-uš a-na ili* (DINGIR) *gul-lul-tu₄*
³⁵ *šá ina lìb-bi-šú mu-us-su-kàt eli* (EGIR) *ili* (DINGIR)*-šú dam-qat*

Das, was gut für einen selbst ist, kann feindliches Handeln gegen Gott sein.
Das, was in seinem (d.h. des Menschen) Herzen schlecht ist, ist für seinen (d.h. des Menschen) Gott(es) gut." ¹⁴

Und in einem anderen Hymnus besitzen wir einen Beleg dafür, dass der Gläubige einzelne Gottheiten durchaus auch als partielle Verkörperungen in der Gottheit wiederfindet, zu der er betet, und somit diese anderen Gottheiten mit seiner eigenen *personifizierte*.

Folgende Verse aus dem vielzitierten Hymnus an den Gott *Ninurta* mögen dieses belegen:

"Deine beiden Augen, Herr, sind Enlil und Ninlil,
Anu und Antu sind Deine beiden Lippen,
Deine Zähne das Siebengestirn,
Deine beiden Ohren Ea und Damkina,
Dein Kopf ist Addu,
Dein Hals ist Marduk ..."

Dieses bedeutete für den Beter, dass er folgerichtig die Existenz anderer Gottheiten eben nicht nur akzeptierte, wenn auch wie in diesem extremen Beispiel lediglich als Körperteile seines persönlichen Gottes *Ninurta*, sondern sich ihnen gegenüber als *positiv* erwies, das Wissen um sie, den Glauben an sie, zumindest als gültig erachtete.

---

[13] Th.R. Kämmerer, *šimâ milka*, Alter Orient und Altes Testament 251 (Münster 1998), S. 216.

[14] W.G. Lambert, Babylonian Wisdom Literature (Oxford 1960), S. 40: *ludlul bēl nēmeqi* II 34-35.

Dass es vom Ende des zweiten und dem Beginn des ersten Jahrtausends dagegen auch Beispiele gibt für einen sehr deutlichen Ausschließlichkeitsanspruch einer einzelnen Gottheit, belegt die Aufforderung: "Auf *Nabû* vertraue, auf einen *anderen* Gott vertraue nicht!"

Doch gingen nur die wenigsten so weit, im Sinne dieser Aufforderung eines hohen *assyrischen* Beamten um 800, anderen Göttern die göttliche Macht abzusprechen.

Ähnlich heißt es auf einer *mittelbabylonischen* Tafel, deren theologische Aussage jedoch einer deutlich älteren, *sumerischen* Tradition entspricht:

É lugal-za-ka è-a
ibila-zu é-gá si-sá-e 'é-en-dib-dib-bé-ne

"Aus dem Hause Deines Herrn kommend,
sollen Deine Erben regelmäßig in *meinen* (d.h. Enlils) Tempel gehen!" [15]

Diese aus *Ugarit* und *Emar* überlieferten gutgemeinten Ratschläge eines Vaters an seinen Sohn *Šūpē-amēli* lassen eine weitere, ganz andere *Nuance* religiöser Toleranz erkennen, die uns aus dem 13. Jahrhundert v. Chr. folgende Worte überliefert:

na-mu-ti ili (DINGIR) *šá la* (NU) *tal-ta-ka-áš e táq-bi* [16]

"Die Verhöhnung eines Gottes, den Du noch nicht auf die Probe gestellt hast, sprich nicht aus"!

Es wird zwar gefordert, dass auch *andere, fremde* Gottheiten zu ehren sind, so sollen grundsätzlich fremde Gottheiten nicht *verhöhnt* werden, doch unterliegt diese religiöse Akzeptanz einer deutlichen Einschränkung: Die Gottheit ist zuerst einer *genauen Untersuchung* zu unterziehen, bevor der Mensch es sich erlauben darf, über sie ein Urteil zu fällen. Ganz bewusst wählt hier der sprechende Vater das Verb *latāku(m),* das eben ganz genau den Umstand des "auf die Probe stellen" umschreibt. Ein mögliches, schließlich *negatives* Urteil scheint dabei als ein in Frage kommendes Ergebnis durchaus akzeptiert worden zu sein. Leider erfahren wir aus den hier vorliegenden mB Sprichwörtern nichts über die Art und Weise einer derartigen "Probe", deren Notwendigkeit auch aus der *babylonischen Theodizee* hervorgeht:

ak-kát-ti-i pak-ki ili (DINGIR) *ú-zu-un-šu ib-ši*

"Für denjenigen, der die Aussage der Überlegung der Gottheit *bestätigt*, war sein Verstand". [17]

---

[15] Th.R. Kämmerer, *šimâ milka,* Alter Orient und Altes Testament 251 (Münster 1998), S. 220.

[16] ders., ebd., S. 184.

[17] W.G. Lambert, Babylonian Wisdom Literature (Oxford 1960), S. 74: The Babylonian *Theodicy* I 49.

Hier wird das Verb *latāku(m)*, "auf die Probe stellen", durch *kattû(m)*, "(die göttliche Aussage durch Vernunft (*uznu(m)*)) bestätigen", gestützt.

So hatte der Gläubige durchaus Mittel (Rituale, Sternkonstellationen BT 243), die für ihn "rational" zu begreifen waren und bei der Überprüfung einer göttlichen Aussage helfen konnten. Denn immerhin galt es als nicht zu unterschätzen, dass es auch "feindliche Gottheiten" gab, deren boshafte Pläne zu erkennen waren:

ina a-mat ilūti (DINGIR-*ti*)-*ku-nu rabūti* (GAL-*ti*)
šá la ut-tak-ka-ru balāṭ (DIN)-*su li-rik*

"Bei dem Wort Eurer großen Götter, die nicht feindlich sind, möge (Gula) sein Leben lang machen." [18]

In diesem Zusammenhang erhält die Formulierung:

ša la tu-ba-a'-ú ṭè-em ili (DINGIR) *mi-nu-ú ku-šìr-ka*

"Wenn Du nicht den Willen (des) Gottes suchst, welchen Erfolg hast Du (dann)? [19]

eine weiterführende Erklärung. Dies führt schließlich auch zum Kernsatz dieser Studie:

man-nu ana šá ta-kil-ú lu ta-kil a-ni-nu a-na ᵈ*Nabû* (AG) *tak-la-a-ni*

"Möge einem jeden (erlaubt sein) an das zu glauben, woran er glaubt, wir glauben an *Nabû*!" [20]

So jedenfalls *rechtfertigt* in neuassyrischer Zeit, damit der 1. Hälfte des 1. vorchristlichen Jahrtausends, der Verfasser eines lyrischen Gedichtes seinen Glauben an *Nabû,* wodurch er den Rezipienten aufhorchen lässt.

Nabû ist uns bekannt als babylonischer Gott der Schreibkunst und Weisheit, als Schutzgott der Schreiber wie gleichzeitig auch als Sohn des Gottes *Marduk*. Für unsere Zeiteingrenzung und Lokalisierung dieser Textstelle ist wichtig, dass die Verehrung des Gottes *Nabû* seit Beginn des 2. Jahrtausends in den antiken Kultorten *Borsippa* und *Sippar* belegt werden kann. Weder in *Ebla* noch überhaupt in *altakkadischer* Zeit, d.h. im 3. Jahrtausend, finden sich Nachweise eines *Nabû*-Kultes. Vom 14. bis zum 11. Jahrhundert wuchs seine Verehrung, und er wurde bekannt auch in *Ugarit, Tell el-Amārna* und *Kalaʿ*. Seit 925 v. Chr. mit dem Aufstieg der *neuassyrischen* Dynastie wurde der Höhepunkt der *Nabû*-

---

[18] W.G. Lambert, Orientalia 36 (Roma 1967), S. 105-132, Z. 196.

[19] W.G. Lambert, Babylonian Wisdom Literature (Oxford 1960), S. 84: The Babylonian *Theodicy* XXII 239.

[20] A. Livingstone, State Archives of Assyria 3 (Helsinki 1989), S. 35: Nr. 14, Z. 1-2.

Verehrung erreicht. Immerhin besaß er unter *Sargon* II. (721-704) in dessen Festung *Dūr-Šarru-kīn*, somit dem zeitweiligen *Regierungssitz* des *neuassyrischen* Herrschers, sein Haupheiligtum. Auch nannten sich namhafte Könige wie *Nebukadnezar* I.+II. (*Nabû-kudurri-uṣur*) und *Nabonid* (*Nabû-na'id*) nach ihm.

Dass in einer Zeit, in der die Verehrung des Gottes *Nabû* nachweisbar ihren Höhepunkt erreicht hatte, sich ein zur gleichen Zeit lebender Assyrer veranlasst sah, seinen Glauben eben an diesen Gott *Nabû* rechtfertigen zu müssen, drängt beim Lesen schon der ersten Zeile dieses lyrischen Gedichtes Fragen auf, die im weiteren Verlauf des Gedichtes eine Antwort finden lassen.

Es wird gerade in der zitierten Präambel des Gedichtes eine religionshistorische Diskrepanz deutlich, die *aus sich* heraus nicht lösbar zu sein scheint. Keineswegs geht es dem Verfasser dieses Gedichtes darum, in *neuassyrischer* Zeit, also zu einer Zeit, wo die Verbreitung des *Nabû*-Kultes im *Alten Vorderen Orient* seine größte Ausdehnung hatte, den Glauben an *Nabû* zu *rechtfertigen*. Auch der *babylonische* König *Nebukadnezar* II. und der Seleukide *Antiochos* I. Soter (281-261) verehrten *Nabû* und beteten zu ihm. So kann der Glaube an den Gott *Nabû* bei den Zuhörern stillschweigend vorausgesetzt werden.

Eine mögliche Erklärung dieser Problematik erhalten wir jedoch, wenn wir unser Gedicht weiterlesen. So heißt es nicht nur: "wir glauben an *Nabû*", sondern: "wir glauben an *Nabû*, wir folgen der *Tašmētu*", wobei *Tašmētu* hier als die göttliche Gemahlin *Nabûs* angesprochen wird.

Und auch diese Erweiterung durch die Nennung der Göttin *Tašmētu* würde kaum helfen, wüssten wir nicht, dass dem Gott *Nabû* zumindest mit Beginn des 2. Jahrtausends eine *weitere* Gemahlin an die Seite gestellt war, nämlich die vor allem in *Uruk* verehrte *Nanaja*, gleichsam wie auch *Tašmētu* wiederum als Gemahlin des Mondgottes *Sîn* galt. Erst zu Beginn des 1. Jahrtausends wurden *Nabû* und *Tašmētu* als göttliches Paar verehrt, so dass es folgerichtig erschien, wenn *Tašmētu* denjenigen, die unter ihrem Schutz standen, somit sie verehrten, die "Kunst des Tafelschreibens" verlieh. Die Priester übertrugen die Funktionen des Gottes *Nabû* auch auf seine Gemahlin.

Nicht die Rechtfertigung des Glaubens an einen oder beide dieser Gottheiten steht im Vordergrund, sondern die Rechtfertigung *beider* Gottheiten als *göttliches Paar* und das gegenüber einer wesentlich älteren Tradition, nach der *Nabû* mit *Nanaja* verbunden war, die vor allem in *altbabylonischer* Zeit, also der 1. Hälfte des 2. Jahrtausends, in *Babylonien* Verehrung fand.

Interessant, weil bislang einzigartig, gilt uns dieser Text als Zeuge für eine als *diachron* begründete Rechtfertigung gegenüber einem anderen Kult, der dann durchaus noch zeitgleich geherrscht haben mag.

Wir haben es hier mit einem Text zu tun, der religionshistorisch an den Übergang eines *Nabû / Nanaja*-Kultes zum *Nabû / Tašmētu*-Kult zu datieren ist. Die Verehrung des göttlichen Paares *Nabû* und *Nanaja* drohte zu verblassen und vor der Verehrung des Götterpaares *Nabû* und *Tašmētu* zu weichen. Damit ist aufs engste diese *Rechtfertigung* mit einer *Toleranzforderung* eben dieses anderen, älteren Kultes verbunden.

Das heißt, genauso wie ein Mensch, der dem *polytheistisch* geprägten Gotteskonzept verpflichtet ist, gegenüber dem Glauben seiner Mitmenschen tolerant zu sein hat, ist er dieses auch gegenüber den Göttern seiner Ahnen. Hier vollzieht sich daher Toleranz sowohl synchron als auch diachron. Denn dem Verfasser dieses Gedichtes muss ja wohl bewusst gewesen sein, dass er einen Glauben vertrat, der eben nicht als *autochthon*, somit als *ursprünglich* zu gelten hatte, sondern der Glaubensausprägung einer *neuen theologischen* Ausrichtung entsprach. Leider sind uns bislang hauptsächlich nur solche literarischen Texte überliefert, die uns Aufschluss geben über eine *synchrone* Reflektion unterschiedlicher Kulte. Opferlisten, Rituale, Omina, aber auch Mythen, Hymnen und Gebete sprechen von eben diesem Verhältnis. So ist die Rede von freundlichen Göttern, aber auch solchen, die dem Menschen feindlich gesinnt waren, weil diese sich von ihren Göttern abgewandt hatten. Der Auszug einer Gottheit aus dem ihr angestammten Tempel und der von diesem Tempel abhängigen Gesellschaft - sei dieses aus eigenem Willen heraus, sei dieses mit Gewalt durch Feinde - bedeutete den Untergang der betroffenen Gesellschaft. So ist es sehr gut zu verstehen, wenn derartige sozio-religiöse Problemstellungen in der Dichtung thematisiert werden. Dieses ist in allen Gesellschaften zu allen Zeiten der Fall gewesen.

Ganz anders jedoch sieht es mit der geistigen Einstellung zum althergebrachten Kult und dessen Glaubensinhalten aus. Während der *Monotheismus* grundsätzlich als sehr konservativ zu gelten hat, sieht man von der ständigen Veränderung und Modernisierung seiner Liturgien einmal ab, so stehen wir beim *Polytheismus* anscheinend vor einer anderen Situation.

Die Reflektion und die sich daraus ergebende Toleranz gegenüber dem Glauben *zeitgleicher*, jedoch grundverschiedener Glaubensinhalte führt im Polytheismus schließlich auch zu einem Nachdenken über *zeitungleiche* Glaubensinhalte. Es wäre interessant, diesen Sachverhalt auch einmal anhand zweier generell verschiedener *kosmologischer Theologeme* zu untersuchen. Hier wären die *Nippur-Tradition* (*emersio*: alles entsteht aus der Vereinigung von Himmel und Erde ohne Schöpfungsakt) und die *Eridu-Tradition* - (*formatio*: ein Schöpfergott erschafft alles) zu nennen. Leider fehlt hierzu das entsprechende Textmaterial, das uns helfen würde, beide Traditionen *bewertend* sowohl *synchron* als auch *diachron* miteinander zu vergleichen. Es bleibt uns daher nur diese kurze, jedoch markante Einleitung zu dem lyrischen Gedicht *Nabû* und *Tašmētu*, die damit so wichtig wird.

Wir erkennen im *Polytheismus* dasjenige Gotteskonzept, dass die Akzeptanz anderer Gottheiten neben dem Glauben an einen Persönlichen Gott grundsätzlich zulässt. Dieses wird auch nicht durch *synkretistische* Tendenzen, wie sie in fast allen Religionen zu beobachten sind, wieder relativiert. So gestattete z.B. die *interpretatio Romana*, also die Wiedererkennung eigener römischer Götter in fremden Gottheiten, die Anerkennung und Einführung von Kulten in Rom durch offizielle Stellen - bzw. bildete sie vice versa nicht nur im *Alten Vorderen Orient* die Annahme von *Hypostasen*, eine legitime Erscheinungsform in *polytheistisch* geprägten Religionen.

Nach *B. Lang* handelt es sich dabei um die "Eigenschaft, Seite oder Erscheinungsform eines Gottes, die als selbständiges Wesen aufgefasst wird, wobei der enge Bezug zur Gottheit, wenn nicht sogar die Identität mit ihr erhalten bleibt". [21]

5. Zusammenfassung

Wenn wir zum Kern der hier gemachten Aussage zurückkommen wollen, so dürfen wir feststellen, dass das *lyrische* Gedicht *Nabû* und *Tašmētu*, ein aus *neuassyrischer* Zeit, somit der ersten Hälfte des ersten vorchristlichen Jahrtausends stammender Keilschrifttext, genau das formuliert, was im *Polytheismus* Toleranz bedeutet:

man-nu ana šá ta-kil-ú lu ta-kil
"Möge einem jeden erlaubt sein, an das zu glauben, woran er glaubt."

Was hier gemeint ist, ist offensichtlich. *Polytheismus* ist mit Toleranz im *weitesten* Sinne gleichzusetzen. In besonderem Maße gilt diese Akzeptanz *auch* den Göttern der *Ahnen* gegenüber, die *synchron,* also zeitgleich, verehrt wurden. Es ist aber *auch* eine Toleranz gegenüber dem *Mitmenschen* und *seinem* Glauben.

Diese *Toleranz* hat dann beim Übergang zum *Monotheismus* im Alten Vorderen Orient viel von ihrem Glanz verloren. Dies gilt auch für das *Christentum,* doch ebenso für den *Islam.* Das Christentum scheint diese Probleme überwunden zu haben, der *Islam* hat sie gerade vor sich. Für das Christentum haben Aufklärung und Säkularisierung im Abendland das Ihrige getan. Aus dem Gefängnis der Intoleranz hat es sich längst befreit, droht jetzt aber einer Toleranz zu erliegen, die zur Selbstaufgabe und Selbstverleugnung führt.

Vordergründig ist mit Toleranz grundsätzlich die *Duldung* des Glaubens gemeint. Dabei liegen im Alten Vorderen Orient in der Verehrung der unterschiedlichen, göttlichen Bezugspersonen stets die gleichen Denkstrukturen zugrunde, die das Verlangen und die Notwendigkeit nach der Entstehung von Glaubenskriegen von vorn herein gar nicht erst aufkommen lassen.

Für den *Islam* dagegen steht immer noch das Gebot der 2. Sure: "Es soll kein Zwang sein im Glauben", mit dem Glaubensgrundsatz: "Gewiss, Wahrheit ist nunmehr deutlich unterscheidbar von Irrtum" und die Anweisung im Widerspruch, wie diese praktisch umzusetzen sind:

"Wer von euch etwas Übles sieht (und gemeint ist dies in religiöser Hinsicht), soll dies mit seiner Hand ändern, wer das nicht kann, dann mit seiner

---

[21] B. Lang, *Hypostase*, Handbuch religionswissenschaftlicher Grundbegriffe (Stuttgart 1993), S. 188.

Zunge, wenn er das nicht kann, dann mit seinem Herzen, dies letzte ist allerdings die schwächste Form des Glaubens."

Das *polytheistische* Bekenntnis der Menschen des Alten Vorderen Orients war grundsätzlich von *Toleranz* geprägt, obwohl sich in ihren Sprachen ein *Lexem* für den Toleranzbegriff bislang nicht finden lässt.

Die Institution der Sonnenjungfrauen bei den Inkas
Ihre Rolle in der Religion und der Gesellschaft

Tarmo Kulmar, Tartu

Die Gesellschaft der Inkas hat eine Pyramide dargestellt. Nach dem peruanischen Wissenschaftler Federico Kauffmann-Doig residierte an der Spitze der Kaiser oder *Sapa Inca* - der Einzige oder Wahre Inka, auf der zweiten Stufe waren die ketschuanischen Vornehmen, die zugleich die nächsten Verwandten des Kaisers waren; auf derselben Stufe, aber auf einer von ihnen etwas niedrigeren Position waren die Stammesführer der unterworfenen Völker. Auf der dritten Stufe standen die übrigen Mitglieder der ketschuanischen Obrigkeit. Auf derselben Stufe, aber etwas niedriger, waren unterworfene verbündete Stämme, die aus irgendeinem Grund dafür privilegiert gehalten wurden. Auf der vierten Stufe befand sich der grösste Teil der Gemeinden der Völker des Imperiums. Auf der fünften Stufe waren die sogenannten *mitimaes* - unterworfene Stämme, die keine Bereitschaft zur Zusammenarbeit an den Tag gelegt haben und die zur Strafe in andere Regionen des Staates umgesiedelt waren. Auf der sechsten und letzten Stufe war die kleine, im Bildungsstadium stehende Schicht der Sklaven (Kauffmann-Doig 1991, 167).

Die gesellschaftlichen Schemata, die seine Landsleute Waldemar Espinoza und Maria Rostworowski für die Inkas entworfen haben, unterscheiden sich inhaltlich nur wenig: Auf der ersten Stufe sind der Kaiser und seine Verwandtschaft, auf der zweiten die Aristokratie der wahren ketschuanischen Inkas, aber auf der dritten die Vornehmen der unterworfenen Stämme und die sogenannten Inkas bezüglich der Vorrechte oder die den Inkas als ersten unterworfenen ketschuanischen Verbündetenstämme (s. z.B. Espinoza 1990, Rostworowski 1992 u.a.).

Bahnbrechend bei der Forschung der Gesellschaftsstruktur der Inkas sind die Werke des deutschen Wissenschaftlers Heinrich Cunow gewesen (s. insbesondere Cunow 1896, gleichfalls 1937, 58 ff.).

Auf Grund der Erforschung der verschiedenen Chroniktexte und der Ergebnisse der wesentlichsten Autoren ist zu erkennen, dass zwischen den sog. wahren Inkas und der Hauptmasse der unterworfenen Völker mehrere Zwischenschichten bestehen: (1) die Aristokratie der unterworfenen Stämme, (2) die durch die Vermischung der Inkas mit den unterworfenen Aristokratiestämmen entstandenen sog. mischblütigen Inkas, (3) die sog. Inkas mit besonderen Vorrechten, und (4) die *aclla*'s oder Sonnenjungfrauen. Ob diese Zwischenschichten auf der

Pyramide vertikal oder horizontal zueinander lagen, ist für die vorliegende Studie nicht von Belang. Ihr Ziel ist zu erforschen, wer die *aclla*'s waren, wie sich diese Mittelschicht zusammensetzte und welche Funktionen sie erfüllt hat.

Zunächst sollte die Regelung der Ehe näher betrachtet werden, die in Tahuantinsuyu, dem Staat der Inkas, gültig war. Die Heirat war sowohl für die Frau als auch für den Mann eine Pflicht. Wenn der junge Mann bis zum 25. und das Mädchen bis zum 18. Lebensjahr keinen Lebensgefährten gefunden hatte, trat der Staat ein. An einem festgesetzten Tag sollten alle ledigen Männer und Frauen in das Administrationszentrum ihrer Region gehen, wo ein entsprechender Beamter aus den Ledigen Ehepaare nach eigenem Ermessen bildete. Es war nicht möglich, gegen eine Zwangsehe dieser Art Einspruch zu erheben. Der Staat der Inkas hat die Entwicklung der Bevölkerung unter strenger Kontrolle gehalten (Busto 1981, 91-102; Espinoza 1990, 220 ff.).

Ausserdem haben im Imperium der Inkas besondere Staatsbeamte - *apo panaca*'s - jedes Jahr die Siedlungen besucht und alle ortsansässigen Mädchen besichtigt. Besonders schöne Mädchen im Alter von 8 bis 10 Jahren wurden ausgewählt (Acosta 1991, Cap. 14). Sie wurden *aclla*'s - Auserwählte - genannt. Die übrigen Mädchen blieben bis zur Heirat mit ihrer Gemeinde - *ayllu* - verbunden. Die ausgewählten Jungfrauen haben das Dorf verlassen und wurden in besondere Internate zusammengezogen. Dort wurden ihnen in einem Zeitraum von vier Jahren Haushaltsarbeiten - Spinnen, Weben, Sticken, Kochen - beigebracht. Wenn die vier Jahre vorüber waren, wurden die Mädchen aufs neue bewertet. Einige wurden nun verdienten Staatsbeamten und Offizieren zur Gemahlin gegeben. Die übrigen, die meisten, mussten das Keuschheitsgelübde ablegen und wurden die sog. Sonnenjungfrauen, die weiterhin im Kloster blieben. Ihr Schicksal konnte in mancher Hinsicht unterschiedlich sein, wie u.a. aus dem untenstehenden Chroniktext ersichtlich wird. Über alle Sonnenjungfrauen des Staates regierte eine Frau im Status einer Oberpriesterin aus dem Geschlecht der Inkas mit dem Titel *coya pasca* (Espinoza 1990, 212-220).

Einer der bekanntesten spanischen Chroniker, Inca Garcilaso de la Vega, widmet dem Problem der Sonnenjungfrauen mehrere Kapitel [1].

> "Die Könige der Inkas und ihr Heidentum und ihre geringfügige Religion haben auch wichtige Aspekte gehabt, die ernster Betrachtung wert sind. Eines davon war das Gelübde der ewigen Jungfräulichkeit, in der Frauen in zahlreichen Häusern gehalten wurden, die für sie in vielen Provinzen des Imperiums errichtet wurden,"

schreibt er (Garcilaso 1988, Libro IV, Cap. I).

Eines der Quartiere in der Staatshauptstadt Cuzco war *acclla huasi*, was das "Haus der Auserwählten" bedeutet. Dort wohnten die Frauen, die bis zum Ende

---

[1] Bei der Wiedererzählung des Chroniktextes von Garcilaso wird versucht, den Stil und den Sprachgebrauch des Autors einzuhalten.

ihres Lebens die Jungfräulichkeit bewahren mussten. Sie wurden auf Grund der Reinblütigkeit und Schönheit aus der Gruppe der ca. 8-jährigen Mädchen ausgewählt. Sie mussten aus der Verwandtschaft der Inkas stammen - die Töchter der Sonne, die dem Sonnengott Inti geweiht waren (S. auch León 1988, Cap.XXXVIII). Es lebten dort über 1500 und ihre Anzahl war nicht begrenzt. Zur Herrscherin des Hauses war die älteste Frau unter ihnen und wurde *mama cuna* genannt [2]. Die Jungfrauen beschäftigten sich dort mit Spinnen, Weben und Kochen, aber auch mit anderen Aufgaben, und sie wurden als Frauen der Sonne angesehen (Garcilaso 1988, ibid.). Sie mussten ihr Leben lang in völliger Abgeschiedenheit leben: Sie durften niemanden besuchen und niemanden empfangen, es durfte sie niemand sehen; sprechen durften sie nur miteinander. Eine Ausnahme bildete nur der *Sapa Inca*, aber auch er hat sich nicht allzu oft getraut, dieses Vorrecht in Anspruch zu nehmen. Die Kaiserin und ihre Töchter durften das Haus der Auserwählten jederzeit besuchen. Der Kaiser hat sie des öfteren dorthin geschickt, um zu erfahren, wie sie leben und was sie brauchen.

Im Haus gab es viele Innenräume, deren Türen sich von zwei Seiten in einen engen Korridor öffneten. Vor den Türen standen Wächterinnen, die den Weg in die Vorzimmer bewacht haben, in denen Mägde arbeiteten. Die Sonnenjungfrauen wohnten in Hinterzimmern. Der Haupteingang des Hauses war nur für die Kaiserin und diejenigen bestimmt, die unter die Auserwählten aufgenommen wurden. Daneben hatte das Haus einen Diensteingang, vor dem 20 Wächter standen, die alle Sendungen empfangen und weitergegeben haben, aber bei Todesstrafe nicht in die innere Tür hereingehen durften, die in das Haus führte. Selbst auf Befehl hätten sie es nicht gewagt hereinzugehen.

Für die Haushaltsarbeiten standen den Sonnenjungfrauen 500 Mägde zur Verfügung, die ebenfalls Jungfrauen sein mussten und aus dem Stand der sog. Inkas stammten. Auch diese Mädchen hatten aus ihrem Stamm eine *mama cuna*, die alt genug war, um ihre Leiterin sein zu können.

Die Sonnenjungfrauen sollten für den Kaiser und die Kaiserin Kleider und andere Gegenstände fertigen, auch den Stoff aus feinstem Gewebe stellten sie als Opfergabe für die Sonne her. Aus ihrer Produktion trug der Herrscher der Inkas als Kopfschmuck ein mit Gold verziertes rotes Fransentuch oder eine Kopfbinde *(llautu)*, ein bis zu den Knien reichendes Tuch *(uncu)*, einen quadratischen Mantel *(yacolla)* und ein Säckchen für die Kookablätter *(chuspa)*. Auch haben sie für die Angehörigen des Herrschergeschlechts den gelben und roten, mit Fransen verzierten Kopfschmuck angefertigt (Garcilaso 1988, Libro IV, Cap. II). Alle diese Gegenstände wurden in grossen Mengen eigentlich für die Sonne angefertigt. Da sie die Sonne aber nicht tragen konnte, so wurde alles, was von den Opferverrichtungen übrig blieb, dem *Sapa Inca*, der *Coya* (der Kaiserin) und der kaiserlichen Familie überbracht. Da diese Gegenstände mit den Händen der

---

[2] Ketschuanisch: *mama* - "Mutter (d.h. diejenige, die die Verpflichtungen der Mutter erfüllt)", *cuna* - Suffix zur Bezeichnung des Plurals. Die ersten Chronisten haben unwissend die Pluralform benützt.

Frauen der Sonne angefertigt waren, waren sie heilig; selbst dem Kaiser war es nicht erlaubt, sie jemandem zu spenden oder zu schenken, der kein reinblütiger Inka war.

Die Sonnenjungfrauen haben auch heiliges Brot *(sancu)* gebacken, das während der wichtigsten Festlichkeiten der Sonne geopfert wurde, ebenso das heilige Getränk *(aca)*, das von den Inkas und den Vornehmen während der Opferfeierlichkeiten getrunken wurde. Sämtliches Geschirr, alle Geräte und Gegenstände im *aclla huasi* waren aus Gold und Silber wie im Sonnentempel selber; wie zum Sonnentempel gehörte auch zu diesem Haus ein Garten, dessen Bäume, Blumen und Gras aus Gold und Silber geschmiedet waren (Cobo 1893, T. IV, Cap.XXXVII).

Eine Sonnenjungfrau, die ihre Unschuld vergab, sollte lebendig begraben, ihr männlicher Partner gehängt werden. Da eine derartige Strafe für einen Mann, der Heiligkeit entweiht hat, für zu gering gehalten wurde, sollten zusammen mit ihm auch seine Frau, seine Kinder, seine Dienerschaft, seinen nächsten Verwandte und Nachbarn, das ganze Dorf und alle Haustiere getötet werden. Seine Mutter, die so einen schlechten Sohn zur Welt gebracht hatte, sollte in die offene Wüste getrieben werden, die Standort des Dorfes zerstört und der Ort selbst verflucht werden. Das war Gesetz. Es sei aber kein Fall bekannt geworden, nach dem man diese Strafe angewandt hätte. Denn die Ehrfurcht der Inkas vor der Heiligkeit der Sonnenjungfrauen war so gross, dass es niemand gewagt hätte, das Gesetz zu verletzen (Garcilaso 1988, Libro IV, Cap. III).

Die Häuser der Auserwählten gab es auch in anderen Provinzen des Staates (León 1988, Cap. XXXVIII). Der Sonne geweihte Häuser gab es auch für die ausserhalb der Ehe geborenen Töchter des Kaisers. Spezielle Häuser sind auch für die Vornehmen unterworfener Völker - *curaca*'s - nachweisbar, ebenso für die schönen Mädchen, die aus dem einfachen Volke ausgewählt und für den Inka persönlich zurückgehalten verwahrt wurden.

Die Eltern waren unsagbar froh, wenn ihre Töchter ausgewählt wurden. Denn die Lebensordnung und Tätigkeit aller ausgewählter Mädchen entsprachen denen der Cuzcoer Sonnenjungfrauen. Auch sie hatten eine *mama cuna* aus ihrem Stand. Auf Wunsch des *Sapa Inca* wurden ab und zu die schönsten von ihnen ausgewählt und in die Residenz des Herrschers gebracht, wo sie zu seinen Nebenfrauen wurden (Garcilaso 1988, Libro IV, Cap. IV).

Die Strafen für das Begehren eines derartigen Eigentums von Inkas waren ebenfalls drastisch. Bekannt ist ein Fall, in dem ein junger Mann die Unschuld einer Nebenfrau des Kaisers Atahuallpa genommen hatte. Beide wurden zum Feuertod verurteilt. Auch die näheren Verwandten der Schuldigen wurden getötet (Zarate 1944, Libro II, Cap. VII). Garcilaso erwähnt, dass Atahuallpa unter dieser Beleidigung mehr gelitten habe, als wegen unter seiner Haft bei den Spaniern (Garcilaso 1988, Libro IV, Cap. IV).

Die Mädchen, die unter den *acclla*'s für den Kaiser als Nebenfrauen ausgewählt wurden, blieben auch nach der Erfüllung ihrer Nebenfrauenpflichten am Hof, wo sie als Hofdamen oder Dienerinnen der Kaiserin gedient haben, bis sie in den Ruhestand versetzt wurden. Danach wurden sie in ihre Heimatorte entlassen, wo sie ein Haus erhielten und ihnen in der Hochachtung gedient wurde, da sie die Nebenfrauen des Inkas selbst gewesen waren.

Die Frauen, die kein Glück hatten, vom Kaiser auserwählt zu werden, blieben in ihrem *aclla huasi* bis ins hohe Alter. Danach konnte sie wählen, ob sie in ihren Heimatort zurückkehren wollten, wo man sich um sie gekümmert hätte, oder ob sie bis zum Tode im Haus der Auserwählten bleiben wollten.

Den Frauen, die für den herrschenden Kaiser bestimmt waren, wurde nach dem Tode des Herrschers der Titel "die Mutter des Nachfolgers des *Sapa Incas*" und *Mama cuna* verliehen. Sie haben die Kinder des Kaisers erzogen und verfügten über eine prächtige Hauseinrichtung; zahlreiches Dienstpersonal kümmerte sich um sie. Heiraten durften sie aber niemals wieder, denn es wäre ja für den Sohn der Sonne erniedrigend gewesen, wenn ein Mann aus niedrigerem Stand diejenigen entweiht hätte, die einmal schon zu Günstlingen des Sohnes der Sonne geworden waren (Garcilaso 1988, Libro IV, Cap. V; Ayala 1980, Cap. 299-301).

Man hat behauptet, dass auch aus den *aclla huasi*'s ab und zu Jungfrauen ausgewählt wurden, um sie als Zeichen der besonderen kaiserlichen Gunst den hohen Aristokraten und Heerführern zur Frau zu geben. Garcilaso versichert, dass dies Falschmeldungen sind. Die Sonnenjungfrauen waren heilig und allein für den Sonnengott oder seinen Vertreter auf Erden, den Kaiser, den Sohn der Sonne bestimmt. Wohl aber hat der *Sapa Inca* seinen ergebenen Dienern Mädchen zur Frau gegeben, die zu den sogenannten mischblütigen Inkas gehörten. Unter denen konnten sogar eigene Töchter sein, deren Mütter nicht aus dem Geschlecht der Inkas stammten. Diese Mütter konnten aber auch selbst *aclla*'s sein. Natürlich gab es wiederholt auch Fälle, in denen der Kaiser das Schicksal eines vom hohen Geschlecht der Inkafamilie stammenden Mädchens ohne die Zustimmung seiner Eltern entschieden hat (Garcilaso 1988, Libro IV, Cap. V-VI).

Auf Grund der Chroniktexte verschiedener Autoren ergibt sich, dass sich die in den *aclla huasi*'s wohnenden Frauen hauptsächlich auf fünf Kategorien verteilten (Ayala 1980, Cap. 299-301; s. auch Espinoza 1990, 219):

Yurac aclla's - die Auserwählten aus dem Geschlecht der Inkas, die als Priesterinnen bei den Riten des Sonnengotts dienten, das heilige Getränk zubereitet haben, und aus deren Reihen leitende *mama cuna*'s ausgewählt wurden. Sie sollten ihr Leben lang ledig bleiben.

Huairuro aclla's - die Mädchen, die aus den Gemeinden aus der Nähe von Cuzco stammten, wo die sog. Inkas auf der Basis des Vorrechts lebten; gleichfalls Mädchen, die Töchter oder Schwestern höherer Beamten und Regionsleiter. Aus ihrer Mitte hat sich der *Sapa Inca* Nebenfrauen gewählt.

Paco aclla's - die Töchter und Schwestern der Leiter der kleineren Administrationseinheiten des Staates und der unterworfenen Stämme. Sie konnten den niedrigeren Aristokraten und Offizieren zu Frauen gegeben werden.

Yana aclla's - in der Regel aus dem einfachen Volke stammende Mädchen, die üblicherweise als Dienerinnen der *aclla*'s aus höheren Kategorien gewirkt

haben; ihr Status konnte sich aber verbessern, wenn sie positiv auffielen.
Taqui aclla's - Mädchen, die Talente zum Singen, Tanzen und Musizieren hatten, und die bei den religiösen Veranstaltungen oder auch am Hof gebraucht wurden.

Die Analyse des Chroniktextes von Garcilaso zeigt allerdings folgendes: Die *aclla*'s wohnten in Häusern, in denen eine strenge Klosterordnung für Nonnen herrschte. Solche Häuser gab es sowohl in der Hauptstadt als auch in den administrativen und religiösen Zentren aller Provinzen. Die *aclla*'s waren eine soziale Gruppe, aus denen der Kaiser seinen Harem komplettierte, die aber auch zu kleinerem Teil für die Aristokratie bestimmt war. Bis auf diese Ausnahme mussten die *aclla*'s bis zum Ende ihres Lebens die Jungfräulichkeit wahren. Die Verletzung dieser Forderung hat eine schwere Züchtigung mit sich gebracht.

Es ist aber offensichtlich, dass nur ein ganz kleiner Prozentsatz von den *aclla*'s zu Nebenfrauen von *Sapa* Inca und der hohen Aristokraten werden konnte. Das legt folgende Überlegung nahe: Wenn es allein in Cuzco ca. 1500, in Huanucopampa zum Beispiel aber mehr als 2000 *aclla*'s gab (Espinoza 1990, 219), dann musste im gesamten Staat, in dem es vermutlich *aclla*-Häuser in jedem wichtigeren Zentrum gab, deren Anzahl wenigstens fünfzigmal grösser sein – verschiedene Chroniktexte erwähnen schon mehr als 38 Siedlungen (s. Busto 1981, 174-180; Espinoza 1990, 219-220). Die genaue Anzahl ist deswegen, weil über die Gesellschaft der Inkas nur die von den Chronisten ermittelten Auskünfte bestehen, nachträglich nur sehr schwer festzustellen. Man kann trotz allem davon ausgehen, dass mehr als 95% der *aclla*'s als Jungfrauen gestorben sein dürften. Das bedeutet aber, dass in einem Staat, in dem nach groben Berechnungen ca. 12 Millionen Menschen gelebt haben (Espinoza 1990, 365) und in dem die vom Staat kontrollierte Ehepflicht herrschte, während in einer Generation ca. 70 Tausend oder mehr Frauen aus den demographischen Zyklus ausgeschaltet wurden.

Die *aclla*'s waren die schönsten Mädchen, die in jungen Jahren aus den Vertreterinnen aller Gesellschaftsschichten ausgewählt wurden. Zu ihnen gehörten sowohl die Töchter der Mitglieder der kaiserlichen Familie, der Vornehmen aus dem Stamm der Inkas und der Führer der unterworfenen Stämme *curaca*'s, als auch die der Familien des einfachen Volkes. Diese Tatsache zeigt, dass die *aclla*'s kein geschlossener und fest umrissener Stand waren, sondern eher eine Pufferschicht zwischen den Ständen, deren Grösse aller Wahrscheinlichkeit nach entsprechend der demographischen Lage des Staates wuchs oder abnam – auf jeden Fall wurde der Prozess vonseiten der Staatsmacht kontrolliert (Trimborn 1969, 121). Zugleich war der gesellschaftliche Status der *aclla*'s hoch: Die Auserwählten waren die Frauen der Sonne und die potenziellen Frauen des Sohnes der Sonne. Ihnen oblagen oft auch verschiedene, den Sonnenkult betreffende religiöse Handlungen, sei es durch Produkte ihrer Handarbeit (die Anfertigung der Opfergaben), durch ihre Talente (Darbieten der heiligen Lieder und Tänze bei Festlichkeiten) oder sogar durch Einsatz ihres Lebens (die Wahl zum

Ritual *capac cocha* oder dem Menschenopfer (Cobo 1893, T. IV, Cap. XXXVII; s. z.B. auch Trimborn 1961, 153; Disselhoff 1972, 218).

Man muss auch die Tatsache beachten, dass die *aclla*'s in ihren Klosterwohnungen arbeiten mussten. Sie haben in Cuzco in grosser Anzahl Kleider, Schmuck, Gerichte und Getränke beigesteuert, die der Hof mit der kaiserlichen Familie an der Spitze ständig gebraucht hat und die auch bei den in der Hauptstadt zwölfmal im Jahr stattfindenden, den ganzen Staat umfassenden religiösen Festlichkeiten verwendet wurden. In den *aclla huasi*'s anderer Orte des Staates wurde derartige Produkte für die an Ort und Stelle residierenden Aristokraten, Beamten, Offiziere und ihre Familien angefertigt, die gleichfalls für die in den Orten stattfindenden religiösen Feierlichkeiten gebraucht wurden (Prem 1989, 188; Hyams&Ordish 1990, 71). Ausserhalb der Hauptstadt gab es sogar noch mehr solcher Festlichkeiten: Dort mussten zusätzlich den zwölf offiziellen grossen Feiertagen der Staatsreligion auch noch die lokalen Gottheiten öffentlich verehrt werden. Im Staat der Inkas hat nämlich eine bemerkenswerte religiöse Toleranz geherrscht: Jedes unterworfene Volk durfte seinen Gottheiten unter der Bedingung weiterhin dienen, wenn sie den offiziellen Kult des Inkastaats erfüllt hatten, deren Empfänger der Schöpfergott Pachacamak oder Wiracocha, der Sonnengott Inti und der Kaiser *Sapa Inca* als der Sohn der Sonne auf Erden waren. Mehr noch: Unter dieser Bedingung wurden die lokalen Gottheiten sogar als vollberechtigt in das Staatspantheon aufgenommen. Daraus wird klar, dass die Häuser der Auserwählten gewissermassen als riesige Manufakturen gewirkt haben. Entsprechend darf die Bedeutung ihrer Produktion im staatlichen Gesamtprodukt nicht unterschätzt werden.

Es ist also sehr schwer, die soziale Lage der *aclla*'s als einer besonderen Schicht der Gesellschafts einzuschätzen. Der soziale Status und der dementsprechende soziale, religiöse und rechtliche Schutz war bei ihnen allen bis zum Ende ihres Lebens gleichermassen hoch - sie waren religiös verehrt und genossen eine personale Immunität. Das gilt auch für ihre soziale Stellung nach ihrem Scheiden aus den *aclla huasi*'s oder dem Hof im Alter - unabhängig von ihrer Herkunft wurden sie ein wichtiger Bestandteil der Hautevolee des Staates (Silverblatt 1987, 81ff.).

Anders verhielt es sich mit der sozialen Position der *aclla*'s im leistungsfähigen Alter. Die überwiegende Mehrheit der Auserwählten musste in der Produktion arbeiten und war vom demographischen Zyklus ausgeschlossen; nur eine kleine Minderheit wurde zu Mitgliedern der Aristokratie und zu Müttern von Kindern des *Sapa Inca* oder der Aristokraten. Man darf die *aclla*'s nicht ausser Acht lassen, die für die Tempelriten oder gar zum Opfer für die Götter ausgewählt wurden (Acosta 1991, Cap. 14) - diese Frauen mussten sehr hohen physischen Anforderungen genügen.

Alle genannten Punkte weisen darauf in, dass die Stellung der *aclla*'s in der Hierarchie der Inkagesellschaft hoch war. Dementsprechend müssen die *aclla*'s in der Gesellschaftspyramide der Inkas zu der dritten der in der Einleitung aufgezählten Zwischenschichten gerechnet werden.

Auf Grund der vorliegenden Betrachtung kann man folgende Schlussfolgerungen ziehen.
1. Die Institution der *aclla*'s oder der Sonnenjungfrauen ist der Meinung der Autoren der Chroniktexte nach vor allem eine religiöse Institution. Im allgemeinen ist das auch richtig, insbesondere wenn man die Tatsache berücksichtigt, dass ein grosser Teil der *aclla*'s zum Erfüllen verschiedener religiösen Pflichten bestimmt war. Daraus darf aber nicht gleichzeitig geschlossen werden, dass in der Religion der Inkas ein Nonnenstand nach christlicher Art existiert hätte. Das hat es bekanntermassen nicht der Fall.
2. Bei der näheren Analyse wird klar, dass die *aclla*'s auch andere Pflichten erfüllen mussten. Ein erster kleinerer Teil von ihnen war zur Zielgruppe bestimmt, auf deren Kosten der Harem des *Sapa Incas* komplettiert wurde, und es ist offensichtlich, dass ein zweite kleinerer Teil von ihnen zu Frauen der höheren Aristokratie bestimmt war. Die überwiegende Mehrheit der *aclla*'s musste in der Produktion arbeiten, wozu sie eine Spezialausbildung bekamen. Das bedeutet, dass die *aclla*'s in der Gesellschaft der Inkas eine wesentliche wirtschaftliche Rolle gespielt haben.
3. Indem man die Tatsache berücksichtigt, dass die überwiegende Mehrheit der *aclla*'s ihr Leben lang ihre Jungfräulichkeit erhalten musste und dass sie also von der demographischen Reproduktion der Gesellschaft der Inkas ausgeschaltet waren, wird offensichtlich, dass das weitestreichende Ziel der Institution der Sonnenjungfrauen die Kontrolle der Einwohnerzahl im Staat war. Dafür sprechen folgende Tatsachen: (1) die gesamtstaatliche Ehepflicht, (2) die hohe Sterblichkeit der ledigen Männer in Verbindung mit den ständigen Eroberungskriegen im Imperium der Inkas, (3) die Sozialpolitik des Inkastaates, mit der die Befriedigung aller elementaren Lebensbedürfnisse für alle Staatsangehörigen gewährleistet werden sollte, (4) das Bedürfnis, die Einwohnerzahl des Staates auf einem gewissen optimalen Niveau zu halten, damit es für das Erfüllen aller Funktionen des Staates und der Gesellschaft Ausführende gäbe. Die Institution der *aclla*'s, deren Menge durch künstliche Methoden gemäss dem Bedürfnis reguliert wurde, hat also ein wichtiges demographisches Ziel erfüllt. Zur Verwirklichung einer solchen Sozialpolitik hat der Staat der Inkas auch für ein Totalitärreich charakteristische Machtmechanismen angewandt (s. darüber z.B. auch Disselhoff 1972, 218-220 (unmittelbar), Rostworowski 1992, 261-282, Espinoza 1990, 483-499 (mittelbar) u.a.).

Literatur

1. Quellen

Acosta, José de. Das Gold des Kondors. Berichte aus der Neuen Welt /1590/. Hgg. und übertragen von Rudolf Kroboth und Peter H. Meurer. Stuttgart-Wien, Edition Erdmann, 1991.

Ayala, Felipe Guaman Poma de. El Primer Nueva Corónica y Buen Gobierno /1615/. Edición crítica de John V.Murra y Rolena Adorno. Traducciones y análysis textual del quechua por Jorge L.Urioste. Ciudad de México, Siglo Veintiuno Editores S.A., 1980.

Cobo, Bernabé. Historia del Nuevo Mundo /1653/. Publicada por primera vez, con notas y otras ilustracciones de D. Marcos Jiménez de la Espada. Tomo IV. Sevilla, Imp. de E.Rasco, 1893.

León, Pedro Cieza de. La Crónica del Perú /1553/. Lima, Promocción Editorial Inca S.A., 1988.

Garcilaso de la Vega, Inca. Comentarios reales de los Incas /1609/. Tomo II. Lima, Editorial Mercurio S.A., 1988.

Zarate, Agustín. Historia del Descubrimiento y Conquista del Perú /1555/. Lima, 1944.

2. Sekundärliteratur

Busto Duthurburu, José Antonio del. Perú Incaico. Lima, Librería Studium Editores, 1981.

Cunow, Heinrich. Die soziale Verfassung des Inkareiches: Eine Untersuchung des altperuanischen Agrarkommunismus. Stuttgart, 1896.

Cunow, Heinrich. Geschichte und Kultur des Inkareiches. Ein Betrag zur Kulturgeschichte Altamerikas. Mit einem Geleitwort von Rudolf Steinmetz. Amsterdam, Elsevier, 1937.

Disselhoff, Hans. Das Imperium der Inka und die indianischen Frühkulturen der Andenländer. Berlin, Safari-Verlag, 1972.

Espinoza Soriano, Waldemar. Economía, sociedad y Estado en la era del Tahuantinsuyo. Lima, Amaru Editores, 1990.

Hyams, Edward; Ordish, George. The Last of the Incas. The Rise and Fall of an American Empire. New York, Dorset Press, 1990.

Kauffmann Doig, Federico. Historia del Perú antiguo. Lima, Kompaktos Editores, 1990.

Prem, Hanns J. Geschichte Altamerikas. - Oldenbourg Grundriss der Geschichte. Hgg. von J.Bleicken, L.Gall, H.Jacobs. Bd. 23. München, R.Oldenbourg Verlag, 1989.

Rostworowski de Diez Canseco. Historia del Tahuantinsuyu. Lima, Instituto de Estudios Peruanos Ediciones, 1992.

Silverblatt, Irene. Moon, Sun, and Witches. Gender Ideologies and Classes in Inca and Colonial Peru. Princeton/New Yersey, Princeton University Press, 1987.

Trimborn, Hermann. Alte Hochkulturen Südamerikas. – H.Trimborn, W.Haberland. Die Kulturen Alt-Amerikas. Frankfurt am Main, Akademische Verlagsgesellschaft Athenaion, 1969.

Trimborn, Hermann. Die Religionen der Völkerschaften des südlichen Mittelamerika und des nördlichen und mittleren Andenraumes. – W.Krickeberg, H.Trimborn, W.Müller, O.Zerries. Die Religionen des alten Amerika. – Die Religionen der Menschheit. Hgg. von Chr. M. Schröder. Bd. 7. Stuttgart, W.Kohlhammer Verlag, 1961.

The current article has been supported by Estonian Science Foundation grant 4893.

The Way to the Bodhisattvahood in *Gaṇḍavyūhasūtra*
with Special Reference to the Term *dharmadhātu*

Märt Läänemets, Tartu

I. The Text

Gaṇḍavyūhasūtra is one of the best-known of Mahāyāna sūtras, put down in India in the so-called Buddhist Hybrid Sanskrit, probably in the 2nd-3rd centuries A.D. [1] In the Buddhist tradition of Nepal, it belongs to the "Nine Dharmas", i.e. the nine most revered sūtras. [2] In China and Tibet, *Gaṇḍavyūha* is known as the last part of the bulky *Avataṃsakasūtra*, or "Garland Sūtra" that is, more precisely, the collection that comprises more than thirty supposedly once independent sūtras. [3]

---

[1] v.: Warder, A. K. *Indian Buddhism*. Delhi: Motilal Banarsidass, 2000, pp.401-402. According to Hajime Nakamura and Torakazu Doi, *Gaṇḍavyūhasūtra* was created no later than the 1st century A.D. v.: Nakamura, H. *Indian Buddhism. A Survey with Bibliographical Notes*. Delhi et. al.: Motilal Banarsidass, 1987, p. 196; Torakazu Doi. *Das Kegon Sutra. Das Buch vom Eintreten in den Kosmos der Wahrheit*. Tokyo, 1978, S. 7-8.

[2] Those are *Aṣṭasāhasrikā Prajñāpāramitā, Gaṇḍavyūha, Daśabhūmīśvara, Lalitavistara, Laṅkāvatāra, Saddharmapuṇḍarīka, Samādhirāja, Suvarṇaprabhāsa, Tathāgataguhyaka*.

[3] *Avataṃsakasūtra* (*Huayanjing* in Chinese) was probably compiled in the 4th century, but certainly not later than the beginning of the 5th century in Central Asia on the basis of the then extant sūtras that were similar in content. The sūtra has not survived in its entirety in Sanskrit. We have information only of *Gaṇḍavyūha* and *Daśabhūmika*, most likely because they were survived in the Nepalese tradition. The full title in Sanskrit is *Mahāvaipulya Budhāvataṃsakasūtra* or *Budhāvataṃsakanāma Mahāvaipulyasūtra*, in Chinese – *Da fang guang fo hua yan jing*, in Tibetan, *Sangs rgyas phal po che shes bya ba śin tu rgyas pa chen po'i mdo*. Three versions of *Avataṃsakasūtra* exist in Chinese: a translation of Buddhabhadra, or '*Huayan* in 60 *juan*', completed around 420 (vol. 9, text no.278 in the Taisho edition of Chinese Buddhist canon); a translation of Shikshānanda from 698, or '*Huayan* in 80 *juan*' (Taisho, vol.10, no.279), and a translation of Prajñā from the end of the 8th century, or '*Huayan* in 40 *juan*' (Taisho, vol. 10, no. 293), containing only *Gaṇḍavyūha* and bearing the subtitle *Ru bu si yi jie pu xian xing yuan pin* or 'The Vow of Samantabhadra Guiding into the Realm of Unthinkable Liberation'. In other Chinese versions *Gaṇḍavyūha* bears the title *Ru fa jie pin*, or 'The Chapter of the Entry into the Realm of Dharmas'. On the translation of *Avataṃsakasūtra* into

The central theme of *Gaṇḍavyūhasūtra*, as of the majority of Mahāyāna sūtras, is the theme of bodhisattva – the 'awakening being' [4], as the active agent and executor of Buddha's teaching. The main emphasis in this text is laid upon the concept of 'way', on how the human being becomes the 'awakening being' in the utmost meaning of this word, whose consciousness and thinking reach far beyond the "other side", beyond the boundaries of the world limited by the conditions of man's physical existence (*saṃsāra*). The most essential message of the sūtra is that the way to the Boddhisattvahood is not an individualistic way, but that it can be achieved only by the support of other human (or mythological) beings more advanced in their spiritual development, the teachers and fellows that are called 'benevolent friends' (*kalyāṇamitra*). Besides the 'way' motif, the sūtra presents an integral survey of Mahāyāna philosophy and the holistic world view, especially elaborate in *Avatamsakasūtra*.

Gaṇḍavyūhasūtra is considered to be a genuine masterpiece of Mahāyāna literature for its artistic structure and style. Its composition is more accomplished and "arranged" than that of most other Mahāyāna sūtras, and its text can be divided into three essentially consistent integral blocks.

Firstly, the introduction (*nidānaparivarta*), which describes the situation in the Jeta grove, the traditional site of proclaiming the teaching of Buddha near Śrāvastī, where many bodhisattvas, śrāvakas and 'lords of the world' (*lokendra*) have gathered to listen. By means of great compassion, Buddha delves into the deep state of concentration (*samādhi*) called 'Roar of Lion' (*siṃhavijṛmbhita*), in which the Jeta grove and the entire universe will be turned into gem-like constellations, and in ten directions of the world wondrous buddha-fields will open, from which innumerable bodhisattvas will arrive to listen to the teaching,

---

Chinese v.: Jan Yun-hua. On Chinese Translation of 'Avatamsakasūtra' from Udra. – *The Orissa Historical Research Journal*. Vol. 7, Parts 3-4, October, 1958 - January, 1959, pp. 125-132.

P.L. Vaidya has published a critical edition of the Sanskrit text of *Gaṇḍavyūhasūtra* in the series *Buddhist Sanskrit Texts*: Vaidya, P. L. *Gaṇḍavyūhasūtra. - Buddhist Sanskrit Texts*. No. 5. Darbhanga: The Mithila Institute, 1960.

The Tibetan text of *Gaṇḍavyūhasūtra* is best available in vol.26 of the Peking version of Kanjour published by D. T. Suzuki: Tibetan Tripitaka (*Bkaḥ-ḥgyur*). Peking Edition. Vol. 26 (Phal-chen II). Ed. by D. T. Suzuki. Tokyo-Kyoto: Tibetan Tripitaka Research Institute, 1958.

There exist two translations of *Gaṇḍavyūhasūtra* into Western languages: the translation of Torakazu Doi into German (*op. cit.*) and the translation of Thomas Cleary into English: Cleary, T. *Entry into the Realm of Reality. A Translation of the Gandavyuha, the Final Book of the Avatamsaka Sutra*. Translated by Thomas Cleary. Boston & Shaftesbury: Shambala, 1989.

[4] In the English-language literature, the word 'enlightening being' has mostly been used as an equivalent of the word *bodhisattva*, and, respectively, 'englightenment' for *bodhi*. However, proceeding from the original meaning of the Sanskrit word *budh* as 'to awake', and the base concept, all *bodhi*- stem words in this article have been translated by means of 'awake'-stem ones.

placing themselves around Buddha in the shape of mandala. In this vision, the universe appears as the 'realm of dharmas' (*dharmadhātu*), which from the point of view of buddha-consciousness is real (*bhūta*), inhabited by buddhas and bodhisattvas, while the 'realm of worlds' (*lokadhātu*) that the common consciousness can perceive is illusory (*nirmita*).

In the 'Roar of Lion' state of concentration, the great bodhisattvas Samantabhadra ('Universally Good'), embodying the power of action enhanced by the compassion of bodhisattvas, and Mañjuśrī ('Sweet Happiness'), embodying the power of wisdom and understanding of the bodhisattvas, act as teachers of the bodhisattvas (while, paradoxically, Buddha himself remains silent). They explain to the assembled bodhisattvas the nature and working of dharmas in the timeless 'realm of dharmas', and why and how the bodhisattvas still keep appearing in the realms of the world in order to help beings and give them this very higher knowledge.

The next and the bulkiest part deals with the benevolent friends, focusing on the journey to them of the "protagonist" of the sūtra, the son of a merchant Sudhana, a novice on the way to Bodhisattvahood, carrying the instructions of the bodhisattva of wisdom Mañjuśrī with him. Having received teaching and instructions from 52 successive benevolent friends of a wide social background, as well as from mythological beings, he has a vision of Samantabhadra who guides him to the similar supreme understanding of the realm of dharmas as achieved by other bodhisattvas in the 'Roar of Lion' buddha-samādhi at the beginning of the sūtra.

Finally, as the culmination of the sūtra, there is the vow of the practice of Samantabhadra (*Samantabhadracaryāpraṇidhāna*), or the vow of the practice of good (*Bhadracarīpraṇidhāna*), made by Sudhana together with Samantabhadra, which marks the real beginning of his way as bodhisattva.

The composition and style of *Gaṇḍavyūhasūtra* are most varied, the visions conveyed in language full of colourful and poetic images interspersed with rational arguments and mātrika-like lists, common "stories" with mythological "time-travels", and the prose written in strict classical Sanskrit alternating with long songs of praise and passages of verse in "irregular" Sanskrit that often reiterate the content given earlier in the prose text.

All this serves as evidence of the fact that the sūtra was compiled and composed of very diverse material that was probably created at different periods of time as well. What is considered to be the most ancient layer consists of passages of verse in simple everyday language that may represent the oral traditional texts of one or several earlier "Proto-Mahāyāna" schools. It is likely that due to the influence of the 'Perfection of Wisdom' (*prajñāpāramitā*) "school" whose teaching was the first of Mahāyāna trends to be put down as sūtra, and in which the glorification of the written text forms a constant theme of its own, [5] the scripture of the *gaṇḍavyūha* "school" was born as a result of collecting the earlier texts and text fragments, philosophical reasoning and the creation of a common compositional canvas. It was later included in *Avataṃsakasūtra*.

II. Methodological Background

One of the most basic and complicated problems connected with Buddhist texts that every researcher faces is the one about the descriptive language: which apparatus of notions, which descriptive method, which background concept to use in order to explicate and interpret, for example, such basic Buddhist concepts like 'buddhahood' (*buddhatā*), 'nirvāṇa' or 'realm of dharmas' (*dharmadhātu*) that lack even the least applicable conceptual equivalents in the cultural paradigm of contemporary humanities.

Linnart Mäll pointed it out already more than thirty years ago that the interpretive models applied in Oriental texts and history of thought very often are inadequate. More or less all of these are based on the premise that the Western scientific and philosophical systems should be applied in interpreting and assessing the Oriental teachings. [6] He suggested a principally new approach, according to which it was necessary to elaborate such interpretive models for Oriental texts that would proceed from these texts themselves, from their own inner logic and message, and would thus enrich and interpret Western theories and doctrines in a novel way. [7] As an example of a model of this kind, he

---

[5] The word "school" has been used here relatively, for there were no known definite historical schools in India that might have been responsible for the development of different Mahāyāna sūtras. Linnart Mäll has dealt with the evolution and sources of *Prajñāpāramitā*, or 'Perfection of Wisdom' sūtras in numerous articles, especially in the following one: Некоторые проблемы возникновения махаяны [Some Crucial Problems of the Foundation of the Mahāyānā, in Russian]. – *Центральная Азия в кушанскую эпоху* [Central Asia in the Kushan Era]. Vol. 2. Moskva: Nauka, 1975, pp. 219-222. See also: Conze, E. *The Prajñāpāramitā Literature*. 'S-Gravenhage: Mouton & Co, 1960.

[6] Mäll, L. Об одном возможном подходе к пониманию *śūnyavāda* [On the One Possible Approach to the Understanding of the *Śūnyavāda*, in Russian] - *Terminologia Indica*. I. Tartu, 1967, lk. 13-24; reprinted in the journal Буддизм России [Buddhism of Russia], No. 35, Spring 2002, pp. 80-84; in French: Une approche possible du *Śūnyvāda*. – *Tel Quel*, 32, 1968, lk. 54-62.

[7] "The phenomena of the East could not be looked any more in the framework of the Western schemes. The possibility of existence of certain parallelisms is, of course, not excluded, but as these are not constructed artificially, they may appear spontaneously and unexpectedly on the new levels. It must be self-evident, that in many spheres of culture the East has reached quite unique results.

Thus the main task of the oriental studies must be the creation of models that make way to the new approach for interpretation of the Western phenomena." (Mäll, L. On the

presents in the cited article an original approach for interpreting Oriental and Occidental cultural phenomena, based on the Buddhist theory of emptyness, or *śūnyavāda*, suggesting even new specific materms – 'zerology' and 'lysiology' – as equivalents for corresponding Ancient Indian terms *śūnyavāda* and *mokṣadharma*.

Linnart Mäll has later successfully used this approach, inspired greatly by the ground-breaking cultural semiotic views of the Tartu-Moscow school of semiotics, especially the ones concerning the broader understanding of the concept of text, for studying and translating Buddhist and Ancient Chinese texts. [8] In his more recent works he has paid much attention to elaborating a model of interpretation for the fundamental concept of Buddhism, *dharma*. He finds it reasonable to interpret a general concept of such level that is hardly ever directly defined in Buddhist texts themselves, by using contemporary fundamental general concepts of the same level, for instance, such as 'text' and 'culture'. [9]

According to Linnart Mäll's semiotic model, *dharma* can be understood unequivocally and uniformly at different levels mainly as a sign that has a meaning within a definite context (likewise, an idea or conscious act expressed by means of signs – in words, writing, pictures, etc.), a word (concept) or phrase as a part of text, a text, a collection of texts, that constitutes culture. Each *dharma* as text or sign has a definite meaning only within a certain definite context or cultural space. When the context changes, the meaning of the definite *dharma* may change as well. For example, when we speak about *buddhadharma* (as a synonym of which the Buddhist texts often simply use *dharma*) within the context of Buddhism, then in contemporary terminology we may understand it as the entire Buddhist culture, or the body of all Buddhist texts. The same word in the plural thus signifies all the elements of this culture, expressed by signs – texts, concepts, ideas, ways of behaviour, etc. It is the same within the context

---

One Possible Approach..., 1967, p. 15.)

[8] A selected bibliography of works by Linnart Mäll has been presented in the given volume as an appendix to his article.

[9] v.: Mäll, L. Дхарма как текст и текстопорождающий механизм [Dharma as Text and the Text-generating Mechanism, in Russian] – Труды по знаковым системам [Works on Semiotics]. Vol. 21 – *Acta et commentationes Universitatis Tartuensis.* Issue No. 754. Tartu, 1987, pp. 22-25; Mäll, L. Semiotics as a Possibility for the Study of Religious Texts in the Conditions of the Communist Dictatorship. – *The Academic Study of Religion During the Cold War. East and West. – Toronto Studies in Religion.* Vol. 27, 2001, pp. 163-170. Among the works on the concept of *dharma* published by other authors in recent decades, the following are of greater interest: Liebenthal, W. Ding und Dharma. – *Asiatische Studien.* Bd. XIV, 1961; Warder, A. K. Dharmas and Data. – *Journal of Indian Philosophy.* Vol. 1, 1971, pp. 272-295; Carter, J. R. Traditional Definitions of the Word Dhamma. – *Philosophy East and West.* Vol. 26, no. 3, July, 1976, pp. 329-337; Masing, U. Dharma as Norm. – *Communio Viatorum.* No. 3-4, 1970, pp. 109-118.

of *Abhidharma*, where dharmas have been listed as if they were elements of the psycho-ontological world. According to the semiotic approach, however, dharmas are considered to be signifying concepts, terms, not ontological entities (that according to the Buddhist theory of dharmas do not exist anyway, or, to be more exact, which are 'essence-less' – *asvabhāva,* or 'empty' – *śūnya,* i.e. they appear as real only at the level of certain conventional consciousness), thus still as signs or parts of text.

Likewise, the well-known clause *sarvadharmaśūnyatā* – 'the emptyness of all dharmas' – does not at all voice ontological nihilism within the cultural semiotic model, but instead, expresses the notional relativity and volatility of concepts and signs. In the 'semiotic space', or 'semiosphere', which could conditionally be used as an equivalent of the Buddhist term *dharmadhātu* ('realm of dharmas')[10] all dharmas or texts (or elements of text) exist as possibilities out of physical time and space, and will become actual only on the level of certain definite states of consciousness. We cannot speak of the existence of dharmas outside consciousness at all. In this sense, dharmas are ontologically empty as well.

Buddhism acknowledges the existence of the hierarchy of states of consciousness, beginning with the absence of consciousness on the level of the so-called physical world to the infinite consciousness, or 'supreme perfect awakening' (*anuttarā samyaksambodhi*) on the level of buddhas and bodhisattvas who are potentially able to actualize all *dharmas*. In the figurative language of *Gaṇḍavyūhasūtra,* the bodhisattvas of this level of consciousness have been

---

[10] The term 'semiotic space' or 'semiosphere' was introduced by Yuri Lotman in the 80-s and it has became very useful in the semiotic studies worldwide. v.: Lotman, Y. M. *Universe of the Mind. A Semiotic Theory of Culture.* London, New York: I.B. Taurus & Co Ltd, 1992, especially the article *Semiotic Space,* pp. 123-130. Lotman defines semiosphere in following way: "The unit of semiosis, the smallest functioning mechanism, is not the separate language but the whole semiotic space of the culture in question. This is the space we term the semiosphere. The semiosphere is the result and the condition for the development of culture" (p. 125).

"As an example of a single world looked at synchronically, imagine a museum hall where exhibits from different periods are on display, along with inscriptions in known and unknown languages, and instructions for decoding them; besides there are the explanations composed by museum staff, plans for tours and rules for the behaviour of the visitors. Imagine also in this hall tour-leaders and the visitors and imagine all this as a single mechanism (which *in a certain sense* it is). This is an image of the semiosphere. Then we have to remember that all elements of the semiosphere are in dynamic, not static, correlations whose terms are constantly changing" (p. 126-127).

"Non-semiotic reality and its space and time can also be enclosed in this system, in order to be made 'semioticizable', i.e. capable of becoming the content of a semiotic text" (p. 133-134).

Thus, using 'semiosphere' seems to me quite fruitful to interpret the Buddhist term *dharmadhātu,* that may also be understood in a similar way as the space of *dharmas* in their dynamic and interdependent correlations.

described as the beings "who had spacelike knowledge, pervading all the realm of dharmas with net of the beams of light" (*gaganasamaprajñāḥ sarvadharmadhaturaśmijālaspharaṇatayā*).[11]

Since the aim of Buddhism is to widen consciousness as much as possible (this tendency is especially prominent in Mahāyāna sūtras), which means the maximum comprehension of *dharmadhātu*, it is the cultivation of those dharmas that contribute to this objective that is valued most in the Buddhist cultural sphere (buddhadharmas). Firstly, being born as man, since only man possesses by birth these dharmas that make the development of consciousness possible at all (in contemporary terminology this means that only man has such highly developed central nervous system and a correspondingly adapted organism that make it possible for him to extend his activity that far beyond the areas connected with the immediate preservation of his biological existence). Secondly, and this is more important still, the cultural environment where buddhadharmas function, i.e. where the respective texts play an active role in culture.

According to the Buddhist tradition, this culture and the text-generating mechanism were founded by the historical Buddha in India about 2500 years ago.[12] This (human) being that has evolved the motivation to develop his consciousness and who finds himself in the favourable cultural environment is called *bodhisattva*, or 'awakening being'. The motivation or inclination to 'awakening' (*bodhi*) is called 'awakening mind' (*bodhicitta*), the process that leads to this, respectively, the 'way to the awakening' (*bodhicaryā*). The state in which the consciousness is widened to the maximum degree, potentially capable of comprehending the entire semiosphere of *dharmadhātu*, i.e. able to explicate any texts in any context and, most importantly, to apply them as buddhadharmas, i.e. as signs and texts that contribute to the 'awakening', is denoted by the above-mentioned term, 'supreme perfect awakening' (*anuttarā samyaksambodhi*).[13]

Proceeding from these introductory remarks, I shall now attempt to give the

---

[11] *Gaṇḍavyūhasūtra* (henceforth GV), p.3; Cleary, p. 12. All text quotations are taken from P. L. Vaidya's text publication (v. reference 3). The English translations of quotations are based on the translation of T. Cleary (v. reference 3), the page numbers of which have been referred to in each case. The author of the present article has only taken the liberty to unify the equivalents of the translated terms.

[12] v. Mäll. Dharma as Text ..., p. 23.

[13] Linnart Mäll defines the term *anuttarā samyaksambodhi* on the basis of the analysis of the text of *Aṣṭasāhasrikā prajñāpāramitā*. (a "working hypothesis", according to his own words) in the following way: "the term *anuttarā samyaksambodhi* denotes, in the opinion of the authors of the sūtras, a state in which the human psyche is conscious to a maximum degree, and in which the subconsciousness plays practically no role in directing human behaviour." v.: Mäll, L. Четыре термина праджняпарамитской психологии [Four Terms of the Psychology of the *Prajñāpāramitā*, in Russian]. Part 2. - Oriental Studies. Vol. 3. - *Acta et commentationes Universitatis Tartuensis*. Issue No. 392. Tartu, 1976, pp. 115.

outline of the basic features of a possible model of description of the way to Bodhisattvahood as presented in *Gaṇḍavyūhasūtra*. While doing this, I shall keep in mind the point of view, according to which the theme of bodhisattva, central in the majority of Mahāyāna texts as it is, is approached differently in each sūtra. These specific emphases overlap to a greater or lesser extent, as far as basic concepts and objectives are concerned. On the level of the described text, however, they may yield very different results. Thus we may even maintain that both Mahāyāna and the bodhisattva theory as such are, in a sense, generalizing abstractions. It is always the definite text itself that matters most, with its usually very explicit and practical instructions for proceeding on the way to Bodhisattvahood, together with theoretical (often mythological, in accordance with the context of the era) substantiation. Naturally, this does not mean that the one who chose to undertake the way had to restrict oneself to the instructions given in one text only (although this was not excluded either, since in principle each text had to instruct the student to move in one direction – towards 'supreme perfect awakening'). Instead, it means that in the Buddhist tradition (at its later stage, at least) one studied different sūtras combined with other texts. But there may have been periods and schools in which attempts were made to systematize and explicate the entire buddhadharma. This was, for example, the case in China during the Tang era where one of the various schools – the *Huayan* school – was based on *Avataṃsakasūtra* (*Huayanjing*) and had an attempt to interpret the whole buddhadharma in the spirit of this particular text.

By way of conclusion, it should be pointed out that for some reason the textological studies of Mahāyāna sūtras are quite rare in contemporary Buddhist studies. While the markedly Eurocentrist (Western) interpretive models no longer seem to prevail in Buddhist studies in general, the philosophical texts and commentaries of later schools still dominate heavily as objects of research. At the same time, very few original interpretations of Mahāyāna sūtras have appeared during the last twenty years. [14] Whenever they are referred to at all, this is

---

[14] For example, a number of excellent works on *Huayan*-Buddhism have appeared during the last 30 years, among which I would like to emphasize three general ones: Chang, Garma C. C. *The Buddhist Teaching of Totality. The Philosophy of Hwa Yen Buddhism*. University Park and London: The Pennsylvania State University Press, 1971; Cook, Francis H. *Hua-yen Buddhism. The Jewel Net of Indra*. University Park and London: Pennsylvania State University Press, 1977; Cleary, Thomas. *Entry into the Inconceivable: An Introduction to Hua-yen Buddhism*. Honolulu: University Press of Hawaii, 1983, as well as the studies of Robert Gimello and others. At the same time, no special investigations of the base text of this school, *Avataṃsakasūtra* have been published, except for the translations by Torakazu Doi and Thomas Cleary referred to earlier on, as well as Cheng Chien Bhikshu. *Manifestation of the Tathāgata. Buddhahood according to the* Avataṃsaka Sūtra. Boston: Wisdom Publications, 1993. The philosophical essays published as prefaces to the volumes of the translation of Torakazu Doi attempt to explicate the spiritual world of *Avataṃsakasūtra* by means of the terms of contemporary critical philosophy, but these, too, are not based on the analysis of terminology, but rather on the analysis of the general concept as seen by a philosopher. In Liu Ming-

done to the extent the sūtras are referred to and explicated in treatises under inspection. Since the treatises (skr. *śāstra*, chin. *lun*, tib. *bstan bcos*) were mostly created centuries later than sūtras, and in an entirely different cultural context, then from the point of view of studying sūtras, the treatises should be viewed as interpretations of the latter. But if at the present time we make conclusions about sūtras only on the basis of the interpretations given in the treatises, we are inevitably dealing with the interpretation of interpretation. Much of the lysiological message originally encoded into the sūtras may get distorted, unnoticed or lost altogether.

This is not to question the importance of studying the texts of philosophical schools from the point of view of comprehending the historical development of Buddhist thought and expanding the interpretive possibilities of sūtras. Rather, this is to emphasize the fact that we cannot confine ourselves to the study of treatises. In order to understand the sūtras more adequately, we will have to find a clue to the problems of their inner structure and basic concepts within the present cultural context, proceeding from the sūtras themselves and the historical context of the period they were created. Śāstras can only serve as auxiliary means here, not as "filters for interpretation". This is where we encounter once again the problem of the language of description. It seems that the process of elaborating the adequate language of description and methodology for studying Mahāyāna sūtras is still at its initial stage in contemporary buddhology. The semiotic approach seems to eliminate many hitherto confusing contradicitons in the interpretation of Buddhist theory of dharmas as the methodological foundation of Buddhism, undoubtedly opens up a new and still unused opportunity for this.

III. Basic Concepts

Below I will confine myself to drawing attention to the three fundamental notions of the *Gaṇḍavyūhasūtra* – *bodhisattva*, *kalyāṇamitra*, and *dharmadhātu*. The substructures of the text based on these three concepts pervades practically the entire text, uniting other substructures, whereby a dynamic and integrative model of the way to Bodhisattvahood is given, beginning with the level at which one develops a wish or readiness to become a bodhisattva (NB! Not to confuse with the ordinary consciousness of common man that is not aware of buddhadharmas and does not contemplate 'awakening'; practically no mention is made of the so-called ordinary consciousness in *Gaṇḍavyūhasūtra*, at any rate it does not belong to the important subjects of the sūtra), and ending with the

---

Wood's study – Liu Ming-Wood. The *Lotus Sūtra* and *Garland Sūtra* according to the T'ien-T'ai and Hua-Yen Schools in Chinese Buddhism. – *T'oung Pao*. Vol. LXXIV, 1988, lk. 47-80 – *Avataṃsakasūtra* is also viewed narrowly within the context of the Chinese *Huayan*-school, especially the works of Fazang.

level of 'supreme perfect awakening' (*anuttarā samyaksambodhi*), that in this sūtra, too, seems to signify the utmost limit or, rather, boundlessness of broadening the possibilities of consciousness. The specific nature of the functioning of such boundless consciousness is often characterized in the sūtra by metaphoric means or expressions that exclude any defining at all, such as 'ocean' (*samudra*), 'cloud' (*megha*), 'space' (*gagana*), 'immeasurable' (*aprameya*), 'innumerable' (*asaṃkhyeya*), 'inconceivable' (*acintya*), 'inexpressible' (*anabhilāpya*), 'infinite' (*ananta*), etc.

The way to Bodhisattvahood is not described by stages in *Gaṇḍavyūhasūtra*, unlike in some other texts [15], but rather as a uniform whole, intertwined on different levels. The aim – the essence of Buddha and the vision pervading the entire realm of dharmas, has in fact been presented at the beginning of the text, before 'setting out'. The way itself has not been described as ascending step by step either, but rather as comparable to assembling a mosaic, into which each *kalyāṇamitra* places a piece in seemingly random order, until at the end of the text, in the powerful visions of the magic tower of Maitreya and Samantabhadra, the "picture" opens as a whole. This "picture" is the very description of the 'realm of dharmas' from the perspective of the level of the 'supreme perfect awakening', that can only be rendered by figurative-mythological means. As mentioned above, the text culminates with the great vow of Samantabhadra (*Samantabhadracaryāpraṇidhāna*), which paradoxically does not express "arrival", but a new setting out, because reaching the 'supreme perfect awakedness' marks the beginning of the real way of bodhisattva. The journey described in the sūtra, taken "by the hand" of benevolent friends, was a mere preparation for that.

The three concepts as basic elements of the substructure for describing the way to Bodhisattvahood in the present model can be defined as follows: *bodhisattva* ('awakening being') as subject or traveller; *kalyāṇamitra* ('benevolent friend') as agent or guide; *dharmadhātu* ('realm of dharmas') as both environment and objective at the same time. In this sense, it is conspicuous and significant that the Chinese version of *Gaṇḍavyūhasūtra* is entitled *Ru fajie pin*, "Entry into the Realm of Dharmas", that in itself stresses the aspect of the way to Bodhisattvahood as discovery of and "pervasion" to *dharmadhātu*.

The three concepts given should not be viewed as isolated in time and space, or even concept-wise. It should be kept in mind that as the process (the way to Bodhisattvahood) proceeds, the content of the concepts evolves and changes as well, which the description and readers of the description should constantly follow. Thus the term bodhisattva stands both for "the beginner", the one setting out, and "the one that has arrived" – the one that has achieved

---

[15] Of the Mahāyāna sūtras, *Daśabhūmika,* or "The Sutra of the Ten Levels of Bodhisattva", which in their own turn form part of *Avataṃsakasūtra,* and a number of very well-known later texts, for example, Śāntideva's *Bodhicaryāvatāra,* or "Setting Out on the Way to Awakening", and Tsongkhapa's *Lamrim,* or "The Steps to Learning" serve as examples of the treatment based on levels or stages.

'supreme perfect awakening' and has entirely entered the 'realm of dharmas'. Except that the "place" that the bodhisattva should reach does not exist, to be more exact, it is undefinable, since the 'realm of dharmas' as semiotic space cannot be defined as "place" in the sense of the perceptible physical world. As the genuine dwelling place of Bodhisattvas, it can be described only in specific "terms of awakening", the most significant of which is *buddhakṣetra,* or 'buddha-field'. Thus it has been said of the bodhisattvas that have "arrived" that they possess "independent sphere of action, pervading all buddha-fields" (*asaṅgagocarāḥ sarvabuddhakṣetraspharaṇatayā*). [16]

IV. *Bodhisattva*

The way to Bodhisattvahood cannot be viewed as movement from "point A to point B", not even as movement from "state A to state B", but rather as transpersonal eternal progress that continues in "worldly" terms (i.e these understood in the level of *lokadhātu*) throughout innumerable human lives, through countless eras and worlds, but which in terms of awakening means the momentary actualization of buddhadharmas in the timeless 'realm of dharmas', where the concepts of time and space peculiar to ordinary consciousness are not valid. As it has been put in "The Vow of Samantabhadra" (verses 32-34):

> May I enter all eons of the future instantly, and may I act in all eons of all times within an instant. May I see all buddhas of all times in one instant and always enter their sphere by magical power of liberation.
> May I produce the arrays of happy fields of all times in an atom, may I thus perceive all the arrays of buddha-fields in all the ten directions. [17]

The specific nature of the consciousness of bodhisattvas that "transcends" in "worldly" terms all concepts, including the concept of time and space, is best characterized by the following passage:

> The sphere of knowledge of bodhisattvas, noble son, is not in the realm of thought, conception, or imagination. It cannot be known in terms of length or brevity of saṃsāra, or in terms of defilement or purity of ages, or in terms of brevity or length of ages, or in terms of multitude or variety of ages, or in terms of variation or differentiation of ages. Why? Because the sphere of knowledge of bodhisattvas is utterly pure in its essential nature, it is outside the net of all conceptions, it is beyond the mountains of all obstructions. It appears in the mind and sheds light on beings who can be guided, according to their mentalities, when the time is ripe for their development.
> It is, noble son, like the sun: there is no reckoning of day and night

---

[16] GV, p. 3; Cleary, p. 12.

[17] GV, p. 432; Cleary, p. 391.

on the sun, but when the sun has gone down that is known as night, and when it has come up that is known as the day. In the same way, noble son, in the nonconceptual sphere of knowledge of bodhisattvas there are no thoughts or concepts of imaginations, or notions of saṃsāra or duration of time frames: but when the will of bodhisattvas arises, then by the light of the sphere of nonconceptual knowledge, and by mastery of timing in development of all sentient beings, conceptual calculations of ages, duration, and saṃsāra are distinguished; in the sphere of nonconceptual knowledge, conceptual calculations of passage of time in past and future ages are distinguished. [18]

Although the consciousness and thinking of the bodhisattvas transcend the notions and concepts of ordinary (saṃsāric) consciousness, it does not mean that the Bodhisattvas exist outside saṃsāra. By the 'supreme perfect awakening' that enables the Bodhisattva to embrace and comprehend the entire 'realm of dharmas', which also means the comprehension and understanding of the thoughts and motives of all beings as dharmas, a dimension opens up in the consciousness of the bodhisattva to an extreme degree, which is called 'compassion' (karuṇā), and which will predominate his consciousness:

At that point, each of those bodhisattvas, illuminated by the light of the concentration of Buddha, entered as many gates of great compassion as atoms in untold buddha-fields, and attained even greater capability to treat all beings beneficially. [19]

By means of 'unprejudiced knowledge' (avikalpajñāna) the bodhisattva grasps the degree of maturity of all beings, and by the power of compassion applies the dharmas characteristic of this particular timing, in order to direct each being towards buddhadharmas and the 'supreme perfect awakening' in the way best suited to this being. Thus the activities of bodhisattvas may involve any areas, for because of compassion they cannot "overlook a single being". Instead, they must find and apply the right dharma for every one of them.

The following example illustrates best the unlimited scope of the social standing and fields of action of the bodhisattvas in the name of the uniform goal – guiding beings towards maturity (paripākana):

Some [bodhisattvas] appeared in the form of mendicants, some in the form of priests, some in bodies adorned head to foot with particular emblematic signs, some in the form of scholars, scientists, doctors, some in the form of merchants, some in the form of ascetics, some in the form of entertainers, some in the form of pietists, some in the form of bearers of all kinds of arts and crafts – they were seen to have come, in their various forms, to all villages, cities, towns, communities, districts, and nations. With mastery of proper timing, proceeding according to the time, by modification of adapted forms and appearances,

---

[18] GV, p. 271; Cleary, p. 248.

[19] GV, p. 34; Cleary, p. 44.

modifications of tone, language, deportment, situation, carrying out the practices of bodhisattvas, which are like the cosmic network of all worlds, illumine the spheres of all practical arts, are lamps shedding light on the knowledge of all beings, are arrays of mystical displays of all realities, radiate the light of all truths, purify the establishment of vehicles of liberation of all places, and light up the spheres of all truths, they were seen to have come to all villages, towns, cities, districts, and nations for the purpose of leading sentient beings to maturity. [20]

Another extract supports the preceding one, stressing the fact that the knowledge of the bodhisattva is inseparable from his great compassion. Due to the former, he sees and understands the illusory nature of being as saṃsāra, due to the latter he himself continues to act in saṃsāra like everybody else, yet never becoming attached to it:

The bodhisattva is ultimately beyond all errors of mistaken conception, thoughts, and views, sees with accurate knowledge of all worlds as dreamlike, realizes all worlds as like magic, has attained knowledge of the realm devoid of beings, sees dharmas as they are, yet by control of great vows of the sphere of vast compassion appears to all sentient beings to guide them to maturity. [21]

The conventional beginning of the way to Bodhisattvahood, marked in the "story" of Gaṇḍavyūhasūtra by the meeting of the "protagonist" Sudhana, a merchant's son (Sudhana śreṣṭidāraka), with Mañjuśrī, the bodhisattva of wisdom, is no beginning in the sense of Buddhist lysiology or dharmadhātu dimensions. This has been preceded (through many lives) by the development, as a result of which certain conditions have been met, which enable him in this life as man to proceed from a certain critical point, to take the so-called qualitative leap to the higher level of bodhisattvas – and this not yet on his own, but with the support of the agents, or 'benevolent friends'. The interior monologue of Mañjuśrī presents a list of those conditions and prerequisites, ten in number (ten is the most frequent numeral criterion used in all kinds of lists in Gaṇḍavyūhasūtra and throughout Avataṃsakasūtra). Sudhana as the representative character of all those that have reached the critical point of the way to Bodhisattvahood has been characterized as a being who:

1. had served past buddhas (pūrvajinakṛtādhikāra);
2. planted roots of goodness (avaropitakuśalamūla);
3. imbued with great zeal of devotion (udārādhimuktika);
4. is intent on following benevolent friends (kalyāṇamitrānugatāśaya);
5. is impeccable in word, thought, and deed (anavadyakāyavānmanaskarmasamudācāra);
6. had engaged in purification of the path of bodhisattvas

---

[20] GV, p.35; Cleary, p. 45.

[21] GV, p. 272; Cleary, p. 248-249.

(*bodhisattvamārgapariśodhanaprayukta*);
7. is heading for omniscience (*sarvajñatābhimukha*);
8. had become a vessel of the buddhadharmas
 (*bhājanībhūto buddhadharmāṇām*);
9. had purified the course of mind (*āśayagamanapariśuddha*);
10. had perfected the independent awakening
 (*asaṅgabodhicittapariniṣpanna*). [22]

As the list demonstrates, on the way to Bodhisattvahood not just anyone can become even a "beginner". It takes only a (human) being that has undergone an immense spiritual development and in whom prerequisites have matured for recognizing 'benevolent friends', above all, and for receiving their teaching and instructions.

According to the simplified (common mythological) model of Buddhist lysiology (represented in Buddhist Jātaka literature, for example), this can be viewed as the maturing of personality in a linear sequence by subsequent births during an extremely long period of time. The lysiological model of Mahāyāna sūtras (including *Gaṇḍavyūhasūtra*) can be interpreted in the same manner. However, it seems that the authors of these texts have meant something different, which explains the paradoxes that occur in the descriptions compiled on the basis of the apparently same simplified model, as the remark about the way to Bodhisattvahood of a benevolent friend, monk Sudarśana once again demonstrates, who says that "in one life I have performed religious practice in the company of as many buddhas as grains of sand in thirty-eight Ganges Rivers." [23] Even for the world view of Indian mythology where extremely big numbers and comparisons are often used, there is a contradiction there, for one definite human life is regarded in this system mostly still in the order of magnitude approximate to human perception of time.

However, this contradiction can be solved quite rationally if we proceed from the prerequisite of the interpretation of *dharmadhātu* via the concept of 'semiosphere', embracing all the 'cultural sphere', which is in itself timeless or beyond time to an utmost degree. Therefore, if one speaks about studying at a myriad of buddhas during one lifetime, or about the past, present and future buddhas meeting within a single moment, or the ripening of the roots of virtue during many earlier lives, then in the light of cultural semiotics these statements can also be interpreted as the way cultural texts work in the individual consciousness, without resorting to the direct descriptive mythology. The cultural texts (dharmas) created in different eras do exist in culture potentially at any moment (compare with the image of museum hall by Y. Lotman, v. reference 10), and the man that has learned (also through culture) certain systems of signs (languages) is capable of recreating any texts in his consciousness and altering

---

[22] GV, p. 40-41; Cleary, p. 50.
[23] GV, p. 100; Cleary, p. 103.

his consciousness as a result of that. Finally, he is capable of enriching the cultural sphere with new (or revived) texts. In Buddhism, emphasis is naturally laid on Buddhist texts, or buddhadharmas, and the expression 'has become the vessel of buddhadharmas' denotes nothing else than a person that has been brought up and educated within the respective cultural tradition in order to be able to realize these texts in his consciousness and culture once again. Therein lies the "eternal nature" of the way to Bodhisattvahood, which from the point of view of cultural semiotics does not certainly mean the "wandering" of certain definite persons from life to life. Rather, it means the functioning of certain types of personality through culture in a way that retains the buddhadharmas in human culture, while continuously increasing their concentration. Certainly, these types of personality are educated or, according to the terms used in *Gaṇḍavyūhasūtra* – 'matured' (*paripākana*) in culture, in a certain cultural situation, where there are pertinent cultural texts and conditions for transmitting those.

V. *Kalyāṇamitra*

Sudhana, the representative character of all neophytes on the way to Bodhisattvahood in *Gaṇḍavyūhasūtra*, while meeting Mañjuśrī, the bodhisattva of wisdom, asks him a number of very practical questions about the activities that should be undertaken on the way to Bodhisattvahood or concerning this. The list of activities is as follows: learning (*śikṣaṇa*), accomplishing (*pratipad*), initiating (*prārambhaṇa*), practicing (*caraṇa*), fulfilling (*paripūraṇa*), purifying (*pariśodhana*), comprehending (*avataraṇa*), developing (*abhinirharaṇa*), following (*anusaraṇa*), keeping (*adhyālambhana*), expanding (*vistaraṇa*), fulfilling (*paripūrṇa*) the circle of bodhisattva Samantabhadra.[24]

As the questions demonstrate, setting out on the way to Bodhisattvahood means, first and foremost, action, both outer and inner activeness. Learning comes first on the bodhisattva list of activities; yet all activities are integrated into the specifically irreversible bodhisattva world view, attitude towards life and behaviour, symbolized by the image bodhisattva Samantabhadra – 'Universally Good' – according to which one is supposed to do good indiscriminately to all beings and to guide them towards the way to awakening, as it has been worded in the vow of bodhisattva Samantabhadra in the end of the sūtra.

Bodhisattva Mañjuśrī, approving of Sudhana's mentality, next gives him some very important advice, according to which one cannot follow the way to Bodhisattvahood alone. In order to progress on this way, one has to find guides and to follow their guidance completely. Such guides are called 'benevolent friends' (*kalyāṇamitra*). Mañjuśrī answers Sudhana's questions like this:

> Therefore, noble son, a bodhisattva is to attain certainty through true benevolent friends for the realization of omniscience. One should

---

[24] GV, p. 46; Cleary, p. 54.

indefatigably seek benevolent friends and be tireless in seeing benevolent friends. One should respectfully follow the appropriate instructions of benevolent friends and should carry out the techniques skillfully devised by benevolent friends, without interruption. [25]

Upon this, Mañjuśrī sends Sudhana on a journey to find benevolent friends, who could answer his questions and would guide him on his way to Bodhisattvahood towards 'supreme perfect awakening'. It is noteworthy that Mañjuśrī, as the bodhisattva of wisdom, could be expected to give the applicant all the knowledge and understanding at once, as the simplified mythological logic would allow us to think, yet he does not do it. Instead, he sends him on a long journey full of hardships.

This constitutes the most significant emphasis of *Gaṇḍavyūhasūtra*, laid on the conviction that knowledge and wisdom cannot be achieved just like that, as a revelation, but only through culture by means of social activity and communication. Benevolent friends are upholders of civilization that preserve and pass on the knowledge and skills retained in culture. From the standpoint of Mahāyāna they are also bodhisattvas. Being a benevolent friend is not a learned or given "profession" or mission. One becomes a benevolent friend through a definite individual relationship. The way to Bodhisattvahood, in turn, is not the way of one-sided knowledge, not even a one-sided religious way, but an all-embracing way. The bodhisattva gets a universal education and diverse skills thanks to the benevolent friends, for according to his vow he must be ready to help all beings in any situations. This is why he must possess a clear understanding of everything and have skills in all fields. No knowledge, no skill or field can be too "low" for a bodhisattva, if it can be used to help other beings.

This is why there are persons of very diverse "social background" and descent among the 52 benevolent friends whom Sudhana visits on his journey. Statistically, they can be divided as follows: 4 bodhisattvas, 6 monks, 1 nun, 2 brahmanas, 1 hermit, 1 scholar, 6 pious women, 3 merchants, 4 landlords, 2 artisans, 1 sailor, 2 kings, 1 viceroy, 11 gods and goddesses. There are only 11 "buddhists" among them, in the narrow sense of the word. It is conspicuous that there are 21 women all in all (including the goddesses). Every one of the benevolent friends gives Sudhana a kind of limited teaching, admitting at the same time that he/she is incapable of offering exhaustive instructions for achieving 'supreme perfect awakening', since he/she has never gained it himself/herself. After this he/she sends him to the next benevolent friend. The circle is fulfilled when Sudhana meets Mañjuśrī again.

The tales and teachings of benevolent friends vary both in content and scope. A detailed analysis of these would be an extensive subject of its own. As one of the important conclusions, it should be pointed out that by such diversity of benevolent friends, *Gaṇḍavyūhasūtra* obviously again wishes to emphasize the fact that the education and preparation of bodhisattvas should be as universal

---

[25] GV, p. 47; Cleary, p. 55.

and versatile as possible. The continuity of one certain teaching line limited in means and methods (as, for example, in later Buddhism, especially in Tibet) is not as important as the preservation and development of the universal cultural continuity. In order to comprehend the entire *dharmadhātu* as the potentially infinite semiosphere, the bodhisattva should acquire as many diverse texts (dharmas) as possible and, what is more important still, the skill to interpret and work with them properly. This is why the instructions of Mañjuśrī mention 'omniscient knowledge' (*sarvajñajñāna*), i.e. the Buddha knowledge, or the knowledge of the essence and workings of all dharmas, as the aim of the help provided by the benevolent friends.

The way to Bodhisattvahood with the support of benevolent friends is by no means an aimless and chaotic gleaning of knowledge. One does not meet benevolent friends by chance, the benevolent friends direct the applicant deliberately to each other, knowing what kind of knowledge he needs most at the given stage of study. And, as already mentioned, the bodhisattva must trust and follow the instructions of the benevolent friends. Comprehension and intellectual disposition play an essential and central role in this process, symbolized by the bodhisattva of wisdom Mañjuśrī, who is both the first and the last benevolent friend, constantly keeping an eye on the student, and being with him. This is why the last one in a row of benevolent friends, bodhisattva Maitreya, sending Sudhana back to Mañjuśrī, says of the latter:

> He will show you, noble son, the real benevolent friend. Why? The best of vows of decillions of bodhisattvas is Mañjuśri's; vast is the outcome of the practice of Mañjuśri; measureless is accomplishment of vows of Mañjuśri; ceaseless is Mañjuśri's achievement of the best of virtues of all bohisattvas; Mañjuśri is the mother of decillions of buddhas; Mañjuśri is the teacher of decillions of bodhisattvas; Mañjuśri is engaged in the perfection of all beings. /.../ Mañjuśri sees all dharmas according to their true significance. /.../ He, noble son, is the progenitor of benevolent friends, who makes you grow in the family of the tathagatas, causes you to establish roots of goodness, shows you the provisions for awakening, introduces you to true benevolent friends, immerses you in all virtues, establishes you in the network of universal vows, causes you to hear of the accomplishment of all vows, shows the secrets of all bodhisattvas, and has similarly practiced the wonder of all bodhisattvas together with you in past lives.
>
> Therefore when you, noble son, go to Mañjuśri, do not be fainthearted, do not become weary in receiving instruction in all virtues. Why? All the benevolent friends you have seen, all the ways of practice you have heard, all the modes of liberation you have entered, all the vows you have plunged into, should all be looked upon as the empowerment of Mañjuśri. [26]

---

[26] GV, p. 428; Cleary, p. 377-378.

The glorification of Mañjuśrī as "the mother of all buddhas" and "teacher of all bodhisattvas" means nothing else than emphasizing ever again knowledge and learning, wisdom and comprehension, in short, the universal intelligence in Buddhist, especially Mahāyāna teachings.

VI. *Dharmadhātu*

As stressed before, the way to Bodhisattvahood supported by benevolent friends means 'entry into the realm of dharmas' in *Gaṇḍavyūhasūtra*, or *dharmadhātu*, the comprehension of the site of dharmas and their true essence by developing one's consciousness. I defined the 'realm of dharmas' both as the goal and environment of the activities of bodhisattvas in the substructure based on the presented three concepts.

Dharmadhātu as one of the basic terms of Mahāyāna Buddhism is among the most complicated terms to interpret at all. At the same time, it is the clue to the comprehension of the world of Mahāyāna sūtras, to begin with. As stressed in the beginning of this article, I proceed from the semiotic interpretive model, according to which dharmas may be interpreted as 'texts' or 'units of culture' in the wider sense of the word, and *dharmadhātu* as the 'semiosphere'. Such an interpretation of reality in terms of signs is in its own turn opposed to the interpretation of reality in terms of ontological physical circumstances, denoted by the term *lokadhātu* – 'the realm of worlds' in Mahāyāna sūtras. The way to Bodhisattvahood in that case would mean the transition from the latter to the former, or the replacement of the ontological paradigm by the semiotic one, which in fact corresponds to the essence of buddha-consciousness. The former, however, is not annihilated but regarded rather as a limited special case of the latter. [27] Entering the realm of dharmas or accepting entirely the semiotic paradigm is accompanied in its own turn by the development of an exceptionally strong imperative ethical dimension in the consciousness of the bodhisattva, which does not allow him to quit the world connected with physical and biological being. Instead, it forces him to remain in it for an indefinite period of time in order to work for the benefit of all beings until everybody has achieved 'supreme perfect awakening'. This goal will probably never be achieved within

---

[27] The translators of the *Gaṇḍavyūhasūtra* have interpreted the term *dharmadhātu* as universe, supreme reality, paying no special attention to its more specific definitions or its very evident opposition to *lokadhātu* in the sūtras. Thomas Cleary (v. reference 3) mostly uses 'realm of reality' as an equivalent of the term *dharmadhātu*, and either 'thing' or 'principle' of the term *dharma*. Torakazu Doi gives 'Kosmos der Wahrheit' ('Cosmos of Truth') as an equivalent. However, they both fail to give a detailed account of what should be understood by 'truth' or 'reality' within the context of *dharmadhātu*. G. C. C. Chang is convinced that *dharmadhatu* is an ontological concept: "There are innumerable universes; earth is only one tiny spot in the vast expanse of Dharmadhātu (the infinite universe)..." (*op. cit.*, p. xiv).

the framework of the ontological and worldly paradigm, since suffering, death and destruction have been encoded into it. It is, however, possible within the semiotic paradigm, for the reality of the 'semiosphere' is timeless and indestructible. Even if one physical world perishes, it will evolve again as soon as any germ of consciousness emerges elsewhere.

We do not encounter any explicit definitions of *dharmadhātu* in *Gaṇḍavyūhasūtra*, yet there are implicit ones that seem to corroborate the interpretive model given above and which do not contradict the semiotic paradigm. Most of the definitions describe the relation of the bodhisattva consciousness with notions connected with *dharmadhātu* or *lokadhātu*. The bodhisattvas are characterized in the following manner:

> they coursed in the knowledge of the unobstructed space of the realm of dharmas (*asaṅgadharmadhātugaganajñānagocarāḥ*); [28]
> they had spacelike knowledge, pervading all the realm of dharmas with net of the beams of light
> (*gaganasamaprajñāḥ sarvadharmadhaturaśmijālaspharaṇatayā*); [29]
> they had attained unimpeded knowledge of all dharmas
> (*sarvadharmānāvaraṇajñānapratilabdhāḥ*);
> they had exposed the knowledge of the ocean of principles of all the realm of dharmas (*sarvadharmadhātunayasāgarajñānaprasāritāḥ*). [30]

The entire ontological sphere (*lokadhātu*), together with living beings, occupies a secondary place in the bodhisattva consciousness. It is derivative and worldly, something that he sees and understands through dharmas as illusory, or virtual (*nirmita*), where everything is reflected in everything, and which he is able to comprehend also in his physical existence all at once. A few characteristic definitions will be given to illustrate this point. According to *Gaṇḍavyūhasūtra*, the bodhisattvas are capable of the following:

> they were in the range of pervading all worlds with one body
> (*sarvalokadhātvekakāyaspharaṇaviṣayāḥ*);
> they were in the realm of seeing the reflections of all worlds and one world contained in each other in a single atom (*ekaparamāṇarajasi sarvalokadhātvekalokadhātupratibhāsasamavaraṇasamdarśanaviṣayāḥ*);
> they had entered the door of nondiscriminatory knowledge of all worlds
> (*sarvalokadhātvasaṃbhedajñānamukhapraviṣṭhāḥ*);
> they demonstrated the mutual interpenetration of all worlds
> (*sarvalokadhātvanyonyasamavasaraṇavikurvitaniryātāḥ*);

---

[28] GV, p. 12; Cleary, p. 21.
[29] GV, p. 3; Cleary, p. 12.
[30] GV, p. 12; Cleary, p. 21.

they knew the various forms of all worlds, subtle and gross, broad and narrow (*sarvalokadhātusūkṣmodāravipulasaṃkṣiptanānāsaṃsthāna-pratividdhāḥ*);
they perceived that al worlds are like emanations (*nirmitopamasarvalokadhātuprasārāvatīrṇāḥ*);
they had attained the knowledge that all realms of beings are like illusions (*māyopamasarvasattvadhātuparijñāpratilabdhāḥ*);
they knew that all existence, states of beings, and births are like dreams (*svapnopamasarvabhavagatyupapattijñānaniryātāḥ*); [31]
they were clear-sighted, knowing the realm of beings to be void of beings or souls (*vitimirār niḥsattvanirjīvasattvadhātuparijñayā*). [32]

I would like to conclude with another eloquent passage from Samantabhadra's vow (3rd stanza), which summarizes the holistic world view of *Gaṇḍavyūha-sūtra* from the point of view of the supreme awakening of buddha-consciousness, in which not only all the realms of worlds are interpenetrated (*samavasaraṇa*) with each other beyond time and space, but from the perspective of *dharmadhātu* also contain potential buddhadharmas and potentially manifest buddhas and bodhisattvas. Which is to say that for a bodhisattva that has entered *dharmadhātu* there is no difference between buddhadarmas and other dharmas. Instead, he is potentially capable of creating contexts in which all dharmas (texts, signs, means) can be applied as buddhadharmas that lead to the 'awakening' of consciousness or, to use *lokadhātu* terms, to the liberation of beings:

In a single atom, buddhas as many as atoms sit in the midst of bodhisattvas; so it is of all things in the realm of dharmas – I realize all are filled with buddhas. [33]

---

[31] Ibid.

[32] GV, p. 3; Cleary, p. 12.

[33] GV, p. 431; Cleary, p. 388.

An Attempt at
Christological Understanding of Humanity
Especially in the Eastern Orthodox and the Lutheran Traditions

Alar Laats, Tartu

During the last fifty years there have been attempts in theology to understand relations between theological doctrines and sociopolitical realities in history, or perhaps it would be better to say between theological doctrines and sociopolitical doctrines. Well-known is the attempt by defenders of the concept of the social Trinity to draw connection lines between the overemphasis of Christian monotheism at the expense of the doctrine of the Trinity and various earthly dominions, especially with an absolutist inclination. [1] Of course, according to contemporary political theologians this influence has not been one-sided. "Reciprocal influence and conditioning is much more frequent." [2] I am not quite convinced that the relations between theology and sociopolitical ideas and conceptions are so straightforward as some theologians with political inclinations think. But I believe that in the course of history some kind of reciprocal influence between these two realms of human thinking could have occurred, for better or for worse. And I believe that Christian theology can in principle influence our sociopolitical ideas for the good of the latter.

In this paper my aim is to point at some possible fruitful impacts of Christology on our ideas about the human being and through it on our understanding of society. Christology has been one of the central doctrines of Christianity but its influence on our understanding of a human being, society and the whole world has been somewhat neglected in comparison for instance with the doctrine of God.

---

[1] Thus Jürgen Moltmann asserts that "The notion of a divine monarchy in heaven and earth ... generally provides the justification for earthly dominion - religious, moral, patriarchal or political dominion - and makes it a hierarchy, a 'holy rule'". And later he continues "Religiously motivated political monotheism has always been used in order to legitimate domination, from the emperor cults of the ancient world, Byzantium and the absolute ideologies of the seventeenth century, down to the dictatorships of the twentieth." Moltmann 1989:191f.

[2] Moltmann 1989:193.

The loss of the concept of inherited guilt and the emergence of individualism

Our society is an individualistic one. Our era is an individualistic era. This is a commonplace knowledge. For us, social relationships and society are less primal and even less real than the individual person. The way of the Western society to our present situation has been long and complicated. There have been a number of decisive steps. We can locate the start of those developments in the era of the Enlightenment or in the era of the Renaissance or even in the Antiquity. Actually we can start with almost all epochs of Western history.

In this paper my aim is not to follow and discuss this development. Here I would like to indicate only to one step that seems to be rather a significant and characteristic sign of this development. One of the strongest attacks of the Enlightenment was made against the idea of original sin [3] In some way the Enlightenment continued the development started already by the Renaissance and interrupted by the Reformation. [4] This critical hostility toward the doctrine of original sin was caused by more than one reason. Tillich is certainly right when he asserts that this doctrine was "criticized because it conflicted with the belief in the progressive improvement of the human situation on earth. [5]

But there was another reason that is relevant to the subject of this paper. The concept of original sin is closely connected with the concept of guilt. At least it was so in the theology of the Middle Ages and of the era of the Baroque. Besides original sin there was also guilt that had passed from the first fallen human beings to all their descendants. As the predecessors were guilty of their fall so all the other human beings after them were also guilty of this primal fall. One of the conceptual devices to explain this was *imputatio*, imputation. [6] God attributes the guilt for the fall to all generations after the fall. This means that there is a certain community or even more, an identity of Adam and Eve with all their descendants. The human nature is in some way identical. And therefore it was fair that God imputed the guilt of some people to all the others.

For the enlightened eighteenth century the assertion of imputation of guilt of one person to another person was no longer acceptable. Even more, this assertion was not understandable. This was absurd. It was morally objectionable that God should impute the guilt of Adam to his descendants even before they had committed any evil act themselves. For the Enlightenment thinking there was an inviolate principle according to which people can be responsible only for acts done by themselves or with their consent. Nobody can be responsible for the acts of others, especially of the ancestors, upon whose conduct they could

---

[3] Tillich 1967:47.

[4] Cassirer 1979:138ff.

[5] Tillich 1967:47.

[6] Muller 1985:149.

have no possible influence.[7] In the eighteenth century Protestant theology largely accommodated itself to this demand of the Enlightenment and abandoned the idea of original sin and inherited guilt.[8] With this development the idea of the identity of all human beings with their first predecessors and therefore with each other has been also lost. An individual and his own deeds became the only reality of which the concepts of sin and guilt were concerned. In later theology the concept of the original sin returned but now it was separated from the idea of guilt. We inherit the distortions but not the guilt. "Increasingly theologians who defend the doctrine of original sin are desirous of dividing between inherited guilt and sin. We may inherit the nature and/or the situation in which sin is inevitable, but we do not become guilty until we act to alienate ourselves from God."[9] The loss of the concept of common guilt that was imputed by God was quite a characteristic step in the direction of modern individualism.

Has Christian theology lost its idea of the unity and identity of humanity in its compliance with the insistence of individualism in Enlightenment thinking? Was the concept of inherited guilt the substantial bulwark against the influx of the modern individualism? In the following parts of this paper my intention is to show that actually there is a powerful undercurrent in Christian theology, especially in Christology that has preserved and still preserves the idea of unity and identity of humanity. I shall present some significant examples from the history of Christian theology that point to it.

The Christological dogma of Chalcedon and the unity of human nature

The doctrine of the inherited guilt was not the only Christian doctrine that was grounded in the concept of identity of the human nature. This identity has been essential in the Christological tradition as well. The normative form and basis of this tradition has been fixed in the definition of Chalcedon that was approved in 451 in the council of Chalcedon. This definition marked the end of a long and complicated Christological development.[10] The faith of Chalcedon has become the basis of Byzantine, Roman-Catholic and Protestant Christology.[11] The definition asserts that Christ is one hypostasis in two natures. For our subject two expressions of the definition are important. In the first part the definition says that Jesus Christ is truly God and truly man, consubstantial with the Father (ὁμοούσιον τῷ πατρί) in Godhead, and consubstantial with us

---

[7] Pannenberg 1994:233.

[8] Pannenberg 1994:233f.

[9] Richardson, Bowden 1989:246.

[10] This definition presents a compromise of different Christological traditions.

[11] Studer 1993:213. On the other hand, this faith and the declaration of Chalcedon has remained to the present day a stumbling block for Monophysite and Nestorian churches.

(ὁμοούσιον ἡμῖν) in manhood.[12] In the second part it asserts that Christ is made known in two natures (ἐν δύο φύσεσιν).[13]

Now the definition of Chalcedon was not merely an end-station of a theological journey. According to Basil Studer "the faith of Chalcedon must in fact be regarded not only as the final point of a long development, but also as the starting point for fresh Christological discussions."[14] And he continues saying that "the council ... opened the way to the doctrine of the hypostatic union."[15] This development did not touch only Christology. It had its impact on theological anthropology as well. If we look at the above presented expressions in the definition then we can discern that it had introduced into the christological language the terminology of the doctrine of the Trinity, e. g., concepts of hypostasis and nature (οὐσία or φύσις). Through Christology these concepts became applicable for anthropology also. A human being was conceivable as consisting from an hypostasis and a nature. Together with the trinitarian conceptuality some ideas that were characteristic of the divinity were introduced to anthropology. The divine nature is in some way a whole in which the three hypostases participate equally. The human nature became to be understood in a similar way - the human nature is a unity, a whole in which all human persons participate.[16]

The history of the development of post-Chalcedonian Christology and together with it anthropology is a complicated and interesting story. There is no space in this paper to give even a precursory treatment. But I would like to offer a short description of the understanding of a human being of Maximus the Confessor as a relevant example of this development. His anthropology was quite characteristic of the later patristic or Byzantine theology. And his ideas on the human being have been rather influential on the theological anthropology of the Eastern Orthodox tradition.[17]

---

[12] DS 301.

[13] DS 302.

[14] Studer 1993:218.

[15] Ibid.

[16] Actually the idea of the human nature as a unity was known in an unconceptualised way in the earlier patristic theology. Already the doctrine of recapitulation of Irenaeus presupposes an idea of humanity as a unity. Kelly 1989:172f., 376f. The whole so-called physical or mystical theory of redemption demands an understanding of humanity as a generic whole. We can discern the role of this doctrine of redemption in Athanasius (Kelly 1989:377f) and in Cyril of Alexandria (Kelly 1989:397f.) In this paper I cannot discuss the influence of Platonic doctrine of real universals on this idea of the unity of the human nature. Cf. Kelly 1989:15f, 375. It is rather likely, that the definition of Chalcedon pushed the old patristic idea of the unity of the human nature in the direction of fuller conceptualisation.

[17] Cf. Meyendorff 1983:37ff., 71f., 138-143.

In the theology of Maximus person or hypostasis is in some measure contrasted to nature. Person is concerned with the way we are and nature demonstrates what we are. [18] According to Maximus the human will did not belong originally to the person or hypostasis but to the human nature. He distinguishes in a real human being between the natural will (θέλημα φυσικόν) and the deliberative will (θέλημα γνωμικὸν, γνώμη). [19] The natural will that is common to the whole nature follows freely the laws of human nature that are good and wise and lead him to the participation in the divinity. [20] The deliberative or gnomic will belongs to the person and it must permanently make choices between various options. According to Maximus various apparent goods attract human beings. They are confused, they need to deliberate and consider. [21] This sort of will appears only as a consequence of sin. [22] Because of sin the unity of human nature is destroyed. The unity of human nature is divided into fragments. [23] According to the interpretation of Thunberg "nature is not completely destroyed, for its *logos* remains, but the outward manifestation of its unity is destroyed." [24] These divisions, caused by sin, occur not only within the individual, the result of which is the emergence of the gnomic will, but these divisions occur also between persons. In itself the human nature is a unity and all human beings participate in the same nature and have the same natural will. [25] The community, unity and indivisibility of the human nature is according to Maximus the basis of social and moral life. Thus Thunberg says that "social life and virtues are seen by Maximus in the light of the nature (*physis*) of man, the nature that is common to all men, and the principle of which (the *logos* of nature) excludes any split or separation within the individual or between different human beings." [26] Thus for Maximus the ethical and sociopolitical dimension of human life is inseparable from the ontological unity and identity of the whole humanity. It has been a rather dominating idea in the

---

[18] Louth 1999:59.

[19] Meyendorff 1987:137.

[20] This will is "the power that longs for what is natural."

[21] Louth 1999:61.

[22] Meyendorff 1987:137. For Maximus, there are two natural wills in Christ, because there are two natures. But there are no "gnomic" will in Christ.

[23] Thunberg 1985:95.

[24] Thunberg 1985:95.

[25] Maximus says even more. For him the whole cosmos is connected with a human being. Human being is a cosmos in miniature, a microcosm. And conversely, the universe is for him a *makranthropos*. Thunberg 1985:73f.

[26] Thunberg 1985:93. And he continues: "The common nature of all men, ruled ontologically by its principle or idea (its *logos physeos*), is the very basis of interhuman morality in Maximus". Ibid.

Eastern Orthodox theology. [27]

The concept of the unity of humankind does not belong merely to a remote history of the Eastern Orthodox theology. In the last century this idea has emerged again and is influential in the neo-patristic school of Eastern Orthodox religious thinking. Thus according to a well-known and influential representative of this theological school, Vladimir Lossky, there is only one human nature common to all human beings. Although in the fallen state this common nature is divided. [28] But in the state of deification all human persons will share the same and whole human nature equally. Thus this eschatological state is in some way analogical to the being of the divine hypostases in the Trinity. [29] The theological anthropology of Lossky is grounded largely in the Christology of the definition of Chalcedon.

The concept of reciprocal responsibility in the Lutheran tradition

The question of the unity of humanity did not belong only to the Patristic and Eastern Orthodox Christology. An idea of some kind of human unity was and still is necessary in the Christology of the Lutheran tradition as well. To demonstrate this I shall treat briefly some topics in Luther's theology.

For Luther's Christology and the doctrine of justification the concept of vicarious suffering is essential. According to Luther human sin demands punishment. Sinner is under God's wrath. But Christ has taken the wrath of God and punishment on himself. He suffers the wrath of God and punishment of sin in our place and for our benefit. [30] The satisfaction in this suffering of the punishment occurs through substitution. [31] This substitution can happen only

---

[27] Here I must admit that Eastern Orthodox theology has understood the unity of human beings differently from Western theology. At the beginning of this paper I spoke about the idea of inherited guilt or common human guilt. In Eastern Orthodox theology there has been no concept of inherited guilt. In the words of John Meyendorff "Greek patristic tradition, in its conception of original sin, ignored the idea of transmittable guilt." Meyendorff 1987:142. But the theological-ontological basis of the Western concept of inherited guilt and the Eastern idea of the unity of humankind is the same - the common human nature. In the East, especially in Maximus sin is rooted with the gnomic or personal will and not in the natural human will that is in principle common to all human beings. Therefore also guilt is always persona.

[28] Lossky 1985:106f.

[29] Lossky 1985:188. Cf. a critical treatment of Lossky's theological anthropology in my study, Laats 1999:115-119.

[30] Althaus 1966:203.

[31] Thus Luther says in one of his sermons that "Christ, the Son of God stands in our place and has taken all our sins upon his shoulders. ... He is the eternal satisfaction for our sin and reconciles us with God, the Father." WA 10^{III},49; LW 51,92.

thanks to incarnation, i. e., because Christ is also a human being.[32] His human nature makes it possible. Thus for Luther in principle one human being can be substituted by another human being.[33] This means that there is certain identity of human beings, at least *coram Deo*. For Luther Christ's sufferings are completely human and real. And even more, the guilt and because of it God's curse are really on Christ.[34] One is bearing truly the guilt and curse of others.[35] God treats him as a sinner and he is really forsaken by God.

There is another concept in Luther that is closely related to the concept of vicarious suffering but that expresses even more clearly the unity of human nature. This is the concept of wonderful exchange.[36]

Here the connection between Christ, his humanity and the Christians is reciprocal. The concept of wonderful exchange was known in the patristic theology and in the theology of Middle Ages.[37] This concept asserts that Christ takes everything, which belongs to fallen human beings, their sin and the agony of their death under the wrath of God upon himself and gives everything, which belongs to him, his innocence, righteousness, and blessedness to human beings as their very own.[38] Luther has developed this idea in his book "The Freedom of a Christian". Here he presents this idea with the help of description of the relations between Christ and a Christian as between bridegroom and bride. They are united so, that all that belongs to one belongs to the other as well and vice versa.[39] In terms of the traditional Lutheran doctrine of justification it means the imputation or attribution of the righteousness of Christ to the Christians.[40] The concept of the wonderful exchange has usually been interpreted as not belonging to mysticism because the person of Christ and the person of a Christian

---

[32] Lienhard 1980:105.

[33] Although we know only one that kind of substitution, that of Jesus Christ, this does not invalidate the principle.

[34] Althaus 1966:205.

[35] Luther asserts that "whatever sins I, you, and all of us have committed or may commit in the future, they are as much Christ's own, as if he himself had committed them." WA 40¹,435; LW 26,278.

[36] *Admirable commercium*. Oberman translates it "joyous exchange." Oberman 1993:78, 184.

[37] Lohse 1995:242.

[38] Althaus 1966:213.

[39] "By the wedding ring of faith he [Christ] shares in the sins, death, and pains of hell which are his bride's. As a matter of fact, he makes them his own and acts as if they were his own and as if he himself had sinned; he suffered, died, and descended into hell that he might overcome them all. ... Thus the believing soul by means of the pledge of its faith is free in Christ, its bridegroom, free from all sins, secure against death and hell, and is endowed with the eternal righteousness, life, and salvation of Christ its bridegroom." WA 7,55; LW 31,352.

[40] Cf. Lienhard 1980:107.

do not become mixed or fused.[41] According to Luther this wonderful exchange takes place only through faith as it is "the wedding ring" through which Christ's marriage with the Christian occurs.[42] Although the exchange takes place not so much in ontological terms, it nevertheless means an exchange *coram Deo* and therefore it indicates a sort of real identity and unity of humanity for God.[43]

Luther does not limit the exchange with the one between Christ and a Christian. Speaking about the community of believers Luther frequently speaks of sharing all the goods we have between one another. But he does not confine it to the external and temporal possessions. He goes further and speaks about the sharing of internal good as well.[44] It is in a certain way an exchange inside the community. This means bearing weakness, sin and guilt of the brother. For Luther the genuinely Christian work is taking the sins of others "upon ourselves and work our way out with them - acting just as though they were our own."[45] And it is not only taking the burden of the other but it is also giving something to the other in exchange. This something one can give to one's brother, to the sinner, is one's righteousness.[46] For Luther, this righteousness is not actually our own, it is a gift to us. And we must give it to the one who does not have it.[47] Luther asserts that the great work of love is the one "in which a godly man uses his righteousness for the sinner and a virtuous woman uses her honor for the benefit of the worse adultress."[48] Every human being is actually created for the sake of the others.[49] For Luther's understanding of a human being the idea of substitutionary love[50] is essential according to which one is able to relinquish the salvation which God has given him and

---

[41] Lienhard 1980:104.

[42] Althaus 1966:213.

[43] Some other concepts in Luther's theology, e. g., the body of Christ or dying with Christ indicate the same sort of unity.

[44] Althaus 1966:308f.

[45] WA 10^{III},218.

[46] In addition to the use of the righteousness of others Luther speaks of the use of the faith of others, of the "alien faith". Cf Obermann 1993:242.

[47] "If there is anything in us it is not our own; it is a gift of God. But if it is a gift of God, then it is entirely a debt we owe to love, that is, to the law of Christ. If it is a debt owed to love, then I must serve others with it. ... Thus my wealth belongs to the poor, my righteousness to the sinners." WA 2,606; LW 27, 303.

[48] WA 10^{III},217.

[49] Althaus 1966:308.

[50] This concept can have substantial implications for ethics. I am afraid the Lutherans have not always lived up to it.

make his neighbour blessed in his own place.[51] Luther develops this idea further in his doctrines of the priesthood and the sacrament of the Holy Communion. Thus speaking about the priesthood of all believers he says that the duty of a priest is "to bear the sins of his brethren just as Christ has borne our sins."[52] In the Holy Communion, according to Luther "all the spiritual possessions of Christ and his saints are shared and become the common property of him who receives this sacrament. Again all sufferings and sins also become common property; and thus love engenders love in return and this mutual love unites."[53] In the sacrament of Holy Communion "we are made part of one another so that one helps the other just as Christ has helped us."[54]

Thus in Luther's theology not only Christ takes our place but human beings can also take the places of one another. There is the exchange between Christ and the Christians and between the Christians themselves. This substitution means transferring sin and guilt, righteousness and blessing from one to another. This does not necessarily demand an ontological unity of human nature. But it certainly means theological unity of human nature, i. e., the unity *coram Deo*. That one member of humankind can substitute in front of God another member means that they are in some way identical and thus one.

The above-mentioned Lutheran idea of substitution of one another does not belong to the remote history of this tradition. One of the representatives of the Lutheran tradition in the twentieth century who has vigorously asserted the unity of humankind was Dietrich Bonhoeffer. His understanding of the unity of humanity, but also his understanding of the humanity generally was christocentric. For Bonhoeffer the being of Christ is first of all being for others.[55] And this being for others is interpreted by him in a way that includes the whole humanity in Christ. Christ is a kind of collective person, or more exactly, Christ existing as the church is the collective person.[56] In this new humanity the disunity of humankind that resulted from sin is overcome. For Bonhoeffer through Christ the relations between human beings are restored.[57] But Bonhoeffer's theology is not confined to abstract assertions about the unity of humanity. One of the central concept for him to describe the relations between human

---

[51] Luther gives as an example Paul's attitude who condemning the Jews nevertheless says "I have desired that I might be damned and eternally rejected if only the people could be helped." WA 10^{III},219.

[52] WA 10^{III},107.

[53] WA 2,743; LW 35,51.

[54] Cf Althaus 1966:321.

[55] The experience of the transformation of the human life is for Bonhoeffer given in the fact "Jesus is there only for the others." Bonhoeffer 1986:381.

[56] Feil 1985:63.

[57] Feil 1985:85.

beings is deputyship. "All human life is in essence a life of deputyship." [58] The deputyship means acting in the place of other human beings or in other words, responsibility for others. And a human being is not responsible only for a particular group of person but he is, according to Bonhoeffer, responsible with respect to the whole humankind. [59] Thus in some way each human being is obliged to act in the place of all other human beings. This being in the place of others or deputyship refers again to the unity of humanity, at least in theological terms.

Conclusion

That the idea of the unity of humanity has almost disappeared from the secular sociopolitical thinking does not mean that it has happened in Christian thinking as well. The Christological dogma of Chalcedon and the doctrine of Christ's vicarious suffering are still confessed to be the truth by most people who consider themselves as Christians.

As we saw, there are significant differences between the Patristic or Eastern Orthodox and the Lutheran approach. The main emphasis in the Patristic and Eastern Orthodox treatment of the unity of humanity is on the unity and identity of human nature. One could call it an ontological approach. In the Lutheran tradition the emphasis has been more on the mutual responsibility of human beings. One could call it a practical approach. Of course, these labels do not convey either the full meanings of these two approaches or the complete indication of their differences. Both approaches to human unity are much more complicated. The Eastern Orthodox approach does not exclude a practical and moral aspect as we noticed in the case of Maximus the Confessor. And in the Lutheran tradition the concept of the human nature has been rather essential in the doctrine of the Lord's Supper. These labels intend to indicate only the differences in the emphases.

In front of the modern or post-modern individualism the two Christological approaches to a human being are united. For both of them human beings are in principle inseparable from one another. The unity of humankind is greater and more essential than its disunity and fragmentation. This is the theological understanding of human being that is still contained in Christian theology, at least latently. It has not been and cannot be the aim of theology to point to empirical or ontic structures of this unity. The aim of theology is rather to conceive a human being *coram Deo* and therefore *coram hominibus*. The unity of humanity should be one of the essential principles of genuinely Christian ethics.

The question is how much has Christian theology influenced Western

---

[58] Bonhoeffer 1985:195.
[59] Bonhoeffer 1985:195.

sociopolitical thinking in the course of history. There is much that Christian theology can contribute to contemporary human understanding of himself. If Christianity would take its own Christological heritage seriously, then it cannot go along with the individualism that has dominated the scene of European sociopolitical thinking during the last centuries.

References

Sources

Denzinger, Henricus and Schönmetzer, Adolfus (eds) (1967), Enchiridion Symbolorum (DS). Barcinone: Herder.
D. Martin Luthers Werke (1883-) (WA). Kritische Gesamtausgabe. Weimar.
Luther's Works (1955-1986) (LW) ed. J. Pelikan, H. C. Oswald, H. T. Lehmann. Philadelphia: Fortress and St. Louis: Concordia.

Books

Althaus, Paul (1966) The Theology of Martin Luther, Fortress Press, Philadelphia
Bonhoeffer, Dietrich (1985) Ethics, SCM Press, London
Bonhoeffer, Dietrich (1986) Letters and Papers from Prison, SCM Press, London
Cassirer, Ernst (1979) The Philosophy of the Enlightenment, Princeton University Press, Princeton
Feil, Ernst (1985) The Theology of Dietrich Bonhoeffer, Fortress Press, Philadelphia
Kelly, J. N. D. (1989) Early Christian Doctrines, A&C Black, London
Laats, Alar (1999) Doctrines of the Trinity in Eastern and Western Theologies, Peter Lang, Frankfurt am Main
Lienhard, Marc (1980) Martin Luthers christologisches Zeugnis, Vandenhoeck & Ruprecht, Göttingen
Lohse, Bernhard (1995) Luthers Theologie in ihrer historischen Entwicklung ind in ihrem systematischen Zusammenhang, Vandenhoeck&Ruprecht, Göttingen
Lossky, Vladimir (1985) In the Image and Likeness of God, St. Vladimir's Seminary Press, New York
Louth, Andrew (1999) Maximus the Confessor, Routledge, London
Meyendorff, John (1983) Byzantine Theology, Fordham University Press, New York
Meyendorff, John (1987) Christ in Eastern Christian Thought, St. Vladimir's Seminary Press, New York
Moltmann, Jürgen (1989) The Trinity and the Kingdom of God, SCM Press, London

Muller, Richard A. (1985) Dictionary of Latin and Greek Theological Terms, Paternoster Press, Carlisle
Oberman, Heiko A. (1993) Luther. Man between God and the Devil, Fontana Press, London
Pannenberg, Wolfhart (1994) Systematic Theology, vol. 2, T&T Clark, Edinburgh
Richardson, Alan, Bowden, John (eds) (1989) A New Dictionary of Christian Theology, SCM Press, London
Studer, Basil (1993) Trinity and Incarnation, T&T Clark, Edinburgh
Thunberg, Lars (1985) Man and the Cosmos, St. Vladimir's Seminary Press, New York
Tillich, Paul (1967) Perspectives on 19th and 20th Century Protestant Theology, SCM Press, London

The Psychological Consequences of Secularization

Tõnu Lehtsaar, Tartu

Abstract

Secularization can be interpreted and defined in a variety of ways. In this article, the general characteristics, causes and stages of secularization are presented. Three different levels of interpretation of secularization, namely the macro, meso and micro level, are discussed. Five possible consequences of the process of secularization, namely powerlessness, anomie, meaninglessness, isolation and self-estrangement, are presented. In the last part the pastoral response to the above-mentioned phenomena is discussed.

What is secularization?

There is no agreement among different scientist on what exactly secularization is, what causes it has and what effects it may have. Dobbelaere (1999) finds that the controversies surrounding the concept of secularization have to do with its distinct use in different disciplines and with different levels of analysis in different sciences. Secularization can be understood as the decline of religion, as the shrinking of the sphere of the sacred, or as a tendency of religion to become worldly. One way to get a general idea of secularization is to bring out the points of apparent agreement between different authors. In this case secularization can be described by six characteristics (Roberts, 1990 p. 304; Shiner, 1966; Stark, 1999).
1. Traditional symbols are no longer a unifying force for industrialized society. This means that different symbols, such as signs, rituals, holidays, buildings and places, are loosing their religious meaning and importance. What was originally understood, developed and used as carrying religious meaning is increasingly becoming just a matter of tradition or aestheticism. For example, Sunday is no longer a HOLY day celebrating faith in God but simply a day when one is not obliged to go to work. A cross on the necklace is no longer a sign of the wearer's religious commitment but of his or her aesthetic taste. A church wedding is no longer a holy act of starting a lifelong union blessed and sanctified by God but a nice custom to celebrate an important event in one's life. As a result, the symbols lose their integrati-

ve religious meaning for society as a whole and are increasingly associated with private aesthetic practices.
2. The modern empirical scientific worldview has supplanted the miraculous religious worldview. Truth and knowledge are gained through double-blind, crossover studies rather than visions or religious intuition. Mythology has given way to empiricism, both in the secular world and within religion itself. The acceptable criteria for truth at both societal and individual level are scientific and empirical rather than religious or visionary. Religious beliefs and institutions are likely to undergo a complete transformation into non-religious forms. One is expected to rely on the psychological concepts rather than personal visions or answers to prayers.
3. People look to science and technology for solutions to their problems. Religion is losing the role and function of solving personal problems. Psychotherapeutic methods are considered more reliable than religious practices. Scientific achievements and technological development are expected to give answers to or at least alleviate existential problems.
4. As a counterbalance, theologians have developed systematic theologies that are logical, coherent and rational. Even religious doctrines are depleted of religious experiences and becoming increasingly formal and rational. This enables one to be an excellent scholar in theology or religious studies without having personal relevance to the subject.
5. The decline of religion whereby the previously accepted beliefs, doctrines and institutions lose their prestige and significance will culminate in society without religion. Institutions like education, the justice system and health care will be independent of religion and in no need for any religious category or framework to render meaning to their work and mission. Greater conformity with "this world" will result in one's attention being turned away from the supernatural to the exigencies and problems of this life. Religious concerns and groups will become indistinguishable from social concerns and groups. The basis for making daily decisions will be utilitarian economical or political considerations rather than religious values, illuminations or doctrines. Religion will withdraw into its own isolated sphere and become a matter of private life, thus ceasing to influence any aspect of social life outside itself.
6. Secularization will cause the world to lose its sacred character. This means that the general worldview will become more and more "thisworldly". The categories for describing the creation, the existence and the end will be borrowed from natural sciences and daily life rather than from religion.

Summing up the characteristics of secularization, it could be said that, in simplified terms, secularization means a movement from sacred to secular society in the sense of abandoning any commitment to traditional values and practices.

The Causes of Secularization

To identify the reasons of secularization would be even more difficult than to define the phenomenon. Again, different reasons are stated by different authors. According to Berger (1967), the roots of secularization can be traced back to the Judeo-Christian way of thinking, in which only God is sacred while the world has been given to humanity to rule over. This way of perceiving the world and understanding life is a good soil for the polarization of the life experience. There are different domains in human life. On the one hand, there is God and the experiences, ideas and behavior directly related to God. On the other had, there is daily life, which is more or less independent of God and belongs to this world. The concentration of religious activities and symbols in one institutional sphere (church) automatically results in the perception of the rest of society as the World. Protestantism may be described in terms of an immense shrinkage in the scope of the sacred in reality, as compared with its Catholic adversary (Berger, 1973 p. 117).

Another possible reason for secularization is pluralism. In the long run, pluralism has promoted secularization rather than religion (Hamilton, 1995 p. 173). This means that from religious perspective the pluralistic worldview is a hidden path to secularization. The possibility of different understandings and experiences is stressed. Religious categories are viewed as appropriate among others. As a result, the religious domain will not establish its own position among others but will decline and become marginalized.

Secularization can be influenced by the organization of social life as well. Wilson (1982) has pointed out the decline of community in the modern urban settings and consequent change in the locus and nature of social control. In large populations the norms and values will be more confused and pluralistic. The role of (religiously grounded) social control will decline. The people feel more impersonal and anonymous in urban settings.

The development of scientific worldview has created an alternative to the religious understanding of life. This means that the possible reasons for secularization can be found at the religious, social and scientific level, and underscores the complexity of the phenomenon.

The stages of secularization

Secularization is viewed as a process in both scientific studies and church practice. The general understanding is that secularization is gradual. It is difficult to estimate the level of secularization from a short-term perspective. Comparing the levels of secularization at longer intervals provides a better picture of the developments. Fenn (1978, 1981) discusses the process of secularization in terms of the boundary between the sacred and the profane in society. It is the boundary which different groups, collectives and individuals seek to establish for their own various purposes.

Differentiation of religious roles and institutions beginning very early and of which the emergence of distinct priesthood is a part.
1. Demand for clarification of the boundary between religious and secular issues.
2. Development of generalized religious symbols which transcend the interests of the various components of society (civil religion).
3. Minority and idiosyncratic (religious) definitions of the situation emerge.
4. Separation of individual from corporate (religious) life.

This short description is one attempt among others to describe the process of secularization. To take some of such attempts as valid ones, it should be possible to predict the future secularization developments in a society. Stark (1999) analyzes the understandings of the process of secularization and finds that for nearly three centuries, social scientists and various western intellectuals have been predicting the end of religion. These predictions have some common characteristics. There is agreement that modernization is the engine that drags the gods into retirement. Secularization prophecies are not directed toward institutions; instead, their primary concern is individual piety. In addition, they stress the role of science in the decline of religion and the irreversibility of secularization.

The experience in modern society shows that religion will change its forms but not disappear despite technological, scientific and social developments. Therefore, the predictive power of the descriptions of the secularization process is relatively low.

Levels of understanding secularization

From the description of the characteristics, reasons and process of secularization, it became evident that secularization concerns different levels of society. The decline in the importance of religion can be studied from the perspective of an individual as well as the society as a whole. Dobbelaere (1999) distinguishes between the macro, meso and micro level in secularization.
- The macro level concerns the fact that modern societies are primarily distinguished along functional lines (economy, politics, science, family). Each of these areas claims autonomy and rejects religiously prescribed rules.
- The meso level concerns the religious market in a society. The keywords are religious competition, relativism and the emergence of new religious movements.
- The micro level concerns the level of the individual, whose religious life is characterized by individualization and alienation from church or lower involvement in church activities.

This article focuses on secularization at the micro level. More specifically, it analyzes people's secularization-related problems, which bring them to counselors.

The micro-level pastoral symptoms of secularization

There are particular psychological problems typical to certain periods and societies. For example, in Freud's time psychoanalytical studies primarily dealt with histrionic reactions. After World War II, the studies of posttraumatic stress came into focus. Consequently, certain human problems assume increased importance in the times of secularization. However, the question still remains whether these problems are the results, by-products or reasons of secularization. Even without answering the question, it is possible to underscore the role of religion in dealing with human problems, including those related to secularization. In this regard, five possible problems could be presented (Fenn, 1978; Roberts, 1990):

1. Powerlessness - a psychological state in which one feels deprived of power, control or influence over what is going on. In this sense a person can be treated as a victim of a certain age. One of the bases of victimization is the elimination of a person's economical, physical, social or spiritual power. Religion can reverse the process by providing a sense of spiritual power and identity.
2. Secularization also leads to changes in social norms. These changes are often confusing. As a result, people may experience anomie, which is defined as a feeling of frustration that results when the rules of the game are unclear. This brings about the breakdown of social structure, general lack of social values and the dissolution of cultural norms. The symptoms are confusion, disorganization and collective insecurity.
3. One of the most important functions of religion is giving meaning to life. Religion can serve as a way of interpreting life events, values, and social processes. If religion is excluded, meaninglessness can become a problem. It signals an existential vacuum, in which one is unable to attach any meaning to the events and relationships in his or her life.
4. Secularization has very practical consequences for human relationships. One of them is isolation – withdrawal from other people or rejection by them. One of the functions of religion is to provide fellowship and a sense of belonging. Staying out of the church is to deprive oneself of one of the guarantees of human relationships.
5. At the very private level, self-estrangement, that is, dissatisfaction with one's own deeds, insecurity and uncertainty about one's own personality can develop. In extreme cases, it can lead to what is called disintegration of identity, which requires therapeutic intervention.

The problems listed above are related to the main functions of religion: the giving of meaning to life, the integration of the self and the worldview and the facilitation of human relationships. The decline of religion has an impact on all of the above areas.

Discussion

The question remains whether all these problems are related to secularization. It could be an oversimplification to ascribe human problems to the decline of religion. If this is the case, religion can be considered as a miraculous panacea for all the complicated problems people have.

This article makes no pretensions to ultimate answers. It just endeavors to provide an overview of the complex process of secularization and its possible psychological consequences. Working with people in educational and counseling settings one often encounters problems that are successfully addressed in religious communities and by religious institutions. This raises the question, at least at the hypothetical level: Are powerlessness, anomie, meaninglessness, isolation and self-estrangement reasons and/or products of secularization?

References

Berger, P.L. (1967). *The Sacred Canopy*. Garden City: Doubleday.
Berger. P.L. (1973). The Social Reality of Religion. Harmondsworth: Penguin.
Dobbelaere, K. (1999). Towards an integrated perspective of the processes related to the descriptive concept of secularization. *Sociology of Religion 3*, 229-247
Fenn, R.K. (1978). *Toward a Theory of Secularization*. Storrs, Conn: Society for the Scientific Study of religion.
Fenn, R.K. (1981). *Liturgies and trials: The Secularization of Religious Language*. Oxford: Blackwell.
Roberts, K.A. (1990). *Religion in sociological perspective*. Belmont: Wadsworth.
Shiner, L. (1966). The concept of secularization in empirical research. *Journal for the Scientific Study of Religion 6*, 207-220.
Stark, R. (1999). Secularization, R.I.P. *Sociology of Religion 3*, 249-273.
Wilson, B. (1982). *Religion in Sociological Perspective*. Oxford: Oxford University Press.
Hamilton, M.B. (1995). *The Sociology of Religion. Theoretical and comparative perspectives*. London: Routledge.

This research was supported by Estonian Science Foundation Grant Number 5238.

The Concept of Humanistic Base Texts

Linnart Mäll, Tartu

The shifts in social life that occur with the passing of time, or history, can be described and explicated from various angles. First and foremost, the choice of the latter depends on which phenomena and tendencies the describer or explicator considers as decisive or, even, motive powers. Thus, for example, changes in production and exchange or, in other words, in economic life, have been regarded as such, or else the events within or between countries (for instance, in diplomacy or battlefields), which is to say, in politics.

Likewise, the alterations, renewals and decay of mythological, religious, philosophical, artistic and ideological ideas, or changes in the spiritual world, have also been held responsible, as have, indeed, many other things. The present author regards humanistic base texts as the greatest influencing factor in the history of the last couple of millennia.

Despite their major impact, the number of humanistic base texts is not really large. They were created, or they appeared or took shape (the use of several words above refers to the complex nature of the formation process of the texts) in various parts of the Old World in a definite period of time. This is characterized by the distinct formation of the new social dimension which had started to evolve much earlier, but was left unrecognized for a long time, denoted by different words in different places back then, but which can at present be termed, in the most general sense, as culture.

It must have become obvious at that period that mankind was more than just a part of the surrounding nature, and that the human being more than merely a member of the tribe or people or *polis* or state, and the transmitter of its traditions and mythological and religious beliefs. The burden of the personal existence must have struck one for the first time at approximately the same time, which found expression in the questions addressed to oneself and other people: "How to be?", "Why to be?", "What to do?", "How to improve or change myself or, how to become different or new?" All these questions presuppose an awareness of the sense of duty and responsibility, and I would like to add at this point that the so-called existential questions in the manner of "To be or not to be?" were probably not popular back then.

Although in the absolute time scale this period and, as a result, the formation of humanistic texts do not exactly coincide by regions, one could still maintain as a generalization that it took place between the 6th century BC and the 2nd century AD, while some of the texts have taken their final shape even later.

Currently I include among such texts from the Chinese tradition "Lunyu" (here and further on all Chinese names and terms will be given in the *pinyin* transcription), from the Indian tradition "Bhagavadgītā" and many Buddhist texts, belonging to the so called Āgama (represented mainly in "Sūtrapiṭaka" or "Suttapiṭaka"), from the Near East tradition the Gospels of Matthew, Mark and Luke. My interpretation of the texts is based on the originals, the majority of which, except for the gospels, I have also translated into Estonian. In this English-language report, however, let me use the generally accepted English translations. "Lunyu" by Chan and Legge, "Bhagavadgītā" by Edgerton, "Suttapiṭaka" - by various translators from The Pali Text Society. Quotations of Gospels are taken from "The New English Bible", edited by Oxford University Press and Cambridge University Press.

Naturally, the above-mentioned list is not closed. And naturally, I would not range the above-mentioned texts by their value, or even claim that the texts written later have been influenced by those written earlier. On the contrary, I think that the writing of each text was connected with the particular cultural context, prevalent in the particular region.

By this particular cultural context we also mean the definite religious background, the traces of which can be detected in the humanistic base texts to a greater or lesser degree. More than that, it is mainly due to this very context that these texts have engendered different religious and ethical-philosophical doctrines, in the course of the development of which over various periods, the humanistic ideas remained entirely unnoticed. We shall now take a closer look at the problems that emerged while studying these texts.

Texts can be studied in various ways and using different methods. This also applies to texts that are commonly called scriptures in some religious traditions and base texts in modern semiotics. When investigating these texts, the tradition itself, and particularly the commentarial and explanatory literature developed within it, are normally taken into account. Undoubtedly, such an approach has yielded brilliant results, and is largely to be credited for the excellent translations through which the scriptures and base texts have been made available to us and continue to have considerable influence on the development of mankind.

However, it is always possible to use other ways and different methods. At this stage I would only like to point out the following: if we eliminate from the texts everything that has to do with the definite cultural environment, the common element that remains is what I have denoted by the term 'humanistic base texts'.

We shall now attempt to sum up the meaning of this notion. The word 'base text' refers, logically enough, to the text that has been a basis for other texts; thus we have a text here that over the ages has functioned as a text generator. A genuine base text has the ability to give rise to an indefinite number of new texts in an indefinite period of time which do not have to be put down in writing but may, as indeed they mostly do, exist either in the form of oral speech or discussion or even as a speculative act (deliberation, reflection, contemplation, meditation).

A humanistic base text has a specific tendency, expressed by the word 'humanistic'. In English, the semantic range of this word has been conveyed by mainly two equivalents: 'humane' and 'human', in the sense of being 'characteristic of man'. The semantic range of these both, as is generally known, is rather vague. Thus, to be more specific, a 'humanistic base text' is a base text that on the one hand is characterized by elevating man as such (in other words, as a species and an individual) to the central and determining phenomenon of existence, on the other hand, by an emphasis on such 'humane' qualities as dignity, philanthropy, compassion, non-violence, responsibility, sense of duty, respect, etc. in human relations.

I will repeat: Although each humanistic base text has evolved within the context of a definite culture, reflecting the latter's influence both in its form and content to such an extent that at first glance it may seem difficult, if not entirely impossible, to find a common denominator for them, there are still enough similarities and common features that allow us to do so, relating to both the formation process and structure of the texts (**A**) and the doctrines they contain (**B**), as well as the direct and indirect impact they make (**C**). We shall now present the most essential ones:

A1. Humanistic base texts evolved in a relatively developed cultural environment, characterized by the existence of the art of writing and a generally accepted and, in some cases, the sole religious and mythological thought system, as well as by an aspiration to establish, in one form or the other, a social hierarchy. At the same time, we can detect a tendency to reinterpret the existing and to present new ideas and doctrines. This is equally true of all these religions within which the humanistic base texts evolved.

By the middle of the first millennium B.C., the urban culture that the invading Aryans had destroyed about a thousand years earlier, had been restored in India. There is enough evidence to presume that the new script had likewise emerged by that time. The dominant religion of India during that period was polytheism that had a rich mythological background and was based on the Aryan holy scriptures, the "Vedas". Yet the monotheistic Brahmanism, initiated by the "Upaniṣads", was rapidly spreading, accepting the caste-based social structure and the supremacy of Brahmans. It seems there was much discontent with such order of things and it was from among the caste of the military-rulers, or the kṣatriya, that several Teachers emerged who laid the ground for new traditions. "Suttapiṭaka", too, contains many references to the different contemporary teachers, many of whom have been commonly classified as *ājīvaka*.

The development of culture had been more consistent in China and no such strictly structured caste-system evolved there as in India. Yet the constant wars were undermining the very basis of culture, and the traditional religion, in which the ancestor-cult played a major part, was disintegrating. There, too, a great number of different Teachers emerged in the middle of the millennium, offering a way out of the predicament. "Lunyu" touches upon several of those.

Palestine was occupied by Rome at the time the Gospels were formed, but since the Judaic tradition was very strong, there was a constant movement for freedom. This served to consolidate the Judaic social order, the leading role in which belonged to the Pharisees. But there, too, the time was ripe for the emergence of new ideas, as the later prophets and sects like the Essenes prove.

A2. These texts have nominal authors, referred to by the same texts and the tradition based on them.

These nominal authors are not Masters themselves but their disciples, or the disciples of their disciples, or, instead, just other persons. It is obvious that the evangelists Mark, Matthew and Luke belonged to the teaching tradition, as did Ānanda who recited suttas in "Suttapiṭaka". The authorship of "Bhagavadgītā" has been ascribed to legendary Vyāsa, the author of the entire "Mahābhārata", but the narrator of the text itself is Sañjaya, though. It is likewise quite evident that Confucius himself did not write down "Lunyu", and that this text was formed on the basis of the notebooks of his disciples.

A3. These texts present a definite Teaching. This Teaching has been given through the mouth of a definite Master, who has a definite mission to preach it.

The texts describe, to a greater or lesser extent, the life story of the Master, but none of those presents the full biography of the Master, least of all "Bhagavadgītā", with Krishna as Master who is mainly called *Śrī Bhagavant*.

"Lunyu" touches upon the life of the Master more often, but mainly in the form of references to the regions he taught at different times. His dicta are mostly preceded by the phrase *Zi yue* that has been translated in a number of ways, for example, as "the Master said". Quite frequently, the name of *Kong Zi* is used, less often *Qiu* and *Kong Qiu*.

We do not find a thorough description of the Master's life in "Tipiṭaka", despite its length, although there are numerous references to separate incidents and the people he met. *Siddhārtha, Gautama, Śākyamuni* – all these names occur there, although *Bhagavant* is the most frequent one. The last days of his life have been described in "Mahāparinibbānasutta".

The Gospels are considerably more biographical in this respect, ranging from the times before the birth of Jesus to the Crucifixion, and even Resurrection. Yet we learn nothing of the boyhood and youth of Jesus there. He is called Jesus (*Iēsous*), Christ (*Christos*), also Lord (*Kyrios*) and Teacher or Master (*Didaskalos*). According to the Gospels, he preferred to call himself simply the Son of Man (*ho hyios tou anthrōpou*).

A4. Although the Teachers must have certainly been literate, due to their origin and education, they preached their Teachings by word of mouth, so that those became fixed in writing only later by their immediate disciples or the inheritors of the teaching tradition. Because the editing process of the texts continued also after that, they acquired their final finished (canonical) form later still.

Buddhist base texts were put down as late as the first century BC, "Bhagavadgītā" possibly even later, most likely in the 2nd-3rd century AD.

There is evidence that of the numerous manuscripts of "Lunyu", only a few copies survived the anti-Confucian massacre towards the end of the 3rd century BC, which served as the basis of the canonical text in the Han era.

The Gospels were probably put down in the beginning of the 2nd century AD, but the process of editing lasted until the beginning of the 4th century AD, when the Church canonized four gospels out of many.

A5. Despite all this, a certain authorial idiosyncrasy can be detected in all humanistic base texts, embracing both descriptions and the way the Teaching is presented. This and other characteristic features of the humanistic base texts have now and again given rise to opinions that the actual proponents of the Teaching are the nominal authors, or the latter are entirely unknown, and that the Master is altogether a fiction or a generalized literary figure.

Personally, I do not support the idea that the Masters of the humanistic base texts never really existed. But it is only natural that the descriptions of them in the base texts, as well as their teaching as presented there, are far from being complete. On the other hand, though, I do not consider it necessary in the present study to make efforts in order to find out what the 'real teaching' of the Masters was, because it was the texts themselves, and not the fantasies about the 'real' life and 'genuine original teaching' of the Masters, that have played an important part in history.

A6. The Master is depicted as an unusual person in some way, to whom extraordinary, supernatural and downright divine qualities are ascribed.

The miracles ascribed to Jesus take up a major part of the Gospels, yet it is Krishna that has been described as the most wondrous, as he reveals his Universal Form: "Of a thousand suns in the sky / If suddenly should burst forth / The light, it would be like / Unto the light of that exalted one..." ("Bhagavadgītā" XI, 12)

Buddha, too, sometimes displays his ability to perform miracles, as, for example, he defends himself against Devadatta's attacks. However, he does not make much of miracles, as a rule. All the same, he is described as an extraordinary man.

The same is true of Confucius, who deliberately avoided the supernatural. "Our Master cannot be attained to, just in the same way as the heavens cannot be gone up to by steps of stairs." ("Lunyu" XIX, 25)

A7. Yet also the human features and even weaknesses of the Masters have been emphasized in the humanistic base texts. They all feel sad at times when they are not understood and they often doubt the expediency of their mission. They do not consider themselves to be unique and superior to other people. Instead, they think and expect that the others should follow them and become like them. This is particularly true of their relations with their disciples, among whom there are always some that are convinced that they surpass the Teacher so much that it gives them even the right to betray.

This in particular concerns Judas, a disciple of Jesus, and Devadatta, a disciple of Buddha, the stories of betrayal of whose are generally known. Krishna mentions more than once ("Bhagavadgītā" VII, 15, 24-25) that he is not understood and his opinion of this could be regarded as quite human: the ones that do not understand him are malevolent, foolish and petty. Jesus has been overcome by doubts in several instances, particularly before his arrest in Gethsemane. But Jesus also participates in the festivities of simple people. The descriptions of Confucius's behaviour in the 10th chapter of "Lunyu" are especially interesting in this respect.

B1. The Teaching presented by any humanistic base text is formally, content-wise and also terminologically related to a certain cultural environment, within which it evolved. According to the Masters themselves, their doctrines are not entirely original, having been preached in one form or other earlier as well.

Confucius, for example, repeatedly hints that his teaching is based on what he terms as *gu* – The Ancient. For cxample, he says in "Lunyu" VII, 1: "I transmit but do not create. I believe and love the ancients."

Likewise, Jesus says that he has come to complete the work of prophets and not to create anything new: "Do not suppose that I have come to abolish the Law and the prophets; I did not come to abolish, but to complete." (Matthew 5, 17)

Buddha speaks on several occasions about the former Buddhas, and even Krishna maintains that he has taught ancient sages in earlier times ("Bhagavadgītā" IV, 1-3).

B2. Yet the novelty of the message of all humanistic texts was quite literally revolutionary, and not just because the Teachings that were proclaimed differed radically from the existing ones, but also partly due to the fact that the situation was right for their emergence.

As I mentioned earlier on, there were many other Teachers in these areas at the time the humanistic base texts emerged, and certain similarities can be detected between their doctrines. Besides everything else, this demonstrates that we need not explain the emergence of the humanistic base texts by foreign influences (for instance, by the view that Jesus had gone to study in India, or, that he received his teaching from his God-Father). Confucius speaks about Guan Zhong (Guan Zi) with great affection. Young Siddhārtha Gautama studied at several outstanding Teachers of his day.

B3. As pointed out earlier, the most significant aspect of these Teachings is their humanism - their humanity and humanness. The main objective of humanistic teachings is to show to man the sense of his existence and what his possibilities and duties are, not only in the physical world, but also in the social and cultural situation at the given moment at the given place; to make the man understand that he as a member of mankind and as a definite personality (but not as *ego*) is something unique in the world, which is why he can and even must, bearing full responsibility, act in a novel way.

B4. The uniqueness of man as a member of mankind is manifested in that gods and other supernatural creatures and phenomena are no longer unequivocally placed above man, but that they are considered equal to him in many ways and sometimes even lower. A god may acquire human shape, appear as a human being, and man may become a god.

Krishna of "Bhagavadgītā" is man, that is, he was born of man and reared as such. And yet he asserts that he is also a god, and not just a god, but the highest of all, the God of gods, the creator of all that exists, who, although in this world, is really outside it.

Buddha proclaimed that only man is capable of attaining the highest state of consciousness – *nirvāna*, and that gods are not able to reach it.

Jesus constantly maintains in the Gospels that he is the **Son of Man** (*ho hyios tou anthrōpou*), who performs deeds that equal the ones accomplished by God, e.g. in Mark 2, 6-12: "Now there were some lawyers sitting there and they thought to themselves, 'Why does the fellow talk like that? This is blasphemy! Who but God alone can forgive sins?' Jesus knew in his own mind that this was what they were thinking, and said to them: 'Why do you harbour thoughts like these? Is it easier to say to this paralysed man, "Your sins are forgiven", or to say, "Stand up, take your bed, and walk"? But to convince you that the Son of Man has the right on earth to forgive sins' – he turned to the paralysed man – 'I say to you, stand up, take your bed, and go home.' And he got up, took his stretcher at once, and went out in full view of them all."

Of Confucius it is said that he "never discussed strange phenomena, physical exploits, disorder, or spiritual beings." ("Lunyu" VII, 20)

B5. The uniqueness of man as a personality is manifested above all in the emphasis of the fact that it is him as a definite person that has been chosen to carry out the Teaching.

For instance, Confucius claimed: "It is a man that can make the Way great, and not the Way that can make man great." ("Lunyu" XV, 28)

According to the Gospels, Jesus was very good at making it clear to his disciples that it was them as definite human beings that were destined to become his disciples. As it is said in Matthew 4, 21-22: "He went on, and saw another pair of brothers, James son of Zebedee and his brother John; they were in the boat with their father Zebedee, overhauling their nets. He called them, and at once they left the boat and their father, and followed him."

Buddha's teachings very often regard definite people, to whom he talks, and the same is true of Krishna whose teachings are addressed to his concrete disciple Arjuna.

B6. This also means that man as an individual has an opportunity to improve himself, to change himself, to become new. Man is not destined to remain the same or to retain his former self. Instead, he has the freedom to choose between remaining the same and becoming new, as well as the freedom of choosing between the various possibilities and means or ways of becoming new.

For example, Jesus says: "Enter by the narrow gate. The gate is wide that leads to perdition, there is plenty of room on the road, and many go that way; but the gate that leads to life is small and the road is narrow, and those who find it are few." (Matthew 7, 13-14)

Describing the way while allowing man the freedom of choice is also characteristic of Confucius and Buddha.

The real ideal of Confucius, of course, is *shengren* (a sage), but he himself claims to lead the way only towards the ideal of *junzi* (this is rendered in different ways, e.g. 'a superior man', but in my opinion, 'a gentleman' would also be a very good translation).

Although Siddhārtha Gautama, or Śākyamuni, applied the term 'Buddha' to himself, in the base texts he teaches the way that leads to the level of Arhat. However, he applied this to himself as well. A lot is said about different ways and goals in the later Buddhist tradition but there are only a few references to such pluralism in "Suttapiṭaka".

B7. In all humanistic base texts, the emphasis has been laid on describing the path or the process of man's renewal. The explication of the path has been preceded by the analysis of the initial situation, that the man inevitably has to proceed from, as well as the more or less exact formulation of where the man will end up.

Already in his first sermon Buddha talks about suffering (*duḥkha, dukkha*), and the need to get rid of it. "Suttapitaka" contains an opposition '*samsāra nibbāna*' (*nirvāṇa*) as the initial and final levels of the way. It should be pointed out that just as in Buddhism in general, where there is a tendency to use as many different terms as possible to describe essential phenomena, these two levels, too, have been called in several ways. The way of Buddhist base texts is, of course, the 'Noble eightfold Way'.

In Confucius we could, with certain reservations, regard the level of 'inferior man' (mean man, small man) (*xiaoren*) as the initial level. Thus the way would be self-development by means of learning, following the customs, and the like. Confucius describes his own development as follows: "At fifteen my mind was set on learning. At thirty my character had been formed. At forty I had no more perplexities. At fifty I knew the Mandate of Heaven. At sixty I was at ease with whatever I heard. At seventy I could follow my heart's desire without transgressing moral principles." ("Lunyu" II, 4)

The teaching of Jesus as presented in the Gospels is likewise the way of common man to the Kingdom of God or Heaven, or, of "becoming his Father's son".

B8. Principally everybody can renew himself, and it does not depend on one's origin or status in the social hierarchy, but above all on how the Teaching or, to put it differently – a new cultural paradigm – has been adopted.

According to Matthew (9, 10-13), Jesus is condemned for not recognizing class distinctions, and Buddha's disciples, too, come from all ranks.

Accordingly, Confucius says: "In education there should be no class distinction." ("Lunyu" XV,38) Perhaps most eloquent of all is the statement of Krishna in "Bhagavadgītā": "For if they take refuge in Me, son of Pṛthā / Even those who may be of base origin / Women, men of the artisan caste, and serfs too, / Even they go to the highest goal." ("Lunyu" IX, 32)

B9. This means that man is culture-centered from the point of view of humanistic base texts: not only does he depend on the current state of culture and recreate the culture, but he also possesses an ability to create and bring to culture utterly new phenomena, and even a completely new cultural whole, something that the Teachers themselves have quite unequivocally accomplished.

Culture is naturally a concept that emerged in the European cultural area, and its meaning has been constantly changing. Most generally speaking, it could be defined as everything created by man, as contrasted to nature. There are terms in the humanistic base texts, the meaning of which partly overlaps with it. One of the most important terms in "Lunyu" is *wen,* that above all denotes written culture. Several European and American sinologists have translated it as 'culture', accordingly. I find it quite reasonable, although the entire scope of this meaning can be attained by adding the concepts that were essential to Confucius, such as rituals (*li*), music (*yue*), education (*jiao*), learning (*xue*), etc – one could even say, the entire positive conceptual whole of "Lunyu". There is no doubt that a synthesis of concepts like that was something extraordinarily new, although most of those terms had been used before. The fact that culture is contrasted to nature is proved by several quotations from "Lunyu" (e.g. XII:8).

The closest notion to culture in "Bhagavadgītā" and "Suttapiṭaka" is *dhamma* (*dharma*), that emphasizes its relation to the spiritual and social values of man, and which is also contrasted to nature (*prakṛti*). It is not right to translate *dharma* simply as 'teaching', because it also involves such aspects as values, norms, assessments, and, more importantly, the conscious and psychic phenomena affected by culture. Buddha contrasted *buddhadharma* (Buddhist culture) with the hitherto prevalent *dharma* (culture) and this contrasting sent out a definite message that an entirely new culture was about to emerge. As we know, due to the tensions that stemmed from this opposition during a long period of Indian history, an enormous amount of cultural riches was created that have enriched the world culture, and are still doing it today.

There was no notion like that in the Near East of the times of Jesus, but Jesus calls the new culture that he himself founded the Kingdom of God (*hē basileia tu theou*), or the kingdom of heaven (*hē basileia tōn ouranōn*), contrasting it with ordinary state or kingdom (*basileia*). The fact that this is nothing mystical is eloquently proved by relevant parables in the Gospels, e.g.: "'What is the kingdom of God like?' he continued. 'What shall I compare it with? It is like a mustard-seed which a man took and sowed in his garden; and it grew to be a tree and the birds came to roost among its branches.'" (Luke 13, 18-19).

B10. At the same time man has to understand that he himself is not the creator of culture, for the process of creation only takes place through him, that is, it is the culture that functions through him. The man must understand that the *ego* that thinks that it has its own thoughts and performs its own acts does not, in fact, exist, so that it has either to be done away with or at least subjected to something that in the given culture is regarded as greater or higher.

Buddha has a simple solution: the *anātman* (*anatta*) doctrine excludes the existence of any ego.

Confucius taught the doctrine of putting one's personal ambitions in the service of the continuity of culture (*wen*) and the ideal of great centralized state. As it is said in "Lunyu": "Confucius was completely free from four things: He had no arbitrariness of opinion, no dogmatism, no obstinacy, and no egotism."

Krishna repeatedly admonishes Arjuna to give up egotism (*ahaṃkāra*). Ego will disappear when a person identifies himself with Brahma or Krishna.

Jesus does the same: "If anyone wishes to be a follower of mine, he must leave self behind; he must take up his cross and come with me." (Matthew 16, 24)

B11. The reason for the emergence of *ego* is the self-protective endeavour of the individual, caused by the fact that man originates from nature, or, in other words, from the animal world. The humanistic base texts accept this fact to a greater or lesser extent, while implying at the same time that the focus of human existence should be located somewhere else, on a cultural level, which also means that the natural nature should be replaced by the cultural one.

In "Lunyu" *junzi* is described as the embodiment of the new cultural orientation, as an *ego*-less person whose aims are located on a cultural level in opposition with 'inferior man' (*xiaoren*), a person who is oriented to the fulfillment of egoistic and material objectives. For example Confucius said, "The superior man does not seek fulfillment of his appetite nor comfort in his lodging. He is diligent in his duties and careful in his speech. He associates with men of moral principles and thereby realizes himself. Such a person may be said to love learning." ("Lunyu" I, 14)

Jesus said: "Do not fear those who kill the body, but cannot kill the soul. Fear him rather who is able to destroy both soul and body in hell." (Matthew 10, 28)

Krishna considers nature (*prakṛti*) an essential part of man that should not be overcome by violent means. One can overcome it only by a peaceful attitude.

B12. It follows from the above that the relations based on physical descent (i.e. genetic information) should not be as important as the culturally determined relations (i.e. cultural information).

B13. This in turn allows us to say that the transmission of cultural information is more important than that of the genetic information. All humanistic base texts view the teacher-disciple relationship as more significant than the parent-child or kinship relations. Studying and passing on the teaching are considered more valuable than procreation and taking care of physical children.

This aspect is most radically presented by Jesus: "You must not think that I have come to bring peace to the earth; I have not come to bring peace, but a sword. I have come to set a man against his father, a daughter against her mother, a young wife against her mother-in-law; and a man will find his enemies under his own roof." "No man is worthy of me who cares more for father or mother than for me; no man is worthy of me who cares more for son or daughter." (Matthew 10, 34-37)

Jesus said of his relatives: ""Who is my mother? Who are my brothers?"; and pointing to the disciples, he said, "Here are my mother and my brothers. Whoever does the will of my heavenly Father is my brother, my sister, my mother."" (Matthew 12, 49-50)

We find equally radical statements in Buddhist base texts as well. For example, "Dhammapada" contains a stanza (294) that is extremely sharp: "Having slain mother, father, two warrior kings, and destroyed a country together with its treasurer, ungrieving goes the holy man." So far it has been regarded as just a figurative comparison, where mother means craving, father egoconceit, etc. But in my opinion it means that the main concepts of old culture must be replaced by concepts of new culture where the new man will live.

The teachings of "Bhagavadgītā" are foreshadowed by an incipient great war between close relatives. Krishna maintains that according to *dharma* it is allowed to kill relatives in a war.

Confucius, of course, is the most benign one. But even in "Lunyu" we come across instances of placing teacher-disciple relationships above the relations between relatives. Confucius's own son was not his favourite disciple: "Chen Kang asked Boyu *(i. e. the son of Confucius)*, saying, "Have you heard any lessons *from your father* different *from what we have all* heard?" Boyu replied, "No. He was standing alone once, when I passed below the hall with hasty steps, and said to me, "Have you learned the Odes?" On my replying "Not yet", he added, "If you do not learn the Odes, you will not be fit to converse with." I retired and studied the Odes. Another day, he was in the same way standing alone, when I passed by below the hall with hasty steps, and said to me, "Have you learned the rules of Propriety?" On my replying "Not yet", he added, "If you do not learn the rules of Propriety, your character cannot be established." I then retired, and learned the rules of Propriety. I have heard only these two things from him." Chen Kang retired, and, quite delighted, said, "I asked one thing, and I have got three things. I have heard about the Odes. I have heard about the rules of Propriety. I have also heard that the superior man maintains a distant reserve towards his son."" ("Lunyu" XVI, 13)

Elsewhere in "Lunyu" the notion of brother has been reduced to one of culture:

"Sima Niu, worrying, said, "All people have brothers but I have none."

Zixia said, "I have heard [from Confucius] this saying: 'Life and death are the decree of Heaven; wealth and honor depend on Heaven. If a superior man is reverential without fail, and is respectful in dealing with others and follows the rules of propriety, then all within the four seas are brothers.' What does the superior man have to worry about having no brothers?" ("Lunyu" XII, 5)

B14. At the same time, the humanistic base texts stress the need for the man to remain humane, meaning that he must treat if not everything that is alive, then at least human beings, with compassion and love.

It is conspicuous that Confucius relates the notion of humanity *(ren)* with love *(ai)*. "Fan Chi asked about humanity. Confucius said, "It is to love men."" ("Lunyu" XII, 22)

In Buddhist texts the terms *mettā (maitrī)* and *karuṇā* - compassion and loving-kindness – are basically used in the similar sense. Both Buddhism and "Bhagavadgītā" make use of the word *ahiṃsā,* that became very famous in the 20th century thanks to Mahatma Gandhi.

The notion of love has an important role in the Gospels as well, where it is rendered by a Greek equivalent *agapē.* It is clearly this very aspect that allows us to classify the texts under inspection in this presentation under the common denominator of 'humanistic base texts'.

B15. But – Compassion and love are notions that have many meanings and that can and may be interpreted rather deliberately. One needs sense to grasp their truly humane significance and to know and employ them as such. Reason, consciousness, comprehension, understanding (i.e. intellectuality) – these are among the most essential concepts in humanistic base texts, the development of intellectual capacities being one of the principal means, as well as objectives, in the process of human renewal (or attaining the higher state of consciousness or repentance).

It is quite obvious that Krishna and Buddha emphasized the significance of intellectual qualities. Such terms as *prajña, jñana, buddhi* in "Āgama" testify to this. The same terms occur in "Bhagavadgītā" as well.

The *zhi* that Confucius uses also denotes high intellectuality.

Things are more complicated with the Gospels, especially because several Christian sects are known for their disapproval of intellect. (Actually, similar features can be found in Vishnuism as well, "Bhagavadgītā" being one of its scriptures, and even in some Buddhist sects.) Jesus has been presented in the Gospels as a wise man, successfully conducting dialogues with the priests.

B16. To sum it all up – the process of becoming a new man or humanization actually means becoming a cultural man. The ideal, however, is not one-sided (specialized) culturalization but a total cultural immersion or absolute culturalization that from the point of view of humanistic base texts means that the natural animalistic or brutal human being has become a superman, saint, blessed, elevated, perfect, Buddha, Bodhisattva, Son of God, God etc. – the name depends on the specific character of the vocabulary of a definite cultural tradition.

C1. The dialogue between the base texts and background cultural environment began already at the first stage of their formation, at the time when the Teacher himself pronounced his Teachings either as sermons or instructions meant for one or another concrete person. Their impact was quite slight at first, becoming manifest mainly in the relatively limited circle of disciples. But their radical difference from the dominant or generally accepted ideology inevitably led to conflicts, which were often accompanied with severe repressions, the most radical of which was the crucifixion of Jesus. But other Teachers, too, to a greater or lesser extent, had to put up with the counteraction of either definite rulers or the representatives of the official ideology.

C2. As time passed, their impact gradually increased, reaching a truly explosive effect after the formation of canonical texts.

C3. Although one cannot detect the direct tendency in the humanistic base texts themselves, several religious, philosophical and other doctrines were formed on the basis of those, as well as certain institutions (churches, temples, monasteries, etc.) that often claimed the exclusive rights of interpreting these texts. In case such institutions managed to attain the dominating position in the society, the humanistic essence of the Teachings has been considerably reduced in the accepted interpretations at the expense of the dominant background system either in the period of the formation of the text or the emergence of the given interpretation.

C4. At the same time we should not underestimate the role of these institutions in spreading both the humanistic base texts, as well as the humanistic ideas, due to which their impact has reached global dimensions by today.

C5. By way of conclusion, let us maintain that even though in the course of history downright human-hating and ego-cult based teachings have been preached under the name of humanism – the latest of those is the implementation of the Leninist-Maoist communism that emerged from Marxism – the direct and indirect impact of humanistic base texts has still been of cardinal importance in the ever-growing influence of humanistic ideas on the development of human society.

Before I wind up, I would once again like to stress the fact that humanistic base texts should not be identified with the institutions in which the same texts serve the function of scriptures. History offers us many terrible examples of the attempts of those institutions to forcefully spread their ideology, and this applies not just to Christianity alone.

Nevertheless, it was due to the same institutions that the humanistic base texts could exert their truly humanizing effect in the course of history, and do this on a global scale. Let me give you but a few examples.

When towards the end of the 17th century "Lunyu" was translated into Latin, it had an almost revelatory effect on the representatives of the European Enlightenment throughout the whole century that followed. Voltaire, for instance, has provided excellent commentaries on the humanistic ideas of Confucius. It would not be an overstatement to assert that the positive impact of this is still there today.

The publication of "Bhagavadgītā" at the close of the 18th century was likewise a great event. The same is true of the Buddhist base texts. The ideas that they contained were first introduced and publicized by such great thinkers like Friedrich von Schlegel and Arthur Schopenhauer in Europe, and Walt Whitman and Henry David Thoreau in North America.

The great Russian writer and humanist Tolstoy disseminated the ideas of the humanistic base texts in Russia, referring both to Confucius, Buddha, "Bhagavadgītā", and the Sermon on the Mount of Jesus. It is interesting to note that the above-mentioned thinkers, especially Tolstoy, caused a definite reaction in the countries where these texts originated. Mahatma Gandhi serves as a good example in this respect.

My personal experience allows me to say that humanistic base texts affected the liberalization process of the communist system in the Soviet Union to a considerable extent, which led to the collapse of this empire. They must have contributed, as one of the factors, to the disintegration of the colonial system in the whole world. Not to mention the spread of non-violence and peaceful solutions on an ever-growing scale.

But the events that have taken place in the world during the last months indicate altogether different developments. This is why I'd like to conclude my lecture with the following: at this very moment we must do everything we can to disseminate the humane ideas of the humanistic base texts everywhere. It is our task to demonstrate that these ideas are universal, inherent to the entire human race, not just a part of it. Maybe this will contribute to the survival of mankind.

Main publications by Linnart Mäll

Books and translations

Bhagavadgītā. "Gītā" kui humanistlik baastekst. Tõlge ja kommentaarid [Bhagavadgītā. New translation into Estonian from Sanskrit with intoductory article "Gītā as The Humanistic Base Text" and commentaries]. – Raamatusari: *Linnart Mälli tõlked* [Series: Translations by Linnart Mäll. Vol. 1]. Tartu: Biblio, 2000, 128 lk. (Earlier translation: *Loomingu Raamatukogu*, 40/41, 1980)

Nulli ja lõpmatuse kohal [Above the Zero and Infinity, in Estonian]. Tartu: Ilmamaa, 1998, 392 pp.

Konfutsius. Vesteid ja vestlusi. Artikkel, tõlge ja kommentaarid [Confucius. Analects. . Translation into Estonian from classical Chinese, introduction and commentaries]. Tallinn: Eesti raamat, 1988, 336 pp

Šukasaptati. Artikkel, tõlge ja kommentaarid [Śukasaptati. Translation into Estonian from Sanskrit, introduction and commentaries]. - *Loomingu Raamatukogu*, 12/13,1983, 128 pp

Šāntideva. Bodhitšarjāvatāra. Artikkel, tõlge ja kommentaarid [Śāntideva. Bodhicaryāvatāra. Translation into Estonian from Sanskrit, introduction and commentaries]. - *Loomingu Raamatukogu*. 3/4, 1982, 88 pp

Lao-zi. Daodejing. Artikkel, tõlge ja kommentaarid [Lao-zi. Daodejing. Translation into Estonian from classical Chinese, introduction and commentaries]. - *Loomingu Raamatukogu*. 27, 1979, 64 pp

Dhammapada. Artikkel, tõlge ja kommentaarid [Dhammapada. Translation into Estonian from Pali, introduction and commentaries]. - *Loomingu Raamatukogu*. 24, 1977, 80 pp

Vetāla kakskümmend viis juttu. Artikkel, tõlge ja kommentaarid [Vetālapañcavimśatika. Translation into Estonian from Sanskrit, introduction and commentaries, together with Uku Masing]. Tallinn: Eesti Raamat, 1969

Papers

Semiotics as a Possibility for the Study of Religious Texts in the Conditions of the Communist Dictatorship. – The Academic Study of Religion During the Cold War. East and West. – *Toronto Studies in Religion*. Vol. 27. 2001, pp. 163-170

On the Concept of Humanistic Base Texts. – *Sign System Studies*. 2000, 28, pp. 290–298

The Role of Form and Content in Understanding and Interpreting Texts of Classical Oriental Thought. - *The Art of Interpretation of Classical Oriental Texts. The Second*

Nordic-Baltic Conference of Orientalists. Tartu, May 19-24, 1994. Abstracts of Papers. Tartu: Estonian Oriental Society, 1994, pp. 25-27

Kul'turnaya model' Tibeta [The Cultural Model of Tibet, in Russian] - *Atlas tibetskoj mediciny* [Atlas of Tibetan Medicine]. Moskva: Galart, 1994, pp. 5-14 (reprint 1998)

1, ∞ i 0 kak generatory tekstov i kak sostoyaniya soznaniya [1, ∞ and 0 as Generators of Texts and States of Consciousness, in Russian] - Trudy po znakovym sistemam [Works on Semiotics]. Vol. 23. - *Acta et commentationes Universitatis Tartuensis*. Issue No 855. Tartu, 1989, pp. 151-152.

Shunyata v semioticheskoi modeli dharmy [Śūnyatā in the Semiotical Model of Dharma, in Russian] - Trudy po znakovym sistemam [Works on Semiotics]. Vol. 22. - *Acta et commentationes Universitatis Tartuensis*. Issue No. 831. Tartu, 1988, pp.52-58

Dharma kak tekst i tekstoporozhdayushchii mehanizm [Dharma as Text and the Text-generating Mechanism, in Russian] - Trudy po znakovym sistemam [Works on Semiotics]. Vol. 21 - *Acta et commentationes Universitatis Tartuensis. Issue* No. 754. Tartu, 1987, pp. 22-25.

Ispol'zovanie teksta kak sredstva psihicheskogo vozdeistviya (po materialam "Ashtasahasriki Pradzhnyaparamity") [The Use of the Text as the Means of Psychological Influence, in Russian] - Trudy po znakovym sistemam [Works on Semiotics]. Vol. 20. - *Acta et commentationes Universitatis Tartuensis.* Issue No. 746. Tartu, 1987, pp. 30-38.

Tõlkekulg [The Way of the Translation, in Estonian] - Poeetilise teksti tüpoloogia, tõlke ja retseptsiooni probleeme [On the Problems of Typology, Translation and Reception of the Poetical Texts]. - *Acta et commentationes Universitatis Tartuensis.* Issue No. 709. Tartu, 1985, pp. 43-60.

Buddiiskaya mifologiya [The Buddhist Mythology. A Serie of Articles, in Russian] - *Mify narodov mira* [The Myths of the Peoples of the World]. I-II. Moskva: Izdatel'stvo "Sovetskaya Enciklopediya", 1982 (reprinted in 1992, 1994, 1997-98)

Dialog v "Bodhicharyavatare" [Dialogue in the "Bodhicaryāvatāra", in Russian] - Trudy po znakovym sistemam [Works on Semiotics]. Vol. 17. - Acta et commentationes Universitatis Tartuensis. Issue No. 641. Tartu, 1984, pp. 45-47

Svetlyi i temnyi put' [The Bright and Dark Ways, in Russian]. - Trudy po znakovym sistemam [Works on Semiotics]. Vol. XVI. - *Acta et commentationes Universitatis Tartuensis.* Issue No. 635. Tartu, 1983, pp. 106-114.

K ponimaniyu "Dao-De-Czina" [Towards the Understanding of "Daodejing", in Russian]. – Oriental Studies. Vol. 6. - *Acta et commentationes Universitatis Tartuensis.* Issue No. 558. Tartu, 1981, pp. 115-126.

Eshchyo raz o Yamantake [Once More on Yamāntaka, in Russian]. - Oriental Studies. Vol. 4. - *Acta et commentationes Universitatis Tartuensis.* Issue No. 455. Tartu, 1978, pp. 43-46.

Nekotorye problemy vozniknoveniya mahayany [Some Crucial Problems of the Foundation of the Mahāyanā, in Russian]. - *Central'naya Aziya v kushanskuyu epohu* [Central Asia in the Kushan Era]. Vol. 2. Moskva: Nauka, 1975, pp. 219-222.

Chetyre termina pradzhnyaparamitskoi psihologii [Four Terms of the Psychology of the *Prajñapāramitā*, in Russian]. Part 1. - Oriental Studies. Vol. 2. *Acta et commentationes Universitatis Tartuensis.* Issue No. 309. Tartu, 1973, pp. 202-213. Part 2. - Oriental Studies. Vol. 3. - *Acta et commentationes Universitatis Tartuensis.* Issue No. 392. Tartu, 1976, pp. 93-124.

K buddiiskoi personologii (bodhisattva v "Ashtasahasrike Pradzhnyaparamite") [On the Buddhist Personology (Bodhisattva in the "Ashtasāhasrikā Prajñāpāramitā", in Russian)]. - Trudy po znakovym sistemam [Works on Semiotics]. Vol. 5. - *Acta et commentationes Universitatis Tartuensis.* Issue No. 284. Tartu, 1971, pp.124-132.

Märkusi pradžnjāpāramitistliku metaloogika kohta [Some Remarks on the Metalogic of the Prajñāpāramitā, in Estonian]. – Oriental Studies. Vol. 1. - - *Acta et commentationes Universitatis Tartuensis*. Issue No. 201. Tartu, 1971, pp. 267-277.

Ob odnom vozmozhnom podhode k ponimaniyu Shunyavada [On the One Possible Way to the Understanding of the *Śūnyavāda*, in Russian] - *Terminologia Indica*. Vol 1. Tartu, 1967, pp. 13-24.

Nulevoi put' [The Zero Way, in Russian] - Trudy po znakovym sistemam [Works on Semiotics]. Vol. 2. - *Acta et commentationes Universitatis Tartuensis*. Issue No. 181. Tartu, 1965, pp. 189-191 (reprint in Buddhism of Russia, 34, 2001, pp. 80-81)

Young Adulthood
Search for a Dream and Need of Mentoring

Einike Pilli, Tartu

Young adulthood is often understood in society as the best period of life. While it is true in physical aspect, that is not the case in other aspects. Socially and emotionally these years are probably more stressful and more difficult than any other part of adulthood. If people look back over their entire adult life and identify the most important events, they list more events in early adulthood as significant as in any other period in their lives. [1] Young adults are often under big pressure because of many important decisions they have to make and new roles they have to learn.

Context

Comparing to previous centuries, world has become much more complicated. Fukuyama [2] describes how technological development and labor market influence relationships in society. Young adults in society are affected by many changes happening around them.

First, parents are not at the same positions of authority than in former times and young people **do not get clear values from home**. Bloom [3] is notifying that even relatively happy (American) families leave their children without vision of the world, without high models of action and profound sense of connection with others. He says, "Children are raised, not educated." [4]

In addition, universities do not always do their job. Allan Bloom writes in his book *The Closing of the American Mind*, that young people at the universities lack an understanding of the past and a vision of the future. Therefore they are living in the impoverished present. He describes: "and our universities, entrusted with their education, no longer provide the knowledge of the great

---

[1] Bee, H. Lifespan Development. Longman, 1998, p 389.

[2] Fukuyama, F. The Great Disruption: Human Nature and the Reconstruction of the Social Order. (In Estonian) Tallinn, 2001.

[3] Bloom, A. The Closing of the American Mind. New York, Simon & Schuster, 1987, p. 57.

[4] Bloom, p 57.

tradition of philosophy and literature that made students aware of the order of nature and of man's place within it. Higher education fails to arouse or to nurture the **self-knowledge** that has always been the basis for serious, humane learning." [5]

Secondly, "the decline of the family, intermediary between individual and society, providing quasi-natural attachments beyond individual" [6], is one reason to **growing individualism**. While "individualism is the corner stone of democracy, it may in its extreme forms affect democracy negatively." [7]

Furthermore, individualism may lead to loneliness, "where people do not have responsibilities to the other society members what would make them to the genuine societies". [8]

The third change is described in generation Y (14-19 years old Europeans). According to GfK research [9] **is one the most important values of contemporary youth freedom**. This freedom means for them tolerance of society and freedom to choose their own way. Tiina Hakman writes: "A lot of freedom and plenty of possibilities creates chaos in young people's heads." [10]

Fourthly, according to Fukuyama, there are two important **changes in people's values**. First, trust to big institutions (police, church, government) has declined gradually. Secondly, the personal moral understanding is getting less honest. As a result, it is complicated to do right decisions alone in this pluralistically thinking context.

These are only some characteristics in young adults' lives today. But it shows well enough the complicatedness of the world they are living in. Questions of this article are, **how do young people deal with this complicated context and how can adults assist them**.

Counter effect of two worlds

During the young adulthood people are in continuous interaction of the context of society and their inner world.

According to Jung, the first half of life, including young adulthood (approximately until 40), is the time of outward expansion. Young adults identify

---

[5] Bloom, p 339.

[6] Bloom, p 86.

[7] Fukuyama, p 69.

[8] Fukuyama, p 60.

[9] Hakman, T. "Description of Generation Y." Magazine *Luup* nr 8, 2001. (In Estonian)

[10] Hakman, ibid.

themselves in terms of the roles they occupy and "try to win as many of society's awards as possible". [11]

In the language of Jane Loevinger's theory, this is a **conformist** stance, characterized not only by external sources of authority but also by a tendency to think in "us-them", stereotyped ways about others and about one's own emotional life. [12]

In the late 30s or early 40s it gives way to what Loevinger calls **self-aware** level and Levinson calls detribalization.

However, the process of finding one's identity and defining one's meaning of life is already going on in young adulthood. During this period young people rely more on external influences than in later part of life. One reason to that is lack of experiences. Young people do not know yet where they are good in and what they can do well. Simultaneously, they have inner thoughts and inborn gifts affecting their choices.

In this article I would like to look on young adults from these two sides: inside thoughts and outside influences.

Inner life   ←------→   Outside world
(the Dream)   (two tasks: work and intimacy [13])

Levinson [14] helps to identify tasks of young adulthood distinguishing four plus one tasks in the young adult period what he describes as the novice phrase (from the early adult transition to the end of the age thirty transition, years 17-33) of adulthood.

These five tasks are (I have changed the order):
1. forming a "Dream" and giving it a place in the life structure
2. forming an occupation
3. forming love relationships
4. forming mutual friendships
5. forming mentor relationships

Firstly, **Forming and living out "the Dream".** Levinson writes: "Dream is the vague sense of self-in-adult-world. It has the quality of a vision, an imagined possibility that generates excitement and vitality. At the start it is poorly articulated and only tenuously connected to reality." [15] Dreams can be: to win a Nobel prize, become a pastor, businessman, the husband-father in a certain kind

---

[11] Crain, W R, Theories of Development. Prentice-Hall International, Inc. 1985, p 201.

[12] Bee, p 389.

[13] Bee, p 390. According to Bee, Freud has defined these two things as "the keys to successful" adult life.

[14] Levinson, DJ et al, The Seasons of Man's Life. New York, A A Knopf., 1978.

[15] Levinson et al, p 91.

of family, highly respected member of one's community etc.

Levinson continues saying that if young people are unable to accommodate their Dream into the initial adult life structure to at least some extent, then the Dream may fade and die, and with the person's sense of vitality and purpose. People can also experience a conflict between a life direction in which their Dream could find expression and real life situation, which is quite different. Levinson believes that those who build their initial adult life structure around their Dream have a better chance of attaining personal fulfillment.

Based to Levinson's understanding of the Dream, we can add some aspects.

Firstly, **Dream is tightly connected with person's identity.** It expresses the most important values and beliefs. In contemporary individualistic society **person's authenticity becomes a new moral ideal**. According to Taylor [16] people who are not authentic, loose the meaning of their life. Self-actualization becomes a key world.

However, forming a Dream is not only inner process.

Secondly, **people form their Dream in relations with external world**. As they do something, they get feedback, if it is done well or poorly. To get to know in what they are good in, they need possibilities to try different things. Taylor affirms it: "To understand one's originality, we need context of meaning." [17] Community where young adult is attending also affects Dream. Values and purposes of faith community often give direction to young person's Dream.

The second task according to Levinson is **forming an occupation.** He makes distinction between choosing an occupation and forming an occupation. Career choice isn't a once-and-for-all decision, especially first career choice. Sometimes young person can struggle for years to transform interests into occupation and the sequence of occupational formation is frequently not the steady, single-track progression. However, Levinson believes that it is important to make firm commitment to certain occupation for late 30s.

Choosing and forming an occupation is affected on person's Dream and possibilities available in concrete society. There is danger that career-decisions will become – individualistically and materialistically – oriented. Young adults do not always realise that real authenticity also means (a) taking into consideration other peoples' needs and (b) having broader background of values than just one's purposes and wishes. [18] Very often young adults do not have enough experience to realise this.

---

[16] Taylor, C. The Ethics of Authenticity. Hortus Litterarum, 2000. (In Estonian)

[17] Taylor, p. 48.

[18] Taylor, p 43.

The third task of young adulthood according to Levinson is **forming love relationship**. Just as the forming of occupation is an extended process, so is the forming a marriage and family.

Erikson defines intimacy as the main task in young adulthood. He defines identity as "the ability to fuse your identity with someone else's without fear that you're going to lose something yourself". [19] Prerequisite to that is that person has achieved identity. In contrary, intimacy supports identity, also.

Love relationship with women may take many forms and fulfill many functions. Levinson believes, that the ideal relationship is where woman is able to support man's Dream. Often the man's dream serves as a vehicle for defining woman's pursuits as well.

Society as described in the context-part of this article puts continuous relationships into big danger. Individualization, changed and pluralistic values, declining role of families, and learned models of family life are all aspects what may make young people confused about their relationship.

The fourth task is **forming mutual friendships.** Levinson found out that young adults had few intimate friends of the kind they recalled fondly from their childhood and youth. He wondered as to the reasons for its rarity and expressed concern as to the consequences of its absence from adult life.

According to GfK research, Y-generation is feeling their connectedness through main brands: Coca-cola, Sony and Nokia [20]. However, this fellowship is not deep enough.

I would like to add one important task to Levinson's list, **forming a value and belief system.**

William **Perry** (1981) [21] suggested that individual differences in student responses to teaching may be conceptualized in terms of student stages of cognitive and moral development. It involves three stages:
1. dualism
2. relativism
3. commitments in relativism

Students at the **lower** stages are characterized by a dualistic view of knowledge. Things are true or false, right or wrong. The teacher knows the truth; the student's job is to learn the truth. Students in the **middle** stages have learned that authorities differ. There seems to be no settled truth; everyone has to be right to his or her own opinions. This stage is succeeded by the recognition that some

---

[19] Evans, R I. Dialogue with Erik Erikson. New York, Dutton, 1969.

[20] Hakman, p 10.

[21] Perry, W G. Cognitive and ethical growth: the making of meaning. In: The modern American College. San Francisco, Jossey-Bass, 1981.

opinions and generalizations are better supported than others. The student's task is to learn the criteria needed for evaluating the validity of assertions in different subject matter fields. His **final** stage involves student commitment to values, beliefs, and goals with the recognition that despite the lack of complete certainty one must make decisions and act on one's values.

Perry sees the middle phase, **relativism**, as the most difficult for young people. Here they need support from others who have gone through this phase.

Looking at today's youth in Estonian society, we see that dualism is comparatively rare and most of youth are relativists. However, **dualism** is not so rare in the context of churches and in their teaching. This applies specially to inside directed communities and charismatic-fundamentalist churches. Coming from such a faith community for instance to theological school with many opinions and understandings can cause a deep crisis of faith.

Also, finding the belief system is not easy. J **Fowler** describes individuative-reflective faith (young adult stage): "The self, previously sustained in its identity and faith compositions by an interpersonal cycle of significant others, now claims an identity no longer defined by the composite of one's roles or meaning to others. To sustain that new identity it composes a meaning frame conscious of its own boundaries and inner connections and aware of itself as a "world view.""" [22]

Fowler describes the previous, synthetic-conventional faith: "While beliefs and values are deeply felt, they typically are tacitly held – the person "dwells" in them and in the meaning world they mediate." [23] Fowler describes transition from the stage three to stage four as a crisis-like, where person has to distance oneself from the secure conformist communities, their value and faith-system and **form independent faith**.

Therefore, one important task in young adulthood is **to form cognitively coherent value and belief system**. Parks writes: "To be human is to seek the meaning of the whole, to make sense of the most comprehensive dimensions we can conceive. We seek a meaningful understanding of the whole of self, world, and cosmos." [24]

Moreover, according to Parks, we do not become adults only with reflectivity of adolescents, but we need the capacity for **critical thought**: the capacity to recognize and to critique our most cherished assumption, theories, and prejudices, and to become self-consciously responsible for what we know and trust – even at the level of ultimate meanings and faith.

She continues: "Meaning and faith are composed **by means of imagination**. It is by means of the disciplined imagination that we search out fitting and right

---

[22] Fowler, Stages of Faith, Harper San Francisco, 1981, p 183.

[23] Fowler, p 173.

[24] Parks, S D, Social vision and moral courage: mentoring a new generation In: Cross Currents 40 (Fall 1990), p 354.

images by which to apprehend truth and compose the meanings we shall live by." [25] This role of imagination is similar to Levinson's concept of Dream. Still, Levinson's Dream differs from Parks' "meaning and faith" by narrower and more person-centered view.

Person depends in this imaging process on the images and dreams available. Therefore Parks asks: Are young adults being **offered** dreams that are worthy of the potential of the young adult soul? In this process of meaning making, Parks believes, young adults continue looking to authorities to lead. They need assistance as they move from uncritical trust to outside authority to a critically aware, inner authority. In other words, **we do not make meaning alone.** The big gap between secular and Christian values makes it even more important to support young adult search for his/her values.

All these five tasks described above are important to fulfill in young adulthood. Still, in the context of contemporary society it is not easy to fulfill these tasks adequately. Person's Dream needs support, making career choices and finding one's place in postmodern society is not easy, and creating lasting love relationship need models which are often lacking in young peoples' homes. Also, person's friendships and sense of community, independently reflected values and beliefs are in danger in current context of society. Young people need support. Therefore there is the sixth task: finding a mentor.

Need of mentoring

Mentors have different functions. Some support young people in their big decisions, help them on their first steps into their career, assist them in their early years of marriage. This is the kind of mentoring which Levinson writes about.

By Levinson, effective mentoring relationship is complex and developmentally important relationship in young adulthood. The mentor is generally 8-15 years, half generation, older. Still many people don't receive perfect mentoring. Levinson believes that women are in worse situation than man. Also, a good mentoring is a temporary phenomenon, where a mentor does something efficient.

The key features of a mentor are, first that he/she is a person of greater relevant experience and seniority, and secondly, that he/she is as a responsible and admired older sibling. Mentor's functions are: being a teacher, a host and guide, role model, and counselor and moral supporter in times of stress. The evidence makes it clear that intense concentration of major tasks in young adulthood carries some emotional price: loneliness and depression are higher in these years that any other. There a mentor can offer his/her help. A mentor is,

---

[25] Parks, p 354.

in best cases, also supporting young adult's Dream.

Still, the role of a mentor can be much profounder. Parks adds: A mentor is one who assists in the transition from conventions of assumed thought to the responsibilities of critical thought. That means that a mentor is helping a person in his/her deeper process of meaning-making and value-forming, from conformist thinking to independent world view.

Parks adds that one mentor is not enough – **nothing less than mentoring community is needed**. People do not usually have only one authority, but several. Even more, they need continuous support to live out their Dream and continue in their meaning-making process which one person cannot always offer. Therefore, religious communities can provide mentoring, so needed in this period of life.

Conclusions

A young adult is forming his/her Dream in the relation with external and internal world. This process is very multifaceted, including forming a job and intimate relationships, finding a Dream and creating a coherent world-view and value system with commitments in relativist background.

This process involves so much energy and effort that often the help from mentor(s) is needed. A mentor is a person who helps through young adult period toward more mature and experienced state of adulthood.

References

- Parks, S D. Social vision and moral courage: mentoring a new generation. In: Cross Currents 40 (Fall 1990), p 350-367
- Fowler, J W. Stages of Faith. Harper San Francisco, 1981
- Bee, H. Lifespan Development. Longman, 1998
- Fukuyama, F. The Great Disruption: Human Nature and the Reconstruction of the Social Order. Tallinn, 2001.
- Bloom A. The Closing of the American Mind. New York, Simon & Schuster, 1987
- Hakman, T. "Description of Generation Y." Magazine Luup (8, 2001)
- Crain, W R. Theories of Development. Prentice-Hall International, Inc., 1985
- Perry, W G. Cognitive and ethical growth: the making of meaning. In: The modern American College. San Francisco, Jossey-Bass, 1981
- Evans, R I. Dialogue with Erik Erikson. New York, Dutton, 1969
- Levinson, D J et al. The Seasons of Man's Life. New York, A A Knopf., 1978
- Taylor, C. The Ethics of Authenticity. Hortus Litterarum, 2000

Living with the Sermon of the Mount
An Uncomfortable Presence of Transcendence

Ain Riistan, Tartu

When we look at most of the New Testament interpretation of the 20th century we see that when it comes to the Sermon of the Mount it is most commonly interpreted and analysed as an outstanding example of the *teaching* of Jesus. Countless commentaries and expositions hail it as the apex of Christian ethics. The main question for the reader then is what to do with the message it presents. And the question, of course, is serious: is it really possible for us to take the demands like "Love your enemies!" and "Do not resist evil!" at face value? Recent developments in the world's political arena do seem to suggest otherwise: after September the 11th there are not too many of those who would consider it to be a realistic and even desirable option. When we focus more narrowly on the New Testament scholarship the picture does not change much. Exegetes have been busy with drawing out different levels in Jesus-tradition, attributing these to different groups in the proposed history of the Early Christianity; others have been more recently arguing that in spite of all possibilities and temptations to cut the Sermon of the Mount into the pieces and interpret it through them the whole passage must be seen and understood as one single piece only because of its literary composition and other factors; and scholars have been, of course, interested in drawing out all kinds of parallels between the message of Jesus and what we know from the literature and literary culture of his day. Much of the New Testament scholarship is based on literary studies.

So we can, for example, follow an interesting and illuminating article in Catholic Biblical Quarterly by Richard J. Dillon [1] from Bronx University, New York, and see how the passage on "Ravens and Lilies" (Matt 6: 25-33) is dependent on the common rhetoric of Jesus' day (known as *qal wahomer*). It starts with an admonition: "Do not be anxious for your life as to what you will eat, nor for your body as to what you will put on." (6. 25a). Then there are two arguments. The first one (verses 25b-26) is argument *a maiori ad minus* (from greater to lesser), which has two parts, and the last one is as follows: "Observe the ravens: they neither sow, nor reap, nor gather into barns, and yet God feeds them: Are you not of *greater* importance than the birds?" (v. 26). Then the second argument (verses 27-30) is of opposite direction, *a minori ad maius* (from lesser to greater). It has again two parts and the last one is as follows:

---

[1] Dillon, Richard J. *Ravens, lilies, and the kingdom of God (Matthew 6:25-33/Luke 12:22-31)* - Catholic Biblical Quarterly 53 (1991), pp. 605-627.

"Learn how the lilies *grow*: they neither toil nor spin; yet I tell you, not even Solomon in all his glory was arrayed like one of these. But if God so clothes the grass in the field, which is there today and tomorrow get thrown into the furnace, will he not do it *much more so* for you, people of little faith?" (v. 28b-30). And then there is the conclusion: "So you must not get anxious, saying: what shall we eat, or what shall we drink, or what shall we put on? For the pagan peoples strive after all these things; and indeed, your Father knows that you need them. But seek first his kingdom, and these things will be granted to you as well." (Verses 31-33).

So far so good. It is certainly enlightening to see that the teaching of Jesus follows the patterns of common Jewish and Hellenistic rhetoric. But what do we make of it? What did the listeners of this Sermon make of it? Dillon's work gives an answer to that question too. I am not going into details here, but in his analysis this passage does not stand alone – when put into the whole context of Jesus' teaching it has to do both with ethics and eschatology. He writes:

> "This passage vibrates with apocalyptic eschatology in arguing the alternative of two mutually exclusive worlds: the one which anxious humans are striving to manage, and the one being shaped even now according to God's ultimate plan of salvation. Jesus' vision of God's kingdom is what alone makes sense of the paradoxes... aimed at shokking the old world's citizens out of their instinctive adherence to its illusions of self-mastery and self-sufficiency." [2]

Dillon's article is thorough and interesting, but it bears strong marks of existentialist thinking. For example this passage about "ravens and lilies" is defined by him to be about "anxiety" and he describes the plight of humans as a set of illusions about their self-sufficiency – he could as well have said that what Jesus did here was to call humans to "authentic existence". There is nothing wrong with existentialism in itself too, but I am not quite certain that the long and honoured bultmannian tradition of existentialist interpretation really does justice to the New Testament in its historical world.

And then there is another and more serious question: this whole way of thinking (and Dillon is just an example here) presupposes that what we have here in the sermon of the Mount is a theological-ethical teaching of Jesus that has some sort of timeless substance. And it is this timeless teaching that had to help Christians of the first century and has to help us in the 21st century also. To put it bluntly: when you are in trouble – became a theologian, do a careful exegesis, apply it to your life, and you are helped!

It just does not work this way. The 20th century had and the 21st century has an unparalleled abundance of theologians – do we live really well today? Or do we theologians live better because of our trade?

Now, the last three decades in the New Testament scholarship have witnessed quite a remarkable shift here. I am speaking of the rise of the discipline of

---

[2] Ibid., p. 626.

the sociological interpretation and analysis of the Scriptures. And the most important difference it has made concerns the understanding of the nature of Biblical texts in general. No longer are they seen as purely and primarily texts about theology and ideas, in first order they are understood as the texts of communication which are rooted thoroughly in the daily life of the most mundane concerns of the Biblical people. The main thrust of this understanding is to say that we cannot and we must not extract theology from daily life as if it could have its independent life of its own. Absolutely everything in the Bible is historical; absolutely everything is culturally conditioned. And – to come back to our previous example – from here it follows that the whole enterprise of existentialist interpretation of the Bible is partly misguided. It is just not possible to extract one certain set of ideas – be they existentialist or orthodox by nature for that matter – from the Bible for our modern usage without significantly changing and therefore distorting them. New Testament scholar Tom Wright says the following in the conclusion of his book about Jesus:

> "... they [i.e. the first Christians] would be people with task, not just an idea. ...That is why a 'history of ideas' will never get to the bottom either of Jesus or of the early church. The model ... [which does justice to the New Testament has to focus] ... not on questions and answers merely, important though they are as part of the whole, but on actions, words-as actions: on praxis and symbol, and the stories which are not 'illustrations' of abstract ideas but are themselves powerful actions, subversive and sustaining. Within that model, 'beliefs' are closely bound up with 'aims'; the aim is not simply to believe as many true things as possible, but to act in obedience, implementing the achievement of Jesus while spurred and sustained by true belief. ... If, then, 'New Testament Theology' were to be true to itself, it would need to understand itself within the broader category of 'New Testament Agendas'". [3]

So when we come to the Sermon of the Mount from this perspective, we must speak of 'Agenda' or 'Agendas' of Jesus and the first Christians. What would it or they be like? Here we have by now several interesting reconstructions made by different scholars. Some of them can be seen as complementary to each other and representing a sort of consensus in some basic matters, but not all. Again, these reconstrucions depend on the methods employed and the presuppositions contained therein. Broadly speaking, we can describe at least three different consensuses or three different "schools".

Into the first belong scholars of so the called Context Group. These are scholars who employ social-scientific methods of interpretation in Biblical

---

[3] Wright, Nicholas Thomas. *Jesus and the Victory of God.* Minneapolis: Fortress Press 1996, p. 660.

studies.[4] This approach uses the models developed in modern anthropology and sociology and applies them carefully to the biblical environment. While some of the first works in this field can be accused of too loose generalisations, the work of the 'Context Group' has been very self-conscious about the limits of the methods employed. Thus, what they usually do is that they take one specific issue or model and apply it to the New Testament. The result is a description of general social values into which a specific biblical message or situation is embedded.

K. C. Hanson has written an article on Matthew's makarisms and reproaches.[5] To illustrate his work I give a short description of his results. First, he argues that makarisms (or 'beatitudes') of the Sermon of the Mount (Matthew 5: 3-10) and reproaches (or 'woes') in Matthew 23:13-36 are to be seen together as they are in Luke 6:20-26 (Sermon of the Field). Then he shows that their cultural and theological functions have been largely misconstructed by previous scholarship and that they do belong organically into the value system of the Mediterranean world, particularly the system of honour and shame and the agonistic nature of that culture. In this context makarisms are to be translated not as "blessed are those, who..." but as "how honourable". Reproaches or woes are not to be translated as condemnations but as "how shameful" or "shame on". They form an honour-shame inclusio around Jesus' public teaching in the matrix of challenge-response transactions. Basically it means that in makarisms certain patterns of behaviour are declared to be honourful and in reproaches others are shameful. Now, honourful patterns belong to Jesus' followers. They may be at odds with society at large, but they are praised within the community. Thus, it means that the matthaean community has turned certain behavioural patterns that could be interpreted by outsiders as shameful (like being meek, which can be a sign of weakness) into honourable ones. Then Jesus himself exemplifies these patterns throughout the Gospel in the face of growing opposition, and in the end (Matthew 23), the opposing patterns (those of the Pharisees) are shown as "what they are" – a shame. One significant result of this is that we cannot speak here of these values as eschatological-theological values that were only proclaimed by Jesus to create a tension that could be resolved only in eschaton. No, these values are thoroughly "this-worldly"; to embrace them is to get an immediate result of being honoured by your own community.

The second "school" or group consists of scholars who belong to the Jesus Seminar.[6] Their agenda, as well as their methods and the presuppositions contained therein are different. Jesus-Seminar fellows follow quite often methods used by social scientists on the one hand, but they combine them with

---

[4] For more information, see their Web page at http://www.serv.net/~oakmande/index.html.

[5] Hanson, K C. *How Honorable! How Shameful! A Cultural Analysis of Matthew's Makarisms and Reproaches* - Semeia 68 (1994), pp. 81-111.

[6] For more information, see their Web page at http://religion.rutgers.edu/jseminar/.

more traditional literary-critical and historical-critical studies on the other. Basically, these are the methods used by most of the traditional New Testament scholars (especially form-criticism). What differentiates them from others is actually their common project called the Jesus Seminar. Although this is a quite diverse group, many fellows share some distinct understandings about how to describe the personality of historical Jesus and the following Early Christian developments. From the viewpoint of our topic the following things should be mentioned. (a) The maintenance of a radical distinction between Jesus and 'Christ'. 'Christ' is a term of interpretation. There are many 'Christs' in the New Testament period. They differ widely from each other and they have little to do with Jesus. Jesus is best described as mere man and – more to the point – not so much in terms of Jewish religion and piety but in terms of comparative religion and anthropological role models. (b) In the field of history of theological ideas some believe that the notions of apocalypticism and eschatological expectations did not belong to Jesus, but were later developments. (c) Consequently, when we come to the New Testament, we have to be aware of at least two things: firstly, New Testament texts as they are present us with the picture of not only thoroughly theologised Christ of the Christian faith but also with a thoroughly "judaized" Jesus. But he was a Galilean, not fully a Jew. Secondly, there is a great difference in what Jesus taught and what he was later said to have taught. [7]

Now in this section I will not present an example of one certain scholar from this group but rather a pastiche of different similar opinions. I do it for the sake of clarity but beware generalisations – they might be misleading. For our understanding of the Sermon of Mount what its significant concerns, of course, not so much 'Christ' as Jesus. Jesus can be described here not as a Jewish prophet but rather as a peasant from Galilee, who in his teaching followed the pattern of Cynic sages who opposed common wisdom with his teaching of subversive wisdom. Common wisdom tries to socialise persons into the fabric of society with all its goods and ills. This is by the way the matrix in which most of the work of Context Group is done. The subversive wisdom of the Cynics was different: their understanding was that society in general is corrupt and worthless and the best thing for humans to do is to radically re-evaluate their attitudes to themselves, their property and their whole lives. There are obvious parallels between several Cynic patterns and Jesus, both in behaviour and in teaching. [8] About behaviour of Jesus J. D. Crossan says the following:

"The radicality of his message was that it operated as much on the sociopolitical as on the religio-institutional levels. What he was opposing was not anything particularly wrong with contemporary Judaism or

---

[7] See Funk, Robert W., Hoover, Roy W. and the Jesus Seminar. *The Five Gospels.* HarperSanFrancisco 1997, pp. 2-5.

[8] Most notably described in Crossan, John Dominic. *The Historical Jesus: The Life of a Mediterranean Jewish Peasant.* HarperSanFrancisco 1992.

even with the Roman imperial system. He was opposing something wrong with culture or civilization itself, and thence with its contemporary (then or now) economic, social, political and religious manifestations. And he can distance himself from civilization only by trying to imagine the transcendent viewpoint of the Kingdom of God – which means, put very simply, what would this world look like if God was in direct, immediate and unbrokered control? His answer is that it would be a world of radical egalitarianism and that it is a vision and program that reduces all of us to stuttering silence. I cannot, quite frankly, imagine anything more transcendent than Jesus vision and program." [9]

Among concrete examples of Jesus' teaching we can come back to the section analysed by Richard Dillon. "Jesus remarks on the birds' carefree life, so does Musonius." [10] And there is more. Jesus speaks about need to love your enemies and be non-violent; the closest analogy we find here is from Epictetus, who is describing the Cynic's life. A Cynic has to lay aside all anger and to be rocklike in the face of insults. Like Jesus, a Cynic philosopher must do without family while still having a new family – the whole humanity. [11] Now, as it was with the results of K. C. Hanson, it is the same here: the teaching of Jesus is not a set of ideas. A Cynic must embody his teaching, and so must his followers. The embodiment, of course, must be radical indeed, but it is never an unattainable ideal; it is the matter of practice.

Of the third group of scholars we cannot use the word "school". What we have here is scholars who in their work sometimes employ methods similar to those of the Jesus Seminar group, but who differ from them in taking seriously Jesus' Jewishness and his eschatologically oriented prophecy. Tom Wright, whom I quoted before, belongs here. Tom Wright's work is interesting and thought-provoking: he puts Jesus and Christians of the 1st century firmly into the matrix of Jewish expectations of the fulfilment of God's covenant with his people and the full return from exile (which in a certain sense still continued as the proclamations of the prophecy about new word after exile had not yet became true). Of the Sermon of the Mount he writes the following words:

"The sermon – take it for the moment as whole – is not a mere miscellany of ethical instruction. It cannot be generalised into set of suggestions, or even commands, on how to be 'good'. Nor can it be turned into a guidemap for how to go to 'heaven' after death. It is rather, as it

---

[9] Crossan, John Dominic. *The historical Jesus: an interview.* - Christian Century 108 (18-25 1991), pp. 1200-1204, p. 1203.

[10] Quotation from Wright, *Jesus and the Victory of God*, p. 68 (discussing the idea that Jesus actually was a Cynic). The Jesus Seminar fellows are not the only ones who see similarities between Jesus and the Cynics.

[11] Theissen, Gerd. *Social Reality and the Early Christians.* Trans. by Margaret Kohl. Edinburgh: T&T Clark 1993, p. 128.

stands, a challenge to Israel to *be* Israel." [12]

The examples are as follows: We start with beatitudes (5: 3-13).

"Israel longs for YHWH's kingdom to come (5. 3). She is ready to work and struggle and fight to bring it in. But the people to whom it belongs are poor in spirit. Israel longs for consolation, for *paraklesis* (5. 4). But YHWH has in mind to give her, not the consolation of a national revival, in which their old wound will be healed by inflicting wounds on others, but the consolation awaiting those who are in genuine grief. Israel desires inherit the earth (5. 5); she must do it in Jesus way, in meekness. Israel thirsts for justice (5. 6) but the justice she is offered does not come by way of battles against physical enemies. It is not a way of anger, of a 'justice' which really means vengeance. It is the way of humility and gentleness." [13]

And so on. When we come to antitheses, we see that in this matrix they do not

"focus on contrast between 'outward' and 'inward' keepings of the law. They are not retrojections into the first century of a nineteenth-century Romantic ideal of religion in which outward things are bad and inward things are good. They emphasise, rather, the way in which the renewal that Jesus sought to engender would produce a radically different way of being Israel in real-life Palestinian situations. There, the ruling interpretation of the Torah would lead to being Israel in the wrong way, the way that would lead to destruction; the way of life he was urging would suggest a totally different approach and result. Thus: ... the soldier who commandeers the services of a Galilean villager must not be resisted or resented, but must be met with astonishing generosity (5. 41); enemies of state are not enemies in the eyes of YHWH, and if Israel is really to imitate her heavenly father she must learn to love and pray for them (5. 44f.)." [14]

In the end

"the real way forward for Israel, therefore (7. 1-6), is to avoid the way of condemnation, whether of gentiles or whether of one another. It is unnecessary; all that is needful will be given to those who ask (7. 7-11)" [15]

So here we have Israel as a whole as a recipient of the Sermon of the Mount and not just individual Christians.

To summarise and also to come to the title of this little essay, I start with just one more short quotation, this time by Gerd Theissen. He discusses the command to love one's enemy in our sermon and says:

---

[12] Wright, *Jesus and the Victory of God*, p. 288.
[13] Ibid.
[14] Ibid., p. 290.
[15] Ibid., pp. 291-292.

> "It is impossible to determine what love of enemies and non-violence mean apart from the social situation in which these demands are made and practised." [16]

We can safely say that this is true of the entire Sermon of the Mount. We cannot in any legitimate way extract from it particular abstract timeless teachings. Rather, what we see is that all these so-called "teachings" are to be understood only in their particular and specific embodiments. As we see from above, New Testament scholars differ quite remarkably among themselves on the question of what these particular embodiments might have been. Context Group sees them in the common and generally accepted cultural values and behavioural patterns of the time; the Jesus Seminar historians see it rather in the subversive wisdom of the Cynic type and the patterns associated with it; others see these embodiments rooted firmly and thoroughly in the particular manifestations of the first century Jewish and Christian attitudes, hopes and agendas.

In one way or another, what all this means for us is that if we really want to take the Sermon of the Mount seriously, these things will even be harder to follow. For we have grown accustomed to the idea that this Sermon is hard live out because of its uncomfortable content. Now we have to admit that we do not even know for sure what that content is. Jesus and his message remain firmly rooted in his time and his cultural situation. Viewed from this perspective the Sermon of the Mount itself remains forever transcendent. Still I do not want to conclude on such a pessimistic note. For this coin has its other side too: this situation still presents us with a possibility – for it means that if we ever want to understand this Sermon we can only do it by our own attempts to embody it (or to be more precise – its elements) in our own lives in our own culture. Whether it comforts us or is it even more uncomfortable I dare not say. It is not a matter of saying anyway – it is a matter of doing.

---

[16] Theissen, *Social Reality and the Early Christians*, p. 130.

"Wastne Testament"
das erste estnischsprachige Neue Testament

Peeter Roosimaa, Tartu

Aus der Sicht der Geschichte der estnischen Bibelübersetzung gab es im XVII. und XVIII. Jahrhundert zwei Sternstunden: 1686 erschien *Wastne Testament* – das Neue Testament in südestnischer Sprache und 1715 *Uus Testament* – das Neue Testament in nordestnischer Sprache. Einen Überblick über die Entstehungsgeschichte dieser Werke macht der Theologiedoktor Toomas Paul in seinem ausführlichen und auf vielen Quellen basierenden Werk „*Eesti piiblitõlke ajalugu. Esimestest katsetest kuni 1999. aastani (Die Geschichte der estnischen Bibelübersetzung. Von den ersten Versuchen bis zum Jahr 1999) Tallinn 1999*". Im Folgenden stütze ich mich zuerst hauptsächlich auf die Angaben Pauls.

Man muss sagen, dass das Übersetzen der Bibel generell eine anonyme Tätigkeit gewesen ist, darum ist es auch ziemlich schwer, alle beteiligten Personen und ihren Beitrag ausfindig zu machen und zu würdigen. Aus dem gleichen Grund können viele Ereignisse zeitlich nicht genau festgelegt werden. Das gilt auch für die ersten estnischen Übersetzungen des Neuen Testaments. Trotzdem hat die Geschichte mehrere Namen deutscher Pastoren überliefert, dank deren Initiative und Mühe die Heilige Schrift auch in die estnische Sprache übersetzt werden konnte.

Der Anfang der Bibelübersetzung in die estnische Sprache (Paul 1999: 299ff.)

An dieser Stelle wäre es angemessen zu erwähnen, dass Estland in ein nördliches Estnisches Bistum und in ein südliches Livisches Bistum geteilt war. Dementsprechend hat sich auch die estnische Sprache in verschiedene Richtungen entwickelt.

Den ersten Versuch, die ganze Bibel in estnischer Sprache herauszugeben, machte Estlands Bischof Joachim Jhering. 1640 hat er die schwedische Regierung über seinen Plan, die Bibel ins Estnische zu übersetzen, benachrichtigt. Ihm wurde empfohlen, mit dem Neuen Testament anzufangen. Unterstützung hat er auch von der estnischen Synode bekommen. Leider ist die Arbeit während der Pest verloren gegangen.

Etwa gleichzeitig hat der livländische Pastor Johannes (Johann) Gutslaff aus Urvaste auf eigene Initiative angefangen, die Bibel in die südestnische Sprache zu übersetzen. Aber auch diese Arbeit wurde nicht gedruckt. Zum Bibelübersetzen haben ebenso Pastor Heinrich Göseken aus Kullamaa und Pastor Christoph Blume aus Hageri ihren Teil beigetragen. Estlands Bischof Jacob Hellwig, Doktor der Theologie, unterstützte ihre Arbeit, die aber nicht druckfertig wurde.

Das Erscheinen des *Wastne Testaments* 1686

Parallel zu den Bemühungen, das Neue Testament im Bistum Estland herauszugeben, beschäftigte man sich damit auch in Livland. Der aus Lübeck stammende Generalsuperintendent Livlands Johann Fischer (1633-1705) arbeitete an der Herausgabe des südestnischen *Wastne Testaments*. Im Auftrag von Fischer fing der junge Adrian Virginius (1663-1706) 1683 an, das Neue Testament zu übersetzen. Die Übersetzung wurde gelesen und nach Kräften von Andreas Virginius (1640-1701) und Johann Nicolaus von Hardung (1636-1702) korrigiert. Im Zusammenhang der Übersetzungsarbeit des *Wastne Testaments* sind außerdem die Namen von Marcus Schütz und Johann Heinrich Neubaud erwähnt worden. Das *Wastne Testament* wurde von Johann Georg Wilcken 1686 in Riga in Johann Fischer´s Druckerei in einer Auflage von 500 Stück gedruckt.

Der Grundtext des *Wastne Testaments*

Es wäre interessant zu wissen, aus welcher Sprache oder aus welchen Sprachen das *Wastne Testament* in die südestnische Sprache übersetzt wurde, und ist es möglich, festzustellen, welche Auflagen dafür benutzt worden sind?

Ausgangspunkt

Im Zusammenhang mit diesen Fragen sollten ein paar wichtige Informationen von T. Paul betrachtet werden. Gemäß einer Mitteilung hat man Johann Fischer vorgeworfen, dass die Übersetzung des *Wastne Testaments* nicht genau der lutherischen Version folgen würde. Daraufhin hat Fischer bestätigt, dass er mehrfach den Urtext, statt den lutherischen als maßgebend nehmen mußte, damit er in reiner estnischer Sprache reden würde. Auf Grund einer anderen Mitteilung hat Professor Christian Korholt die Tatsache gelobt, dass Fischer wahrheitsgemäß aus dem Urtext übersetzen würde (Paul 1999: 379). Aus diesen Hinweisen kann man schließen, daß man sowohl die griechische als auch die deutsche Sprache als Übersetzungsgrundlage benutzt hat. Welche dieser Sprachen tatsächlich zur Grundlage genommen worden war, kann aus diesen Hinweisen nicht ganz festgelegt werden.

Wenn man bei dem deutschsprachigen Text ohne Zweifel davon ausgehen kann, dass man die Übersetzung von Martin Luther benutzt hat, bleibt doch die Frage, mit welcher Ausgabe man es bei dem griechischen neutestamentlichen Text zu tun hat. Es waren ja damals verschiedene Ausgaben des griechischsprachigen Neuen Testaments im Umlauf. Sicherlich war es eine, die vor dem

Jahr 1686, wahrscheinlich sogar vor 1683 herausgegeben worden war.

Um eine mögliche Antwort zu finden, habe ich verschiedene griechische Texte untersucht, die in der Estnischen Nationalbibliothek aufbewahrt werden. Die Texte stammen von 1563 (herausgegeben vom Drucker Nicolai Brylinger aus Basel), 1618 (redigiert von Erasmus von Rotterdam), 1633 (herausgegeben von dem niederländischen Verleger und Drucker Guilielmus Blaeu) und 1657 (herausgegeben von Christian Kirchner), sowie die Ausgaben der lutherischen Bibeln von 1641, 1649 und 1661. Diese Texte habe ich anhand des 1. Petrusbriefes verglichen.

Das Vergleichen der griechischen Texte ergab, dass die meisten Unterschiede bei der Interpunktion zu finden waren. Man könnte glauben, dass verschiedene Verleger die Satzzeichen nach ihrer besten Auffassung gesetzt haben. Auch bei der Benutzung von Aspirations- und Akzentzeichen war man nicht konsequent. Die inhaltlichen Unterschiede der Texte bestanden zum Beispiel darin, dass man oft wir und ihr verwechselt hat (z.B. 1Petr 1,12 u.a.); dass die Reihenfolge einzelne Wörter unterschiedlich war (z.B. 1Petr 1,23 u.a.), oder dass verschiedene Formen der Wörter benutzt wurden (z.B. 1Petr 3,7: ζωῆς - ζώσης = Leben – Errettung, Erlösung). An einer Stelle (1Petr 2,7-8) waren die Texte unterschiedlich in Verse eingeteilt worden.

Der Vergleich der deutschsprachigen Texte untereinander ergab, dass sie inhaltlich alle identisch waren. Die hauptsächlichen Unterschiede befanden sich in der Orthographie und in der Interpunktion. Nur bei 1Petr 2,23 hat man bei drei Verben unterschiedliche Zeiten benutzt. Für die weitere Analyse habe ich mich für die Herausgabe von 1661 entschieden.

Beim Vergleichen des *Wastne Testaments* mit den griechischen Texten hat sich herausgestellt, dass sich die größte Übereinstimmung mit dem Text von 1633 ergab. Dabei ist es wichtig, dass die Verseinteilung von 1Petr 2,7-8, die sich von den anderen betrachteten griechischen Texten, sowie von lutherischen Texten unterscheidet, hier übereinstimmt.

2,7. …/ nink kä Pähnulga Kiwwiß om sahnu/ <u>üts Puttusse Kiwwi/ nink Pahandusse Paas:</u>	2,7.... οὗτος ἐγενήθη εἰς κεφαλὴν γωνίας, <u>καὶ λίθος προσκόμματος, καὶ πέτρα σκανδάλου</u>·	2,7. …/ und zum Eckstein geworden ist/
2,8. kumma hendä Sönna külge taukwa/ nink ei ussu mitte/ kummale nemmä kah omma pantu.	2,8 οἳ προσκόπτουσι τῷ λόγῳ, ἀπειθοῦντες, εἰς ὃ καὶ ἐτέθησαν.	2,8. <u>Ein Stein deß Anstossens/ und ein Fels der Ergernis</u>/ die sich stossen an dem Wort/ und gläuben nicht dran/ darauff sie gesetzet sind.

Wahrlich, die Verseinteilung von 1Petr 3,15-16 ist bei dem südestnischen Text und bei dem griechischen Text von 1633 unterschiedlich, aber die südestnische Verseinteilung unterscheidet sich an dieser Stelle auch von den anderen betrachteten griechischen Texten und von dem lutherischen Text.

3,15. ... Ent olge ikkes walmi eggäüttele kostma/ kä teist Arwo püwwäb se Lohtusse perräst/ kumb teije sissen om/ <u>Tassausse ning Peljoga:</u>	3,15. ... Ἕτοιμοι δὲ ἀεὶ πρὸς ἀπολογίαν παντὶ τῷ αἰτοῦντι ὑμᾶς λόγον περὶ τῆς ἐν ὑμῖν ἐλπίδος,	3,15. ... Seyd aber allezeit bereit zur Verantwortung jederman/ Der Grund fordert der Hoffnung/ die in euch ist/
16. Piddäge hähd Süddäme Teedmist: ...	16 μετὰ πραΰτητος καὶ φόβου· συνείδησιν ἔχοντες ἀγαθήν· ...	16. Und das mit <u>Sanfftmütigkeit und Furcht/</u> und habt ein gut Gewissen/ ...

Die Verseinteilung von 1Petr 1,4-5; 4,7-8 unterscheidet sich nur von dem lutherischen Text.

1,4. Ilmhukkaminnemättä/ nink pürretämättä nink erränärwämättä Perrändusseß/ kumb <u>meile Taiwan om tallele</u> pantu.	1,4 εἰς κληρονομίαν ἄφθαρτον καὶ ἀμίαντον καὶ ἀμάραντον, τετηρημένην ἐν οὐρανοῖς <u>εἰς ὑμᾶς,</u>	1,4. Zu einem unvergänglichen und unbefleckten und unverwelcklichen Erbe/ das behalten wird im Himmel/
1,5. Kumbe Jummala Wäen läbbi Ussu hoijetas Önnistusselle/ ...	1,5 τοὺς ἐν δυνάμει Θεοῦ φρουρουμένους διὰ πίστεως, εἰς σωτηρίαν ...	1,5. <u>Euch/</u> die ihr aus GOttes Macht durch den Glauben bewahret werdet zur Seligkeit/ ...

4,7. Ent kige Asja Ots om lähünu. <u>Sis olge nühd targa nink kaine Palwusselle.</u>	4,7 Πάντων δὲ τὸ τέλος ἤγγικε. <u>Σωφρονήσατε οὖν καὶ νήψατε εἰς τὰς προσευχάς.</u>	4,7. Es ist aber nahe kommen das Ende aller Dinge.
4,8.	4,8	4,8. <u>SO seyd nun mässig und nüchtern zum Gebet.</u> ...

Ein inhaltlicher Unterschied ist in 1Petr 1,4 zu finden, wo statt des südestnischen *wir* in allen anderen betrachteten Texten und auch in dem lutherischen Text *ihr* steht. Dieser Unterschied befindet sich auch in 1Petr 2,21, wo zwei mal statt *ihr*, so wie es in dem griechische Text von 1633 steht, die *wir*-Form benutzt wurde. An dieser Stelle ist anscheinend die lutherische Übersetzung benutzt worden.

Als Zusammenfassung des o.g. kann man sagen, dass der 1633 von dem niederländischen Verleger und Drucker Guilielmus Blaeu herausgegebene Text oder ein mit ihm verwandtes Neues Testament als griechischer Grundtext des 1. Petrusbriefes gedient hat.

Die Kriterien der Analyse

Beim Vergleich der Texte habe ich die Aufmerksamkeit hauptsächlich auf folgende Sachverhalte gelegt:
1. Wie ist der Satzbau, die Satzstruktur? Gibt es Besonderheiten, woraus man schließen könnte, dass hier ein griechisches Partizip, eine *a.c.i.*-Konstrukion oder etwas ähnliches weitergegeben wird, oder ob Einflüße aus dem deutschen Satzbau zu finden sind?
2. Welche inhaltlichen Unterschiede oder Übereinstimmungen der betrachteten Texte sind zu finden, aus denen man deuten kann, welcher Text beim Übersetzten des Neuen Testaments benutzt worden ist?
3. Gibt es einzelne Wörter, die nicht direkt in dem zu übersetzenden Text zu finden sind, die aber vermuten lassen, von welchem Text man ausgegangen ist? Zum Beispiel, welche Wörter sind an den Stellen benutzt worden, bei denen im griechischen Text die Kopula fehlt?
4. Gibt es andere Beobachtungen, die auf einen benutzten Text hinweisen?

Die Analyse

Um mehr Klarheit über die Ausgangssprachen und die benutzten Texte zu bekommen, habe ich eine synoptische Tabelle über den 1. Petrusbrief aufgestellt, in der sich der Text des *Wastne Testaments* von 1686, der griechische Text von 1633 und die lutherische Übersetzung von 1661 befinden. Die Tabelle habe ich unter den obengenannten Kriterien untersucht. Um untereinander entsprechende Wörter, Satzteile, Teilsätze besser hervorzuheben, habe ich verschiedene Unterstreichungen gebraucht.

Der deutschsprachige Text

Dafür, dass die lutherische Übersetzung als Ausgangstext für das *Wastne Testament* gedient hat, möchte ich folgende Beobachtungen nennen.

1. Die Struktur des Satzes
a) Bei vielen Versen entspricht der Satzbau dem der lutherischen Übersetzung. Ich bringe hier einige Beispiele:

1,11. Nink omma juhrdlenu/ kumba echk mähräst Aiga se Kristusse Waim/ kä neide sissen olli/ täendäß/ kä ette om errä tunnistanu neid Kannatussi/ kumma Kristussen omma/ nink perräst neid Auwustust:	1,11 ἐρευνῶντες εἰς τίνα ἢ ποῖον καιρὸν ἐδήλου τὸ ἐν αὐτοῖς Πνεῦμα Χριστοῦ, προμαρτυρόμενον τὰ εἰς Χριστὸν παθήματα, καὶ τὰς μετὰ ταῦτα δόξας.	1,11. Und haben geforschet/ auff welche und welcherley Zeit deutet der Geist Christi/ der in ihnen war/ und zuvor bezeuget hat die Leiden/ die in Christo sind/ und die Herrligkeit darnach/

In 1Petr 1,11 wurden die griechischen Partizipkonstruktionen ἐρευνῶντες und προμαρτυρόμενον mit Hilfe von Teilsätzen *Nink omma juhrdlenu – Und haben geforschet* und *kä ette om errä tunnistanu – und zuvor bezeuget hat* weitergegeben, wobei man der Satzstruktur des lutherischen Textes folgte. Eine Ausnahme bildet das Wort *täendäß*, dessen Standort sich von dem Wort *deutet* unterscheidet. Die Bedeutung des Wortes kommt aber auch eher aus der deutschen als aus der griechischen Sprache ἐδήλου (Imperfekt von δηλόω - *offenbar machen, aufdecken, kundtun, zu erkennen geben, erklären, deutlich machen.*) Auch das Anfangswort *nink* entspricht dem Wort *und* aus dem lutherischen Text. Die Attribute ἐν αὐτοῖς und εἰς Χριστὸν zu den Ausdrücken τὸ ... Πνεῦμα und τὰ ... παθήματα sind so wohl in deutscher als auch in estnischer Sprache mit Nebensätzen weitergegeben: *kä neide sissen olli – der in ihnen war* und *kumma Kristussen omma – die in Christo sind*. Im Ausdruck *se Kristusse Waim* entspricht das Wort *se* dem Artikel *der* im Ausdruck *der Geist Christi*.

1,12. Kummille se om awwaldetu/ et nemmä sega ei olle hendä essi/ enge meid orjanu/ mes teile nühd om kuhlutetu/ neide läbbi/ kumma teile Armo Oppust omma juttustanu/ läbbi pöhä Waimo/ kä Taiwast om lähätetu/ kumma sisse kah Englil Himmo om kajeda.	1,12 Οἷς ἀπεκαλύφθη ὅτι οὐχ ἑαυτοῖς, ἡμῖν δὲ διηκόνουν αὐτά, ἃ νῦν ἀνηγγέλη ὑμῖν διὰ τῶν εὐαγγελισαμένων ὑμᾶς ἐν Πνεύματι ἁγίῳ ἀποσταλέντι ἀπ' οὐρανοῦ, εἰς ἃ ἐπιθυμοῦσιν ἄγγελοι παρακύψαι.	1,12. Welchen es offenbaret ist/ denn sie haben nicht ihnen selbst/ sondern uns dargethan/ welches euch nun verkündiget ist/ durch die/ so euch das Evangelium verkündiget haben/ durch den heiligen Geist/ vom Himmel gesandt/ welches auch die Engel gelüstet zu schauen.

In 1Petr 1,12 entspricht die Satzstruktur völlig dem lutherischen Text. Abweichungen finden sich nur in Bezug auf einzelne Wörter. Für das Wort *sega* (*somit*) fehlt im lutherischen Text ein entsprechendes Wort; *vom Himmel gesandt* ist mit dem für die estnische Sprache charakteristischen *kä Taiwast om lähätetu* ausgedrückt; der Ausdruck *kumma sisse* entspricht mehr dem griechischen εἰς ἃ als dem deutschen *welches*.

2,1. Sis heitke nühd errä kik Kurjust/ nink kik Pettust/ nink Kawwalust/ nink Kaddeust/ nink kik Keelepesmist/	2,1 Ἀποθέμενοι οὖν πᾶσαν κακίαν καὶ πάντα δόλον καὶ ὑποκρίσεις καὶ φθόνους καὶ πάσας καταλαλιάς.	2,1. SO leget nun ab alle Bosheit/ und allen Betrug/ und Heuchelen/ und Neid/ und alles Affterreden/

Die eins-zu-eins Entsprechung der Satzstruktur mit dem lutherischen Text ist auch in 1Petr 2,1 zu finden. Eigentlich haben hier alle drei Sprachen die gleiche Satzstruktur. Dabei sollte man anmerken, dass das Partizip ἀποθέμενοι – *ablegend* nach dem deutschen Vorbild als Imperativ übersetzt worden ist: *leget ... ab – heitke ... errä*.

b) Dass man beim Übersetzen nicht mechanisch den lutherischen Text gefolgt ist, und dass man nicht nur die deutsche Ausgabe benutzt hat, das bezeugen die folgenden Beispiele:

2,11. Arma/ minna mannitse teid/ kui Külläleisi nink Teekeüjid/ hoitke hendä lehalikko Himmo eest/ kumma Henge wasta tapplewa:	2,11 Ἀγαπητοί, παρακαλῶ ὡς παροίκους καὶ παρεπιδήμους, ἀπέχεσθαι τῶν σαρκικῶν ἐπιθυμιῶν, αἵτινες στρατεύονται κατὰ τῆς ψυχῆς·	2,11. Lieben Brüder/ ich ermahne euch/ als die Frembdlingen und Pilgern/ enthaltet euch von fleischlichen Lüsten/ welche wider die Seele streiten/

In 1Petr 2,11 ist man ansonsten dem lutherischen Text gefolgt, auch das Objekt *teid* ist vom deutschen Text übernommen, nur dass das am Anfang des Verses stehende Wort *Arma* nicht aus dem deutschen Text *Lieben Brüder*, sondern aus dem griechischen Wort Ἀγαπητοί kommt. Man kann auch sagen, dass ἀπέχεσθαι (Infinitiv) als Imperativ ins Deutsche übersetzt ist; dem folgt auch die estnische Übersetzung *enthaltet euch – hoitke hendä*.

2,12. Nink piddäge hähd Keüki Pagganide seän: Et ne/ kumma teist Kurja pajatawa/ kui Kurjateggijist/ teije Hähd Tekko nätten/ Jummalat kittässe Koddo otsmisse Peiwäl.	2,12 τὴν ἀναστροφὴν ὑμῶν ἐν τοῖς ἔθνεσιν ἔχοντες καλήν· ἵνα ἐν ᾧ καταλαλοῦσιν ὑμῶν ὡς κακοποιῶν, ἐκ τῶν καλῶν ἔργων ἐποπτεύσαντες, δοξάσωσι τὸν Θεὸν ἐν ἡμέρᾳ ἐπισκοπῆς.	2,12. Und führet einen guten Wandel unter den Henden/ auff daß die/ so von euch affterreden/ als von Übelthätern/ eure gute Wercke sehen/ und Gott preisen/ wenns nun an den Tag kommen wird.

Auch in 1Petr 2,12 folgt man dem deutschen Satzbau nach dem Vorbild der deutschen Sprache ist das Partizip ἔχοντες als Imperativ *piddäge – führet*, das Partizip ἐποπτεύσαντες als Indikativ *nätten – sehen* übersetzt, aber das am Ende des Verses stehende *Koddo otsmisse Peiwäl* steht dem griechischen ἐν ἡμέρᾳ ἐπισκοπῇ – *an dem Tag des Rechenschaftsgebens* viel näher als dem deutschen Text *wenns nun an den Tag kommen wird*.

c) Es gibt auch Verse, deren Satzbau nicht eindeutig erkennen lässt, aus welcher Sprache sie übersetzt worden sind. Zum Beispiel 1Petr 2,17.

2,17. Auwustagge eggämehst: Armastage Wellitsid: Peljäke Jummalat: Auwustage Kunningat.	2,17 Πάντας τιμήσατε. Τὴν ἀδελφότητα ἀγαπᾶτε. Τὸν Θεὸν φοβεῖσθε. Τὸν βασιλέα τιμᾶτε.	2,17. Thut Ehre jederman. Habt die Brüder lieb. Fürchtet Gott. Ehret den König.

In diesem Vers gibt es eine Reihe kurzer, einzelner Anordnungen, in denen die natürliche Wortfolge sowohl in der estnischen als auch in der deutschen Sprache *Prädikat – Objekt* ist. In der griechischen Sprache ist es aber umgekehrt: *Objekt – Prädikat*. Das Wort *eggämehst* kommt wahrscheinlich aus dem deutschen Wort *jederman* und gibt damit dem deutschen Text als Vorbild einen Vorteil.

2. Die Übersetzung einzelner Wörter

Zusätzlich zum deutschähnlichen Satzbau vieler Verse gibt es auch genügend einzelne Worte, die die Annahme unterstützen, dass der Text aus der deutschen Sprache übersetzt wurde. Hier bringe ich einige Beispiele:

a) Das Ἐν ᾧ ἀγαλλιᾶσθε aus 1Petr 1,6, das im Präsens steht, ist nach dem deutschen Vorbild in die Zukunftsform übersetzt worden: *Kumman teije **sahde** röhmsa **ollema** – In welcher ihr euch **freuen werdet**;* in 1Petr 1,8 ist dagegen ἀγαλλιᾶσθε als Präsens übersetzt worden **röhmustate hendä** (vgl. *so* **werdet** *ihr euch* **freuen** - Zukunft), wobei das reflexive Wort *hendä* wahrscheinlich von der deutschen Variante oder Denkweise stammt.

b) Sichtbare deutschsprachige Einflüße sind in 1Petr 1,12 zu finden: *läbbi pöhä Waimo – durch den heiligen Geist*; vgl. ἐν Πνεύματι ἁγίῳ.

c) In 1Petr 2,22 steht *Kä **ütteke** Pattu ei olle tennu*. Das Wort *ütteke* kommt hier aus der deutschen Sprache *keine – Welcher **keine** Sünde gethan hat*; vgl. ὃς ἁμαρτίαν οὐκ ἐποίησεν.

d) In 1Petr 3,6 ist ἧς ... τέκνα nach dem deutschen Vorbild übersetzt worden *kumma Tüttriß – welcher Töchter*.

e) In 1Petr 3,21 ist συνειδήσεως ἀγαθῆς ἐπερώτημα εἰς Θεὸν als *häh Süddame Teedmisse **Lepping** Jummalaga* übersetzt worden. Zweifelsfrei entspricht hier das Wort *Lepping* dem deutschen Wort *der Bund – der Bund eines guten Gewissens mit Gott*.

f) In 1Petr 4,5 kommt die estnische Wortwahl ***Arwo** sahwa andma* eher aus dem deutschen Ausdruck *werden **Rechenschafft** geben* als aus dem griechischen ἀποδώσουσι λόγον. Das gleiche kann man auch über 1Petr 4,18 sagen: *Nink kui Öige waiwalisse **üllespeetäs** – Und so der Gerechte kaum **erhalten** wird*. Vgl Καὶ εἰ ὁ δίκαιος μόλις σῴζεται – *errettet man*.

g) In 1Petr 5,13 ist das Personalpronomen der zweiten Person Plural nur einmal vorhanden: Ἀσπάζεται ὑμᾶς ἡ ἐν Βαβυλῶνι συνεκλεκτή. In dem *Wastne Testament* aber zwei Mal – ***Teid** terwitäb se teijega **üttenerräwallitsetu*** – genauso wie auch im deutschen Text – *Es grüssen **euch**/ die sampt **euch** außerwehlet sind*.

3. Von den anderen Beobachtungen möchte ich folgendes anmerken. Im südestnischen Neuen Testament befinden sich bei 1Petr 2,20 und auch bei 1Petr 5,11 am Ende der Verse einzelne Klammern. Gleiche Klammern gibt es auch am Ende der entsprechenden Verse im lutherischen Text von 1661. So eine einzelne Klammer steht auch am Ende von 1Petr 2,25 in dem südestnischen Neuen Testament, eine Entsprechung bei den betrachteten Ausgaben gab es aber nicht.

Zusammenfassend kann man sagen, dass die deutschsprachige lutherische Übersetzung als einer der Grundtexte zur Übersetzung des *Wastne Testaments* gedient hat.

Der griechische Text

Dafür, dass der griechische Text als Ausgangstext für das *Wastne Testament* gedient hat, möchte ich folgende Beobachtungen nennen.

1. Wie sich bereits herausgestellt hat, entspricht die Verseinteilung des *Wastne Testaments* mehr der des griechischen als der des lutherischen Textes. Dieses

weist darauf hin, dass auch der griechische Text als Grundlage zur Übersetzung benutzt wurde.

2. Die Struktur des Satzes

Im Vergleich zur lutherischen Übersetzung gibt es zwischen dem *Wastne Testament* und dem griechischen Text viel weniger satzstrukturelle Entsprechungen. Trotzdem weisen die vorhandenen Entsprechungen auf das Griechische als Grundtext hin. Die spezifischen griechischen Satzteilen und Satzkonstruktionen (Partizipen, *a.c.i.*), die oft als Nebensätze übersetzt werden, machen das Vergleichen der Texte kompliziert. Zum Beispiel:

| 3,10. Sest kä om Ello tahab armastada/ ninck hüwwi Peiwi nättä/ se hoidko omma Keeld Kurja eest/ ninck omme Huhli Pettust pajatamast. | 3,10 Ὁ γὰρ θέλων ζωὴν ἀγαπᾶν, καὶ ἰδεῖν ἡμέρας ἀγαθὰς, παυσάτω τὴν γλῶσσαν αὐτοῦ ἀπὸ κακοῦ, καὶ χείλη αὐτοῦ, τοῦ μὴ λαλῆσαι δόλον· | 3,10. Denn wer leben wil/ und gute Tage sehen/ der schweige seine Zunge/ daß sie nichts Böses rede/ und seine Lippen/ daß sie nicht triegen. |

Das Partizip θέλων am Anfang von 1Petr 3,10 ist sowohl in die estnische als auch in die deutsche Sprache mit Hilfe eines Nebensatzes übersetzt worden. Doch die Übersetzung des entsprechenden Gliedsatzes *Sest kä om Ello tahab **armastada*** entspricht mehr dem griechischen Ὁ γὰρ θέλων ζωὴν ἀγαπᾶν als dem deutschen Text *Denn wer leben wil*. Der ins Estnische übersetzte Text *se hoidko omma Keeld Kurja eest* aus der zweiten Hälfte des Verses ist in die deutsche Sprache mit Hilfe eine Satzfolge vom Hauptsatz und Nebensatz gesetzt worden: *der schweige seine Zunge/ daß sie nichts Böses rede*, vgl. παυσάτω τὴν γλῶσσαν αὐτοῦ ἀπὸ κακοῦ. Die gleiche Form hat man auch bei *nink omme Huhli Pettust pajatamast* benutzt: *und seine Lippen/ daß sie nicht triegen*, vgl. καὶ χείλη αὐτοῦ, τοῦ μὴ λαλῆσαι δόλν. So kann man sehen, dass sowohl die Versstruktur als auch die Übersetzung aus der griechischen Sprache und nicht aus der lutherischen Übersetzung gewonnen wurden.

| 4,7. Ent kige Asja Ots om lähünu. Sis olge nühd targa nink kaine Palwusselle. | 4,7 Πάντων δὲ τὸ τέλος ἤγγικε. Σωφρονήσατε οὖν καὶ νήψατε εἰς τὰς προσευχάς. | 4,7. Es ist aber nahe kommen das Ende aller Dinge. 4,8. SO seyd nun mässig und nüchtern zum Gebet. |

In 1Petr 4,7-8 folgt das *Wastne Testament* der Verseinteilung des griechischen Textes, zusätzlich entspricht auch die Übersetzung *olge ... targa* mehr dem griechischen Wort Σωφρονήσατε – *seid erwägend, vorausschauend*, als dem deutschen Ausdruck *seyd ... mässig*.

| 4,14. Kui teije Kristusse Nünme perräst Tikko kannatate/ sis ollete önsa: Sest se Auwustusse nink Jummala **Waim** hengäb teije pähl: Neide man teotetas temmä kül/ ent teije man auwustetas temmä. | 4.14 Εἰ ὀνειδίζεσθε ἐν ὀνόματι Χριστοῦ, μακάριοι· ὅτι τὸ τῆς δόξης καὶ τὸ τοῦ Θεοῦ Πνεῦμα ἐφ' ὑμᾶς ἀναπαύεται· κατὰ μὲν αὐτοὺς βλασφημεῖται, κατὰ δὲ ὑμᾶς δοξάζεται. | 4,14. Selig sendt ihr/ wenn ihr geschmähet werdet über dem Namen Christi/ denn der **Geist**/ der ein **Geist** der Herrligkeit und Gottes ist/ ruhet auff euch. Ben ihnen ist er verlästert/ aber ben euch ist er gepreiset. |

Die Versstruktur von 1Petr 4,14 entspricht dem griechischen Text. Der erste Teil des Verses *Kui teije Kristusse Nünme perräst Tikko kannatate/ sis ollete önsa* folgt der Gedankenentwicklung des griechischen Textes. Im deutschsprachigen Text steht der Seligkeitsgedanke dagegen am Anfang des Satzes: *Selig send ihr/ wenn ihr geschmähet werdet über dem Namen Christi*. Auch der zweite Versteil *Sest se Auwustusse nink Jummala **Waim** hengäb teije pähl* folgt dem griechischen Text. Wenn in der estnischen Sprache das Wort *Waim* einfach mit untergeordneten Satzgliedern wie *Auwustusse nink Jummala* charakterisiert wird, dann wird in der deutschen Sprache an dieser Stelle ein Zwischensatz angewendet, der zugleich die Wiederholung des Wortes *Geist* verursacht: *denn der **Geist**/ der ein **Geist** der Herrligkeit und Gottes ist/ ruhet auff euch*. Die Struktur des Satzendes *Neide man teotetas temmä kül/ ent teije man auwustetas temmä* passt im Prinzip sowohl mit dem griechischen als auch mit dem deutschen Text zusammen, dabei kann in dem Wort *kül* eine Entsprechung zum griechischen Wort μὲν und im Wort *ent* eine Entsprechung zum deutschen Wort *aber* aus dem lutherischen Text gesehen werden.

| 5,4. Nink kui Pähkarjus hendä sahb awwaldama/ sis sahde erränärwämättä Auwustusse Wannikut sahma. | 5.4 Καὶ φανερωθέντος τοῦ ἀρχιποίμενος, κομιεῖσθε τὸν ἀμαράντινον τῆς δόξης στέφανον. | 5,4. So werdet ihr (wenn erscheinen wird der Ertzhirte) die unverwelckliche Krone der Ehren empfahen. |

Der in 1Petr 5,4 stehende absolute Genitiv φανερωθέντος τοῦ ἀρχιποίμενος ist sowohl in die estnische als auch in die deutsche Sprache mit Hilfe von Nebensätzen *kui Pähkarjus hendä sahb awwaldama – wenn erscheinen wird der Ertzhirte* übersetzt worden. Das *Wastne Testament* folgt der Reihenfolge der Gliedsätze aus dem griechischen Text, dagegen steht in der deutsche Sprache der entsprechende Nebensatz als Schaltsatz im Hauptsatz. Was die Zeitform Zukunft bei *sahde ... sahma* betrifft, so stammt ihre förmliche Seite wahrscheinlich aus der deutschen Sprache *werdet ... empfahen*. Der Ausdruck selbst steht aber auch in der griechischen Sprache im Futurum.

3. Die Übersetzung einzelner Wörter

Zusätzlich zum griechischähnlichen Satzbau der Verse gibt es auch einzelne Wörter, die den Gedanken unterstützen, dass der Text aus der griechischen Sprache übersetzt wurde. Vielmehr ist die Situation aber so, dass man sehen kann, dass beim Übersetzen sowohl der griechisch- als auch der deutschsprachige Text benutzt worden ist. Einige Beispiele:

| 2,24. Kä essi meije Pattu omman Ihun om kandnu Puh pähl/ et meije Pattule erräkohlden Öigusselle ellässe: Kumma Raigi läbbi teije ollete süttitetu. | 2.24 Ὅς τὰς ἁμαρτίας ἡμῶν αὐτὸς ἀνήνεγκεν ἐν τῷ σώματι αὐτοῦ ἐπὶ τὸ ξύλον· ἵνα ταῖς ἁμαρτίαις ἀπογενόμενοι, τῇ δικαιοσύνῃ ζήσωμεν· οὗ τῷ μώλωπι αὐτοῦ ἰάθητε. | 24. Welcher unser Sünde selbst geopffert hat an seinem Leibe/ auff dem Holtz/ auff daß wir der Sünde abgestorben/ der Gerechtigkeit leben/ durch welches Wunden ihr seyd heyl geworden. |

Die Struktur und der Inhalt von 1Petr 2,24 entspricht generell dem lutherischen Text; man kann aber sehen, dass die Aussage *meie Pattu...om kandnu Puh pähle* aus dem griechischen Text τὰς ἁμαρτίας ἡμῶν ... ἀνήνεγκεν ... ἐπὶ τὸ ξύλον (ἀναφέρω – Grundbedeutung: *hinaufbringen*) abzuleiten ist und nicht aus dem lutherischen *unser Sünde ... geopffert hat ... auff dem Holtz*. In der ersten Hälfte des Verses gibt es auch Unterschiede in Bezug auf die Reihenfolge der Satzglieder: *omman Ihun **om kandnu*** vgl. ***geopffert hat*** *an seinem Leibe*.

| 3,6. Nida kui Sara Abrahamil sönnawötlik olli/ ninck kuts teddä Essandaß/ kumma Tüttriß teije ollete sahnu/ kui teije Hähd tehde/ nink ei pelgä ütteke Hirmotamist. | 3,6 ὡς Σάρρα ὑπήκουσε τῷ Ἀβραάμ, κύριον αὐτὸν καλοῦσα· ἧς ἐγενήθητε τέκνα, ἀγαθοποιοῦσαι, καὶ μὴ φοβούμεναι μηδεμίαν πτόησιν. | 3,6. Wie die Sara Abraham gehorsam war/ und hieß ihn Herr/ welcher Töchter ihr worden seyd/ so ihr wohl thut/ und nicht so schüchtern seyd. |

Wie wir es vorne gesehen haben, ist im 1Petr 3,6 das Wort *Tüttriß* nicht aus dem griechischen τέκνα, sondern aus dem deutschen Wort *Töchter* übersetzt worden, auch die Satzstruktur passt mit der deutschen Übersetzung zusammen. Dagegen entspricht das am Ende des Verses geschriebene *nink ei pelgä ütteke Hirmotamist* dem griechischen καὶ μὴ φοβούμεναι μηδεμίαν πτόησιν und nicht dem deutschsprachigen *und nicht so schüchtern seyd*.

3:18. Sest Kristuseke om ütskörd Pattu eest kannatanu/ Öige Köwweride eest: Et temmä meid Jummalalle wihß/ nink om kül erräsurmatu Leha perrä/ ent elläwäß tettu Waimo perrä:	3,18 ὅτι καὶ Χριστὸς ἅπαξ περὶ ἁμαρτιῶν ἔπαθε, δίκαιος ὑπὲρ ἀδίκων· ἵνα ἡμᾶς προσαγάγῃ τῷ Θεῷ, θανατωθεὶς μὲν σαρκὶ, ζωοποιηθεὶς δὲ τῷ Πνεύματι.	3,18. SIntemal auch Christus ein mal für unser Sünde gelidten hat/ der Gerechte für die Ungerechten/ auff daß er uns Gott opfferte/ und ist getödtet nach dem Fleisch/ aber lebendig gemacht nach dem Geist.

Die Struktur von 1Petr 3,18 des *Wastne Testaments* entspricht dem deutschen Text. Die Übersetzung der Partizipien θανατωθεὶς und ζωοποιηθεὶς ist eindeutig aus der deutschen Sprache übernommen worden: *nink om kül erräsurmatu Leha perrä* – und **ist getödtet** nach dem Fleisch und *ent **elläwäß** tettu Waimo perrä* – aber **lebendig gemacht** nach dem Geist. Es ist hier bemerkenswert, dass das Personalpronomen im Ausdruck *für **unser** Sünde* am Anfang des Verses nicht übernommen worden ist. Das Personalpronomen fehlt an dieser Stelle auch in dem griechischen Text. Weiter ist zu erwähnen, dass das estnische *Et temmä meid Jummalalle **wihß*** mehr dem griechischen ἡμᾶς προσαγάγῃ τῷ Θεῷ (προσάγω – *zu etwas führen, zu etwas bringen*) als dem deutschen Text *auff daß er uns Gott opfferte* entspricht. Doch, prinzipiell kann *zu Gott bringen* auch *opfern* bedeuten.

3,20. Kumma ennemuste es ussu/ kui Jummala Pikmeel ütskörd oht Noa Peiwil/ kui Kirst walmisteti/ kumman weidi (se on kattesa) Henge hoijeti Ween.	3,20 ἀπειθήσασί ποτε, ὅτε ἅπαξ ἐξεδέχετο ἡ τοῦ Θεοῦ μακροθυμία ἐν ἡμέραις Νῶε, κατασκευαζομένης κιβωτοῦ, εἰς ἣν ὀλίγαι, τουτέστιν ὀκτὼ ψυχαὶ διεσώθησαν δι' ὕδατος.	3,20 Die etwa nicht gläubeten/ da Gott einsmals harret/ und Gedult hatte/ zu den Zeiten Noe/ da man die Archa zurüstet/ in welcher wenig/ das ist/ acht Seelen behalten wurden/ durchs Wasser/

Am Anfang von 1Petr 3,20 kommt es *ussu* aus dem deutschsprachigen *nicht gläubeten*; vgl. ἀπειθήσασι Aorist Partizip aus dem Wort ἀπειθέω – *ungehorsam sein*; dagegen entspricht *kui Jummala **Pikmeel** ütskörd **oht*** dem griechischen ὅτε ἅπαξ ἐξεδέχετο ἡ τοῦ Θεοῦ μακροθυμία, vgl. *da Gott einsmals **harret**/ und **Gedult hatte**.*

4. In Bezug auf die anderen Beobachtungen möchte ich anmerken, dass es in 1Petr 3,21 Klammern gibt, die dem griechischen Text genau folgen, im lutherischen Text aber nicht vorhanden sind.

Zusammenfassung

In diesem Jahr sind 315 Jahre seit der Herausgabe des südestnischen *Wastne Testaments* vergangen. Mit Bewunderung und Dankbarkeit denke ich an die Leute aus der Vergangenheit, die Großes für die Entwicklung der estnischen Schriftsprache geleistet haben, aber auch wegen ihrer Übersetzung, da seitdem auch eine so kleine Nation nun die Heilige Schrift in ihrer Muttersprache lesen kann. An dieser Stelle möchte ich vor allem den jungen Adrian Virginius hervorheben, der damals genau so jung war, wie ein Großteil der Studenten unseres Instituts, seinen Vater Andreas Virginius und andere, die beim Übersetzen, wahrscheinlich vor allem aus der griechischen Sprache, und beim Korrigieren der Übersetzung mitgeholfen haben. Gleichermaßen möchte ich den Generalsuperintendent Johann Fischer wegen seiner Initiative und seines Vertrauens in den jungen Mann hervorheben.

Obwohl diese Untersuchung nur den Ersten Petrusbrief betrifft, kann man davon ausgehen, dass man beim Übersetzen des ganzen *Wastne Testaments* dem gleichen Muster gefolgt ist. So kann man als Zusammenfassung sagen, dass zusätzlich zur lutherischen Übersetzung auch das griechische Neue Testament als einer der Grundtexte zur Übersetzung des Neuen Testaments in die südestnische Sprache benutzt wurde.

Wenn man jetzt zurück zu den Angaben aus dem Buch von T. Paul (Paul 1999; 379) kommt, kann man sagen, dass die Meinung von Professor Christian Korholt, Fischer hätte wahrheitsgemäss aus der Ursprache übersetzt, nicht stichhaltig ist. Was mit der jetzigen Analyse im Einklang steht, ist die Version, dass der benutzte Grundtext zur Übersetzung des *Wastne Testaments* das deutschsprachige von M. Luther übersetzte Neue Testament war, und dass dabei in großen Maßen der griechische Urtext benutzt wurde, so wie es auch Johann Fischer selbst bestätigt hat. Aller Wahrscheinlichkeit nach war der zugrunde gelegte griechische Text der von Guilielmus Blaeu 1633 herausgegebene ΤΗΣ ΚΑΙΝΗΣ ΔΙΑΘΗΚΗΣ ΑΠΑΝΤΑ. Dieses Ergebnis stimmt auch mit der Behauptung überein, dass der wesentliche Übersetzer der junge, zwischen 20 und 30 Jahre alte Adrian Virginus war, von dem man auch noch keine genügenden griechischen Sprachkenntnisse erwarten konnte. Auf diesem Gebiet haben wahrscheinlich sein Vater Andreas Virginius und Johann Nicolaus von Hardung einigermaßen, vielleicht auch andere Personen ihren Beitrag geleistet.

Da die eigentliche Grundlage der Übersetzung der deutsche Text war, die der Texteinteilung aber das griechische Neue Testament, könnte man meinen, dass man ursprünglich das *Wastne Testament* aus dem Griechischen übersetzen wollte, dieser Plan aber leider nicht umgesetzt werden konnte.

Literatur- und Quellenverzeichnis

Novum Testamentum Graecè & Latinè. Des. Erasmo Roterodamo interprete. Cum summariis, concordantiis & explicationibus difficiliorum vocabulorum, & aliis in hac editione praestitis, uti ex sequenti praefatione & ipsius operis impressione apparet. – Wirebergae [Wittenberg]: Typis haeredu Seuberlichij; impensis haeredum Selfischii, 1618.

Novum Testamentum, Graecè & Latinè. Desid. Erasmo Roterodamo interprete. Cum Summariis, Concordantiis & explicationibus difficiliorum vocabulorum, & aliis in hac editione praestitis, uti ex sequenti praefatione & ipsius operis impressione apparet. – Wirebergae [Wittenberg]: Impensis Haered. Samuel Selfisch, 1635

Novum Testamentum Graecum, cum vulgata interpretatione Latina Graeci contextus lineis insertis : Quae quidem interpretatio cum a Graecarum dictionum proprietate discedit, sensum, videlicet, magis quam verba exprimens, in margine libri est collocata : atque alia Ben. Ariae Montani Hispalensis opera e verbo reddita, ac diverso characterum genere distincta, in ejus est substituta locum. Accesserunt & huic editioni Libri Graece scripti, qui vocantur Apocryphi ; cum interlineari interpretatione Latina ex Bibliis Complutensis pepromata. – Lipsiae [Leipzig] : Impensis Christiani Kirchneri ; Typis Johannis Wittigau, 1657

ΤΗΣ ΚΑΙΝΗΣ ΔΙΑΘΗΚΗΣ ΑΠΑΝΤΑ. Novum Jesu Christi Testamentum Graece, collatis non paucis venerande fidei exemplaribus, accuratiâima nunc lima editum. Additis summis rerum et sententiarum, quae singulis capitibus contienter: variis item lectionibus, mutuisq, testimoniis, quae laborem in legendo ac conferendo magnopere subleuabunt. – Basileae [Basel]: Per Nicol. Bryling, 1563

ΤΗΣ ΚΑΙΝΗΣ ΔΙΑΘΗΚΗΣ ΑΠΑΝΤΑ. Amsterdami [Amsterdam]: Apud Guiljelmum Blaeu, 1633

BIBLIA – Das ist: Die ganze Heilige Schrift/ verteutschet durch D. Martin Lutherum. Mit Churfürstl. Sächs. Auch Brannschw. Lüneburgischem PRIVILEGIO. Lüneburg/ Beŋ den Sternen. 1641

BIBLIA – Das ist/ Die ganze Heilige Schrift/ Altes und Newes Testaments Deutsch/ D. Martin. Luther. Zu Amsterdam Gedruckt und Verlegt beŋ Joachim Rosche Buchdrucker/ wohnende in der Harlemmer-Strassen/ in der Hochdeutschen Bibel. 1649.

BIBLIA – Das ist/ Die ganze H. Schrift Alten und Neuen Testaments/ Deutsch D. Martin. Luthers/ Sampt D. Hutteri Summarien/ der Biblischen Bücher und Capitel richtiger Eintheilung/ verbesserten Registern und Concirdantʒen nütʒlich zugerichtet/ und mit dem Exemplar/ so zu erst nach Lutheri Sel. Todt/ im Jahr Christi 1546. in Wittenberg gedrucket/ jetʒo mit allem Fleiß conferiret von der Theologischen Facultet zu Wittenberg/ Mit deroselben Vorrede/ Und Churfürstl. Sächs. Gnädigster Befreŋung Wittenberg/ In Verlegung Balthasas Christoph Wustens/ Buch-Druck- und Händlers in Franckfurt am Mäŋn. Im Jahr Christi M.DC.LXI

PAUL, Toomas. Eesti piiblitõlke ajalugu. Esimestest katsetest kuni 1999. aastani (Die Geschichte der estnischen Bibelübersetzung. Von den ersten Versuchen bis zum Jahr 1999) Tallinn 1999

Auf dem Wege zu neuzeitlicher Toleranz und Gewissensfreiheit
Randbemerkungen zur Frage der (Nicht)tolerierung der Täufer in der Reformationszeit

Andres Saumets, Tartu

Wir leben heute sowohl in Estland als auch in Deutschland in einer nach dem Demokratischen Prinzip geordneten Gesellschaftsordnung, zu deren Grundlagen auch verschiedene von Staat grundgesetzlich garantierte Grundrechte [1] wie z.B. Religions- und Gewissensfreiheit [2] gehören. Der demokratische und freie Staat will also diese Freiheiten schützen; sie sollen einen offenen, politischen Prozeß in der Gesellschaft ermöglichen. Eigentlich geht dies aber nur auf der Grundlage der Gleichwertigkeit aller Kräfte im Staat, die das Grundgesetz als Rahmenordnung für das menschlich-gesellschaftliche Zusammenleben vorbehaltlos akzeptieren. Insofern spricht das Grundgesetz nicht nur vom religiösen, sondern auch vom weltanschaulichen Bekenntnis. Die diversen religiösen und weltanschaulichen Bekenntnisse sind jedoch nicht staatstragend; das verbietet die normierende Redeweise von der religiösen und weltanschaulichen Neutralität des Staates. Demnach kann es in Deutschland oder in Estland weder einen "evangelischen", noch einen "katholischen", auch keinen "christlichen" oder "muslimischen" Staat geben. Die unterschiedlichen Bekenntnisse sind aber auch nicht uninteressant für Staat und Gesellschaft, sondern sind im Gegenteil Ausdruck der inneren Lebendigkeit der Gesellschaft. Was nutzt die Religionsfreiheit, wenn es

---

[1] "Grundrechte sind verfassungsrechtlich gewährleistete subjektive Rechte, die als Freiheitsrechte die individuelle Freiheitssphäre vor dem Zugriff der Staatsmacht schützen oder als Gleichheitsrechte rechtliche Gleichheit schützen.". - H. Avenarius, Kleines Rechtswörterbuch, 7. Aufl., Bonn 1992, S. 214.
   Das Grundrecht der Religionsfreiheit ist durch Art. 4 GG gewährleistet. Danach sind die Freiheit des Glaubens, des Gewissens und die Freiheit des religiösen und weltanschaulichen Bekenntnisses unverletzlich (Abs. 1); die ungestörte Religionsausübung wird garantiert (Abs. 2). Art. 4 GG schützt sowohl das religiös fundierte als auch das von einer Weltanschauung unabhängige Gewissen. - H. Avenarius, Kleines Rechtswörterbuch, 7. Aufl., Bonn 1992, S. 207.416.

[2] Die Gewährleistung voller Religionsfreiheit ist eine Grundvoraussetzung freien Geisteslebens, in das einzugreifen dem Staat verboten ist. Die Gewissensfreiheit, die in engem Zusammenhang mit der Religionsfreiheit steht, umfaßt nicht nur die Freiheit der inneren Gewissensentscheidung, sondern auch die Freiheit, diese Entscheidung nach außen zu bekunden und ihr gemäß zu handeln.

keine wachen Gemeinden oder Bekenntnisgruppen gibt, die in freier Weise ihre Religion ausüben: *free exercise and voluntary commitment?* Eine Gesellschaft, der religiöse Initiative fehlt, ist auf dem besten Weg in die Unfreiheit quasireligiöser und/oder ideologischer Establishments.[3] Die Neutralität entspringt somit weder einem Desinteresse noch einer Indifferenz des Staates gegenüber religiösen und weltanschaulichen Gruppen, sondern sie bildet den Ermöglichungsgrund sowohl für die Freiheit des Staates als auch für die Freiheit der Religionen und Weltanschauungen. Denn nur die *Neutralität* des Staates garantiert, daß dieser keinem Klerikalismus und keiner Ideologie unterliegt und ermöglicht gerade deshalb die freie und ungehinderte sowie ungezwungene religiöse und/oder weltanschauliche Entfaltung der Persönlichkeit[4]. Ein freier Staat, d.h. ein nicht-totalitärer, neutraler, für den politischen Prozeß offener, auf die religiöse und politische Mündigkeit der Bürger und deren politischer Partizipation setzender Staat wäre ein Stück unfreier ohne Religionsfreiheit, bzw. ohne freie Kirchen oder Weltanschauungsgruppen.

Dieser grundrechtlich verankerte Schutzbereich ist das Ergebnis eines historischen, aber keineswegs linearen und kontinuierlichen Prozesses, der im Abendland in der frühen Neuzeit deutlich bemerkbar einsetzt und sich seit dem ausgehenden 18. Jahrhundert beschleunigt. Mit der Einleitungsphase der Neuzeit steht aber im strukturellen Zusammenhang die Reformation. Bedingend für die Neuzeit wurde die Reformation u.a. auch durch Ein- und Auswirkungen des kirchlich-religiösen Phänomens Reformation auf alle gesellschaftlichen Bereiche.[5] So interessiert uns bezüglich dieser Ausführungen vor allem die Frage: gibt es unter den demokratischen Grundkategorien unserer Gegenwart Phänomene, die historisch begründet mit der Reformation und deren Auswirkungen in Verbindung gebracht und als unverändert gültig bewertet werden können? In diesem Sinne bietet sich unter unmittelbarer Bezugnahme auf den Speyerer Reichstag von 1529 das Problem der *Gewissensfreiheit* an, das Fragen nach Religionsfreiheit sowie generell nach *Toleranz* einbezieht[6].

Nach Helmut Burkhardt ist Toleranz als Aushalten der Spannung, die durch das Anderssein anderer Menschen in Denken, Wollen und Empfinden entsteht, eine soziale Tugend, die überall unumgänglich nötig ist, wo Menschen zusam-

---

[3] E. Geldbach, Religion und Politik: Religious Liberty, in: Gott und Politik in USA, hg. von K.-M. Kodalle, Frankfurt a.M., 1988, S. 238.

[4] Die menschliche Freiheit ist durch Art. 2 GG als Grundrecht gewährleistet: Jeder hat das Recht auf die freie Entfaltung seiner Persönlichkeit (Abs. 1). - H. Avenarius, Kleines Rechtswörterbuch, 7. Aufl., Bonn 1992, S. 170.

[5] Vgl. R. Wohlfeil, Bedingungen der Neuzeit, in: Gewissensfreiheit als Bedingung der Neuzeit. Bensheimer Hefte 54, Göttingen 1980, S. 7-24.

[6] In diesen Ausführungen beschränkt sich der Begriff 'Toleranz' auf die christliche Tradition und auf die abendländische Entwicklung, und zwar deswegen, weil im Abendland in der frühen Neuzeit sich eine Situation ergeben hat, die für die Entwicklung der Toleranzgedanken eine besondere Herausforderung bedeutete.

menleben [7]. In der Religionsgeschichte begegnen wir zwei verschiedenen Arten der Toleranz und ihres Gegenteils: die *formale* und die *inhaltliche* Toleranz und Intoleranz. Erstere meint das bloße Unangetastetlassen fremder Religion und (Glaubens-)Praxis. Vom tolerierten Objekt aus spricht man dann von Glaubens- oder Religionsfreiheit. Die formale Intoleranz zwingt die Bekenner fremden Glaubens zur Unterwerfung unter eine sakrale Institution des Staates oder einer Kirche, bzw. einer Konfession, deren formale Einheit durch abweichenden Glauben und Kultus gestört werden würde. Die inhaltliche Toleranz beschränkt sich nicht auf bloße Duldung, sondern ist darüber hinaus die positive Anerkennung fremder Religion als echter Möglichkeit der Begegnung mit dem Heiligen. [8]

Der exklusive Wahrheitsanspruch der sog. Universalreligionen, zu denen auch das Christentum gehört, führt zumeist zur Intoleranz im formalen und auch inhaltlichen Sinne und in extremen Formen sogar zum Fanatismus. In der Geschichte des Christentums hat sich der Toleranzgedanke erst im Übergang vom Mittelalter zur Neuzeit herausgebildet. Obgleich das Christentum dem Römischen Reich gegenüber für sich selbst Toleranz forderte und schließlich durchsetzte, blieb das Christentum im Verhältnis zu Andersgläubigen und Häretikern trotz pragmatischen Regelungen weitgehend intolerant und gewalttätig [9]. Die Häresie galt als krimineller Akt. Bezüglich der im allgemeinen feh-

---

[7] H. Burkhardt, Art. Toleranz, in: Evangelisches Lexikon für Theologie und Gemeinde, Bd. III, hg. von H. Burkhardt und U. Swarat, Wuppertal und Zürich 1994, S. 2018. Toleranz ist nicht zu verwechseln mit Gleichgültigkeit in der Wahrheitsfrage.

[8] G. Mensching, Art. Toleranz, I. Religionsgeschichtlich, in: Die Religion in Geschichte und Gegenwart, Bd. VI, 3. Aufl., hg. von K. Galling, Tübingen 1986, S. 932f.
Es gibt aber auch andere Vorschläge zur Typisierung: 1) die pragmatische Toleranz; 2) die Konsensus-Toleranz; 3) die dialogische Toleranz. Vgl. E. Stöve, Art. Toleranz. I. Kirchengeschichtlich, in: Theologische Realenzyklopädie, Bd. XXXIII, hg. von G. Müller, Berlin 2002, S. 647.

[9] Vgl. M. Hengel, Christus und die Macht. Zur Problematik einer "Politischen Theologie" in der Geschichte der Kirche. Stuttgart 1974, besonders S. 46-60. Hengel stellt fest: "Daß der *eine* Gott, das *eine* Reich und der *eine* Herrscher dann auch zu *einem* Glauben und *einer* Kirche hindrängten, war auf Grund dieser neuen "christianisierten" Herrschaftsideologie nur zu verständlich. Daß die Christen einst selbst gegenüber der Staatsräson um Toleranz gebeten hatten, vergaß man leider gar zu schnell." (a.a.O., S. 55f). Das Profil von Toleranz im Christentum ist durch zwei Tendenzen gekennzeichnet: Einerseits wird Glaubenszwang gegenüber Nichtchristen abgelehnt (nicht immer konsequent), andererseits werden Häretiker in den eigenen Reihen unerbittlich verfolgt. Ein klassisches Beispiel dafür ist Konstantins Häretikergesetz aus der Zeit um 326: "Was sollen wir also länger solche Frevel [ihr Novatianer, Valentianer, Markionisten, Paulianer, Kataphryger] dulden? Unsere lange Nachsicht bewirkt ja nur, daß auch die Gesunden wie von einer pestartigen Krankheit befallen werden. Warum also nicht durch öffentlich bewiesene Strenge so rasch wie möglich dieses große Übel sozusagen mit den Wurzeln ausrotten?" Zitiert nach A. M. Ritter, Alte Kirche. Kirchen- und Theologiegeschichte in Quellen, Bd. I, 5. Aufl., hg. von H. A. Oberman u.a., Neukirchen-Vluyn 1991, S. 139.

lenden Toleranz bestimmt eine starke Interdependenz von kirchlicher und weltlicher Herrschaft das Mittelalter. Kaiser Friedrich II. z. B. erklärt Häretiker zu Staatsfeinden (*Liber Augustalis*, 1231) [10], Päpste Gregor IX. (1231) und Innozenz IV. (1252) sanktionieren und verbreiten seine Ketzergesetze [11]; es entsteht ein wirkungsvolles und monolithisch christliches Rechtsganzes. Thomas von Aquin unterscheidet Unglauben, Häresie und Abfall. Die Ungläubigen dürfen nicht zum Glauben gezwungen werden, denn *credere voluntatis est*. Der Kult der Ungläubigen, z. B. der Juden, kann toleriert werden, wenn ihre Zahl groß ist; Häretiker dagegen sind mit dem Tode zu bestrafen. Die Häresie ist gesteigerte Falschmünzerei, also ein Majestätsdelikt; die Häretiker verbreiten einen Infekt, der die Seele verdirbt [12]. Die Rezeption griechischer und arabischer Philosophie brachte in die scholastische Theologie einige Elemente der Konsensus-Toleranz [13], die in der Mitte des 15. Jahrhunderts einen Höhepunkt in Nikolaus von Kues' religionsphilosophischen Schrift *De pace fidei* (1453) findet. Er hat der Idee der Konsensus-Toleranz eine konkrete Formulierung gegeben: Einheit der Religionen bei Verschiedenheit der Riten (*religio una in rituum varietate*) [14]; aber das Häretikerproblem blieb von diesen Gedanken unberührt.

---

[10] "...ordnen wir zuerst an, daß man das Verbrechen der Häresie... unter die Staatsverbrechen zähle. Denn wahrhaftig muß von allen ein Verbrechen gegen unsere Majestät besonders abschreckend bestraft werden, weil ein solches Attentat als Verletzung der Majestät Gottes zu gelten hat... Denn wie das Verbrechen des Hochverrates Personen und Besitz der Bestraften trifft und auch noch das Andenken der Toten nach ihrem Hinscheiden verflucht, so wollen wir auch, daß bei dem eben erwähnten Verbrechen...es allerwege gehalten werde... Niemand soll es wagen, bei uns für derartige [Verbrechen] Fürsprache einzulegen; wir werden gegen jeden, der so handelt, die Schärfe unserer wohlverdienten Ungnade richten." Zitiert nach R. Mokrosch/ H. Walz, Mittelalter. Kirchen- und Theologiegeschichte in Quellen, Bd. II, 4. Aufl., hg. von H. A. Oberman u.a., Neukirchen-Vluyn 2001, S. 160f.

[11] Vgl. M. Lambert, Ketzerei im Mittelalter. Häresie von Bogumil bis Hus, Augsburg 2001, S. 145-164.

[12] Vgl. H. Bornkamm, Art. Toleranz II. In der Geschichte des Christentums, in: Die Religion in Geschichte und Gegenwart, Bd. VI, 3. Aufl., hg. von K. Galling, Tübingen 1986, S. 935.

[13] Sie sucht nach Übereinstimmung im Kernbereich, um die nicht vergleichbaren Punkte (in der äußeren Ausprägung) als sekundär oder äußerlich zu entschärfen.

[14] Nach seiner Anschauung haben Christentum, Judentum und Islam einen Kernbestand gemeinsamer Überzeugungen, auch wenn die jeweilige Frömmigkeitspraxis ganz unterschiedlich ausfällt. Aber der gemeinsame Kernbestand ist (natürlich!) ganz aus der Sicht des christlichen Dogmas formuliert. Für Nikolaus sind Trinität, Inkarnation, Rechtfertigung unaufgebbare Glaubenswahrheiten, und die eine, wahre Religion ist im Christentum allerdings in vollkommenster Weise enthalten. Nikolaus scheint ein System einzuleiten, das die Humanisten später verkünden werden: Die Union der Kirchen und der Sekten ungeachtet ihrer Verschiedenheiten auf der Grundlage einiger großer gemeinsamer Wahrheiten, einiger "fundamentaler Artikel". Er strebt es jedoch weniger als ein zu schließendes "Konkordat" an, sondern als ein Ideal, dem es ohne Unterlaß zu folgen

Eine deutliche Wende im Verständnis der Toleranz bahnt sich erst im 16. Jahrhundert mit der Reformation und mit dem Humanismus an [15]. Die Reformation als in erster Linie kirchengeschichtliche Bewegung [16] resulierte in gemeineuropäisch geschichtlicher Komplexität: 1) aus vorangegangenen geistig-geistlichen, kirchlich-religiösen und politisch-sozialen Auseinandersetzungen und daraus erwachsenen Erneuerungshoffnungen; 2) aus der Polarität zwischen tiefer christlicher Verwurzelung in den bewußtseinsbestimmenden Glauben und dem Unbefriedigtsein mit den überlieferten Formen der Heilsvermittlung; 3) aus der Spannung zwischen dem Ideal eines gut christlichen Lebens aller Mitglieder des *Corpus Christianum* und deren Verhaltensweise im konkreten Geschehen mit der daraus sich ergebenen Forderung nach Reform von Sitten und Moral. Aus der unterschiedlichen Rezeption des individuellen Denkens, ureigenen Wollens und konkreten Wirkens Luthers und anderer Reformatoren - zu denen auch die führenden Denker der verschiedenen Täuferbewegungen gehören - ergab sich die Mannigfaltigkeit ihrer direkten und mittelbaren, beabsichtigten und unerwünschten Anstöße und Wirkungen mit ihren Folgerungen auf allen gesellschaftlichen Ebenen. [17]

Das Christentum ist in seiner Geschichte immer wieder vor die doppelte Aufgabe gestellt worden, Toleranz zu erringen und Toleranz zu gewähren. So befand sich auch die Reformation in der gleichen Situation: Sie mußte Toleranz fordern und wurde bald gefragt, ob sie selbst sie gewähren wollte. In seiner berühmten Adelsschrift (1520) hat Luther verlangt: *"So sollte man die Ketzer mit Schriften, nicht mit Feuer überwinden, wie die alten Väter getan haben. Wenn es eine Wissenschaft wäre, mit Feuer Ketzer zu überwinden, dann wären die Henker die gelehrtesten Doktoren auf Erden, dann brauchten auch wir nicht mehr zu studieren, sondern wen den andern mit Gewalt überwände, könnte ihn*

---

gilt, sei es auch hienieden nicht zu erreichen. - H. G. Senger, Nikolaus von Kues. In: Gestalten der Kirchengeschichte, Bd. IV, Stuttgart 1993, S. 291, vgl. auch J. Lecler, Geschichte der Religionsfreiheit im Zeitalter der Reformation, Bd. I, S. 181f.

[15] Freilich bringt die frühe Neuzeit noch keine Duldung in modernem Sinne, aber es zeigen sich die ersten Ansätze zu ihr. Einerseits versagen die traditionellen Mechanismen der Einheitsstiftung, andererseits ist Religion immer noch ein öffentliches Gut und noch nicht als Religionsfreiheit, wie in den modernen Verfassungen, privatisiert. Weil der Staat den christlichen Glauben als die eine und wahre Religion betrachtet, gewährt er keine Religionsfreiheit; es besteht "Staatszwangskirchentum". Die Kirche ihrerseits bedient sich des weltlichen Armes, um abweichende religiöse Auffassungen zu bekämpfen. - R. P. de Mortanges, Art. Religionsfreiheit, in: Theologische Realenzyklopädie, Bd. XXVIII, hg. von G. Müller, Berlin 1997, S. 565f.

[16] "Reformation (lat.) 'Wiederherstellung'; die kirchengeschichtliche Bewegung, die gegen die Mißstände in kirchlicher Lehre und Praxis des Spätmittelalters die Erneuerung der Kirche von ihrer Grundlage, der Heiligen Schrift... her betrieb." - J. Hanselmann u.a. (Hg.), Fachwörterbuch Theologie, Wuppertal 1987, S. 145f.

[17] R. Wohlfeil, a.a.O., S. 16f.

verbrennen." [18] Luther löste sich von der für das mittelalterliche Ketzerstrafrecht gundlegenden Auffassung der Häresie als Mord an den Seelen. Er konnte anerkennen, daß auch die Irrgläubigen und Schwärmer nach ihrem Gewissen handeln und deshalb nicht durch Gewalt, sondern durch die Heilige Schrift zu überwinden seien. *"Denn Ketzerei kann man nimmermehr mit Gewalt abwehren. Es gehört ein anderer Griff dazu, und es ist hier ein anderer Streit und Handel als mit dem Schwert. Gottes Wort soll hier streiten... Ketzerei ist ein geistliches Ding, das kann man mit keinem Eisen zerhauen, mit keinem Feuer verbrennen, mit keinem Wasser ertränken. Es ist aber allein das Gotteswort da, das tut's..."*, sagt Luther in seiner Schrift *Von weltlicher Obrigkeit* (1523) [19]. Die unerzwingbare Freiheit des Glaubens, die Natur des Gotteswortes und die Trennung des Geistlichen vom Weltlichen (Zwei-Reiche-Lehre) machen bei Luther dem kirchlichen Inquisitionsverfahren und der staatlichen Verfolgung *ketzerischer Lehre* ein Ende [20]. Wie weit Luther aber damit noch von einem politisch-rechtlichen Verständnis der Toleranz entfernt war, zeigt der Umstand, daß er unter dem Eindruck der - mit dem Auftreten der Täufer verbundenen - Unruhen die politische Gewalt zu unnachsichtigem Eingreifen aufforderte. E. Stöve stellt fest, daß die reformatorische Theologie, ob in Wittenberg oder in Zürich, ihren Glaubenssubjektivismus mit politischem Konservatismus verbunden hat. Diese Verbindung brachte es mit sich, daß der sog. "linke Flügel" der Reformation aus dem neu sich bildenden protestantischen Kirchenwesen ausgeschieden und die anfangs Verfolgten dann selber zu Verfolgern wurden [21].

Luther ging von einer empirisch begründeten Sorge vor der Zerstörung der staatlichen Ordnung durch Zwiespalt in Lehre und Gottesdienst aus. Die *politische Gefahr der Ketzerei* reichte für Luther über die entstehende Unruhe bis in den Bereich des Zornes Gottes über ein Land, in dem die Blasphemie der Messe, Synagoge oder schwärmerischen bzw. täuferischen Predigt zugelassen wird. Die Obrigkeit muß hier um des Landes willen Ordnung schaffen, nicht um des Evangeliums willen, das keinen Schutz braucht. Nach Luthers Auffassung sollte der evangelische Fürst einer dreifachen Rolle für die Ausbreitung und Organisation des Evangeliums gegenüberstehen: 1) nach besten Kräften die Predigt der Schrift zu begünstigen; 2) die Predigt falscher und häretischer Lehrer zu verhindern und gleichzeitig alles zu unterdrücken, was von außen der Ehre Gottes abträglich sein konnte; 3) Sorge zu tragen, daß alle das wahre Wort Gottes hören und sie notfalls dazu zu zwingen. Diese Vorschriften griffen nach Luthers Meinung die Glaubensfreiheit in keiner Weise an! [22]

---

[18] WA 6, 455, 21f; zitiert nach: Martin Luther. Ausgewählte Schriften, Bd. I, hg. von K. Bornkamm und G. Ebeling, 2. Aufl., Frankfurt a.M., 1982, S. 221.

[19] WA 11, 268, 22ff, zitiert nach: Martin Luther. Ausgewählte Schriften, Bd. IV, hg. von K. Bornkamm und G. Ebeling, 2. Aufl., Frankfurt a.M., 1982, S. 69.

[20] H. Bornkamm, a.a.O., S. 937.

[21] E. Stöve, a.a.O., S. 652.

[22] J. Lecler, a.a.O., S. 241.

Unter allen Reformatoren hat sich Luther am ausführlichsten mit der Frage des Gewissens und der Gewissensfreiheit beschäftigt. Gewissensfreiheit ist nach Luthers bzw. nach reformatorischer Auffassung nichts anderes als die Umschreibung des erkennenden und vertrauenden Glaubensverhältnisses zu Gott, das durch sein befreiendes Wort im Evangelium konstituiert wird [23]. Wir müssen also merken, daß Luther die Freiheit des Gewissens keinesfalls als allgemeines Recht des Einzelnen im Sinne von Religionsfreiheit, also zu glauben und eine Religion zu leben ohne jedweden äußeren Zwang, sondern ausschließlich als Befreiung des Gewissens durch das Evangelium als einziger objektiver Wahrheit verstanden hat. Durch das Wort Gottes blieb das Gewissen jedoch "gefangen", also fest gebunden an die Bibel als seine einzige Autorität. In diesem Sinne berufen sich die protestierenden Reichsstände 1529 in Speyer auf das Gewissen; keineswegs verstanden sie in Übereinstimmung mit Luther unter dessen Forderung nach Gewissensfreiheit das Recht ihrer Untertanen als Individuen auf ein persönliches Gewissen oder ein zumindest eigenverantwortliches religiöses Leben jedweden Glaubens. Grundlage der Gewissensfreiheit bildet für Luther und für die evangelisch-lutherischen Reichsstände nur das Evangelium im Verständnis des Reformators, jede Berufung auf ein anderes wies Luther als "erdichtetes Gewissen" ab und stritt damit grundsätzlich gegen die Auffassung von Katholiken und Anhängern reformatorischer Bewegungen, die sich von ihm emanzipiert hatten, sich auf ihr Gewissen zu berufen. [24] Luther verlangte also nicht die Anerkennung seiner subjektiven Gewissensentscheidung als solcher, sondern die Anerkennung seiner exegetisch und vernünftig begründeten Entscheidung, an die er sich im Gewissen gebunden fühlt, solange er nicht eines Besseren belehrt wird.

Die Reformation ist im Ansatz eine sowohl kirchenzerstörende als auch kirchenbegründende und in der Folge eine neue Linie der Weltgeschichte mitbegründende Theologiereform [25]. Die neue Bibeltheologie Luthers führte sogleich zur Entstehung einer Mehrzahl gleichgerichteter, doch nicht identischer reformatorischer Theologien, so daß man von einem neuen reformatorischen Typus der Theologie reden kann, der in sich wiederum Variationen und Gegensätze auch kirchenbildender Art enthält. Die Theologien des Schweizers Zwingli und des Franzosen Calvin begründen eine eigene Form protestantischer Kirchenbildung. Sie haben mit der Theologie Luthers und vieler anderen Reformatoren unter anderem gemeinsam, daß sie die mittelalterliche Wirklichkeit einer Gesamtchristenheit der getauften und der sich zum Christentum bekennenden Herrschaftsgewalt akzeptieren und nur von innen neu gestalten wollen. Daneben stehen, ebenfalls biblisch begründete Gemeinschaftsbildungen, die sich nur an

---

[23] Fr. Krüger, Art. Gewissen III, in: Theologische Realenzyklopädie, Bd. XIII, hg. von G. Müller, Berlin 1984, S. 222ff.

[24] R. Wohlfeil, a.a.O., S. 19.

[25] Vgl. K.-V. Selge, Einführung in das Studium der Kirchengeschichte, Darmstadt 1982, S. 118ff.

den einzelnen wenden und die christliche Gesamtgesellschaft, ja die christliche Obrigkeit als eine echte Möglichkeit zum Teil ablehnen [26]. Nach Hans-Jürgen Goertz waren die polygenetisch entstandenen täuferischen Bewegungen, die ihr gemeinsames Merkmal in der Praxis der Glaubens- und Bekenntnistaufe und in der Bemühung um Wiederherstellung des "wahren Christentums" hatten, "weder katholisch noch protestantisch", sondern eine deutliche *Alternative* zu beiden großen Kirchen [27]. Eine erneuerte Christenheit konnten sie sich nur als eine radikale Alternative zur bestehenden Kirche und Gesellschaft vorstellen. Die Verweigerung der Kindertaufe und die Durchführung der Glaubenstaufe, der Ruf in die Nachfolge Jesu Christi, das Modell der separatistischen Gemeinschaft: all das sind kirchen- und gesellschaftskritische Ausdrucksformen eines alternativen Christentums. Mit ihren Alternativen brachten die Täufer eine Unruhe in die geistlich-weltlichen Mischformen des Corpus Christianum [28]. Der Bruch mit der verfassten Kirche, die massive Kritik an der gesellschaftlichen Situation der Zeit und ihr Eintreten für eine "gesamtgesellschaftliche Erneuerung der Christenheit" weist den Täufern ihren eigenen Ort in der Reformationsgeschichte zu [29]. Die Täufer reihten sich in die "radikale Reformation" ein, die eine Überwindung der gesellschaftlichen Grundordnung des 16. Jahrhunderts anstrebte und in den Unruhen "des gemeinen Mannes" von 1525 ihren prägnantesten Ausdruck fand [30]. Demzufolge waren die Täufer Reformer, die ihre Radikalität aus dem antiklerikalen Milieu der frühen Reformationsjahre bezogen und von ihrer Vision einer besseren Kirche und Gesellschaft nicht lassen wollten. Sie wollten die Welt und die Obrigkeit nicht dämonisieren. Aber wer nach dem Gesetz der Welt lebte, konnte ihrer Meinung nach das Gesetz Christi nicht

---

[26] Als eigenen reformatorischen Typus, der an der Wurzel des Umbruchs zur Neuzeit 150 Jahre später stehe, hat einst Ernst Troeltsch in seinem bedeutenden Buch *Die Soziallehren der christlichen Kirchen und Gruppen* (Tübingen 1912) diese von ihm vor allem als "Täufer" angesehenen Gruppen ins Licht gestellt.

[27] H.-J. Goertz, Die Täufer. Geschichte und Deutung, Berlin 1988, S. 14. Vgl. auch J. Stayer, W. Packull, K. Deppermann, From Monogenesis to Polygenesis: The Historical Discussion of Anabaptist Origins, in: Mennonite Quarterly Review 49, Goshen 1975

[28] Die Gläubigentaufe wurde zum Signal für die Auflösung und Beendigung des allgemein anerkannten, durch ihre Praxis als Säuglingstaufe herbeigeführten Verstehens- und Lebenszusammenhanges von Kirche als alle Menschen umfassendem Leib Christi, als *Corpus Christianum*.

[29] "...die bedeutendste Seitenbewegung der Reformation, die abseits der großen Konfessionen bis in die Gegenwart fortlebt...", so Johannes Wallmann, Kirchengeschichte Deutschlands seit der Reformation, 5. Aufl., Tübingen 2000, S. 51.

[30] Luther erschienen die Täufer im steigenden Maße nicht nur als Ketzer, sondern wie Müntzers Wirkung im Bauernkrieg erwiesen hatte, als Aufrührer, obwohl sich die täuferische Bewegung als ganzes von der Müntzerischen Utopie wegbewegt hatte. Luther warnte immer davor, die Welt mit dem Evangelium regieren zu wollen. Ein gewaltsamer Aufstand mußte Luther schädlich erscheinen auch wegen der Diskreditierung der Reformation, die Luther für die weitaus wichtigste Sache auf dieser Welt hielt.

erfüllen. Dieser die reformatorische Zwei-Reiche-Lehre ablehnende Dualismus von Welt und Gemeinde findet sich sowohl bei den von Zürich ausgehenden oberdeutschen Täufern wie bei den anderen großen, in der Folgezeit sich bildenden Täufergruppen, den Hutterischen Brüdern und den Mennoniten. Man vertraut darauf, daß Gott Leute bestellt, die die Welt leiten und für Ruhe und Sicherheit der großen Menge sorgen. Sich selbst weiß man berufen, Gottes Wort ohne Abstriche zu befolgen, die unverfälschte Taufe zu vollziehen und das Abendmahl als Gemeinschaftsmahl in brüderlicher Liebe zu feiern, sich von den Bösen durch den Bann zu trennen und ein durch selbstgewählte Laienprediger geordnetes Gemeindeleben zu führen. Die auf der Kindertaufe gegründete Volkskirche ist für die Täufer ein fauler, dem Evangelium widersprechender und mit dem Verlust der Wahrheit erkaufter Kompromiss mit der Welt. *"Es ist viel besser"*, so Konrad Grebel, einer der Begründern des Täufertums in Zürich, *"wenn wenige durch das Wort Gottes recht unterrichtet werden, recht glauben und in rechten Tugenden und Bräuchen wandeln, als wenn viele durch verfälschte Lehren einen falschen und trügerischen Glauben haben."* [31]

Der schon oben genannte Zweite Speyerer Reichstag von 1529 ist in die Geschichte gegangen als *"Geburtsstunde des Protestantismus"* und ein Meilenstein auf dem Wege zu neuzeitlicher Gewissensfreiheit. Er ist aber auch eine Wegmarke in der Geschichte der Intoleranz gegenüber Andersgläubigen und Nonkonformisten, sofern diese ohne politischen Einfluß waren. Mit dem Speyerer Reichstag wurde also die Sterbestunde des Täufertums eingeläutet. [32] Das Wiedertäufermandat wurde einmütig sowohl von Katholischen und als auch von Evangelischen zum Reichsgesetz erhoben und dem Reichsabschied einverleibt [33]. Begründet werden Straftat und Strafmaß mit dem Hinweis auf den *Codex Justinianus* aus dem 6. Jahrhundert, in dem die Ketzerei der Manichäer und Donatisten, auch die dort geübte Praxis der Wiedertaufe, unter die Todes-

---

[31] Zitiert nach J. Wallmann, a.a.O., S. 52.

[32] H.-J. Goertz, a.a.O., S. 121.

[33] (1) Wer wiedertauft oder sich der Wiedertaufe unterzogen hat, ob Mann oder Frau, ist mit dem Tode zu bestrafen, ohne daß vorher noch ein geistliches Inquisitionsgericht tätig zu werden braucht. (2) Wer sein Bekenntnis zu den Wiedertäufern widerruft und bereit ist, für seinen Irrtum zu sühnen, soll begnadigt werden. Er darf jedoch nicht Gelegenheit erhalten, sich durch Ausweisung in ein anderes Territorium einer ständigen Aufsicht zu entziehen und eventuell rückfällig zu werden. Die hartnäckig auf der Lehre der Täufer Beharrenden werden mit dem Tode bestraft. (3) Wer die Wiedertäufer anführt oder für deren Verbreitung sorgt (Fürprediger, Hauptsacher, Landlaufer und die aufrührerischen Aufwiegler) soll "keineswegs", also auch bei Widerruf nicht, begnadigt werden. (4) Wer nach einem ersten Widerruf rückfällig geworden ist und abermals widerruft, soll nicht mehr begnadigt werden. Ihn trifft die volle Strafe. (5) Wer die Taufe für seine neugeborenen Kinder verweigert, fällt ebenfalls unter die Strafe, die auf Wiedertaufe steht. (6) Wer von den Täufern in ein anderes Territorium entwichen ist, soll dort verfolgt und der Bestrafung zugeführt werden. (7) Wer von den Amtspersonen nicht bereit ist, nach diesen Anordnungen streng zu verfahren, muß mit kaiserlicher Ungnade und schwerer Strafe rechnen. Zitiert nach H.-J. Goertz, a.a.O., S. 121f.

strafe gestellt worden war [34]. Bei der Modernisierung des Rechts auf der Grundlage des römischen Rechts im 16. Jahrhundert hat dieser Tatbestand ein trauriges und blutiges Nachspiel erfahren. Das Delikt ist eine kultische Handlung, und Delikt ist zugleich die Wirkung, die davon ausgeht: Unfriede und Uneinigkeit im Reich. Der Kaiser erläßt das Mandat, um *"fried und einigkeit im heiligen reich zu erhalten."* [35] Diese Bestimmungen sollen die Rechtspraxis auf Reichsebene vereinheitlichen und vereinfachen. Erneuert und erweitert wurde dieses Mandat noch auf den Reichstagen von 1544 und 1551.

Das Speyerer Mandat hat eine Vorgeschichte. Das erste Mandat gegen die Täufer wurde am 7. März 1526 in Zürich erlassen [36]. Die eidgenössische Schweiz war übrigens ein Ursprungsland des Täufertums, und Zürcher Täuferbewegung entstand in einem Bibelkreis um den dortigen Reformator Huldrych Zwingli. Da sie die Kindertaufe ablehnten und seit Januar 1525 die (Wieder)taufe an Erwachsenen vollzogen, blieben die Verfolgungen nicht aus. Zwingli selbst mußte seine früheren Freunde bekämpfen. Die Obrigkeiten duldeten die Trennung von der kirchlich-bürgerlichen Gemeinde, welche immer noch eine Einheit bildete, nicht. Das Mandat bildete die rechtliche Grundlage für das Todesurteil; im Januar 1527 wurde Felix Manz als erster Täufer vom Zürcher Rat zum Tode verurteilt und in der Limmat ertränkt. Der Zürcher Rat zog es vor, das rigorose Urteil mit dem Verstoß gegen bürgerliche Gesetze begründen zu lassen [37]. Zwinglis Kommentar zu diesem Mandat lautete so: *"...wer sich von jetzt an noch taufen lasse, der werde ganz untergetaucht; das Urteil ist schon gefällt."* [38] Damit begann die erschütternde Leidensgeschichte der Täufer [39], an denen sich das Wort von der fortzeugenden Kraft des Märtyrerbluts

---

[34] Vgl. R. Bainton, David Joris, in: Archiv für Reformationsgeschichte, Ergänzungsband VI, Leipzig 1937, S. 11: "Zwingli bestand auf der beschimpfenden Benennung ("Anabaptistici", d.h. Wiedertäufer), um die Radikalen unter die Reichsgesetze zu bringen, welche den alten Donatisten Todesstrafe auferlegte (sic!), weil sie Konvertiten von der katholischen Kirche wiedertaufen."

[35] Zitiert nach H.-J. Goertz, a.a.O., S. 122.

[36] H.-J. Goertz, a.a.O., S. 123.

[37] Aus dem Mandat des Zürcher Rates gegen die Täufer: "...einige von ihnen aber ganz uneinsichtig und entgegen ihren Eiden, Gelübden und Versprechungen bei ihrer Meinung geblieben sind und sich gegenüber dem obrigkeitlichen Regiment mit nachteiligen und zerstörerischen Folgen für den gemeinen Nutzen und das christliche Wesen als ungehorsam erwiesen haben...", zitiert nach H.-J. Goertz, a.a.O., S. 194.

[38] Zitiert nach H.-J. Goertz, a.a.O., S. 123.

[39] Über die Todesarten der Täufer im Geschichtsbuch der Hutterer: "Einige hat man gereckt und gestreckt, so daß die Sonne durch sie hindurchscheinen konnte, einige sind an der Folter zerrissen und gestorben, einige sind zu Asche und Pulver als Ketzer verbrannt worden, einige an Säulen gebraten worden, einige mit glühenden Zangen gerissen, einige in Häusern eingesperrt und alles miteinander verbrannt worden, einige an Bäumen aufgehängt, einige mit dem Schwert hingerichtet, erwürgt und zerhauen worden. Vielen sind Knebel in den Mund gesteckt und die Zunge gebunden worden, damit sie nicht

bewahrheiten soll [40]: nach wenigen Jahren gab es in und außerhalb der Schweiz vielerorts Täufergemeinden, die Bewegung war nicht aufzuhalten und breitete sich überall aus. Im habsburgischen Österreich wurde gegen alle Reformbewegungen, vor allem aber gegen die *"new erschrockenlich unerhört leren"* der Täufer, auf der Rechtsgrundlage des Wormser Edikts vorgegangen. Das erste österreichische Mandat, das sich speziell gegen die Täufer wendet, wurde im Oktober 1527 erlassen. In diesem wurde gesagt, daß von diesen Ketzern nicht nur die christliche Einheit in Mitleidenschaft gezogen werde, sondern daß von ihnen auch *"widerwillen, auffruer, abfallung der obrigkeit und besunderung des gemain mans"* ausgehen könne [41]. So tritt allmählich neben den Ketzervorwurf auch der Vorwurf des *Aufruhrs*. Am 4. Januar 1528 wird schließlich ein kaiserliches Mandat in Speyer erlassen. Es wird gesagt, daß nach geistlichem und weltlichem Recht die Todesstrafe auf Wiedertaufe steht und daß die Wiedertäufer den Umsturz und die Abschaffung der Obrigkeiten im Schilde führten. Dieses Mandat ist das erste auf Reichsebene und der unmittelbare Vorläufer des Wiedertäufermandats von 1529. [42]

Die Beratungen der beiden gegenüber feindlich gesinnten Religionsparteien, die auf dem Reichstag zu dem Wiedertäufermandat geführt haben, scheinen unproblematisch zu sein. Hans-Jürgen Goertz hat versucht, das zu erklären [43]. Mit ihrer Zustimmung zu einem strengen Wiedertäufermandat konnten die evangelischen Stände *erstens* den Ketzervorwurf von sich auf die Täufer ablenken und zeigen, wie widersinnig es sei, die Erneuerung des Wormser Edikts zu betreiben, um Ruhe und Frieden im Reich zu gewährleisten. Dieses Ziel ist nicht mit dem Wormser Edikt, sondern mit einem Wiedertäufermandat zu erreichen. *Zweitens* konnten sie unterstreichen, wie abwegig es sei, den Konsens des Ersten Speyerer Reichstags von 1526 aufs Spiel zu setzen, der gefunden worden war, um Aufruhr und Empörung des gemeinen Mannes zu beseitigen. Nicht die Anhänger des neuen Glaubens, d.h. die Evangelischen, sondern die "aufrührerischen" Täufer seien die wahren Feinde des Reichs und der Christenheit, gegen die mit aller Entschiedenheit *gemeinsam* vorgegangen werden müsse. Und *drittens* ließen sich auch die evangelischen Stände gern von einem Reichstag indirekt bestätigen, daß die geistlich-kirchliche Jurisdiktion eine Angelegenheit der weltlichen Gewalt ist. Wenn es die Aufgabe der Obrigkeit sei, auf Ketzerei zu befinden, dann, so müßte man schließen, konnte diese Obrigkeit doch selber nur orthodox sein.

---

reden und sich verantworten konnten. So sind sie zu Tode geführt worden... Wie die Lämmer führte man sie oft haufenweise zur Schlachtbank und ermordete sie nach des Teufels Art und Natur..." - Zitiert nach H.-J. Goertz, a.a.O., S. 197.

[40] Der Graf von Alzey in der Pfalz soll, nachdem er ca. 350 Täufer hinrichten ließ, ausgerufen haben: "Was soll ich bloß tun? Je mehr ich töte, desto größer wird ihre Zahl." - Zitiert nach G. Wehr, Reformation der Täufer, in: Die Kommenden, 25.11.1983.

[41] Zitiert nach H.-J. Goertz, a.a.O., S. 124.

[42] H.-J. Goertz, a.a.O., 125f.

[43] A.a.O., S. 127f.

Auf das Reichsgesetz gegen die Täufer wurde in den einzelnen Territorien und Städten unterschiedlich reagiert, obwohl es von allen Ständen einmütig beschlossen worden war. [44] Es ist bemerkenswert, daß dieses Mandat in aller Härte eben in Kursachsen, dem Unsprungsland der Reformation, durchgeführt wurde. Noch 1528 ließ Luther nur das Exil, die Ausweisung aus dem Territorium zu; dennoch machte bei den deutschen Führern der Reformation bald der Gedanke der Todesstrafe seinen Weg. 1530 schreibt Melanchthon, dessen Versöhnungsbereitschaft sonst allgemein bekannt war, in einem Brief an Myconius: *"Ich finde, daß jeder, der ausgesprochen lästerliche, wenn auch nicht aufrührerische, Artikel verteidigt, durch die zivile Autorität zum Tode geführt werden sollte"* [45]. Er war einer der entschiedensten Kämpfer für die Todesstrafe gegen die Täufer. Der sächsische Kurfürst konnte sich auf ein von ihm angefordertes Gutachten (1531) berufen, das Melanchthon angefertigt und dem Luther zugestimmt hatte. Melanchthon bemerkte, daß gewisse Häretiker aufrührerische Lehren gegen die Fürsten verbreiten; deshalb kann man sie wie Rebellen behandeln und mit dem Tode bestrafen. Selbst die Täufer, denen keine aufrührerischen Lehren nachgewiesen werden konnten, seien eindeutig mit dem Tode zu bestrafen, weil *"sie das öffentlich ministerium verbi (d.h. Predigtamt) verwerfen, und lehren, man soll sonst heilig werden ohne Predigt und Kirchenamt. Das zerstört die Kirche und bedeutet Aufruhr gegen die kirchliche Ordnung. Dieser Versuch muß ebenso wie andere Aufstände verhindert und unterdrückt werden..."*. [46] Die Verachtung des *"öffentlich ministerium verbi"* sei Gotteslästerung und müsse mit dem Tode bestraft werden. Melanchthon verschiebt also die Begründung von "Ketzerei" auf "Gotteslästerung"; und Gotteslästerung und Aufruhr rücken wiederum eng zusammen. Luther hat dieser Schrift seine Billigung gegeben: *Placet mihi Martino Luthero*, und hat das Gutachten seines Kollegen so kommentiert: *"Wiewohl es crudele anzusehen, daß man sie mit dem Schwert straft, so ist doch crudelius, daß sie ministerium verbi damniren und keine gewisse Lehre treiben, und rechte Lehr unterdrucken, und dazu regna mundi zerstören wollen."* [47] Vor Jahren noch hatte Luther es Thomas Müntzer nicht durchgehen lassen, die Ausrottung der Gottlosen mit dem mosaischen Gesetz zu rechtfertigen; jetzt stört es ihn nicht, wenn Melanchthon die Hinrichtung der öffentlichen Gotteslästerer mit eben demselben Gesetz

---

[44] Zum Beispiel hat der einflußreiche Landgraf Philipp von Hessen in seinem Territorium eine relativ tolerante Haltung gegenüber Andersgläubigen gezeigt; es ist nicht bekannt, daß dort jemals ein Täufer zum Tode verurteilt worden wäre. Nach Claus-Peter Clasens Errechnung wurden außerhalb der Schweiz im Reich mit Bestimmtheit 715 und mit Wahrscheinlichkeit 130 weitere Täufer hingerichtet, mehr als 400 in den Habsburgischen Erblanden. Nicht berücksichtigt wurde dabei allerdings der niederdeutsche Raum. - C.-P. Clasen, Anabaptism. A Social History, 1525-1618. Schwitzerland, Austria, Moravia, South and Central Germany, London 1972, p. 370.

[45] Zitiert nach J. Lecler, a.a.O., S. 247f.

[46] Zitiert nach J. Lecler, a.a.O., S. 248f.

[47] Zitiert nach H.-J. Goertz, a.a.O., S. 129.

begründete. Schon im Jahre 1530 hat Luther in seiner Auslegung des Psalms 82 im Zusammenhang mit schweren Formen der Häresie an die furchtbaren Strafmaßnahmen des mosaischen Gesetzes gegen die öffentlicher Lästerer erinnert. Diese Strafen können im Normalfall gegen aufrührerische Häretiker, bzw. gegen Täufer, angewandt werden. *"...will er predigen, so beweise er den Beruf oder Befehl... Will er nicht, so befehle die Obrigkeit solchen Buben dem rechten Meister, der Meister Hans heißt (= dem Henker)."* [48] Derselbe Luther, der zehn Jahre zuvor erklärt hatte: *Haereticos comburi est contra voluntatem Spiritus,* fordert nun gegen die Täufer die Todesstrafe. Im Jahre 1536 verfaßten die Wittenberger Theologen [49] eine Denkschrift, die folgenden Titel trägt: *Ob Christliche Fürsten schuldig sind, der Widerteuffer unchristlichen Sect mit leiblicher straffe, und mit dem schwert zu wehren.* Die Antwort ist zustimmend: *"Jedermann ist schuldig nach seinem stand und ampt, Gottes lesterung zu verhüten und zu wehren... Da zu dienet auch der text Levit 24: Wer Gott lestert, der sol getödtet werden."* [50]

Mit der (gewissen) Duldung anderer Lehre und der Freigabe des Gewissens überwand Luther das Mittelalter; in der politischen Sorge vor öffentlicher Toleranz blieb er mittelalterlich. Die politische Gefahr der Täufer erhellt für Luther aus der Ablehnung der obrigkeitlichen Ämter, des Eides, des Kriegsdienstes, z. T. des Eigentums, aber auch des geordneten Predigtamtes (*ministerium verbi*), in dem er eine Hilfe für den inneren Frieden sah. Wenn die Täufer den offiziellen Amtsträgern mißtrauten und ihre Predigten und Gottesdienste mieden, mußte das ja noch nicht heißen, daß sie grundsätzlich das *"ministerium verbi"* verwarfen. Sie hatten nur eine andere Vorstellung von Funktion und Wesen dieses Dienstes. Eine obrigkeitlich angeordnete und überwachte Visitation der Amtsträger war in den Augen der Täufer alles andere als biblisch zu rechtfertigen. So nützlich es den Reformatoren erscheinen mochte, die Begründung der täuferischen Straftat von Ketzerei auf Gotteslästerung umzustellen, so problematisch war dieser Schritt. Eindeutiger konnte die reformatorische Entdeckung der Zwei-Reiche-Lehre, die ein hohes biblisches Recht für sich hatte, nicht desavouiert werden. Die Entscheidung für das Speyerer Mandat, die von den evangelischen Ständen gefällt und den kursächsischen Reformatoren nachvollzogen wurde, stand unter einem paradoxen Zeichen. Die evangelischen Stände haben sich auf den Reichstag gegen die altgläubige Zumutung, das Wormser Edikt zu erneuern, gerade im Namen der Trennung von Geistlichem und Weltlichem gewandt, die sie den Täufern selber zum Verhängnis werden ließen, da sie in ihren eigenen Territorien den bereits eingeschlagenen Weg zu

---

[48] WA 31 I, 189ff.

[49] Diese Denkschrift ist von Luther, Bugenhagen, Melanchthon und Creutziger unterzeichnet und gibt Antwort auf die Frage, die Philipp von Hessen an diese Theologen richtete: Was soll man mit den Wiedertäufern tun, die verhaftet worden sind?

[50] Zitiert nach J. Lecler, a.a.O., S. 250.

einem landesherrlichen Kirchenregiment ungestört fortsetzen wollten. [51] Die Wittenberger Theologie büßte nach und nach ihre innere Unabhängigkeit ein und wurde zur Rechtfertigungsideologie ihres weltlichen Schutzherrn.

Mit der Reformation stehen erstmals mehrere Konfessionen mit dem Anspruch auf Alleinvertretung der Wahrheit nebeneinander. Die Reformatoren halten am Absolutheitsanspruch evangeliumsgemäßer christlicher Verkündigung ebenso wie an der Einheit von Kirche und Welt, bzw. Staat fest. Die *Unum-Corpus-Christianum*-Idee wurde durch die Reformation grundsätzlich nicht in Frage gestellt, weil die Reformation diese Idee auf territorialer Basis fortführte. Hinfort ist nicht mehr das ganze Reich, sondern sind die einzelnen, evangelisch gewordenen Territorien kleine einheitliche christliche Körper. Ein Staatswesen ist unregierbar, so lautet die Rechtfertigung dieser Lösung bei Luther und anderen Reformatoren, wenn es in sich durch verschiedene Religionsparteien zerstritten sei. *Ein* Landesherr, *ein* Territorium, *eine* Religion für die Landeskinder: das ist das typisch europäische Modell des Verhältnisses von Staat und Religion, das die Täufer mit aller Entschiedenheit abgelehnt haben.

Über Luther und die protestierenden Reichsstände von 1529 führt kein unmittelbarer Weg zur neuzeitlichen Freiheit des Gewissens als unantastbarem individuellen Recht des Gewissens. Johannes Kühn hat eine interessante Analyse der Reichstagsakten von 1529 vorgenommen: *"Wer die Protestierenden zu Verfechtern der Gewissensfreiheit macht, der trifft ihren Sinn nicht... Wenn sie selbst sich auf ihr Gewissen berufen, so tun sie das nicht nur als Einzelpersonen, sie tun es als Obrigkeiten. Sie schließen dabei ohne weiteres ihre Untertanen mit ein. Sie setzen voraus, daß Menschen, die den evangelischen Glauben haben, in ihrem Gewissen nicht anders empfinden können als sie selbst. Die ihn aber nicht haben - und sie hatten doch alle noch solche Untertanen in ihrem Land - denen würden sie auch nur ein irrendes Gewissen zusprechen können, das keine Beachtung verdient. Gewissensfreiheit und Berufung auf das Gewissen sind nicht ein und dasselbe."* [52]

Auch in den Augsburger Verhandlungen von 1555 hatten beide Religionsparteien die Gewissensfreiheit nicht problematisiert, der Religionsfrieden gewährte nur das Recht der Gläubigen, unter Berufung auf das Gewissen aus dem Herrschaftsbereich einer andersgläubigen Obrigkeit abzuziehen (*ius emigrandi*). Das alles bedeutete einen gewaltigen Fortschritt gegenüber der totalen Intoleranz des Mittelalters, aber doch nur einen ersten Schritt in der Richtung auf wirkliche Toleranz, da neben dem Existenzrecht der beiden Konfessionen - Reformierte, Täufer u.a. waren übrigens vom Religionsfrieden ausgeschlossen - das Prinzip des *Cuius regio, eius religio* rechtlich begründet wurde. Die Reformation brachte daher "nicht Glaubensfreiheit, sondern Glaubenszweiheit" [53]. Das führte zu gravierenden zwischenstaatlichen und innerstaatlichen Problemen, u.a. auch zu

---

[51] H.-J. Goertz, a.a.O., S. 134f.

[52] J. Kühn, Die Geschichte des Speyerer Reichstags 1529, Leipzig 1929, S. 257ff.

[53] R. P. de Mortanges, a.a.O., S. 566.

den blutigen konfessionellen Kriegen. Von bleibendem Wert ist aber die Tatsache, daß Luther eine Diskussion anregte, geführt von Kräften, die evangelische Freiheit anders begriffen und damit auch späterem individualistischen Verständnis von Gewissensfreiheit die Bahn eröffneten. Durch die Reformation aufgeworfen wurde zunächst das Problem der religiösen Toleranz, die Gewissens-, Glaubens- und Religionsfreiheit erst ermöglicht. Und erst das unaufhebbare, den bisherigen Zustand von Grund auf verändernde Nebeneinander von Kirchen schuf die Möglichkeiten für eine künftige Entfaltung der Toleranz.

Welche Rolle haben die Täufer in dieser Entwicklung gespielt? Man kann sagen, daß die Täufer gewissermaßen zu den ersten Wortführer der neuzeitlichen Toleranz gehörten, und zwar nicht nur als die Verfolgten, sondern auch auf Grund ihrer Auffassung der Lehre Jesu und der Absonderung der Christenheit von der Welt. In ihrer internen Auseinandersetzung mit Thomas Müntzer schieden sie sich darum von dessen eschatologischer Intoleranz, die das Reich Gottes durch die Herrschaft der "Auserwählten" über die "Gottlosen" herbeizwingen wollte. Der Schatten Müntzers überdeckte leider die echte Gestalt des Täufertums, da er für den Blick der Reformatoren mit ihm verschmolz. Der wichtigste Beitrag der Täufer zur Toleranz lag darin, daß sie unermüdlich Duldung forderten und durch ihr Leiden dafür eintraten. *"Um ihrer Leiden willen kann daher gesagt werden, daß sie unmittelbar zur Durchsetzung der Religionsfreiheit beigetragen haben"*, so der bekannte Kirchenhistoriker Roland Bainton [54]. Die Täufer haben das Martyrium vorausgesehen und als ein notwendiges Kennzeichen der wahren Kirche und als einen Weg angenommen, auf dem sich die Vision einer erneuerten Christenheit am Maßstab des Urchristentums verwirklicht. Sie sind mit dem Bekenntnis zu Jesus Christus, ja wegen dieses Bekenntnisses gestorben, so unbeholfen und theologisch fragwürdig sie es oft auch formuliert haben. Entscheidend für die Frage nach dem Martyrium ist nicht die "doctrina", entscheidend ist das Bekenntnis, das in den Loyalitätskonflikten des Christen in dieser Welt eindeutig durchgehalten wird und Zeugnis dafür ablegt, daß das Leben, das Gott will, noch anders ist, als das Leben, das Menschen einander bereiten. [55] Der große Täufer-Theologe Balthasar Hubmaier, der ehemalige Schüler Johann Eck's und Prorektor der Ingolstädter Universität, verfaßte z.B. 1524 die Schrift *"Von Ketzern und ihren Verbrennern"*. Diese Schrift war ein flammendes Plädoyer gegen jede Art inquisitorischer und gewaltsamer "Bekehrung" zum "richtigen Glauben der Kirche" und ein früher und wichtiger Ansatz zum Toleranzgedanken! Die Vermischung von weltlichen und geistlichen Argumenten und Kompetenzen sollte um des Evangeliums willen ein Ende haben und mehr Geduld in der Bemühung um die Wahrheit des Glaubens walten. Der angefochtene Glaube ist für Hubmaier nicht schon Häresie, sondern Station auf dem Wege zur Wahrheit, die sich am Ende durchsetzen wird. Sein

---

[54] R. H. Bainton, Der täuferische Beitrag zur Geschichte, in: G. F. Hershberger (Hg.), Das Täufertum. Erbe und Verpflichtung, Stuttgart 1963, S. 304.

[55] H.-J. Goertz, a.a.O., S. 136.

Lebensmotto lautete: *"Die Wahrheit ist untödlich! (untötbar)"*.[56] Hubmaier wurde am 10. März 1528 in Wien als Ketzer und Aufrührer verbrannt; seine Frau ertränkte man drei Tage später in der Donau. Die Mennoniten, eine auf Menno Simons zurückgehende Täuferbewegung im holländischen Friesland, die heute in vielen Gebieten der Erde verbreitet ist, haben auf dem europäischen Boden aus eigenstem Interesse als erste den Gedanken konfessioneller Toleranz vertreten. Der niederländische Täuferführer David Joris erklärte Glaubenszwang und gewaltsame Unterdrückung für unvereinbar mit dem christlichen Liebesgebot. Diese Gedanken haben reiche Früchte getragen besonders im angloamerikanischen Raum, wo man im Umgang mit religiösen Minderheiten viel früher zu einem betont *individualrechtlichen* Verständnis der Religionsfreiheit gelangt als z. B. in Deutschland[57]. Thomas Helwys, ein englischer Theologe und "Nonkonformist", der von der anglikanischen Staatskirche verfolgt wurde und 1608 nach Amsterdam flüchtete, kam dort mit den hiesigen Mennoniten in Berührung. Er empfing die Glaubenstaufe und gründete mit dem Kollegen John Smyth 1609 die älteste Baptistengemeinde[58]. Als Helwys 1611 nach England zurückkehrte, nahm er mit sich ein von ihm verfaßtes Buch für den Verkauf in England, das den Titel trug: *Eine kurze Erklärung des Geheimnisses der Ungerechtigkeit (A Short Declaration of the Mistery of Iniquity)*. Es ist der erste in englischer Sprache gedruckte Aufruf zu völliger Glaubensfreiheit für alle: *"Unser Herr, der König, ist nur ein irdischer König und er hat als König Autorität nur in irdischen Dingen, und wenn die Leute des Königs gehorsame und wahre Untertanen sind, die allen von Königs erlassenen menschlichen Gesetzen gehorchen, so kann unser Herr, der König, nicht mehr verlangen; denn die Religion der Menschen zu Gott besteht zwischen Gott und ihnen selbst, der König soll dafür nicht Rede stehen, noch soll der König Richter sein zwischen Gott und Mensch. Sollen sie Ketzer, Türken, Juden oder sonst etwas sein, es steht der irdischen Macht nicht zu, sie im geringsten Maße zu bestrafen."* Noch kühner war Helwys in der Widmung an König James I, die er mit eigener Hand schrieb: *"...Der König ist ein sterblicher Mensch und nicht Gott, und deshalb hat er keine Gewalt über die unsterblichen Seelen seiner Untertanen, für sie Gesetze und Ordnungen zu schaffen und geistliche Herren über sie zu*

---

[56] Vgl. Ch. Windhorst, Balthasar Hubmaier - Professor, Prediger, Politiker, in: Radikale Reformatoren, hg. von H.-J. Goertz, München 1978, S. 129.

[57] Das Aufkommen der Independenten in Großbritannien im 17. Jahrhundert, die jegliche Form des Staatskirchentums ablehnen, gab dem Verlauf der Dinge eine neue Wende. 1647 wurde ein Verfassungsentwurf von historischer Bedeutung zusammengefaßt, weil er die Religionsfreiheit als Menschenrecht bezeichnete. Der Entwurf war geprägt vom individualistischen Gedankengut der Independenten; Religionsangelegenheiten gehören zu den "native rights", welche der Einwirkung der Obrigkeit entzogen sind.

[58] Vgl. W. R. Estep, Why Baptists? A Study of Baptist Faith and Heritage, Fort Worth 1997

setzen...".[59] So sind auch die Baptisten von Anfang an die Verfechter der Religionsfreiheit sowie der Trennung von Kirche und Staat gewesen[60], und infolge der Emigration der Glaubensflüchtlinge verbreitete sich dieses Gedankengut bald auch in der "Neuen Welt". Da setzte sich das sog. *freikirchliche Modell* des Verhältnisses von Staat und Kirche, das dem Staat überhaupt keine Machtbefugnisse in religiösen Angelegenheiten zubilligt, weil die Religion nicht zu den staatlichen Hoheitsaufgaben gehört, in der Tat durch. Zuerst wurde dieses Modell greifbar im 17. Jahrhundert in der Kolonie Rhode Island, wo ein englischer Puritaner und Gründer der ersten baptistischen Kirche der Kolonien, Roger Williams, einen Freistaat auf der Grundlage der Gewissensfreiheit und religiöser Toleranz gründete. Williams Begründung war sehr tiefsinnig: Das Wirken des Heiligen Geistes in Erwählung und Wiedergeburt erfordert völlige Glaubensfreiheit, die weltliche Natur des Staates absolute Trennung von der Kirche. Wenig später machte es ihm der Quäker William Penn in seiner Kolonie Pennsylvania nach. Dieses Modell wird dann bei Gründung der neuen Republik trotz allen Widerstands in den Verfassungsrang erhoben.[61] Im *First Amendment* von 1791 wird der Kongreß darauf verpflichtet, *"to make no law respecting an establishment of religion, or prohibiting the free exercise thereof"*, was als strike Trennung von Staat und Kirchen interpetiert wird.[62] Im Gegensatz zu den europäischen Modellen einer Trennung - Französische Revolution, Russische Revolution, Laizismus - geschieht es in Amerika nicht, um Religion das Absterben zu erleichtern, sondern im wohlverstandenen Interesse der Religion. Die Religion gedeiht besser, wenn sie keiner ihr wesensfremden Macht unterworfen oder von dieser abhängig ist[63].

Zum Schluß nochmals zurück in die frühe Neuzeit. Das Bekenntnis der Täufer hat die Gesellschaft des 16. Jahrhunderts herausgefordert, ihre Grundla-

---

[59] Zitiert nach J. D. Hughey, Die Baptisten. Einführung in Lehre, Praxis und Geschichte, Kassel 1959, S. 116.

[60] "Baptisten legen großen Wert auf die Trennung von Kirche und Staat und auf die Religionsfreiheit, weil sie überzeugt sind, daß das Evangelium in Freiheit von politischen, gesellschaftlichen, nationalem, gesetzlichem und religiösem Zwang oder Gebundenheit empfangen und gelebt werden muß." - Baptisten und Lutheraner im Gespräch. Bericht der Gemeinsamen Kommission des Baptistischen Weltbundes und des Lutherischen Weltbundes, Genf 1990, S. 33.

[61] Vgl. E. Geldbach, Religion und Politik: Religious Liberty, in: Gott und Politik in USA, hg. von K.-M. Kodalle, Frankfurt a.M., 1988, S. 230ff.

[62] R. P. de Mortanges, a.a.O., S. 569.

[63] Demnach muß man auch zwischen Freiheit und Toleranz unterscheiden, wie es auf der baptistischen Weltbundkonferenz des Jahres 1923 festgestellt wurde: "...Glaubensfreiheit schließt das Prinzip der religiösen Toleranz aus. Die Gewalt und das Ansehen des Staates eine Form der Religion zukommen zu lassen und die anderen bloß zu dulden, bedeutet nicht Glaubensfreiheit. Das ist religiöse Nötigung... Gleiche Rechte für alle und besondere Vorrechte für keinen, das ist das wahre Ideal." - Zitiert nach J. D. Hughey, Die Baptisten. Einführung in Lehre, Praxis und Geschichte, Kassel 1959, S. 119.

gen neu zu überdenken und zu verändern. Und die Verfolgung von Täufern im 16. Jahrhundert beweist einen großen Mangel an Engagement für Religionsfreiheit, einen Grundsatz, der heute von allen bekräftigt wird, obwohl es sowohl in Estland als auch in Deutschland immer noch an der Gleichbehandlung bzw. an der Gleichsetzung mangelt. Der Kampf um die Freiheit des Glaubens und der Religion ist nie ein für allemal gewonnen. Der Beispiel der Täufer sorgt aber hoffentlich für die Einsicht, daß Toleranz und Religionsfreiheit nicht Forderungen sind, die eine Gesellschaft zerstören, sondern vermenschlichen.

Heilige Geschichte als Paradigma am Beispiel von Jerusalem

Sergei Stadnikow, Tallinn

1. Zum Geleit

Seit Jahrtausenden wohnte dem 'Fruchtbaren Halbmond' eine höchst intensive religiös-schöpferische Kreativität inne. In dieser Gegend entstanden drei Weltreligionen — Judentum, Christentum und Islam. Die heilige Geschichte des Judentums, dieses ältesten erhaltenen monotheistischen Glaubenssystems, hat wesentlich die Historiosophie des Christentums und Islams beeinflußt.

Den Kern der jüdischen heiligen Geschichte bildet die Auffassung ein Volk zu sein, das durch Gott Jahwe auserwählt ist, durch eine besonderen sakralen Vertrag an ihn gebunden und als 'Heiliges Land' Juda-Israel ewiger Besitz von ihm zu sein. Von einer solchen Überzeugung wurde entscheidend auch die am Ende des 19. Jahrhunderts entstehende zionistische politische Bewegung (mit religiöser Färbung) getragen. Schon im Jahre 1919 sagte einer der führenden Repräsentanten des Zionismus, der spätere erste Staatspräsident Israels, Chaim Weizmann, in der Friedenskonferenz zu Versailles: *"Unser Recht ist die Thora!"* Dieser Ausspruch klang in den Ohren vieler Politiker der Sieger-Staaten wie eine schöne Musik.

Als die UNO unter der starken Lobbyarbeit der USA und der Sowjetunion 1947 beschloß, den Staat Israel zu gründen, wurden die etwas profanisierten Versionen der 'heiligen Geschichte' zu untrennbaren Teilen der offiziellen und halboffiziellen Ideologie. In vielen Lebensbereichen sind seither Staat und Religion miteinander verbunden. So wird z.B. das Glaubensbekenntnis im Bürgerpaß fixiert, was in einem demokratischen europäischen Land ganz unmöglich wäre – bemerkenswert ist übrigens, daß auch in Ägypten ist in den Pässen die Konfession in Form einer Kodenummer festgehalten ist.

Der feste Glaube an die Rechte der historischen Heimat war meines Erachtens der Hauptgrund für den Ausbau von Israel in eine technologisch moderne Gesellschaft – das nicht nur mit Hilfe von außen. Denn es half auch der starke national-religiöse Geist der Israelis selbst, einige Kriege gegen die Koalitionen arabischer Staaten zu gewinnen und innerlich die fortdauernde Besatzung der palästinischen Territorien mit Vertreibung vieler ansässiger Araber aus ihren Häusern zu rechtfertigen. Bis in die letzte Zeit hinein kontrollierte Israel weitgehend die geopolitische Lage im Nahen Osten.

Dann aber begann im Jahre 1987 der erste Aufstand der Palästinenser, die sogenannte Intifada, der Steinkrieg. Spätestens jetzt haben die Israelis (zumindest die meisten von ihnen) verstanden, daß sie sich mit der künftigen Existenz eines unabhängigen Palästinas irgendwann doch abfinden müssen.

Ein ernsthaftes Problem bildet der staatlich-politische Status von Jerusalem. Hier macht sich die Realpolitik die 'heilige Geschichte' breit, die in der Tat jedweden Kompromiss ausschließt, weil sowohl in jüdischer als auch islamischer Überlieferung diese Stadt eine höchst wichtige göttlich-himmlische Bedeutung hat (vornehmlich natürlich im Judentum). Eine solche geistig-religiöse Haltung geht letztlich auf die Grundlagen beider Religionen als äußerst puristisch-monotheistische zurück, nach denen der transzendente Einzelgott das Weltall geschaffen und der Menschheit die festen Gebote gegeben hat und alle Geschehnisse in der Welt nach wie vor bestimmt. Diese Situation scheint fast auswegslos zu sein. Vielleicht sollen dort die internationalen Friedenstruppen intervenieren – USA, Europäische Union und vielleicht auch Rußland.

2. Geschichtlicher Überblick über die Stadt Jerusalem

Die frühesten Siedlungsspuren im östlichen Teil der Stadt stammen aus dem 4. Jahrtausend v.Chr. Aus der 1. Hälfte des 2. Jahrtausends vor Christus datieren erste Spuren einer Stadtmauer, und gegen Ende des 2. Jahrtausends war Jerusalem eine Festung der Jebusiter, einer vorisraelitischer Bevölkerung. Zu Beginn des 2. Jahrtausends v.Chr. wurde die Stadt erstmals in ägyptischen Ächtungstexten erwähnt. Um 1000 v.Chr. gelang den Israeliten unter David die Eroberung von Jerusalem, die Stadt wurde daraufhin zur Residenz der israelitischen und später judäischen Könige.

Der unter Salomo (um 950 v.Chr.) erbaute Jahwe-Tempel befand sich im Norden der Stadt. 587-586 v.Chr. wurde Jerusalem vom babylonischen Heer erobert und zerstört. Fast die ganze Bevölkerung wurde deportiert, kehrte teilweise seit 538 v.Chr. mit der Genehmigung des persischen Königs Kyros II. sukzessive wieder zurück. In der 2. Hälfte des 5. Jahrhunderts v.Chr. konnten die Stadtmauer von Jerusalem und der Tempel wieder aufgebaut werden. Gegen den Hellenisierungszwang unter dem Seleukiden Antiochus IV. Epiphanes leisteten die Makkabäer erfolgreich Widerstand. Der idumäische Usurpator Herodes der Große leitete einen Tempelausbau und befestigte Stadt zusätzlich. Nach der Zerstörung Jerusalems durch die Römer im Jahre 70 n.Chr. sowie nach der Niederschlagung des Bar Kochba-Aufstandes im Jahre 135 n.Chr. fand die Umwandlung Jerusalems in die römische Kolonie Aelia Capitolina statt. In ihr darf nunmehr nur bleiben, wer sich nicht auf jüdische Weise mit der vom Tempel verbürgten Heiligkeit der Stadt identifiziert. Ab 638 n.Chr. war Jerusalem unter islamisch-arabischer Oberhoheit, von 1517 bis 1917, also rund 400 Jahre, Provinz des Osmanenreiches. Daran schloss sich bis zum Jahre 1948 die britische Besetzung und Mandatszeit an. Seit Dezember 1949 ist Jerusalem Hauptstadt des Staates Israel. Bis zum 'Sechstagekrieg' im Jahre 1967 waren West- und Ostteile Jerusalems von Israel und Jordanien okkupiert. Vor vierzehn Jahren hat Jordanien auf alle Ansprüche auf Palästina und Jerusalem verzichtet.

Ost-Jerusalem soll künftig Hauptstadt des palästinensischen Staates werden. Allerdings hat Israel bis heute nichts Entsprechendes getan. [1]

---

[1] Zur ältesten Geschichte Jerusalems s. K. Armstrong, Jerusalem: One City, Three Faiths. New York, 1996; B. Mazar, Der Berg des Herrn. Bergisch Gladbach, 1979; K.L. Schmidt, Jerusalem als Urbild und Abbild. In: Eranos Jahrbuch, Bd. 18, 1950, S. 207-248; E. Otto, Jerusalem. Die Geschichte der Heiligen Stadt. Stuttgart, 1980; S. Abramsky u.a., Jerusalem. In: Encyclopaedia Judaica, Bd. IX, Jerusalem, 1985, S. 1378-1593; S.D. Goitein, Al-Kuds, History. In: Encyclopedia of Islam, Bd. V, Leiden, 1960ff., S. 322-339; O. Grabar, Al-Kuds, Monuments. In: Encyclopedia of Islam, Bd. V, Leiden 1960ff., S. 339-344; U. Berger u.a., Jerusalem: Symbol und Wirklichkeit. Berlin, 1982; R.J.Z. Werblowsky, Die Bedeutung Jerusalems für Juden, Christen und Muslims. Jerusalem, 1986; T. Kollek, M. Pearlam, Jerusalem. Frankfurt/Main, 1985; K. Kenyon, Digging up Jerusalem. London, 1974; Ch.W. Wilson, T.W. Saunders, Jerusalem: Ancient and Modern. London, 1874; W. van Leer, Jerusalem. Haifa, 1969; F.J. Salmon, Jerusalem: the Old City. Tel Aviv, 1936/75; D. Haines, A new map of the Land of promise and the holy city of Jerusalem. Philadelphia, 1828; Panorama of Jerusalem on the day of the crucifixion. Philadelphia, 1890; J.F. Thrupp, Ancient Jerusalem. Cambridge, 1855; Josephus Flavius, Jüdischer Krieg. München, 1980; Ch. Warren, Underground Jerusalem. London, 1877; Ch.W. Wilson, Ordonance survey of Jerusalem. Southampton, 1866; A. Jeremias, Das Alte Testament im Lichte des Alten Orients. Leipzig, 1916, S. 464-488; N. Avigad, Discovering Jerusalem. Nashville, 1983; H. Gera (Hrg.), Ancient Jerusalem revealed. Jerusalem, 1994; M. Gilbert, Jerusalem illustrated history atlas. Ilford, 1994; J.D. Purvis, Jerusalem, the Holy City. A bibliography. London, 1991; K. Kenyon, Royal Cities of the Old Testament. London, 1971; K. Kenyon, Archaeology in the Holy Land. London, 1979; T. Benson, A Visit to Ancient Jerusalem. In: The Testimony, March-June, 1988; R. Carr, Jerusalem: excaveting 3,000 years of history. In: The Testimony, April, 1972; Jerusalem revealed: archeology in the Holy City. In: The Testimony, June, 1976; J. Collyer, Jerusalem: in the time of the kings. In: The Testimony, March, 1935; C.S. Knopf, The Name of the City. In: The Testimony, March, 1935; R. Mellowes, Digging up Jerusalem. In: The Testimony, December, 1980; F.E. Mitchell, A.D. 70. In: The Testimony, March, 1935; F.E. Mitchell, Jerusalem in Old Testament times. In: The Testimony, May-August, 1952; F.E. Mitschell, The Siege of Jerusalem. In: The Testimony, August, 1978; F.E. Mitchell, Zion and Jerusalem. In: The Testimony, July and October, 1945; E.W. Newman, Jerusalem and the Western Wall. In: The Christadelphian, May, 1972; W.J. Owen, Jerusalem: the city of the great king. In: The Testimony, February-March, 1931, L. Ritmeyer, Locating the original Temple Mount. In: Biblical Archaeology Review, March/April, 1992; L. Ritmeyer, The temple and the ark of covenant. In: The Testimony, February, 1996; H. Shanks, Jerusalem: an archaeological biography. New York, 1995; G.A. Smith, Jerusalem: the topography, economics, and history from the earliest times to A.D. 70, Bd. 1 2, London, 1907; J.W. Thirtle, A Jewish account of the destruction of Jerusalem. In: The Christadelphian, March, 1881; H.A. Thompson, Jerusalem: in the beginning. In: The Testimony, March, 1935; J.G.M. Thorne, Jerusalem shall be trodden down until ... In: The Testimony, February, 1975; W.J. Young, The temple of Ezekiel's prophecy. In: The Testimony, March, 1935; Jerusalem in History (Hrg. K.J. Asali), New York, 1986; N. Avigad, Discovering Jerusalem. New York, 1983; D. Bahat, C.T. Rubinstein, An Illustrated Atlas of Jerusalem. New York, 1990; M. Benvenisti, Jerusalem: the Torn City. Jerusalem, 1976; B. Brande, B. Lewis, Christians and Jews in the Ottoman Empire. New York, 1982; R.E.

Jerusalem kommt im gesamten jüdischen Glauben die zentrale Bedeutung zu, die im Kontext der heilsgeschichtlichen Kategorien Gott, Bund, Volk und Land zu sehen ist. Darauf weisen zahlreiche Texte. Von den Gebetstexten bezieht sich insbesondere die Bitte des 'Schechmonaeserhu' auf Jerusalem:

"Nach deiner Stadt Jeruschalaim kehre in Erbarmen zurück, wohne in ihr, wie du gesprochen hast, erbau sie bald in unseren Tagen als ewigen Bau, und Davids Thron gründe schnell in ihr. Gelobt seist du, Ewiger, der du Jeruschalaim erbaust."

Ebenso wird die Bedeutung Jerusalems im Abend- und Morgengebet sowie in der Pessach-Haggada hervorgehoben mit ihrem Wunsch *"Das kommende Jahr in Jerusalem!"*, das bedeutet: *"Im wiederaufgebauten Jerusalem!"* Also ist Jerusalem ein wichtiges Symbol für die Existenz des jüdischen Volkes.[2]

Clements, God and Temple. Oxford, 1965; A. Cohen, Jewish life under Islam: Jerusalem in the sixteenth century. Cambridge-London, 1984; C.R. Conder, The City of Jerusalem. New York, 1971; H.J. Franken, Jerusalem in the Bronze Age, 3000-1000 BC. In: K.J. Asali (Hrg.), Jerusalem in History. New York, 1990; M. Gilbert, Jerusalem, rebirth of a city. London, 1985; J. Jeremias, Jerusalem in the time of Jesus: an investigation into economic and social conditions during the New Testament period. London, 1969; K. Kenyon, Jerusalem: Excavating 3000 years of history. New York-London, 1967; S. Lane-Poole, Saladin and the fall of Jerusalem. London-New York, 1898; J.D. Levenson, The Jerusalem temple in devotional advisionary experience. In: A. Green (Hrg.), Jewish spirituality, Bd. 1, London-New York, 1986; R.M. Mackowski, Jerusalem, city of Jesus. Michigan, 1980; F.E. Peters, Jerusalem: the Holy City in the eyes of chroniclers, visitors, pilgrims and prophets from the days of Abraham to the beginning of modern times. Princeton, 1985; F.E. Peters, Jerusalem and Mecca: the typology of the Holy city in the Near East. New York-London, 1986; F.E. Peters, The distant shrine: the Islamic centuries in Jerusalem. New York, 1983; Ch. Raphael, The walls of Jerusalem: an excursion into Jewish history. London, 1968; E.T. Richmond, The Dome of the Rock in Jerusalem. Oxford, 1924; A.L. Tibawi, Jerusalem: its place in Islam and Arab history. Beirut, 1967; P.W.L. Walker, Holy City, Holy Places? Christian attitudes to Jerusalem and the Holy Land in the fourth century. Oxford, 1990; Ch. Warren, Underground Jerusalem. London, 1876; M. Barker, The Gate of Heaven: the history and symbolism of the temple in Jerusalem. London, 1991.

[2] Im Verlauf vieler Jahrhunderte gab es keine ernsthaften Spannungen zwischen Juden und Muslims in Jerusalem. Die Juden glaubten, daß der von den Römern zerstörte Jahve-Tempel vom Messias wiederaufgebaut werde. Sie hatten anfangs sogar keine spezielle Bezeichnung für den Bereich ihres ehemaligen Hauptheiligtums; die Muslims nennen ihn Haram al-Scharif ('Das edelste Heiligtum'). Seit dem 16. Jahrhundert wurde zum heiligsten Ort der jüdischen Welt die Klagemauer – sie liegt unter dem Felsendom und ist der Rest der gewaltigen Fundamente des von Herodes (reg. 37-4 v.Chr.) im ersten Jahrhundert v.Chr. errichteten Tempels. Der ottomanische Sultan Suleiman der Herrliche (1494-1566) erlaubte den Juden, dort ein offizielles Heiligtum zu bauen. Unter anderen zeichnete der griechische Hofbaumeister Sinan selbst zeichnete die Gebetsstätte (s. K. Armstrong, Battle for God ..., S. 347).

Der arabisch-israelitische politisch-religiöse und militärische Konflikt unterbrach die ruhigen Beziehungen zwischen zwei Religionen. Seit dem Anfang der 20er Jahre des letzten Jahrhunderts fanden in der heiligen Stadt zahlreiche Gewalttaten statt. In der Zeit

In christlicher Tradition ist Jerusalem unlösbar mit Person und Werk Jesu verbunden: Letztes Mahl, Kreuzigung, Auferweckung, Geistsendung. Jerusalem bleibt für die Christen daher die heilige Stadt mit zahlreichen heiligen Stätten. Papst Johannes Paul II. drückt in seinem 'Apostolischen Schreiben über die Stadt Jerusalem' vom 20.4.1984 die christliche Wertschätzung dieser Stadt u.a. so aus:

> *"Jerusalem ist 'als der Ort, wo nach dem Glauben die unendliche Transzendenz Gottes und das Erschaffene zusammenkommen, das Symbol des Zusammentretens und der friedlichen Verbindung der gesamten Menschenfamilie'. Folglich gehört es zur ökumenischen Aufgabe aller Christen, zur Verwirklichung dieser Hoffnung beizutragen."*

Im Koran kommt der Ortsname Jerusalem nicht vor. Die Stadt heißt al-Kuds, 'die Heilige', und ist nach Mekka und Medina die drittheiligste Stadt des Islam. Nachdem Muḥammads missionarische Bemühungen um die Juden und Christen gescheitert waren, änderte er erbittert die Gebetsrichtung (*kibla*) von Jerusalem nach Mekka. Obwohl er selbst nie in Jerusalem war, wird die Verehrung der Stadt vor allem durch die Nachtreise von Mekka nach Jerusalem (*isra*) begründet, wie sie im Koran 17,1 überliefert wird:

---

der jordanischen Okkupation von Ostjerusalem und der Altstadt (1948-1967) konnten die gläubigen Juden vor der Klagemauer nicht beten und alle Synagogen im jüdischen Stadtviertel wurden abgerissen. Doch sollte man folgendes stets im Auge behalten: Eines der Ergebnisse des ersten arabisch-israelitischen Krieges war die Vertreibung von ca. 750.000 Palästinensern aus ihrer Heimat. Das ist nur die Erklärung, keinesfalls die Rechtfertigung des beschriebenen Phänomens.

Als die israelitischen Truppen Ostjerusalem und dessen Altstadt 1967 eroberten, wurde der Weg zur Klagemauer für die Juden frei. Es war eine der ergreifendsten Erfahrungen dieses Krieges sogar für die weltlich orientierten Israelis. Auf Grund der Sondergesetze ('Gesetz zum Schutz der Heiligen Stätten' vom 27.6.1967 und 'Jerusalem-Gesetz', 30.7.1980) wurde der ungehinderte Zugang zu allen heiligen Stätten vom Staat Israel garantiert. Die administrativ-religiöse Kontrolle über Haram al-Scharif führten die Muslims aus. Allerdings entstehen von Zeit zu Zeit Konflikte zwischen israelitischen Staatsbehörden und verschiedenen Konfessionen beispielsweise wegen der Eigentumsfragen u.s.w. Die meisten Palästinenser sind mit dem herrschenden rechtlichen Status von Ostjerusalem ganz unzufrieden, weil sie dieses als künftige Hauptstadt ihres Staates ansehen.

Als offizielle religiöse Feste sind nur die jüdischen Feiertage anerkannt, obwohl die Nichtjuden mindestens 20% der ganzen Bevölkerung Israels bilden.

In den 70er-80er Jahren des 20. Jahrhunderts versuchten die jüdischen religiösen Extremisten den Felsendom zu sprengen, um die eifrig erwartete Ankunft des Messias zu beschleunigen. Letzterer sollte dann den Jahve-Tempel wiederaufbauen (s. zum Thema K. Armstrong, Battle for God..., S. 347-359; E. Sprinzak, The ascendance of Israel's far right. Oxford-New York, 1991, S. 94-98; G. Aran, Jewish Zionist Fundamentalism. In: E. Marty, R.S. Appleby (Hrg.), Fundamentalism observed. Chicago-London, 1991, S. 267-268; A. Ravitsky, Messianism, Zionism and Jewish Religious Radicalism. Chicago-London, 1993, S. 133-134.

"Gepriesen sei der, der mit seinem Diener bei Nacht von der heiligen Kultstätte (in Mekka) nach der fernen Kultstätte (in Jerusalem), deren Umgebung wir gesegnet haben, reiste, um ihn etwas von unseren Zeichen sehen zu lassen! Er ist der, der (alles) hört und durchschaut."
Nach dieser Initiationsreise betete Muḥammad mit allen ihm vorausgegangen Propheten und wurde auf einem wundersamen Geschöpf in den Himmel geführt.

Nach der Eroberung Jerusalems durch den Khalifen Omar im Jahre 638 n.Chr. liegt die Stadt im 'Haus des Islam'. Omar erbaute nahe dem Tempelfelsen eine Gebetsstätte. 691 n.Chr. vollendete der Omayadenkhalif Abd al-Malik b. Marwan hier den Felsendom (Ḳubbat al-Ṣakhra), später auch Omar-Moschee genannt. Nach späterer Tradition ist der Felsen deshalb heilig, weil Muḥammad bei der Himmelreise auf ihn seine Füße gesetzt habe. Die Moschee am Südende des Tempelplatzes wird al-Akṣa genannt und mit der 'fernen Kultstätte' (vgl. 17,1) identifiziert. Aufgrund der Sukzession und Substitution auf dem Tempelplatz übernimmt der Islam nun jüdische und christliche Bezeichnungen für Jerusalem, wie etwa 'Bait al-Maḳdis' (= 'Haus der Heiligkeit'). Diese Gleichsetzung hatte primär religiöse, nicht jedoch politische Gründe: Die muslimischen Heiligtümer sollen die christlichen Kirchen, insbesondere die Grabeskirche, an Bedeutung und Pracht übertreffen. [3]

Nach muslimischer Theologie liegt der Tempelfelsen genau unter Allahs Thron und über einer Höhle, in der sich alle Seelen der Verstorbenen zweimal wöchentlich versammeln. Der Felsen ist der Ort, an dem Noahs Arche stand und auf dem Abraham den Ismael opfern wollte. Er ist Mittelpunkt des ganzen Weltalls und erhält von daher eschatologische Bedeutung.

---

[3] Die Forderung der Befreiung Jerusalems gehört zu den außenpolitischen Prioritäten fast aller arabischen politischen Bewegungen. Zu den arabisch-jüdischen Verhältnissen s. H.-J. Fischer, Die Geschichte von Juden und Arabern in Palästina. In: Frankfurter Allgemeine Zeitung vom 14. März 1975; S.D. Goitein, Jews and arabs. New York, 1955; G. v. Paczensky, Unser Volk am Jordan. Frankfurt/Main, 1971; C. Sykes. Cross roads to Israel. London, 1965; M. Burrows, Palestine is our business. New York, 1956; E. Berger, The Jewish dilemma. New York, 1946; A. Lilienthal, What price Israel. Chicago, 1953; C. Weizmann, Trial an error. New York, 1949; D. Ben Gurion, Rebirth and destiny of Israel. New York, 1954; M. Sid-Ahmed, Nach vier Kriegen im Nahen Osten — Thesen zu einer offensiven Friedenspolitik. Reinbek bei Hamburg, 1977; E. Vogt, Israel-Kritik von Links. Dokumentation einer Entwicklung. Wuppertal, 1976; R. Tawil, Mein Gefängnis hat viele Mauern. Bonn, 1979; M. Krupp, Zur Siedlungsgeschichte in Palästina/Israel. In: Zionismus. Beiträge zur Diskussion (Hrg. M. Stöhr), München, 1980, S. 43-68; M. Wolffsohn, Wem gehört das Heilige Land? Die Wurzeln des Streits zwischen Juden und Arabern. München, 2002; F. Schreiber, M. Wolffsohn, Nahost. Geschichte und Struktur des Konflikts. Opladen, 1991; F. Schreiber, Die Palästinenser. Berlin 1992; W. Laquer, Der Weg zum Staat Israel. Wien, 1975; P. Scholl-Latour, Lügen im Heiligen Land. München, 2000; B. Morris, The birth of the Palestinian refugee problem 1948-1949. Cambridge, 1987; M. Begin, The Revolt. Mash, 1972; B. Morris, The causes and consequences of Arab Exodus from Palesine. - In: Middle Eastern Studies, Bd. XXII, January 1986, S. 5-19.

3. Jerusalem und das Völkerrecht

Am 29. November 1947 beschloß die UNO mit ihrer Resolution Nummer 181, Jerusalem zu teilen und gab der Stadt einen Sonderstatus. Im Namen dieser Weltorganisation mußte die administrative Macht dort einen Vormundschaftsrat einsetzen. Auf Initiative der arabischen Staaten begann 1948 der erste arabisch-israelische Krieg.[4] Im Laufe der Kampfhandlungen nahmen die israelischen Truppen West-Jerusalem ein.

Im Dezember 1949 verkündete Israel West-Jerusalem als seine Hauptstadt und im Jahre 1951 wurde dorthin das höchste gesetzgeberische Machtorgan, die Knesset, verlegt. Die Knesset steht nach Überzeugung der örtlichen arabischen Bevölkerung auf den von Palästinensern konfiszierten Grundstücken - israelische Machthaber bestreiten dies allerdings. Seit jener Zeit arbeitet in West-Jerusalem auch die israelische Regierung. 1967, während des Sechstagekriegs, eroberte die israelische Armee Ost-Jerusalem[5]; 1980 proklamierte die Knesset Jerusalem als ewige, unteilbare Hauptstadt Israels. Die Weltöffentlichkeit hat diese Annexion jedoch nicht akzeptiert, sogar die Botschaft der Vereinigten Staaten von Amerika befindet sich in Tel Aviv, nicht in Jerusalem.

Die UNO hat mehrmals die Frage von Jerusalem unter ihren religiösen, politischen, demographischen und historischen Aspekten behandelt. Als Ergebnis der Diskussionen wurde die israelitische Siedlungspolitik in den okkupierten Gebieten wiederholt scharf kritisiert, z.B. in den Resolutionen Nummer 242, 338 und 452.[6]

---

[4] Eine grundsätzliche Anmerkung: Palästina als staatliches Gebilde existiert noch nicht. Arabische Staaten wurden damals nicht als gleichwertige politische Partner betrachtet. Zusätzlich hatten die Araber zu jener Zeit schon den gut organisierten zionistischen Terror durch paramilitärische Einheiten kennengelernt (vgl. N.S. Haddad, Die Geschichte Palästinas und das Recht der Palästinenser auf ihre Heimat. In: Zionismus (Hrg. M. Stöhr), München, 1980, S. 111).

[5] Die jüdischen religiösen Schulen (Jeschibot) begannen geheim das Eigentum der Araber im muslimischen Stadtviertel aufzukaufen und alte Synagogen dort wieder einzurichten (K. Armstrong, The battle for God ..., S. 287; s. zusätzlich S. Heilman, Guides of the faithful: contemporary religious Zionist Rabbis. In: R.S. Appleby (Hrg.), Spokesmen for the despised: fundamentalist leaders of the Middle East. Chicago, 1997, S. 339). Von der rechtlichen Stellung der Palästinensischen Minderheit in Israel s. den Sammelband Legal violations of Arab minority rights in Israel. Jerusalem, 1998; A. Rubinstein, The constitutional law of Israel. Tel Aviv, 1996; B. Bracha, Administrativ law. Tel Aviv, 1996.

[6] Zur Frage des politischen Status von Jerusalem s. A.H. Mahdi, The future of Jerusalem — a Palestinian perspective. In: Shu'un Tanmawiyyeh, vol. 5, 1995/1996, S. 11-16; A.H. Mahdi, The ownership of Jerusalem: a Palestinian view. In: Jerusalem today: what future for the peace process? Jerusalem, 1996; M. Benvenisti, N. Chasan, J. Dakkak, In search of solutions: a roundtable discussion. In: Palestina-Israel Journal, vol. 2, No. 2, 1995, S. 87-96; A.O. Adnan, Two capitals in an undivided Jerusalem. In: Foreign affairs, Bd. 70, 1992, S. 183-188; A. Arafah, A Rahman, Projection of the future status of Jerusalem. In: Shu'un Tanmawiyyeh, Bd. 5, No. 2-3, S. 2-10; C. Albin, M. Amirav, H. Siniora, Jerusa-

Die Basis für eine solche Politik ist nicht das Völkerrecht, sondern die stark religiös fundierte historische Vision mit dazugehörender 'wir und die Umwelt'-Stammesethik. Das aber schuf einen gefährlichen Präzedensfall für andere Weltreligionen.

Man muss auch den demographischen Faktor im Auge behalten — in dieser Hinsicht ist Israels Zukunft ganz unbefriedigend. Selbst Kernwaffen können nicht weiterhelfen, weil die Konfliktterritorien zu klein sind. Ich persönlich unterstütze den Vorschlag des Papstes Johannes-Paul II., nach dem Jerusalem eine internationale heilige Freistadt sein sollte. Das ist natürlich ein idealistischer Vorschlag, aber alle anderen Lösungen dieses Problems führen zu einem permanenten Blutvergießen.

Aus der Sicht der christlichen Theologie hat Karl Ludwig Schmidt die religiöse Wichtigkeit von Jerusalem tiefsinnig folgendermaßen zusammengefaßt:

"In Apk. 21,10 ist das neue Jerusalem, wie es vom Himmel herabkommt, das Gegenstück der Weltstadt Babel, von deren Turm aus die Menschen in titanischer Hybris in den Himmel hinaufsteigen wollten. Dieses Babel, das dabei der Deckname für Rom ist, wird einige Male in der Johannes-Apokalypse für die 'große Stadt' genannt, und zwar im Anschluß an die aramäische Aussage Dan. 4,27. In Apk. 11,8 wird

---

lem: an undivided city as dual capital. In: Israeli-Palestinian peace research project, working paper series, No. 16, 1991/1992; G. Baskin, R. Twite (Hrg.), The future of Jerusalem. Proceedings of the first Israeli-Palestinian international academic seminar on the future of Jerusalem. Jerusalem, 1993; B. Yossi, Touching peace: from the Oslo accord to a final agreement. London, 1999; Ch.F. Emmet, The status quo solution for Jerusalem. In: Journal of Palestine Studies, Bd. 26, Nr. 2, 1997, S. 16-28; Problema Jerusalima. In: Blizne-vostotčnyj vestnik, Bd. 4, Moskau, 1993; R. Friedland, R. Hecht, To rule Jerusalem. Cambridge, 1996; D. Gold, Jerusalem: final status issues. In: Israel-Palestinian study, Bd. 7, S. 1995; M. Hirsch, D. Housen-Couriel, R. Lapidoth, Whither Jerusalem? Proposals and positions concerning the future of Jerusalem. London, 1995; M. Klein, Doves in the skies of Jerusalem. Jerusalem, 1999; T. Kollek, Jerusalem. In: Foreign Affairs, 1977, Nr. 55, Nr. 4, S. 701-716; A. Latendresse, Between myth and reality: Israeli perspectives on Jerusalem. In: Shu'un Tanmawiyyeh, Bd. 5, 1995/1996, S. 2-10; J. Lustick, Reinventing Jerusalem. In: Foreign Policy, Bd. 93, 1993/1994, S. 41-59; J. Quigley, Jerusalem in international law. In: Jerusalem today: what future for the peace process. Jerusalem, 1996; R. Shuqair, Jerusalem: its legal status and the possibility of a durable settlement. Ramallah, 1996; J. Whitbeck, The Jerusalem question: condominium as compromise. In: The Jerusalem Times, Nr. 24, 1998, S. 5; *"Israel and the occupied territories: report on human rights practices for 1997"*. In: U.S. Department of State, 30 January 1998 at 9; *"The protection of Jewish holy sites regulation (1981)"*. In: Legal violations of Arab minority rights in Israel, Jerusalem, 1998, S. 83; J.L. Kraemer (Hrg.), Jerusalem: problems and perspectives. New York, 1980; M. Romann, A. Weingrod, Living together separately: Arabs and Jews in contemporary Jerusalem. Princeton, 1991; A.L. Tibawi, Anglo-arab relations and the question of Palestine, 1914-1921. London, 1978; A.L. Tibawi, The Islamic pious foundations in Jerusalem: origins, history and usurpation by Israel. London, 1978.

dieses Babel-Rom auch einmal Jerusalem, die sonst heilige Stadt, die sich mit Sünden befleckt hat, die 'große Stadt' genannt und dazu mit Sodom gleichgesetzt (vgl. dazu in den prophetischen Drohreden Jes. 1,9; Ezechiel 16,46.49) und schließlich mit Ägypten. Entsprechendes findet sich in der Verkündigung Jesu, der einerseits das irdische Jerusalem, wie jeder damalige Jude, die heilige Stadt nennt, der aber andererseits doch betont, daß dieses Jerusalem verspielt hat. Die Frommen, die 'auf Jerusalems Erlösung warten' (Luk. 2,38), müssen ihr Gesicht einem anderen Jerusalem zuwenden. Bei einer Annäherung an Jerusalem hat Jesus auf seiner Wallfahrt über sein Verhältnis zu dieser heiligen, aber nun unheilig werdenden Stadt wegen ihres bevorstehenden Untergangs geweint und das Nähere darüber in umfassender apokalyptischer Rede (Mark. 13) ausgeführt. Was in Gal. 4,25f. über die Ablösung des 'jetzigen Jerusalems' durch das 'obere Jerusalem' knapp behauptet und in der Johannes-Apokalypse bis in die Einzelheiten hinein entfaltet ist, hat seinen geschichtlichen Grund in der Geschichte von Jesus Christus.

Es ist also die himmlische Stadt Jerusalem, die Heimat der Christen, bei aller Verbundenheit mit der jüdischen Ausdrucksweise etwas anderes als die Jerusalem-Stadt der Juden und die Babel-Stadt der Heiden. Damit wird apokalyptisch unterstrichen und gesichert, was oben über das eschatologische politeuma im Himmel der Christen gegen Juden und Heiden gesagt ist. Die in solchem Zusammenhang gegebenen sittlichen Weisungen bekommen von der Sicht des himmlischen Jerusalems her Richtung und Kraft. Die obere, die neue, die heilige, himmlische Stadt Gottes ist das Ziel, aber auch der Grund des ganzen Heilsgeschehens von Ewigkeit zu Ewigkeit". [7]

Karen Armstrong betrachtet die heutige religiös-politische Bedeutung der Stadt so:

"*Since 1948 the gradual return of the Jewish people to Zion had resulted in the displacement of thousands of Palestinians from their homeland as well as from Jerusalem. We know from the history of Jerusalem that exile is experiences as the end of the world, as a mutilation and a spiritual dislocation.*

Everything becomes meaningless without a fixed point and orientation of home. When cut off from the past, the present becomes a desert and the future un-imaginable. Certainly the Jews experienced exile as demonic and destructive. Tragically, this burden of suffering has now been passed by the State of Israel to the Palestinians, whatever its original intentions. It is not surprising that Palestinians have not al-

---

[7] K.L. Schmidt, Jerusalem als Urbild und Abbild. In: Eranos-Jahrbuch, Bd. XVIII, 1950, S. 230-231.

ways behaved in an exemplary manner in the course of their own struggle for survival. But, again, there are Palestinians who recognize that compromise be necessary if they are regain at least part of their homeland." [8]

---

[8] K. Armstrong, Jerusalem: one city, three faiths. New York, 1996, S. 425-426.

Hexenprozesse und der Werwolfglaube in Estland

Tiina Vähi, Tartu

Die Popularität des Hexenglaubens und die Entstehung der Hexenprozesse hat man in Europa mit der religiösen oder politischen Verfolgung verbunden, die ihren Höhepunkt im 15.-16. Jahrhundert in Form der Inquisition erreicht hat.

Zu den wichtigsten Gründen für die Verbreitung der Hexenprozesse zählt die wachsende Spannung zwischen Protestanten und Katholiken, die zum Krieg geführt haben. Der Hexenwahn war am auffälligsten in den Regionen, in denen scharfe soziale Gegensätze sich mit Glaubensfeindschaft verbunden haben und in denen Katastrophen wie Sturm, Pest und Hungersnot die Spannungen in der Gesellschaft gesteigert haben. Besonders grausam war sowohl die kirchliche als auch die weltliche Anfeindung von Hexen in katholischen Regionen Europas wie zum Beispiel in Frankreich, wo die lange Tradition der Ketzerprozesse zur Begründung für die gerichtliche Verfolgung der Hexen wurde (Russell 2001: 99).

Die das ganze Europa erfassende Hexenjagd hat auch die peripheren Gebiete nicht unberührt gelassen, fiel dort aber viel bescheidener aus. Die massenhafte und systematische Verfolgung der Hexen gehörte mit der zu diesem Zweck geschaffenen Inquisition und den Inquisitionsgerichten in die Welt des spätmittelalterlichen und früh-neuzeitlichen Europas.

Die Zugehörigkeit Estlands zur Peripherie Europas weitab vom Zentrum der Hexenprozesse hat es mit sich gebracht, daß die Inquisitionswellen abgeschwächt erst etwas später hierher gelangten. Die mittelalterliche katholische Inquisition Europas der klassischen Form – insbesondere in ihrer blutigen spanischen Variante – ist samt Heiligem Tribunal gar nicht erst bis Estland gelangt.

Die in Estland jahrhundertelang andauernde Bestrafung und Hinrichtung der Hexen kann als bescheidene schwedische Kolonialinquisition bezeichnet werden, die mit der spanischen und portugiesischen Kolonialinquisition auf dem amerikanischen Kontinent oder der Kolonialinquisition in der schwer zugänglichen Rand- und Gebirgsgebieten Europas verglichen werden kann, deren Einwohnerschaft den christlichen Glauben nur formal nach dessen (oft gewaltsamer) Einführung kennengelernt hatte (Trevor-Roper 1967: 108, 116).

Ebenso wie die Hochgebirgsregionen Spaniens, die europäischen Alpen und andere "Randgebiete" gehörte das Baltikum zur Peripherie Europas, in denen die religiösen Überzeugungen, Sitten und Bräuche des Volksglaubens noch Jahrhunderte nach der Annahme des Christentums erhalten geblieben sind. Auf dem

Hintergrund der in Europa und letztlich auch in Estland stattgefundenen Hexenprozesse haben zu Beginn der Neuzeit auf Grund des Übergangs von den veralteten Feudalbeziehungen zum aufkommenden Kapitalismus und der Reformationskriege begleitet von Epidemien, Hungersnöten und Naturkatastrophen grosse soziale Umbrüche im gesellschaftlichen Leben stattgefunden. Ausserdem wurden die lokalen Verhältnisse und die Geisteswelt durch Kriege beeinflusst, die im 16. und 17. Jahrhundert in Alt-Livland ausgetragen wurden und zu politisch territorialen Umgestaltungen und zu religiöser Wirrnis beigetragen haben. Diese haben statt des erhofften Fortschritts und klarer Verhältnisse vielmehr das materielle und geistige Chaos mit sich gebracht und zur Verbreitung einer pessimistischen Lebenssicht beigetragen. Die Folge davon waren zerstörte zwischenmenschliche Beziehungen, gegenseitiges Misstrauen und Furcht, die zur Überschätzung des Hexenglaubens sowohl im Volk als bei den Machthabern geführt haben.

Ein Überblick über die in Estland stattgefundenen Hexenprozesse

Es ist unmöglich, die Gesamtzahl der in Estland durchgeführten Hexenprozesse auszumachen, da ein Teil von Gerichtsunterlagen aus der früheren katholischen Zeit und der zweiten Hälfte des 16. Jahrhunderts, teilweise auch die aus dem 17. Jahrhundert durch Kriegsereignisse verlorengegangen oder im Laufe der Reformation vernichtet worden ist. Daher sind über die Hexenprozesse der katholischen Zeit hierzulande nur einige Dokumente erhalten. Sie geben Anlass zur Vermutung, dass in Estland Hexenprozesse auch schon früher stattgefunden haben, wenn vielleicht auch nicht in demselben Umfang wie anderswo in Europa. Es ist anzunehmen, dass die Kampagne zur Vernichtung von Hexen auch in Alt-Livland begonnen wurde, nachdem die Hexenbulle *"Summis desiderantes"* (1484) von Papst *Innocentius VIII* und das Handbuch zur Vernichtung der Hexen *Malleus Maleficarum* "Hexenhammer" (1487) der Inquisitoren Jacob Sprenger und Heinrich Institoris, die zur ideologischen Grundlage für die gesamte Aktion waren, in ganz Europa grosse Popularität erlangt hat. Wie eifrig die Lehren des Papstes und der berühmten Inquisitoren im mittelalterlichen Alt-Livland angewendet wurden, bleibt leider Gegenstand von Vermutungen.

Über die Anzahl der in Europa durchgeführten Hexenprozesse und die der Opfer gehen die Meinungen auseinander, zumal die letzten Untersuchungen vermuten lassen, dass die diesbezüglich überlieferten Zahlen seit der Aufklärung aus humanistischen Erwägungen heraus übertrieben sind. Die Verbrechen der Inquisition waren nicht so schrecklich und opferreich, wie man sie dargestellt hat. Sicherlich hat es keine Millionen, auch nicht Hunderttausende von Delinquentinnen gegeben. Die wirkliche Anzahl der Prozesse liegt wohl zwischen 100- und 200-Tausend und die der Opfer bei ca. 60- bis 100-Tausend (Nenonen 1992: 31). Dasselbe gilt auch für Estland. Nach gegenwärtigen Angaben sind in Estland im Laufe von dreihundert Jahren (16.-18. Jahrhundert) 145 Prozesse mit 218 Angeklagten und 65 zum Tode Verurteilten zustandegekommen (Madar

1987: 126). Somit ist der Umfang der in Estland durchgeführten Prozesse tausendmal kleiner als im sonstigen Europa – dabei ist zu bedenken, dass Estland flächenmässig und bevölkerungsmässig bedeutend kleiner ist.

Die erste Mitteilung über die Verbrennung einer Hexe stammt aus dem Jahre 1527 in der Nähe von Tallinn auf der Grenze der Güter Saha und Maardu, die zweite aus dem Jahre 1531 aus dem Kirchspiel Äksi und die dritte aus dem Jahre 1542 nach einen in Rakvere durchgeführten Hexenprozess, der 5 Menschen zum Feuertod verurteilt hat. Aus der ersten Hälfte des 16. Jahrhunderts sind nur diese drei Prozesse bekannt, aus der Zeit des livländischen Krieges kennt man keinen einzigen (ibid. 126).

Wie anderswo in Europa, so haben auch in Estland die Reformation und die darauf folgende Periode des religiösen Wirrnis Hexenprozessen Vorschub geleistet. So wurden im Jahre 1596 in der Stadt Tartu einige Hexen verbrannt, wie eine Nachricht der Jesuiten an ihr Zentrum zu verstehen gibt (Helk, V., Salupere 1998: 13).

So widersinnig das auch sei, eine richtiggehende Hexenjagd begann in Estland erst als der "guten alten Zeit" bekannten schwedischen. Damals stellte die Verfolgung der Hexen einen Teil der Unterdrückungspolitik der schwedischen Regierung und der Kirchenmächte gegenüber den Einwohnern des estnischen Gebietes dar, was sowohl durch die Gesetzgebung der Leibeigenschaft als auch durch die Verstärkung der kirchlichen Disziplin verwirklicht wurde. Diese Tätigkeit der Schweden in Estland wurde durch die 'epidemische Kampagne' der Verfolgung der Hexen in ganz Europa während dieser Zeit positiv beeinflusst (Kahk 1987: 165).

Überraschend ist es festzustellen, dass die ideologische Grundlage für die Hexenprozesse im Baltikum und in Skandinavien auch durch die damalige Theologie der Tartuer Universität - *Academia Gustaviana* - gelegt wurde. Denn die später in Aland beschäftigten Richter Nils Pilsander und insbesondere der in Finnland berüchtigt gewordene Veranstalter der Hexenprozesse, der Prokanzler der Turuer Universität *(Åbo Akademi)* und Turuer Bischof Johannes Gezelius [1], erhielten in der *Academia Gustaviana* ihre "dämonologische Ausbildung" – letzterer hat vor seiner Tätigkeit in Finnland als Generalsuperintendent in Livland gearbeitet und hier eine bedeutende Rolle bei der Verbreitung und Ausführung reaktionärer Standpunkte der Kirchenpolitik gespielt (Kahk 1987: 155).

---

[1] **Johannes Gezelius** (der Ältere), geboren 1615 in Värmland. Zuerst studierte er an der Universität zu Uppsala. Im Jahre 1638 ging er zur Universität Tartu, wo er 1641 Magister wurde und schon im selben Jahr Professor für griechische und hebräische Sprachen und 1643 Professor für Theologie. Zwischenzeitlich hatte er in Schweden gearbeitet. 1660 wurde er zum Generalsuperintendent Livlands und zum stellvertretenden Kanzler der Tartuer Universität ernannt (Heikkinen 1969: 165).

Der soziale Hintergrund der Hexenprozesse.
Die Angeklagten und die Anklagen

In den siebziger und achtziger Jahren des vorigen Jahrhunderts haben sich die meisten Historiker auf die Erforschung der Sozialgeschichte der Hexen konzentriert. Dank ihrer Ergebnisse hat sich herausgestellt, dass die Entstehung der Vorstellungen über Hexerei aus den realen gesellschaftlichen Verhältnissen entwickelt hat (Russell 2001: 131).

Viele Forscher haben Antworten auf die Verbreitung des Hexenwahns sozial zu begründen versucht. Zum Beispiel zieht A. Macfarlane, der die Hexenprozesse der Grafschaft Essex in England erforscht hat, den Schluss, dass *"sich die Gegensätze und Spannungen, die zwischen den Nachbarn herrschten, schliesslich mit der Beschuldigung des Hexens verbanden"* (Macfarlane 1970: 170). Seiner Meinung nach gehörte der soziale Gegensatz zwischen dem Ankläger und dem Angeklagten zum Grund der Hexenprozesse zu einer Zeit, als an die Stelle der traditionellen und statischen Gemeinde eine lebendigere, variablere und gegenüber Sonderwerten duldsamere Gesellschaft zu treten begann (Macfarlane 1978: 1-2, 189).

Auch französische Forscher haben festgestellt, dass vor allen Dingen ärmere Dorfbewohner der Hexerei verdächtigt wurden. Der Meinung von R. Muchembled nach ist *"die Hexerei die Tochter der Armut"*. Soziale Feindschaft findet sich im jedem Menschenkollektiv, das Spannungen zwischen Reichen und Ärmeren aufweist. Neid und Gegensätze aller Art bewirken ein entsprechendes Denken (Muchembled 1979: 159; Kahk, ibid. 149).

Nach J.B. Russell ist eine Verbindung zwischen Hexen und Klassenzugehörigkeit nicht überzeugend. Diesen Zusammenhang könne man nicht überall erkennen. Wenn in England die Hexe meistens ärmer war als ihr Kläger, die Hexen zumeist aus dem Volk der Knechte stammten und ihre Kläger zumeist Freibauern waren, so wurden im Südwesten Deutschlands sowohl die Reichen als auch die Armen angeklagt; so hat es unter den Verurteilten Reiche und Arme zu ziemlich gleichen Teilen gegeben. Auf Grund der Untersuchung der Verhältnisse im Südwesten Deutschlands hat es den Anschein, als hätten die Anklagen meistens Personen mit ungewöhnlich schlechtem oder gutem Ruf getroffen, also waren Menschen, die auf irgendeine Weise aufgefallen sind, am meisten gefährdet. Meistens wurden Diebe, Sexualverbrecher, Unruhestifter und Hebammen der Hexerei beschuldigt. Andererseits wurden aber ebenso oft auch Ratsmitgliedern, Kaufleute und Lehrer schuldig befunden (Russell 2001: 134).

Gesellschaftswissenschaftler haben vermutet, dass der Hexenglaube eine soziale Funktion hatte, die sich nach unbewussten Bedürfnissen richtete, jemanden aus der Not des Alltagslebens heraus zu beschuldigen. Also habe die Hexerei die Schuld von der abstrakten und verstandesmässigen auf die persönliche Sphäre gewälzt, die man bestrafen konnte. Die Verurteilung der Hexe und ihre Hinrichtung hätten den Zauber vertrieben, so daß man danach ruhig weiterleben konnte. Diese religiös-psychologische Meinung erkläre auch die grosse Anzahl von Hinrichtungen (Russell 2001: 132).

Wie anderswo in Europa, sind auch in Estland die Anklagen aus den innerdörflichen sozialen Spannungen heraus gewachsen. Die meisten Hexenprozesse begannen mit einem Streit zwischen den Bauern und mit Beschuldigungen, Schaden mittels Hexerei angerichtet zu haben. Wegen des Misstrauens, das im Volk herrschte, und wegen des gegen einander gerichteten Neids oder ethnozentrischer Ansichten hat es zu allen Zeiten sowohl Ankläger als auch Zeugen gegeben. Trevor-Roper hat bemerkt, dass dann, wenn eine Gemeinde von "grosser Angst ergriffen war, sie erwartungsgemäss angefangen hat, den Feind unter sich zu suchen" (Trevor-Roper 1969: 190).

Es hat den Anschein, als ob die in Estland und auch in Finnland durchgeführten Hexenprozesse mit der Hinwendung von Mitgliedern des Volks an die Mächtigen um Hilfe begannen, nicht aber als Folge einer Anzeige durch Hexenjäger zu sehen sind. Örtliche Machthaber - Gutsherren und Pfarrer - haben Bauern selten beschuldigt (Madar 1987: 136) – die innerdörfliche soziale Kontrolle hat auch ohne die Initiative und Aktivität seitens von Machthabern und Geistlichen gut geklappt. Die Gutsbesitzer, Geistlichen und Richter führten den Rechtsvollzug und die Sanktion durch, wobei sie sich auf die herrschende Ideologie und die geltenden Gesetze stützten.

Heutige wissenschaftliche Abhandlungen richten ihr Augenmerk auf die Erfassung sozialpsychologischer Gegebenheiten der Angeklagten, erforschen deren gesellschaftliche Position und Reputation – auch ihre geschlechtliche Zugehörigkeit ist ein Thema.

Die Hexerei in Westeuropa galt jahrhundertelang als eine vornehmlich weibliche Tätigkeit. Das gilt besonders für England, da hier die Hexen zu 80% Frauen waren (Russell 1987: 420). Die Beschuldigung der Frauen mit Hexerei stammt aus den mittelalterlichen und späteren dämonologischen Lehren und erklärt sich zunächst daraus, dass man sich den Teufel als eine männliche Person vorstellte, der sich eine Hexe sexuell unterwarf. Hier ist aber auch zu die Tatsache zu erwähnen, dass im 14. Jahrhundert Frauen und Männer noch zu gleichen Teilen beschuldigt wurden, es im 15. Jahrhundert jedoch unter den Angeklagten mehr Frauen gab (Russell 1972: 279; Cohn 1975: 227-229). In den Jahren 1450-1750 waren es auf jeden Fall meisten Frauen, die als Hexen bekannt wurden (Levack 1987: 124-128).

Im Laufe der Zeit haben sich international stereotype Vorstellungen herausgebildet, nach denen Hexen alte, hässliche und böse Weiber sind, die zänkisch und verdriesslich waren und Verfluchungen aussprachen. Obwohl die Hexen auf Spottbildern als hässliche alte Weiber dargestellt wurden, hat das Aussehen eines Menschen keinen Grund dafür abgegeben, jemanden der Hexerei zu beschuldigen. Der Hexerei wurden zwar gerne alte Frauen verdächtigt, die sich mit dem Heilen oder Betteln beschäftigten, weil sie dann, wenn sie den gewünschten Lohn oder die Almosen nicht bekamen, Flüche ausstiessen. So galt beispielsweise in Schweden als Prototyp einer Hexe eine alte Frau, die zwar keine Gefahr in der sozialen Konkurrenz darstellte, die aber sowohl unter den Kindern als auch unter den Erwachsenen Widerwärtigkeit und Angst hervorrief

(Heikkinen 1969: 60). Ausserdem haben die Forscher beobachtet, dass es unter denen, die der Hexerei beschuldigt wurden, wiederholt solche Frauen gab, die nicht mehr fruchtbare Frauen im Alter der Menopause waren und sich um Kleinkinder kümmerten - oft waren es Hebammen.

In England verdächtigte man auch oft Häusler- und Bettlerfrauen, die zu Hochzeiten, Totenfeiern oder anderen wichtigen Ereignissen im Leben der Dorfbewohner nicht eingeladen waren und darum den Nachbarn Unglück wünschten (Thomas, K. 1971: 553-556).

Derlei Beispiele spiegeln sich deutlich in estnischen und finnischen Volkstraditionen wider. Zu ihnen gehören auch Motive von Werwolfsagen, die sich ebenfalls in den Materialien der Hexenprozesse finden.

Aus den Protokollen der estnischen und finnischen Hexenprozesse ergibt sich, dass die Hexerei in den nordischen Ländern nicht nur dem Wirkungskreis der Frauen zugehörte, sondern selbstverständlich – und vielleicht überwiegend – auch in den der Männer. Nach heutigen Erkenntnissen waren unter den 206 Angeklagten in Estland, deren Geschlecht bekannt ist, 59,9 Prozent Männer. In den Gerichten Estlands war der Anteil der Männer und Frauen beinahe gleich, 49,1% zu 50,9% (Madar 1987). Bedeutend grösser war der Anteil von männlichen Angeklagten in Livland (69,1%). Auch in Island und Russland war der Anteil von Männern an der Hexerei grösser als der Anteil der Frauen (Nenonen, 1992: 32).

Das Übergewicht der Männer unter denen, die der Hexerei beschuldigt wurden, hat man für Skandinavien auf dem Hintergrund der entsprechender schamanistischer Praktiken zu erklären versucht (Hertzberg, 1889). Hier sind die Forscher jedoch unterschiedlicher Ansicht. So war beispielsweise nach Meinung von Martti Haavio die schamanistische Hexereikultur zur Zeit der Durchführung der finnischen Hexenprozesse im 17. Jahrhundert schon aus dem Volksglauben verschwunden (Haavio 1967). Entsprechend der Angaben des bedeutenden Forschers von finnischen Hexenprozessen, M. Nenonen, gibt es in den Protokollen der neuzeitlichen Hexenprozesse wenig Hinweise über schamanistische Seancen, weswegen er den Einfluss der schamanistischen Tradition bei der Beschuldigung der Hexerei bei Männern für gering hält. Er hält die Gründe dafür, dass Männer in die Hexenprozesse geraten sind, eher für gesellschaftspolitisch. Es gehöre zum steropyen Verständnis des finnischen Hexenmeisters, dass Männer durch Verhexung Schaden zufügten und Frauen durch Magie heilten. Nachdem die letzte verurteilt worden sie, habe man auch die Männer der Magie beschuldigt. Dementsprechend seien auch ihnen Anklagen über die Beschäftigung mit der Hexerei angehängt worden. Den Grund für die Zunahme des Anteils der Frauen sieht er nicht in einer speziell gegen die Frauen gerichteten Verfolgung, als vielmehr in der Ausdehnung des staatlichen Einflusses auf das Gebiet des Alltagslebens, auf den Bereich der häuslichen Tätigkeit der Frauen im Bereich der Familie, der Verwandtschaft oder der Dorfgemeinschaft. Als Grund dafür, dass der Typ des männlichen Hexenmeisters aus den Gerichten immer weiter verschwunden ist, hält M. Nenonen die Einführung einer neuen Hexentheorie: Um die Mitte des 17. Jahrhunderts erscheinen plötzlich überall die zum Hexensabbat fliegenden weiblichen Hexen (Nenonen 386-388).

In den wissenschaftlichen Abhandlungen fehlen derart grundlegende Beobachtungen über die estnischen Hexenprozesse. Wenn man aber im Auge behält, dass Estland und Finnland damals zum Schwedischen Königreich gehört hat, dann ist anzunehmen, dass hier wie dort etwa dieselben Faktoren für die Hexenprozesse galten. Dies wird auch durch die bekannte gewordenen estnischen Angaben bestätigt, die zeigen, dass im Blick auf die Geschlechtszugehörigkeit unter den Beschuldigten der Jahre 1590-1629 das Übergewicht auf der Seite Frauen lage, in den Jahren 1630-1709 jedoch wesentlich mehr auf der Seite der Männer. Wenn man in denselben Perioden die zum Tode Verurteilten einander gegenüberstellt, dann ergibt sich dasselbe Verhältnis.

Die Ankläger waren meistens Bauern (zu 82,7% Männer), die behauptet haben, der Verdächtigte habe ihnen oder ihrer Familie in Bezug auf ihr Hab und Gut mit Verhexung irgendeinen Schaden zugefügt (Madar 1987). Aus den finnischen Untersuchungen geht hervor, dass der Ankläger ebenfalls meistens ein Mann war, der hauptsächlich andere Männer des Dorfes, seltener Frauen beschuldigt hat. Die Frauen haben einander gegenüber selten Beschuldigungen erhoben, noch seltener gegen Männer. Die Bedeutung der geschlechtlichen Angehörigkeit in den Hexenprozessen war in verschiedenen Regionen und in verschiedenen Zeiten allerdings unterschiedlich (Nenonen 1992: 184). Dasselbe kann man bei estnischen Hexenprozessen beobachten.

Die Protokolle der estnischen Hexenprozesse sind wenig informativ und spiegeln das Alter, den Familienstand, den sozialen Zustand usw. der Beschuldigten nicht genau wider. Am häufigsten wurden in mittlerem Alter stehende oder ältere verheiratete estnische Bauern und Bäuerinnen der Hexerei beschuldigt (Madar 1987). Dasselbe gilt im generell auch für die anderen skandinavischen Länder – Schweden, Dänemark, Norwegen –, doch konnte hier und da der Anteil von ledigen Frauen oder Witwen grösser sein (Ankarloo 1987: 273-275; Birkelund 1983: 60-62; Levack 1987: 131-132). Was das Alter betrifft, so scheint dieses kaum zu ermitteln. Da es in Augen der Rechtsprechenden offensichtlich keine besondere Rolle gespielt hat, ist es meistens auch nicht genau bestimmt worden (Nenonen 1992: 189). Nach Angaben aus Mitteleuropa waren Angeklagten wenigstens 50-60 Jahre alt (Levac 1987: 128-131). Man glaubte, dass die Zauberkraft mit dem zunehmenden Alter wuchs.

Auf Grund von finnischen Beispielen ist ebenso wie in Estland das Alter selten genau erwähnt worden. Häufig waren es sehr jungen Menschen, Teenager, sehr alte. Vermutlich hat man im 17. Jahrhundert sein eigenes Alter oder das seines Nächsten nicht schätzen können. Wenn der Mensch körperlich und geistig gesund war, machte es offenbar keinen Unterschied, ob er 40, 50 oder 60 Jahre alt war. Im allgemeinen wurden über 60 Jahre alte Leute schon für alt gehalten. Man kann vermuten, dass dann, wenn das Alter in den Protokollen nicht genau genannt wurde, der Angeklagte weder besonders jung noch besonders alt war, also den Mittelalten gehörte (Nenonen 1992: 185, 187).

Aus den estnischen Hexenprozessen sind Fälle bekannt, nach denen Angeklagte aus anderen Nationen stammten - zum Beispiel gab es da vier Finnen, drei Schweden, zwei Deutsche, einen Litauer, einen Russen und einen Polen (Madar 1987: 135). Daraus ist zu schließen, dass der Ethnozentrismus sich eher aus den folkloristischen Vorstellungen belegen lässt als aus den Anklagen in den Hexenprozessen.

Unter die Beschuldigten geriet man nicht ganz zufällig. Gewöhnlich hatte die entsprechende Person oder jemand in ihrer Familie schon den Ruf einer Hexe, Heilerin o.ä. Bei 22 Männern und 10 Frauen wusste man von Fähigkeiten des Heilens, und man hatte sich an sie auch früher um Hilfe gewandt. Die Zauberkunst und der Ruf der Hexe schien auch von einer Generation auf die nächste übergegangen zu sein.

Die Fähigkeit der Verhexung wurde häufig auch beiden Partnern einer Ehe zugeschrieben. Denn in vielen Fällen wurden beide Gatten zusammen beschuldigt (ibid.).

Der dämonologische Hintergrund des Hexenglaubens und der Hexenprozesse

Nach Ansicht von Jeffrey Burton Russell nach haben drei Faktoren den europäischen Hexenglauben geformt: Zauberei, Heidentum und Folklore. Zusätzlich nennt er als vierten Faktor die Häresie (Russell 2001: 65). Das Volk hat sich Klagen vor Gericht normalerweise auf drei Faktoren gestützt: Volkstümliche Glaubensvorstellungen von der schädigenden Magie – von Verhexung in Krankheit oder Tod mit Hilfe eines bösen Auges, von der übernatürlichen Fähigkeit der Menschen, sich in Werwölfe oder -bären zu verwandeln, oder mittels der Magie sich Gewinn zu verschaffen oder Diebstahl zu begehen – auf diese Faktoren bauen die Anklagen normalerweise auf.

Von seiten der Richter wurden bei Verhexungsanklagen an erster Stelle der Abfall vom richtigen Glauben und der Kirche vorgebracht. An diesen Verfehlungen konnten in gleicher Weise sowohl die Weisen und Beschwörer schuldig sein, die an den vorchristlichen magischen Überzeugungen festgehalten hatten, ebenso Ketzer und Sektierer, die die Lehre der an Ort und Stelle herrschenden Kirche nicht anerkannt haben (Kahk 1987: 151).

Die volkstümliche Magie und das Beschwörung wurde mit der satanischen Hexerei gleichgesetzt, die Hexerei wiederum mit der Ketzerei. Mit der Gleichsetzung von Hexerei und Ketzerei wurden die Grenzlinien für das Christentum gezogen, die den Zusammenhalt aller Christen gewährleisteten, um den schrecklichen und mächtigen Truppenmassen unter Anführung des leibhaftigen Satans entgegentreten zu können (Russell 2001: 132).

Die Inquisition war in ihren Anfangsjahrhunderten in erster Linie gegen die Ketzer gerichtet. Erst ein Hundert Jahre später begann man mit der Ketzerei auch das Hexerei zu verbinden. In der estnischen Geschichte fehlen Auskünfte über die hierzulande tätigen ketzerischen Sekten und die katholische Rechtsprechung über sie.

Je mehr die Inquisition in den christlichen Ländern Fuss gefasst hat, desto mehr begann man davon zu sprechen, dass Verhexung und Beschwörung die Krieger des Satans seien, die in die sogenannte "Synagoge des Satans" gehörten. In der zweiten Hälfte des 14. Jahrhunderts war in den dämonologischen Traktaten eine recht klares Konzept über die ketzerische Sekte der Hexen-Magier ausgearbeitet. Als deren Gründer wurde Satan angesehen. Entscheidend wurde die Idee, mit Satan einen Vertrag zu schliessen, die dem dämonischen Treiben der Beschwörer die Krone aufgesetzt hat. Von nun an war der *Maleficus* ein Mensch, der mit Satan einen Vertrag geschlossen hat (Russell 2001: 65).

In eine neue Etappe, die den Höhepunkt markiert hat, ist die katholische Dämonologie gegen Ende des 15. Jahrhunderts eingetreten, als der Papst Innocentius VIII. mit seiner im Jahre 1484 herausgegebenen Hexenbulle *Summis desiderantes affectibus* den Kampf gegen die Sekte der Hexen verstärkt hat (Inquisitoren waren nämlich der Meinung, dass eine solche Sekte existierte).

Die autoritativsten Dämonologiespezialisten der Kirche aller Zeiten, die deutschen Inquisitoren *Jacob Sprenger* (1436-1495) und *Heinrich Institoris Krämer* (1430-1505) bekamen den Auftrag, den Kampf mit den Hexen und Zauberern aufzunehmen. Diesen päpstlichen Auftrag haben sie in ihrem Traktat, der berüchtigten Anleitung zur Vernichtung von Hexen, dem *"Hexenhammer"* (*Malleus maleficarum* 1487) vorgestellt, wo sie die Grundlinien der Dämonologie formuliert haben, in denen der Hauptfaktor ein Vertrag mit dem Teufel war. Die Autoren bestätigen, dass der Mensch, der mit dem Teufel einen Vertrag geschlossen hat, zur Brut des Satans, zur Hexe oder zum Magier wird und fähig ist, den ihn umgebenden Menschen Schaden und Unglück zuzufügen.

Ausser den destruktiven Taten können Ketzer und Hexen auch angenehme Dinge zustandebringen: Erfolg in der Liebe garantieren, Schönheit geben, von der Unfruchtbarkeit heilen, durch Wunder reich machen, usw.

Nach Sprenger und Institoris ist der Grund von jedweder Ketzerei die Tätigkeit des Teufels, der Irrlehren sät. Die Hexerei wurde von ihnen als eine Form der Ketzerei angesehen. Auch auf die Frage, wie die satanische Hexerei in den religiösen Werwolfüberzeugungen zum Ausdruck kommt, können wir aus ihrem Buch eine Antwort finden. Im I. Teil des *Hexenhammers* behandeln die Autoren ausführlich das Wesen der Hexerei, ihre Verbundenheit mit dem Teufel und ihre Äusserungen, unter denen auch die Verwandlung in den Werwolf eine Form ist.

Die von ihnen gestellte neunte Frage behandelt die Verhexung in Tiere: *Können die Hexen Menschen in Tiere verwandeln und können die Hexen als Tiere vor den Menschen erscheinen?*

Diese Frage wird beantwortet, indem man sich auf hier wichtigste rechtliche Urkunde *Canon episcopi* (Kap. XXVI, 5) stützt, die die Hexerei behandelt: Dies sei unmöglich. Nach scholastischer Methode trägt man die Standpunkte dazu von drei Wissenschaftlern zusammen und kommt zu dem Ergebnis, dass der Teufel einen Menschen durchaus in einem solchen Grade täuschen kann, dass ihm bei Sinnestäuschung ein Tier erscheint (Sprenger, Institoris 1991: 135).

Gleichzeitig hat man in der Dämonologie den Teufel zum Konkurrenten

Gottes gemacht, zum grössten Magier, Zauberer und Beschwörer, der dank seiner ätherischen Eigenschaften andere Gestalten annehmen könne – nicht nur die Gestalt eines Menschen und verschiedener Tiere, sondern auch von Gegenständen –, auch könne er verduften und in einem einzigen Augenblick grosse Räume durchqueren. Nach den damaligen Deutungen der kirchlichen Dogmen konnten die Metamorphosen des Teufels ein Mann, eine Frau, Tiere und Ungeheuer sein. Nach Rudwin tritt der Teufel in zeitlicher Folge zuerst als Tier, dann als Tierhybride (Ungeheuer) und zum Schluss als Mensch auf (Rudwin 1973: 38).

In der Dämonologie sind Bestialität, Sexualität und Satanität eng miteinander verbunden und werden mit der Inversion der Heiligen Dreifaltigkeit vergleichen (Russell 1988: 126). Die tierischen Züge des Teufels könne man im christlichen Rahmen als wilde, unorganisierte und unbeherrschte Natur deuten, die die menschliche Kultiviertheit und organisierte Kultur zu vernichten versuche (Wolf-Knuts 1992: 109-114). Das Transformationsvermögen könne als das zentrale Kriterium der Supranormalität des Teufels angesehen werden, da archaische Menschen und Tiergestalten auf Grund einer übernatürlichen Metamorphose oft auch für böse Geister erklärt würden (Ivanits 1989: 39-40).

Nach demselben Grundsatz gewann die Vorstellung der Tiermetamorphose im Volksglauben - der Werwolf - in der Dämonologie eine diabolische Bedeutung. Die Menschen, die für Werwölfe gehalten wurden, wurden zugleich als Hexen im Dienste des Teufels gehalten, die aus einer vom Teufel verursachten Sinnestäuschung heraus glaubten, dass sie die Gestalt eines Wolfes angenommen hätten.

Das Christentum hat nun eine Hexe, die freiwillig dem Teufel dienen und mit Hexerei dem Menschen Schaden zufügen wollte (Cohn 1970, 11), und das mythische Wesen, das auf verschiedene Weise – sei es als Werwolf, Schrat, Windhose oder etwas anderes aus dem dämonenhaften Volksglauben stammt – auftrat, gleich beurteilt.

Zwischen der Kirche und des Hexenglaubens herrschte eine enge Verbindung. Die Elemente des Hexenglaubens, die aus den Vorstellungen des Volksglaubens kamen, fanden eine Entsprechung in den Dogmen des Christentums, durch dessen Einwirkung Hexerei und Ketzerei miteinander verbunden wurden. Die Universalität der mittelalterlichen Kirche als einer übergreifenden Institution hat die wesentliche Voraussetzung dafür geschaffen, dass der Hexenglaube zu einer das ganz Europa umfassenden Erscheinung wurde. Auch die in Estland durchgeführten Hexenprozesse münden als Parallelerscheinungen in diesen grossen Strom der Entwicklung Europas ein (Mark 1938: 20-21).

Die in den estnischen Hexenprozesse vorgebrachten Beschuldigungen entsprachen im allgemeinen den im damaligen Europa verbreiteten theologisch-dämonologischen Ansichten vom Vertrag zwischen dem Teufel und dem Menschen, andere Menschen und Tiere zu schädigen. Auch wenn in den von Bauern beim Gericht eingereichten Anklagen gewöhnlich der diabolische Teil der Beschuldigung fehlt, hat sich dieser im Laufe des Gerichtsprozesses herauskristallisiert.

Lokale Richter und Pfarrer liessen sich gemäss der Hexendoktrin von den religiösen Überzeugungen über den Vertragsschluss mit dem Teufel und dem Besuch des Hexensabbats leiten und versuchten, diese im Laufe des Verhörs mit entsprechenden Fragen an die Angeschuldigten, in die Sachverhalte zu projizieren. Die Menschen haben sich trotz Folterung nicht immer zu solchen Vorstellungen bekannt (Kahk 1987: 164).

Aus den Hexenprotokollen Österreichs und der Schweiz geht hervor, dass die Menschen solche Zeugnisse nicht aus eigener Initiative abgelegt haben (Horsley 1979: 693). Auch in Estland gibt es mehrere Protokolle mit Aussagen, aus denen man das Vorhandensein der Sabbatvorstellungen folgern könnte, aber es hat den Anschein, dass diese nur unklare Anspielungen auf die Sabbatvorstellung der Hexendoktrin sind. Konkrete, mittels Folterung erwirkte Geständnisse über die Teilnahme an Hexensabbaten gibt es nur in wenigen Protokollen, z.B. in dem des Jahres 1616 aus einem in Tartu durchgeführten Prozess (s. Salupere 1998: 16-23). Viel charakteristischer für die alte volkstümliche religiöse Überzeugung sind die mit der Magie verbundenen Vorstellungen, die von der Schädigung durch das böse Auge, das Wort oder andere Kunststücke berichten. Auch Werwolfgeschichten finden in den Protokollen der Hexenprozesse einen bemerkenswerten Reflex, obwohl sie in der offiziellen Stellungnahme der Hexenjagd verhältnismässig schwach vertreten sind.

Nach den Recherchen von M. Madar wurden in den zurzeit bekannten 145 Prozessen am häufigsten Anklagen wegen der Verhexung in Krankheit und Verkrüppelung (45) oder in den Tod (36) eines Menschen erhoben; auch wurde des Diabolismus (26), der Verhexung in Tod oder Krankheit von Tieren (21), der Schädigung als Werwolf (18) beschuldigt. Die übrigen Anschuldigungen waren Diebstahl, Brandstiftung oder das Verhexen der Ernte, der Felder, der Milch, des Biers, des Boots, der Branntweinbrennerei oder einer anderen Sache (Madar 1987: 137).

Werwolfprozesse

Der Meinung des finnischen Hexenprozess-Forschers A. Heikkinen nach *"scheint der charakteristische Zug der Hexenprozesse des Baltikums gerade die Konzentration der Beschuldigungen auf die Schädigung als Werwolf zurückgeht ... // Baltische Länder sind weithin für die Hexen bekannt, die sich in Werwölfe verwandelt haben."* (Heikkinen 1969: 42).

Woher rühren solche Jahrhunderte alte stereotype Ansichten? Sind sie auch wahr?

Gewiss haben der Herausbildung eines solchen Rufs die Ausführungen der einheimischen Dämonologen-Geistlichen Paul Einhorn und Hermann Samson über Hexen-Werwölfe Vorschub geleistet. Unserem Volk dürften auch die früheren klischeehaften Auskünfte von Olaus Magnus (1555), Caspar Peucerius (1560), Sebastian Münster (1544) u.a. über die Werwölfe Livlands in Europa einen derartigen Ruf eingebracht haben. Alt-Livland gewann dank der Abhandlungen von Männern wie Hermann von Bruiningk, der viel über die Hexenprozesse Livlands geschrieben hat, unverdient den Ruf *des Eldorados der Werwölfe* (Bruiningk 1924: 186).

Dass dieser Ruf nicht immer unverdient war, hat schon der Folklorist Walter Anderson betont, der sowohl die lokalen als auch die europäischen Folkloremateralien besser als von Bruiningk kannte und in ihnen Belege für die reichlich nachweisbare Existenz des Werwolfglaubens in Alt-Livland erkannt hat (Anderson 1924: 152-153).

Auch heutige wissenschaftliche Abhandlungen zur Folklore und Untersuchungen über Hexenprozesse zeigen, dass sich der Glaube an Werwölfe sowohl in der damaligen Folklore als auch in den Protokollen der Werwolfprozesse recht eindeutig wiederfindet. Nach Angaben von M. Madar sollen nämlich in 18 Prozessen Dorfbewohner (18 Männer und 13 Frauen) als Werwölfe des Stiftens von Schäden beschuldigt worden sein (Madar 1987: 138). Diese 18 bisher bekannt gewordenen Prozesse könnten somit auch als Werwolfprozesse bezeichnet werden. Auch bei fast allen anderen Hexenprozessen kamen neben den üblichen Beschuldigungen bezeichnenderweise auch die vor, die das Werwolflaufen oder den Weg zum Werbären betrafen (Madar 1980: 74) – Am Ende werde ich einige Beispiele über die Hexenprozesse vorstellen, in denen Beschuldigungen des Werwolflaufens belegt sind.

Welches Bild zeichnet der angeführte Überblick über die Hexenprozesse über den Werwolfglauben? Können wir den Gelehrten des 16. Jahrhunderts zustimmen, dass in Alt-Livland der Glaube an Werwölfe verbreitet war, der auf einem Vertrag mit dem Teufel und der Zusammenarbeit mit ihm stand? Oder treten hier im volkstümlichen Denken und Verhalten völlig andere Gedankenkonstruktionen über die Dämonologie an den Tag?

Jedenfalls bestätigt die Analyse der Materialien über die Hexenprozesse, dass die Menschen unabhängig von der offiziellen Lehre und den Hexendoktrinen an die Existenz der Werwölfe geglaubt und sich gegenseitig der Werwolfaktivitäten bezichtigt haben. Bei näherer Betrachtung der erwähnten 16 Prozessurkunden wird klar, dass es weniger Beschuldigungen in Sachen Werwolfaktivitäten gibt als Vorwürfe. Das bedeutet, dass die Menschen auf Grund anderer ernster *Maleficum*-Hexenbeschuldigungen wie etwa die Verhexung in Krankheit und Tod vor das Gericht gebracht worden sind und dass sie sich erst im Laufe des Prozesses als Folge von Folterungen auch zu Werwolfaktivitäten bekannt haben, weil sie diese für ihre erste und kleinere Versündigung gehalten haben. Dies ist jedenfalls 1617 im Prozess von Kiviloo mit Alit, 1623 im Prozess von Merimõisa mit Klati Jaak, 1628 im Prozess von Undla mit Maret und später noch in allerlei anderen Prozessen geschehen. Im Prozess von Kiviloo waren die Werwolfaktivitäten zunächst ein Nebenmotiv, wurde dann aber zur Hauptbeschuldigung, die sieben Menschen in den Feuertod trieb. Dieser Prozess, von dem eindrucksvolle Materialien überliefert sind, ist in der Geschichte der Hexenprozesse als der berühmteste Werwolfprozess Estlands bekannt (Luce 1829: 187-189).

Bei der Lektüre dieser Protokolle bekommt man den Eindruck, als ob die Werwolftätigkeit im Vergleich mit anderen eingereichten Anklagen ein Verbrechen von viel leichterem Gewicht gewesen sei, dem sowohl die Angeklagten als auch die Richter keine besondere Bedeutung beigemessen haben. Häufig bekannte man sich zum Werwolflauf zusätzlich zu anderen Beschuldigungen, wie es ausdrucksvoll im Idavere-Prozess von 1651 zum Ausdruck kommt: Hier war die Hauptbeschuldigung gegenüber der Mutter Else die Verhexung eines Menschen in Tod, die Nebenbeschuldigung dagegen das schon über Jahre andauernde Werwolfaufen zusammen mit ihrem Sohn Hans. Oder: Laiske Mart kann man ja verstehen, wenn er in den Jahren 1641-1642 im Prozess des Pärnuer Landgerichts nach dem Todesurteil gewissermaßen nebenbei aussagte, dass er bei seinem "Herren", dem Teufel, als Werwolf beschäftigt war. Bei anderen Angeklagten, deren Schicksal noch nicht entschieden war, fallen solche Geständnisse allerdings als verhältnismässig unbesonnen auf. Die Werwolfgeschichten schien man vor dem Hexengericht ziemlich leichtfertig und ohne grosses Engagement, schwungvoll fabulierend erzählt zu haben, selbst dann, wenn die Aussagen Bekannte und Nachbarn betraf. So scheint es, dass man die Aufmerksamkeit der Richter mit lustigen Werwolfgeschichten von den Verbrechen wie etwa den Diebstahl von Vermögen zu lenken versuchte, die sich auf eine bestimmte Person bezog, oder damit die Hoffnung verband, eine gegen sich gerichtete Schuldenlast leichter zu machen. Bemerkenswert ist noch die Tatsache, dass man dann, wenn man sich zum Werwolf bekannt hat, eine Kettenreaktion ausgelöst hat: Die Beschuldigung von Bekannten hat dazu geführt, dass diese wiederum andere Dorfbewohner als Werwölfe anzeigten, die bisher nicht involviert waren.

Was steht hinter diesen Werwolf-"Geständnissen"? Geschahen sie nur deswegen, weil die psychischen und physischen Kräfte wegen der Folterung nachließen? Oder kamen hier in extremer Lage noch alte Modelle des mythischen und kulturellen Denkens zum Ausdruck, die zum kollektiven Gedächtnis, zur höchsteigenen Mentalität gehörten?

Auf das Werwolfaufen direkt bezogene Beschuldigungen, dessentwegen die Menschen beim Gericht verklagt wurden, gibt es nach Ergebnissen der gegenwärtigen Untersuchungen wenig. Von den 16 angeführten Prozessbeschreibungen kann eine Beschuldigung des Werwolfaufens nur aus dreien direkt herausgelesen werden – im Protokoll von 1632 tritt eine Beschuldigung wegen des Verhexens in einen Werbären an den Tag, und in dem des Prozesses in Nabala von 1695 die des Werbärlaufens. Zweimal wurde vor dem Gericht Anklage wegen Werwolfaktivitäten erhoben: 1615 wegen Werwolf- und 1633 wegen Werbärlaufens. In allen übrigen Prozessunterlagen kommt der Werwolfglaube nur in erwirkten Geständnissen der Angeklagten zum Ausdruck.

Welches ist der Grund dafür, dass sich der Werwolfglaube so häufig in Geständnissen findet, nicht aber in Anklagen und Beschuldigungen? Merkwürdig ist auch die Tatsache, dass in den Geständnissen der Menschen, die mehrerer Hexereiverbrechen beschuldigt werden, Werwolfaktivitäten im Vordergrund stehen. Es hat den Anschein, als seien Schädigungen auf diesem Weg eher erlaubt gewesen als auf anderen.

Offenbar wurden mehrere Faktoren auf einen gemeinsamen Nenner gebracht, die der Mentalität, der Sinnesart und der kollektiven Bewusstseins der Bevölkerung entgegenkamen und durch althergebrachte Rechtsbräuche und Ermessen der herrschenden Schichten unterstützt wurde. Auf jeden Fall stützen sie sich auf Prinzipien der Moral und der Gerechtigkeit, die von einem genuin volkstümlichen, religiös-mythologischen Weltbild ausgingen, das sich deutlich von dem des Christentums unterschied.

Die "Mentalität des Werwolflaufens" war dem Volk viel eher eigen als der klassische "Teufelsglaube". Denn sie baute in der Regel nicht auf einen Pakt mit dem Teufel, der nicht vollends verboten war. Die Klärung der glaubenspsychologischen und mythologischen Hintergründe dieser Mentalität sollte späteren wissenschaftlichen Abhandlungen vorbehalten bleiben.

Schlussfolgerungen

Aus den Materialien über Hexenprozesse geht hervor, das die Hexerei und die Magie fest im Alltagsleben des estnischen Bauern verankert waren. Gegen die Hexerei musste sich jeder schützen – das tat er am besten mit eigener Hexerei. Es herrschte die sogenannte "Wolfsmoral", in der der Talionsgrundsatz "Zahn um Zahn, Auge um Auge" herrschte. Der Mensch dieser Epoche kannte sich in der Magie aus, war eine Hexer, der sich vor anderen Hexern fürchtete.

Hexerei war eine Gefahr, mit der man sowohl an Werk- als auch an Feiertagen rechnen musste. Das musste im Verhältnis zwischen Mensch und Mensch berücksichtigt werden. Schlechte Beziehungen untereinander, Streit und unerwartete Erkrankung wurden oft mit der Hexerei verbunden. Im Denken der Bauern standen Gesundheit und Krankheit von Mensch und Haustier im Mittelpunkt. Die Bewirkung von gesundheitlichen oder anderen Schäden war üblicherweise der Grund für den Beginn eines Hexenprozesses. Der Schadenszauber galt schon lange vor der Epoche der Hexenprozesse als Verbrechen und hat schon in alten Zeiten zur Verdammung durch das Volkes geführt.

Die Einstellung der Dorfgemeinschaft gegenüber einer als Hexe bekannten Person war insofern meistens negativ, als man von ihr annahm, dass sie Gott gegen das Böse ausgetauscht habe, dass sie Unsittlichkeiten beging, Hab und Gut ihres Nächsten begehrte oder ihre Nachbarn und deren Tiere mit Krankheiten verwünschte. Hexen haben die ethischen Normen der Bauerngesellschaft in verschiedener Hinsicht verletzt. Für einen gewöhnlichen Dorfbewohner war die Hexe somit der Prototyp für soziales und kulturelles Übel. Über die Hexe als einen "Antimenschen" konnte gespottet und verurteilt werden, weil er ausserhalb der Gesetze der Gesellschaft stand und dem Unglück anheimgestellt war. Das einfache Volk war davon überzeugt, dass Hexen eine ihnen eigene Hexenkraft besassen – die gelehrten Kirchenvertreter und Richter erklärten diese Kraft als Gabe des Teufels (Sarmela 1994: 143).

Die Forschungsergebnisse aus den Materialien der estnischen Hexenprozesse zusammenfassend, kann man erkennen, dass die aus der Dämonenkunde abgeleitete Hexendoktrin, die die Verhexung als das Ergebnis eines Paktes mit dem Teufel ansah, für das estnische Bauernvolk nie ganz überzeugend war. Das hatte mehrere Gründe. Zum einen, dass die estnischen Bauern ebenso wie die anderer europäischer Dorfgemeinschaften geglaubt haben, dass Hexen als besondere Menschen sowohl Schaden als auch Gutes anrichten konnten. Man hat in der Magie, die zum Alltag gehört hat, nichts Unzulässiges gesehen. Die Ausübung von Hexenstreichen und das "Possen" war eine zum Privatleben eines jeden gehörende Angelegenheit. Die Wissenden und Weisen, die sich mit Hexerei befasst haben, wurden nach volkstümlicher Anschauung unterschiedlichen Kategorien zugerechnet, so dass die Hexerei einen ambivalenten Charakter hatte: So war die schädigende Magie auch im Bewusstsein des Volkes zwar als verwerflich und strafbar eingestuft, wurden aber nicht mit solcher Strenge verurteilt, wie dies die Lehre der Kirche und die weltlichen Gesetze vorgeschrieben haben.

Obwohl in der Lehre der Kirche und in der Gerichtspraxis die Übergänge zwischen der "schwarzen" und der "weissen" Magie fliessend waren, wurde vom Volk einhellig der Standpunkt vertreten, dass es notwendig sei, die "schwarze", schädigende Magie zu bekämpfen. Hierin gab es keine Meinungsverschiedenheiten. So hat das Volk mit den Hexenklagen vor Gerichten der offiziellen Einstellung Vorschub geleistet und zur Durchführung von Hexenprozessen beigetragen. Als die Kirche begann, auch die Vertreter der "weissen Magie" wie beispielsweise Volksärzte zu verfolgen, wurden in den Gerichten selbst aus ihnen Handlanger des Teufels gemacht.

Das Volk und die Kirche hatten in Sachen Magie und Hexerei unterschiedliche moralisch-rechtliche und religiöse Einstellungen. So ist festzustellen, dass das Volk trotz seines Bekenntnisses zu den Grundwahrheiten des Christentums altertümliche animistische Vorstellungen von der Kraft der Natur, der Tiere und der Seelen beibehielt. Dazu gehörten die Überzeugungen vom religiösen Charakter der Werwölfe, Schrate, Gutsschlepper und anderer mythischer Wesen, mit deren Hilfe der Bauer seine Lebensverhältnisse zu bessern hoffte. Obwohl diese Überzeugungen im Bewusstsein des Volkes eher eine negative Bedeutung hatten, wurden sie mit Zurückhaltung doch nicht für so unerlaubt gehalten wie dies offiziell geschah. Denn wusste im Volk offensichtlich nicht immer, ob die hiermit verbundenen Praktiken der "schwarzen" oder der "weissen" Magie zugerechnet werden sollten. Es hing schliesslich alles davon ab, ob eine Erscheinung aus dem Blickwinkel des Gewinners oder Verlierers betrachtet wurde. Diese ambivalente Einstellung kommt besonders klar beim Werwolf und bei vergleichbaren Überzeugungswesen zum Ausdruck.

Die reichlich schweren Lebensverhältnisse der Bauern brachten es mit sich, dass die Natur rational und nicht nach Grundsätzen der kirchlichen Lehre betrachtet wurde. Dies äusserte sich nicht zuletzt in der Verwandlung in Tiere, ein Phänomen, das von der Dämonenlehre nicht sorgfältig erfasst war und als vom Teufel bewirkte Sinnestäuschung abgetan wurde. Das Volk glaubte an die Tatsache der körperlichen Verwandlung, wofür das Geständnis des jungen Mannes Hans im Prozess zu Idavere von 1651 ein hervorragendes Beispiel ist. Es hat den Anschein, als folge nach Ansicht des Volks die Verwandlung in einen Werwolf ganz andere Grundsätze als von der Dämonenlehre erfasst. Das spiegeln die eingestandenen Bekenntnisse zum Werwolf in den Hexenprozessen wider, die davon ausgehen, dass sie für das Volk eher annehmbar und natürlicher waren als für die von der Dämonenlehre erfassten Vorstellungen des Hexensabbat, an dem laut klischeeartiger Beschuldigungen in mitteleuropäischen Hexenprozessen mit dem Teufel gefeiert und gehurt wurde.

Die Werwolfvorstellung hatte in den folkloristischen Überlieferungen Estlands keine so schreckenerregende und blutrünstige Bedeutung wie bei vielen anderen Völkern Europas, wo der Werwolf Menschen tötete. Hier beschränkten sich die Werwölfe auf das Reissen von Tieren und begründeten dies auch meisten rational: Es sollte die tägliche Kost mit frischem Fleisch angereichert werden. Wenn wir von der folkloristischen Überlieferung ausgehen, dann hatte das Werwolflaufen religiöse Aspekte. Es war weit verbreitet und natürlich begründet, weswegen es im Bewusstsein des Volkes auch keine eindeutig verurteilende Einstellung einnahm. Offensichtlich hatten die in der Volkstradition "unschuldigen" Werwolfgeschichten, die vom Grade ihres Verbrechens aus gesehen, nicht mit den aus der Dämonenlehre stammenden kannibalistischen Teufelsgeschichten vergleichbar waren, die Geständnisse der Hexenprozesse dahingehend beeinflusst, dass die Angeklagten sich eher zu dieser "Sünde" bekannten als zu einer anderen, weil sie davon ausgingen, dass ihre Strafe dann leichter ausfiel. In der Tat sind in einigen Fällen die Werwolfläufer dem Feuertod entkommen und haben eine leichtere Strafe verbüsst – dafür ist wiederum der oben erwähnten junge Mann Hans ein Beispiel, der zur Strafe nur zehn Paar Rutenschläge bekam. Offensichtlich hat das Gericht, bei dem auch Bauern Schöffen waren, beim Strafmass diese Schuld zugrundegelegt, da es eine anderen schrecklicheren Beschuldigungen gab – wie etwa das massenhafte Zerfleischen von Haustieren oder die Verhexung von Menschen in Tod.

Eine interessante Tatsache ist, dass die estnischen Hexenprozesse nicht so oft auch andere mythische Wesen des Volksglaubens wie Gutsschlepper, Schrate usw., erwähnen. Das Werwolflaufen war jedenfalls eine stereotype Beschuldigung und ein allgemein übliches Geständnis, das sowohl von den Klägern als auch von den Angeklagten gerne zusätzlich zu anderen Anklagen wegen Hexerei benutzt wurde. Aus der Sicht der Richter ist das dadurch erklärbar, dass der Werwolf als ein zur Vorstellung der Tiermetamorphose des Menschen gehöriges Wesen gut mit dem von ihnen vertretenen dämonologischen Konzept zusammenpasste, nach dem die Verwandlung in einen Werwolf ein Bund mit dem Teufel und seine Fähigkeit voraussetzte, Sinnestäuschungen hervorzurufen. Schliesslich wurde der Teufel in der Gestalt eines reissenden Tieres, oft eines Wolfes dargestellt.

Die Popularität des Werwolfs in den Anklagen, Geständnissen und Rechtssprüchen der Hexenprozesse weist darauf hin, dass dieses mythische Wesen damals zwar sowohl im Weltbild des estnischen Volks als auch in dem der Kirche bekannt war, in beiden Bereichen aber eine unterschiedliche Beurteilung erfuhr. Leider bieten die verhältnismässig wortkargen Hexenprozesse nicht viel

Vergleichsmaterial dazu, ob und in welchen Masse die volkstümliche Werwolfvorstellung unter dem Einfluss des Gerichtsverfahrens und der Dämonenlehre Wandlungen erlebt hat. Es ist auf jeden Fall zu beobachten, dass sich laut Hexenprozesse auf Grund der von Richtern geforderten, der Hexenlehre entnommenen Anklagen eine neue, sogenannte Hexenfolklore herausgebildet hat, die sich später mit der angestammten Volkstradition vermischt hat. In den 16 von mir analysierten Protokollen von Werwolfprozessen kommen 5 Hinweise auf die Verbundenheit mit dem Teufel vor. Als Beispiel sei hier das in den Jahren 1641-1642 vom Layske Mart im Pärnuer Landgericht gegebene Geständnis gebracht, in dem er in Verkleidung eines Werwolfs als "Lieferant" (Fleischbringer) den Sumpf Röhma besucht habe, um seinen Herren zu verehren. Ein weiteres Beispiel sei dessen Geständnis mit Nennung der Frau eines Mannes namens Matz, einer Hexe, des Küchenmädchens und der Geliebten des Teufels. In den früheren Prozessen aus den Jahren 1617 und 1619 gibt es eindeutige Hinweise auf den Hexensabbat. Hier kann man deutlich die Einflüsse der Dämonenlehre auf die Definition der Dienste von Werwölfen beim Teufel und der Teilnahme am Hexensabbat erkennen.

Im Prozess der Pärnuer Landgerichts von 1696 spricht man von einer grossen Zunft der Werwölfe, zu der aus den Dörfern der Umgebung 11 Menschen gehört hätten. Der Anführer der Zunft sei der Bauer Lible Matz gewesen (Madar 1987: 139; ERAKA f. 915.n.1. S 331.L.6). Dieses Dokument ist bisher das einzige Protokoll der Hexenprozesse, das auf eine organisierte Gruppe von Werwolfläufern in Estland hinweist. Dazu passt die Hundert Jahre ältere Auskunft des Olaus Magnus (1555) über die Werwölfe Alt-Livlands, die nachts truppweise herumlungern, viele wilde Taten begehen und Bierkeller leertrinken. Vielleicht könnte man aus diesen beiden Angaben Hinweise auf die Tätigkeit jener ketzerischen Geheimsekte herauslesen, die über Hexenprozesse und Dämonenlehre in den religiösen Vorstellungen des Volkes Fuss gefasst haben.

Die Hexenprozesse hatten sicher einen negativen Einfluss auf die Entwicklung der estnischen Werwolfvorstellung. Die auf der Dämonenlehre der Richter beruhende Auffassung hat die Werwolfvorstellung auch des Volkes verändert und ihr allmählich die ihr eigene, ursprüngliche Bedeutung fast vollständig geraubt. Einer vergleichbaren Veränderung unterliegt die Tradition des Fruchtbarkeitskults der *Benandanten* in Italien, die sich wegen des 50 Jahre andauernden ideologischen Drucks der Inquisition zu den ursprünglich fremden Hexereivorstellungen und schließlich sogar zur üblichen Form des Hexensabbats bekannt hat (Ginzburg, 1990). Entsprechend hat sich die volkstümliche Werwolfvorstellung Estlands an ein Modell der Dämonenlehre angepasst, das ihr die Inquisition über Jahrhunderte oktroyiert hat.

Auch wenn geistige Vorstellungen nach Meinung mancher Forscher eine sich langsam wandelnde Struktur haben (Siikala, 1992: 27, 29; Bloch 1968: 129), so sind sie doch nicht unveränderlich und können auf Dauer nicht einer gewaltsamen Indoktrination standhalten oder unbeeinflusst von ihr bleiben. Die Hexenprozesse könnte man für Schmelztiegel der Religionen halten, in dem der Akkulturationsprozess der Verschmelzung der eigenen und der fremden Kulturen gewaltsam und blutig verlaufen ist.

Wenn man die estnischen Hexeprozesse mit denen vergleicht, die zur selben Zeit in Europa geschehen sind, dann kann man sowohl Ähnlichkeiten, als auch Unterschiede erkennen. Die Gründe für die Hexenprozesse, die geistigen Voraussetzungen für ihre Durchführung und die Methoden waren die gleichen. Die Beschuldigungen wurden vereinheitlicht und der bäuerischen Vorstellungswelt aufgedrängt. Unterschiede gab es je nach Zeit und Gegend. Massenhysterien wie in Spanien, wo zu Zeiten des Grossinquisitors Torquemada innerhalb von etwa zehn Jahren ca 10 000 Menschen liquidiert wurden, oder in Süd-Europa, Frankreich und der Schweiz während des 16. Jahrhunderts, wo Menschen dorfweise und zu Hunderten auf Scheiterhaufen geschickt wurden, hat es in Estland nicht gegeben. Die grössten Prozesse haben etwa zehn Personen betroffen.

In einem für Estland typischen Hexenprozess hat es entweder einen, zwei oder vier Angeklagte gegeben. Im Laufe von dreihundert Jahren wurden bekanntlich in 145 Prozessen mit 218 Angeklagten 65 zum Tode verurteilt (Madar 1987: 133) – es ist allerdings nicht sicher, ob diese Zahlen vollständig sind. Die ganze Wahrheit werden wir wohl nie erfahren, da die einschlägigen Dokumente verlorengegangenen sind.

Der Glaube an die Hexen erreichte gemäss vorliegender Angaben im 17. Jahrhundert seinen Höhepunkt, als in Estland die meisten Hexenprozesse (127) durchgeführt wurden. Ab dem 18. Jahrhundert ging er zurück. Noch am Ende des 18. Jahrhunderts und am Anfang des 19. Jahrhunderts wandten sich Bauern an Gerichte und zeigten Verhexungen an. Gegen die Angeklagten wurde die Todesstrafe allerdings durch leichtere Strafen wie etwa Prügel, Anprangern am Schandpfahl oder Ausweisung ersetzt (Madar 1987: 140).

Die religiösen Vorstellungen über Hexen und Werwölfe haben sich auch nach dem Ende des Zeitalters der Hexenprozesse im Bewusstsein des Volkes noch über Jahrhunderte gehalten. Das kann durch Unterlagen bestätigt werden, die gegen das Ende des 19. Jahrhunderts und in der ersten Hälfte des 20. Jahrhunderts gesammelt worden sind.

Die schreckliche Erinnerungen an Hexen auf den lodernden Scheiterhaufen sind im Gedächtnis der Menschen erhalten geblieben, und in Archiven werden Protokolle von Hexenprozessen, die uns von dem jahrhundertealten Werwolf- und Hexenglauben berichten, aufbewahrt.

* * *

Ausgewählte Beispiele von Werwolfprozessen

Beispiel Nr. 1: Der Prozess vm 20.-21. Juni 1617 in Fegefwer

Der baltisch-deutsche Historiker Luce schreibt am Ende des 19. Jahrhunderts, dass der einzige bisher bekannte Werwolfprozess am **20.-21. Juni 1617 in Fegefwer (Kiviloo im Gut Harju-Jaani)** stattgefunden habe. 7 Bauern (6

Frauen und 1 Mann) waren hier angeklagt und wurden dessen beschuldigt, als Werwölfe umhergelaufen und viel Schaden angerichtet zu haben. Sie alle wurden zum Tode verurteilt (Luce 1827: 187-189).

Der Prozess begann damit, dass einige Bauern des Gutes Kiviloo eine Frau namens *Alit* die Gattin eines Bauern zum Tod verhext habe. Alit bekennt sich schuldig und gesteht zusätzlich, dass sie vor 10 Jahren als Werwolf gelaufen sei und viel Schaden anrichtet habe. Zusammen mit zwei anderen Hexen habe sie in Läänemaa zwei Paar Ochsen, zwei Pferde und andere Haustiere getötet. Auf die Frage der Richter nach dem Besitzer dieser Tiere antwortet Alit lachend, dass ein Wolf doch nicht die Tiere fragen wird, wem sie gehörten. Später erwähnte sie, dass sie auch Kälber von Engelbrecht Mekken zerfleischt habe.

Hinsichtlich des Verzehrs der Tiere erzählte sie, dass sie vor dem Kochen des Fleisches den Wolfsbalg beiseite gelegt und dann das Fleisch gekocht habe. Zusammen mit ihr seien drei Frauen als Werwolf gelaufen: Ann, die Frau eines Bauern namens Anti aus dem Dorf Kiviloo, die Frau von Mäeküla Aderkass aus dem Gut Rassi des Dorfes *Piecfall*, schliesslich Ann, die Frau von Jaan, aus dem Dorf *Vessell (Vosell)*. Die Hexenkunst habe sie von einem alten Mann gelernt, dessen Name Matz Lübbe (Lübber, Libe?) sei. Die von Alit genannten Mitbeschuldigten wurden vor das Gericht gerufen, um Stellung zu nehmen. Ann aus dem Dorf Vessel gestand, dass sie eine Hexe sei; die Hexerei habe sie von der Frau des Kaika Jaan gelernt. Sie gestand ausserdem, dass sie zusammen mit Liukert (Liuke) beim Teufel gegessen habe. Kaika Jaan und die Frau eines anderen Hausherrn hätten die Hexerei von diesem Teufel gelernt. Lübbe Matz leugnet seine Schuld, die beiden Frauen erklärten ihn aber aufs neue für schuldig. An Matz wird nun eine Wasserprobe veranstaltet: Wenn er wie eine Ente auf die Wasseroberfläche schwimme, sei schuldig. Während eines neuen Verhörs und offensichtlich als Folge von Folterung bekent er sich schliesslich doch schuldig und stirbt. Das Gericht war der Meinung, dass der böse Feind ihn getötet habe, damit er nicht noch andere Hexen anzeigen könne.

Die Frau von Kaika Jaan und die Frau des anderen Hausherrn leugneten, dass sie zusammen mit Liuke beim Teufel gegessen hätten, aber die Wasserprobe bezeugte, dass sie schuldig waren. Ann aus dem Dorf Vesseli gesteht dann, dass sie eine Woche vor Pfingsten im Dorf von Jakob von Lund (Linden) in "Pergeli" versammelt waren, wo sie gemeinsam Schafe und Schweine in ihrem Heimatdorf totgebissen hätten. Auf Grund der Geständnisse, die im Laufe der gerichtlichen Untersuchung und der Folterungen gemacht wurden, und auf Grund der Wasserproben wurden 6 Menschen vom Gericht zum Feuertod verurteilt. Die Schöffen im Gericht waren einheimische estnische Bauern (Eisen, 1923: 1588/9).

Beispiel Nr. 2: Der Prozess am 24. Juli 1623 in Merimõisa

Am 24. Juli 1623 wurde in Merimõisa im Kirchspiel Keila vor dem aus fünf Deutschen und sieben Bauernrichtern zusammengesetzten Gericht über Klati

Jaak gerichtet: Er wurde beschuldigt, fünf Bauern durch die Hexerei geschädigt zu haben. Jaak hat anfangs seine Schuld der Hexerei abgelehnt, gestand aber nach der vierten Folterung das Werwolflaufen gemeinsam mit Anne, der Frau von Tammeaugu Hendrik.

Dies wird folgendermassen geschildert: *"Am Samstagabend vor Pfingsten sei er auf das Feld gegangen, habe dort Hendriks Frau Anne getroffen und sich mit ihr so lange unterhalten, bis sie beide in Werwölfe verwandelt worden seien. Die beiden haben darauf das Pferd von Toomas Raudsepp totgebissen".*

Die Frau von Hendrik wurde vor das Gericht gerufen und dem Jaak gegenübergestellt. Jaak habe gefordert: *"Anne darf nicht lügen, sie muss ebenso wie ich die Wahrheit sagen! Ich bestätige nochmals, dass wir beide sind Werwolf gelaufen sind."* Auf diese Beschuldigung hin hat Anne nichts anderes geantwortet und nur gerufen: *"Oh du Menschenkind, oh du Gottes Hoffnung! Warum lügst du!"* Danach habe sie geschwiegen.

Jaak ging zum Heiligen Abendmahl und bekannte sich schuldig. Vom Gericht wurde Jaak aber hauptsächlich deswegen zum Feuertode verurteilt, weil er verdächtigt wurde, eine Schlange in das Bier gehext zu haben.

Annes Verhör ging weiter. Nun kam zur Anzeige von Klati Jaak noch die von zwei Männern hinzu, die Anne bedroht hätte. Das veranlasste die Männer, sie für eine Hexe zu halten. Anne rechtfertigte ihre Drohung damit, dass ihr Unheil zugefügt worden sei. Weil sich ihr Befinden verschlechtert habe, habe sie Bedrohungen gegen den Gefängniswächter ausgesprochen: *"Falls ich unschuldig sterbe, so müssen auch andere sterben!"* Später leugnete sie diese Drohung. Trotzdem sei sie merkwürdigerweise aus den Fesseln frei gekommen.

Danach sei sie zur Folterung in der Marterkammer verurteilt worden. Dort habe sie gestanden, dass sie vier Jahre lang Werwolf gelaufen sei – ausser einem Pferd habe sie aber nur kleinere Tiere getötet. Der Wolfsbalg, den sie benützt habe, sei auf dem Felde unter einem Stein versteckt. Ein Junge habe sie im Namen des Teufels aus den Fesseln im Kerker befreit. Zuletzt habe sie auch über ihren Mann gestanden, dass dieser manchmal als Wolf, manchmal auch als Bär gelaufen sei. Dieses Geständnis habe sie vor dem Heiligen Abendmahl wieder zurückgenommen und gesagt, dass sie es nur wegen der grossen Schmerzen gemacht hätte.

Anne wurde schliesslich auch für den Scheiterhaufen verurteilt. Die Lage des Tammeaugu Hendrik wurde aber auch kritisch, als gegen ihn zwei Frauen vor Gericht auftraten und ihn als einen gefährlichen Hexenmeister und einen, der gegen das kirchliche Sakrament, das Heilige Abendmahl, aufhetze, bezeichneten. Damit habe er der Hexerei schuldig gemacht (Winkler 1909: 326-330; Eisen 1923: 1589; ERAKA, f. 2. Nim 2. Sü. 1,1, 26 p.).

Beispiel Nr. 3: Der Prozess am 3.-5. November 1628 in Undla

Am 3.-5. November 1628 haben in Undla im Kirchspiel Kadrina 10 Adelige und 4 Bauernrichter über Marret (Maret), die Frau eines russischen Mannes Kannas das Urteil gesprochen, nachdem sie durch Fabian von Tiesenhausen der Hexerei beschuldigt wurde. Maret sei mit der weit und breit bekannten Beschwörerin Anne in Streit geraten. In einem Wutanfall hätten sich die beiden Frauen als Hexe beschimpft.

Als Tiesenhausen Maret fragte, ob sie tatsächlich eine Hexe sei, habe diese geantwortet: *"Falls ich sterben müsste, werden einige andere mit mir verbrennen, die reicher sind als ich!"* Die Angeklagte hat ihre Schuld abgestritten. Dann wurden Zeugen vorgeladen, aus deren Reden klar wurde, dass Anne ihre Kontrahentin Maret darin beschuldigt habe, dass sie Schafe gestohlen habe, die dem Junker Fabian gehörten. Daraufhin habe Maret in der Mühle die Hände gerungen und weinend gesagt: *"Der Junker hat mich zur Hexe geschimpft!"*

Nach dem Verhör hat das Gericht beschlossen, eine Wasserprobe zu veranstalten. Beide Frauen seien wie Enten auf der Wasseroberfläche geschwommen. Darauf wurde mit der Folterung begonnen. Maret hat nun gestanden, dass sie zusammen mit zwei anderen Frauen und den beiden Männern Ivan und Conrad Werwolf gelaufen sei und einige Schafe totgebissen habe. Die Verwandlung in einen Werwolf habe sie letzthin am Margaretentag an der Kirche von einer Frau gelernt, die sie dort getroffen habe.

Auch Anne hat sich schuldig bekannt: Zusammen mit einem unbekannten Bettler habe sie den Leuten als Werwolf viel Schaden zugefügt. Die vor das Gericht gebrachten Männer haben ihre Schuld aber hartnäckig geleugnet. Bei der Wasserprobe ist Ivan untergegangen, Conrad aber nicht. Danach wurden sie beide in den Flur der Mühle gebracht. Beim Ankleiden sei dem Ivan die Flucht gelungen und sei damit dem Schicksal der anderen entkommen. Conrad dagegen habe sich bei der Folterung schuldig bekannt. Alle drei Angeklagten – *Maret, Anne und Conrad* – wurden zum Feuertod verurteilt (Madar, 1980: 14; ERAKA f. 2. nim. 2. sü. 45,1.1-4; Winkler, 1909: 333, 334; Saarse, 1958, Nr. 5, S. 17).

Beispiel Nr. 4: Der Prozess von 1651 in Idavere

Im Jahre 1651 wurde im Prozess im Kirchspiel Haljala zu Idavere eine Frau namens Else beschuldigt, die Wirtin von Otto Loden in den Tod verhext zu haben und zusammen mit ihrem 18-jährigen Sohn Hans jahrelang Werwolflaufen begangen zu haben. Hans hat das Gericht als Strafe für das Werwolflaufen 10 Paar Ruten an der Kirchensäule zugeschrieben (Toll, 1839: 257-263).

Interessant sind ist das Geständnis von Hans über seine Aktivitäten als Werwolf: *"Er ist zwei Jahre als Werwolf herumgelaufen und hat kleinere Tiere totgebissen. Den Wolfbalg hat er von einem schwarz gekleideten alten Mann bekommen, der diesen am Bach in einem Mauseloch versteckt hatte. Die Richter interessierten sich dafür, ob auch der Körper des Hans am Werwolflaufen teilgenommen habe oder nur seine Seele. Der Junge hat versichert, dass er selbst in den Wolfsbalg geschlüpft sei, und als Beweis hat der die Narbe eines Hundebisses am Bein gezeigt, die er als Werwolf davongetragen habe. Auf die Fragen der Richter, ob er sich in der Zeit, als er als Werwolf gelaufen ist, verstandesmässig als Mensch oder als Tier gefühlt habe, antwortete der Junge, dass er sich als Tier gefühlt habe."* (Toll; 1839: 257-263); Madar 1987: 138).

Protokolle der Hexenprozesse im Estnischen Geschichtsarchiv

ERAKA f.915, nim.1.,sü. 1.1. 60-61.p.
ERAKA f.915, nim.1., sü. 1.1. 88-89
ERAKA f. 915. n.1. S 331.L.6.
ERAKA,f. 2. nim 2. sü.1,1. 26p.
ERAKA f. 2. nim. 2. sü. 45,1.1-4;

Literatur und Archivmaterialien

Anderson, W. 1924. Uus töö Balti libahundiprotsesside kohta. - Ajalooline Ajakiri III.
Ankarloo, B.; Henningsen, G. 1987 (1980). A. History of Witchcraft, Heretics and a Pagans. from Antiquity to Primitive Christianity. London.
Ankarloo, B.; Henningsen, G. 1990. Early Modern Eyropen Witchcraft. Oxford.
Arbusow, L. 1919-1921. Die Einführung der Refomation in Liev- und Est- und Kurland. Riga.
Arbusow, L. 1924-1926. Die altlivländische Bauernrechte - Mitteilungen aus der livländischen Geschichte. Bd. 23. S-60-61. Riga.
Birkelund, M. 1983. Trold kvinden og hendes anklagere. Dannske hekseprocesser I det 16. og 17. århunderderde med et bilag om processerne I østjylland. Arusia- Historiske skrifter III. (Århus N.).
Bloch, M. 1968. La Société féodadale. Paris.
Bruiningk, H. von 1924. Der Werwolf in Livland und das letzte im Wendenschen Landgericht und Dörptschen Hofgericht i. J.1692 deshalb stattgehebte Stratverfahren. - Mitteilungen aus der lievländische Geschichte. Band 22.3. Heft 163-220. Riga.
Cohn, N. 1975. Europes Inner Demons. An Enquiry Inspired by the Great Witchhunt. London.
Eisen, J.M. 1915. Nõid Tint Hans - Päevaleht, nr. 180.
Eisen, J.M. 1923. Eestimaa nõidade põletamine. - Agu, nr. 49, 50. Tallinn.
Eliade, M. 1994. Mõningaid täheldusi Euroopa nõiakunsti kohta. - Vikerkaar 4/5 (in: "History of Religions", 14, lk. 149-172).
Ginzburg, C. 1990. Ecstasies Deciphering the Witches Sabbath. New York.
Gurevits, A. 1992. Keskaja inimese maailmapilt. Tallinn.
Gurevitš 1999 = Гуревич А. Избранные туды. Том 2. Средневековый мир. Москва - Санкт-Петербург.
Haavio, M. 1967. Suomalainen mytologia. Porvoo-Helsinki.

Hasselblatt, G. 1837. Ein Verhör in einem Hexenproceß. - Das Inland, 3. Jg., Nr.47. Dorpat.
Heikkinen, A. 1969. Paholaisen liittolaiset. Noita ja magiakäsituksia ja oikeudenkäynteja Suomessa 1600 luvun jälkipuoliskolla (n. 1640- 1712) Historiallisia tutkimuksia LXVII. Porvoo.
Heinsohn, G. - Steiger, O. 1989 (1985). Om häxförföljelse, sexualitet och människoproduktion. Översättning Gunnar Sandin. Uddevalla.
Hertzberg, R. 1889. Vidskepelsen I Finland på 1600 talet. Kulturbilder zur Finlands historia II. Helsingfors.
Ivanitš, L. 1989. Russian Folk Belief. New York.
Jacoby, M. 1974. Wargus, vargr. "Verbrecher", "Wolf", eine sprach- und rechtsgeschichtliche Untersuchung. Uppsala.
Jung, J. 1879. Eesti rahva vanast usust, kombedest ja juttudest. Tartu.
Kahk, J. 1987. Ristiusk, teadus ja nõiaprotsessid 17. sajandil. Religiooni ja ateismi ajaloost Eestis. Artikite kogumik III. Tallinn.
Kahk, J. 1983. Inimesed ja olud "vanal heal" Rootsiajal- - Looming, 8.
Kahk, J.; Salupere, M. 1991. Nõiamoorid, pisuhännad ja maatargad. - Akadeemia, nr. 3.
Kruus, H. 1926. Eesti ajaloo lugemik II: Valitud lugemispalad Eesti ajaloo alalt 1561.-1721. a. Tartu.
Leesment, L. 1931. Piinamise ja tortuuri kaotamine Eestis ja Liivimaal. - Ajalooline ajakiri. Tartu.
Levack, B.B. 1987. The witch-hunt in early modern Europe. Longman: London – New York.
Luce, J.W.L. 1829. Beitrag zur Geschichte von Oesel. Pernau.
Macfarlane, A. 1970. Witchcgaft in Tudor and Stuart England: A regional and comparative study. London.
Macfarlane, A. 1978. The Orings of English Individualism. Oxford.
Madar, M. 1980. Nõiaprotsessid Eestis 16.-19. sajandini. Diplomitöö (käsikiri).
Madar, M. 1987. Nõiaprotsessid Eestis XVI sajandist XIX sajandini. Religiooni ja ateismi ajaloost Eestis: Artiklite kogumik III. Tallinn.
Mark, L. 1938. Nõiaprotsessidest Eestis VIII sajandi lõpul ja XIX sajandi alguses. Ajalooline ajakiri nr.
Monter, W. E. 1976. Witchcraft in France and Switzerland. The Borderlands during the Reformation. Cornell University Press.
Muchembled, R. 1979. La Sorcière au village (XVe-XVIIIe siècle). Paris.
Nenonen, M. 1992. Noituus, taikuus ja noitavainot Ala-Satakunnan, Pohjois-Pohjanmaan ja Viipurin Karjalan maaseudulla vuosina 1620-1700. Historiallisia Tutkimuksia 165. Helsinki. Jyväskylä.
Nenonen, M; Kervinen, T. 1994. Synnin palkka on kuolema. Suomalaiset noidat ja noitvainot 1500-1700 - luvulla. Helsinki.
Olaus Magnus. 1840 (1567). Historia de gentibus septtentrionalibus. Basel, 1567, lib. VIII CAP. 46) LK. 235/6, "Der Jäger", nr. 59.
Olaus Magnus. 1845. Des Olaus Magnus Bericht über die lievländische Verwölfwe., (Überstz.Ed.Pabst) Archiv für die Geschichte Liv-Esten und Cur-

lands, herausgegeben von Dr. Gr.Brunge, Band IV. Dorpat.
Peters, E. 1978. The Magian, the Witch and the Law. University of Pennisylvania Press.
Riesmann, O. 1879. Nõiad ja sortsid Tallinnas 17. aastasaja hakatusel.- Eesti Postimees, nr. 22. 30.
Rudwin, M. 1973. The Devil in Legend and Literature. Illinois.
Russell, J. 1987. Witchcraft. Eliade, M. (ed.) The Encyclopedia of Religion, vol. 15. NY.
Russell, J. B. 1972. Witchcraft in the Middle Ages. London.
Russel, J.B. 2001. Nõidus ja nõidususk Euroopas. Tallinn.
Saarse. 1958. Siis kui lõõmasid tuleriidad.-Nõukogude Naine, nr. 5, lk. 17.
Sarmela, M. 1994. Suomen perinneatlas. Suomen kansankulttuurin kartasto 2. Helsinki.
Setälä, P. 1999. Keskaja naine. Tallinn.
Smolinsky, H. 1993.Kirchengeschichte der Neuzeit I. Düsseldorf.
Thomas, K. Anthropology and the study of english witchcraft. Douglas, M (ed) Witchcraft, Conessions Accusations. ASA Monographs 9. London.
Thomas, K. 1971. Religion and the Decline of Magic: Studies in popular Beliefs in sixstiinth and seventeenth century England. London.
Toll, F. von 1839. Zur Geschichte der Hexenprocesse: Auszug aus dem Protocoll der Wier- und Jerwschen Manngerichts. - Das Inland, 4. Jg., Nr.17.
Trevor-Roper, H. 1967. Religion, the Reformation and Social Chance. London.
Trevor-Roper, H. 1969 (1956). The European Witch-Craze of the Sixteenh and Seveneenh Centuries and Other Essays. London - New-York, 1969.
Uuspuu, V. 1937. Nõiaprotsesse Pärnu maakohtu arhiivist kuni 1642. - Usuteadusline Ajakiri. 3/4.
Uuspuu, V. 1938. Surmaotsused eesti nõiaprotsessides - Usuteadusline Ajakiri. 1938.
Winkler, R. 1909. Über Hexenwahn und Hexenprotzesse in Estland während der Schwedenherrschaft. - Baltische Monatschrift. Band 67. Heft 5.
Wolf-Knuts, U. 1968. Varulvföreställingen på finskspråktigt område. Budkavlen organ för brages sektion för folklivsforskning och Institutet för Nordisk Åbo Akademi.

Religious Education through the Eyes of Pupils, Teachers and Headmasters [1]

Pille Valk, Tartu

The development of Religious Education (RE) in Estonian schools, which began again about ten years ago, has encountered vivid public interest. In the situation in which the influences of the Soviet atheistic past are still recognisable in peoples' mentality (Valk, 2000), where discussions about RE brought out several prejudices, fears and lack of knowledge (Valk, 1999), the study of the context in which RE has to be taught becomes substantially important.

In the following article one aspect of such a study, based on empirical research into the attitudes towards and expectations for RE among upper secondary school pupils, teachers and school headmasters, is presented.

1. INTRODUCTION TO THE RESEARCH

The current article is primarily based on the three following surveys.
1. *A questionnaire of pupils* (henceforth '*pupils questionnaire*') was carried out at the end of 1998 by Outi Raunio-Hannula (Raunio-Hannula, 2001). 288 upper secondary school pupils from 15 classes in 8 different schools were asked about their attitudes towards RE. The sample of schools contained both, town and rural schools in different parts of Estonia. 65% of respondents were female, 35% were male students; 10% of respondents were members of the Church. All pupils attended RE classes.
I would hereby like to express my gratitude to O. Raunia-Hannula for the kind permission to use the results of her research in my work.
Two other surveys were carried out by P. Valk in 2000 – 2001.

2. *The questionnaire of teachers* (henceforth '*teachers' questionnaire*') was performed in 11 schools in 2001. Schools were chosen according to the following principles:
- To cover different parts of Estonia. The sample of schools contained schools in larger cities (Tartu, Tallinn, Pärnu and Viljandi) as well as in

---

[1] The article introduces a part of research 'Development of the Contemporary Concept of Religious Education for the Estonian Schools', funded by Estonian Science Foundation grant NR. 4634.

rural areas (in Ahja, Pärnu-Jaagupi and Turba).
- To present different school types. Nine of the schools were upper secondary schools (Gymnasiums), eight had all 12 grades, and one had grades 10 to 12. Two schools in the sample were Basic Schools (grades 1 – 9).
- To present both schools with and without RE. Seven schools in the sample had and four didn't have RE classes.

  163 respondents, 144 women and 19 men with an average age of 42 were teachers of different subjects. Most of them had worked at the school for about 15 years. 31% (51) of the respondents were Church members (44 Lutherans, 1 Catholic, 1 Baptist, 1 Orthodox, 1 Adventist).

3. *The questionnaire of school principals* (henceforth *'principals' questionnaire'*) was carried out in 2000 - 2001 *via Internet* using e-mail. Questionnaires were sent out to all schools whose addresses were available from the Estonian Schools website. 115 principals returned fulfilled questionnaires, 56 of them were women and 69 men. The average age of the respondents was 47. 20% of respondents were members of the Church (22 Lutherans, 1 Catholic).

In addition to the above mentioned researches, Lii Lilleoja's survey about the development of RE in Estonian schools in 1989 – 1997 has been used to complement data about the teaching methods (Lilleoja 1998).

Some remarks about the research method

The aim of the surveys carried out among teachers and principals was to obtain a first survey about the attitudes towards and expectations for RE, to chart the very general outlook of the research field and to determine some problems and 'common ground' for dialogue and future development of RE. This aim justifies the using of convenience sampling where the specific rate of returned questionnaires is not of such importance (Tooding 2001, 168; Bryan & Cramer 1992, 105). This approach also determined the parameters of generalisation from the subsequent data analyses. As long as one can avoid the temptation of drawing profound and sweeping conclusions about the respondent's competence in the specific issues of RE and the clear backgrounds of their attitudes, collected data could be considered sufficient. The surveys enabled to point on the issues of educational policy, RE curriculum development and teacher training.

Questionnaires were analysed using the data processing program STATISTICA.

Before presenting the main results of the analyses, some comments have to be made about some grouping variables. If one takes into consideration the official rate of church membership in Estonian society, which totals about 15% (Au & Ringvee, 2000), one can note the higher proportion of church members among the responded teachers and also principals. Analyses didn't reveal any remarkable differences between the answers of church members' and the non-members' ones. Thus, one can assert that the church members were more eager to answer the questionnaires but their attitudes towards and expectations for RE didn't depend on their belonging to the Church.

Also the gender and age of respondents didn't correlate with any certain answers.

2. DOES RE HAVE TO BE TAUGHT IN SCHOOL?

This question was asked in all three surveys (pupils' questionnaire, teachers' questionnaire and principals' questionnaire). The answers, illustrated in graph 1, show a remarkably positive attitude towards the need for RE.

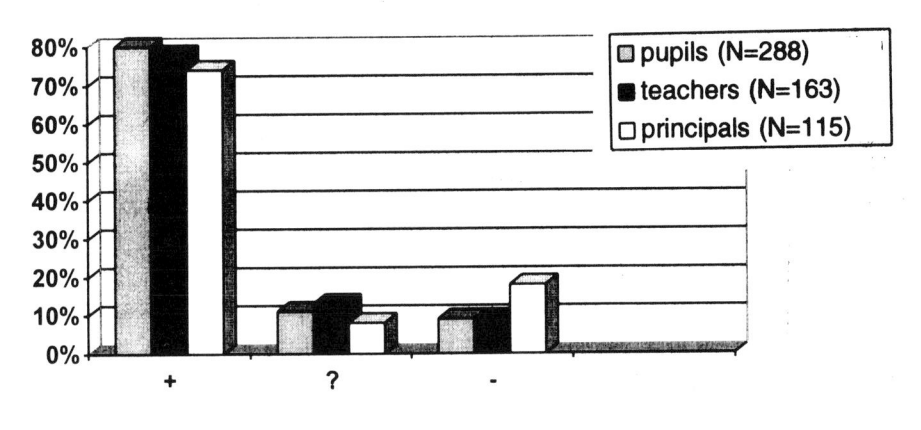

Graph 1
Attitudes towards the need for RE

80% of students, 78% of teachers and 74% of principals found that RE should be taught in school. The percentage of respondents who didn't have a clear attitude was 11% among pupils, 13% among teachers and 8% among directors. 9% of pupils and teachers and 18% of principals found that there is no need for RE in schools. One can note quite a remarkable difference – two times higher - in the rates of negative opinions between principals and two other groups of respondents. The reasons for such a difference require future research.

It is interesting to compare this telling data with the results form the broader survey 'Concerning life, belief and religious life in Estonia', carried out twice, in 1995 and 2000 (Hansen, 2000, 8; 2001, 29) where the same question yielded the following answers:

The percentage of supporters of RE was 86% in 1995 and 88% in 2000. The proportion of respondents who found RE unnecessary decreased from 12% to 9%. Particular research also pointed to some differences among the age groups. The group that was most critical towards RE was the youngest group – respondents up to 25 years of age. 21% of them found RE in schools to be unnecessary.

The figures are wonderful and promising but the reality is different. RE is not a very widespread subject in Estonian schools. Statistics from the Ministry of Education about the 2000/2001 school year indicate that RE was officially taught in only 41 of approximately 700 schools. For unknown reasons several schools where RE is taught were absent from the list. According to the latest data, the subject is offered in approximately 70 schools (Lilleoja 2002). RE is taught mostly in primary and upper secondary school classes.

3. WHY IS THE POSSIBILITY TO STUDY RE SO RARE?

In their questionnaire principals were asked why RE is not taught in their schools. They named the following reasons:
- Parents and pupils are not interested (mentioned 33 times)
- The lack of competent teachers (mentioned 28 times)
- The curriculum is overloaded (mentioned 24 times)
- Some of the reasons mentioned were quite surprising, like the following - there are no churches in the region.

The first three arguments deserve a closer look.

The **first** of them, lack of interest, raises some questions. As presented above, there is a generally positive attitude in society towards the need for RE. Secondary school pupils also found it necessary. The case seems to have a more complicated, and to a certain extent even hidden background. One of the reasons for this could be the incompleteness of the legal framework of RE, which does not sufficiently clearly define the obligations of schools in organising RE. Schools are by law obliged to organise RE classes when there are at least 15 pupils at the school level who themselves or who's parents are interested in it (Riigi Teataja I 1999, 24,358). But the procedure and precise responsibilities are unspecified. There are several ways to avoid real initiative or to put the question in a manner that pre-determines expected negative answers. For example: if pupils have no experience and knowledge of the aims and content of RE, if they have to choose between one more lesson or going home, if they have to choose between RE and, for example, computer training or other familiar and attractive subjects, one can be quite sure about the answers. The real question is - are principals really motivated to organise RE classes? Regretfully, positive attitudes towards RE don't lead always to direct action.

The **second** reason, the lack of competent teachers, is a more serious one. RE teacher training began in 1989 and now there are teacher-training programs in all Estonian theological institutions of higher education. The number of trained RE teachers is approximately 300, but only about 50 of them work as RE teachers (Lilleoja, 2001, 67). The feedback from the teachers speaks of the difficulty of finding work as a RE teacher. They were told that there are no finances, no time table limit for lessons or the school is not interested in organising RE classes because nobody had asked for it. Several times RE teacher candidates have mentioned a rather distrustful atmosphere when meeting school authorities and asking for the job. Some schools have also experienced failures with RE. When the teaching of RE was first permitted, many eager people without teaching experience and professional skills rushed to teach it. Unfortunately individual failures have been exaggerated and generalised and pointed to as reasons for leaving RE off the curricula in many schools. A similar problem also occurred in the pupils' survey. The main reason for disappointment with RE was related to the low level of teachers' professional skills (Raunio-Hannula 2001, 86).

Thus RE teacher training faces serious challenges. We need well-trained and highly motivated teachers, personalities who are able to overcome such objective and subjective difficulties. To guarantee the possibility to teach RE in all schools, many more teachers must be prepared. Also, the legislative framework of RE needs to be more specific. This is a question of educational politics.

The **third** reason, connected with the overloaded curriculum, is the most important and complicated one. Teachers mentioned that it is almost impossible to find space for one more lesson in the school timetable. It is also a question of priorities. In the current situation schools are strongly orientated towards the results of the state exams at the end of the upper secondary level, which serve as a kind of 'quality certificate' to evaluate the formal teaching level of the school. Thus, all available lessons are divided between these subjects. The capability of RE to contribute a lot through integration with the other subjects and thus also to play a part in preparation for the final exams by supporting the development of the whole person, knowledge and skills, is almost completely unrealised. One more personal and delicate issue has to be mentioned here. As long as teachers are paid according to the number of the lessons they give, most of them are interested in as many lessons as possible. Losing lessons to somebody else can create a great deal of tension between colleagues. Thus this is also a problem that needs to be solved through the changes at the level of the national curriculum. And it is also a question of educational politics.

4. How do teachers understand the aims of RE?

In the teachers' questionnaire respondents were asked to point out three aims for RE in order of significance. The aim that came in first place on the list was evaluated in the analyses with 3 points, the second with 2 points and the third with 1 point. During the analyses the aims were grouped into three larger blocks: 1) imparting knowledge; 2) aims connected with Moral education; 3) deeper learning skills. In all blocks five more specific groups were formed.
Table 1 provided an overview of the aims of RE as teachers saw them. The first column presents the blocks and groups of the aims. The second column indica-

tes how many times the current aims were mentioned (N). The third column exhibits the weightiness of the aims presented - the number shows a sum of the points earned by the current aims.

Aims	N	Points
Imparting knowledge	*169*	*276*
Broaden students' outlook, general knowledge of religions	55	134
Relationships between religion and culture	48	97
World religions	31	70
Christianity	26	55
Philosophy of religion	9	17
Aims connected with Moral education	*121*	*285*
Moral education	68	169
Developing virtues and attitudes	26	61
Knowledge of ethics	13	29
Development of personality	12	24
Religious nurture	2	2
Deeper learning skills	*29*	*52*
Formation of worldview	11	21
Orientation in religious questions	9	16
Analytical skills	4	7
Decision-making skills	3	4
Evaluation skills	2	4

Table 1

Aims of RE through the eyes of Teachers

Analyses of the above-mentioned aims brought out the key word among the aims - 'to know' - first the knowledge of religions, the broadening of outlook, the recognition of the relations between religion and culture. These types of aims were mentioned 169 times (276 points). Among others, imparting knowledge about world religions was mentioned 31 times (70 points), the need to learn more about Christianity 26 times (55 points).

The other main group of aims was connected with Moral Education, which was mentioned 121 times (285 points). Deeper learning skills, such as for example, analysing, understanding and supporting the development of one's personal worldview, were mentioned only 29 times (52 points).

Emphasising knowledge proves indirectly that our school system is very deeply knowledge-centred. It could be that in the case of RE this is even more strongly amplified. Here one can presumably identify the fears and shadows of the totalitarian educational system – painful experiences from our recent history. People are afraid of new ideology and 'brainwashing'. Such an interpretation could be supported by analyses of the debates over RE in the media (Valk 1999). In several discussions about RE, the fear of converting pupils and a hidden mission has been a clear 'red line'. In RE, knowledge seems to be a neutral ground. The validity of such an opinion could easily be questioned, but it not a topic in this article. Nevertheless, this circumstance is a very important one that must be taken into consideration in developing the concept of RE as well in RE teacher training.

The other remarkable outcome of the previous analyses is the weight assigned to moral education. Supporting pupils' moral development has always been a central aim of RE. When looking at the general aims of education as determined by the national curriculum, one can mention the clear emphasis on moral qualities and the education of the whole person (Põhikooli ja gümnaasiumi riiklik õppekava). It is evidence that RE can play a certain role in the framework of the national curriculum. Its potential to support achieving the general aims of education deserves much more attention and needs more explanatory work to bring it into peoples' consciousness. Especially in the situation where RE teachers are almost the only ones whose training includes courses in ethics (!).

5. WHAT KIND OF RE IS ACCEPTED?

This It is a question of the nature of RE. Corresponding questions were included in the teachers' questionnaire. They were asked whether RE should be linked to a particular confession. 88% of teachers argued for **non-confessional** RE. At the same time, most of them had nothing against positive co-operation between school and church in developing RE. Only 18% of respondents find such co-operation useless.

The other question – should RE be **a compulsory or an optional subject** – gave the following result: 72% of teachers argued for optional RE, 22% for compulsory subject.

The reasoning of the choice brought forward the following motives:
1. Supporters of the subject being optional emphasised the necessity of giving pupils the possibility to make a free choice (36 cases) and alluded to religious freedom (31 cases), while 9 respondents wrote that the curriculum is already too overwhelmed to add one more compulsory subject to it, 6 respondents argued that RE is a matter for the Church.
2. Supporters of the subject being compulsory referred to the necessity to offer

knowledge about religion to everybody (17 cases) and 9 respondents wrote that there are too many prejudges, and that lack of knowledge prevents real choices. 8 respondents emphasised the need for moral education.

It was surprising that not one of the respondents mentioned RE as a guarantee of religious freedom. This aspect of RE deserves to be made more widely known. The question is – how can the principle of religious freedom be observed in a society where people are religiously uneducated?

Thus the idea of compulsory RE can encounter serious opposition. At the same time here lies the ground for the most serious obstacles to the development of RE, a real 'vicious circle'. It is a combination of several problems: the scope of lessons available for RE, the prestige of the subject, the motivation of principals to organise classes, the number of places in RE teacher training, getting a job as an RE teacher, money for continuing education and the publishing of study materials etc, etc.

I personally see one of the possible solutions of the problem in the situation where RE will be to at least some extent compulsory. This could involve courses on ethics, world religions and religions and culture. Why? – the answer emerges in the following section of the article.

6. HOW ARE DIFFERENT TOPICS IN RE EVALUATED?

Teachers and principals were asked to evaluate different topics in RE curricula. The results are presented in table 2, where 'T' indicates teachers' answers and 'H' those of principals.

	+ % Very important + important		? % Don't know		- % Not important + unnecessary	
	T	H	T	H	T	H
Bible studies	75.5	54	18	18	6.5	28
Church history	58	53	25.5	22	16.5	25
World religions	92	91	5	3	3	6
Ethics	95	95	4	3	1	2
Religion and science	62	76	20	10	18	14
New religions	50	55	30	18	20	27
Religion and culture	92	81	5	11	3	8
Dogmatics	41	30	25.5	28	33.5	42

Table 2
Evaluation of different topics in RE

Thus the topics Ethics, World religions and Religion and culture were most highly evaluated. Among teachers they earned positive evaluations from more than 90% of respondents. Preferences among the principals were similar. The highest place, given to Ethics, indicates the recognised concern about moral developments in the school and society. Here lies the 'common ground' for co-operation between religious educators and the school. It is clear that the aspect of Moral education has to find a central place in the entire RE curriculum.

The most unpopular topic was Dogmatics. It is noteworthy that this topic also obtained the greatest number of 'Don't know' answers. These attitudes most likely indicate an objection to clearly church-related content in RE. The low evaluation of New Religions topics was somewhat surprising. On the other hand this may be proof that New Religious movements are more topical in Church circles than in society as a whole.

The notable difference between attitudes towards Bible studies among teachers and principals is remarkable. The reasons for this need to be more closely examined in future surveys.

To complete the 'topic of RE topics', I would like to add the Top-10 of pupils' favourites from O. Raunio-Hannula's research. Pupils were asked to evaluate different topics on a scale of one to five (from 1- not at all interested to 5 – very interested). As the next step they had to evaluate how much attention teachers devoted to the same topics in RE lessons. The scale also had five steps (from 1 – not at all, to 5 – much attention).

Topics	Average evaluation	Attention paid in lessons
Sexuality, relations between boys and girls, marriage	3.9	2.0
Love	3.9	2.2
UFOs and life in the Universe	3.8	1.5
World religions (Judaism, Hinduism, Buddhism, Islam, Religions in China and Japan)	3.7	4.1
Destiny	3.7	2.4
Is there life after death?	3.7	2.7
Alcohol and drugs	3.7	2.1
The soul, spirits and ghosts	3.7	1.9
Reincarnation	3.7	2.5
Problems of violence	3.6	2.1

Table 3
Top-10 of pupils' favourite topics for RE

The most unpopular themes among pupils were Mission (average evaluation 2.3/ attention paid in lessons 1.6), Christian festivals (2.3/ 2.4), Prayer and praying (2.3/2.4), Church history (2.2/ 2.7), Nurture of the personal religious life (2.2/1.8), Christian worship (2.1/2.1), Church life (2.0/1.7). The maximum mark for a specifically Christian theme was obtained by Bible history with 2.8/2.8; the life of Jesus gained 2.6/3.0 points.

If one adds some topics where the difference between the average value and that offered by teachers were remarkable, the following themes should be added. End of the World 3.5/2.2; The meaning of life 3.3/2.6; Abortion 3.3/1.6 (!); Human relationships and the Christian way of life 3.3/2.3; Euthanasia 3.2/1.8; The environment 3.1/1.5; New Age and New Religious Movements 3.0/1.8.

Thus one can see quite a clear gap between pupils' expectations and real lessons. It was especially sad to note that several issues of moral education obtained much less attention from teachers than students had expected. This circumstance points to serious didactical problems and has to be taken into consideration in RE curriculum development, where pupils' interests must find more response. This does not mean that the question of the content of RE has to be solved by pupils. But bearing in mind the constructivist theory of learning (Seppälä 1998, 105), I argue that taking pupils' interests into consideration is an important source of study motivation and helps to make the learning process more targeted.

7. How should RE be taught?

Thanks to the research of O. Raunio-Hannula (Raunio-Hannula 2001, 76) there is a possibility for the first charting of the teaching methods through the eyes of pupils. She asked upper secondary school students to evaluate different teaching methods on a scale from one to five and at the same time to indicate how often teachers use them. A mark of '1' indicated in the first case the least attractive methods and in the second case indicated that teachers never use them; a mark of '5' indicated the opposite. A selection of some of her findings is presented in table 4.

Methods	Evaluation by pupils	Used by teachers
Field trips	4.0	1.4
Free conversation	3.8	3.0
Visits of quests and experts	3.7	1.5
Group work and discussion	3.5	2.4
Using music (singing, recordings)	2.9	1.2
Storytelling	2.8	1.9

Games	2.8	1.1
Interviews performed by pupils	2.7	1.2
Drawing and handwork	2.6	1.2
Holding exhibitions	2.6	1.1
Teacher's oral presentation + pupils taking notes	2.3	3.2

Table 4
Evaluation of teaching methods in RE
and their use from the viewpoint of secondary school students

The overview above reveals a clear prevalence of active and creative teaching methods in students' expectations. Two of the first four methods that gained more than 3 points indicate the longing for discussion and interaction. The 3.7 points given to visitors indicate interest in meeting different people who could share their knowledge and attitudes with adolescents. The highest score, given to field trips and the biggest gap with the reality has to be a serious reminder for teachers and to encourage them to organise such activities. It is notable that even secondary school pupils desire more music, stories and games in RE lessons. The last row in the table points to a sad circumstance – it was the only method with the much higher rate of use in comparison with its evaluation by students.

Lii Lilleoja's research can be used to obtain some overview of the teaching methods at the basic school level, especially in the primary classes, (Lilleoja, 1998). She questioned 62 RE teachers, most of whom worked with primary classes. According to the responses, the most widespread teaching method was conversation about different life issues. 60 respondents wrote that they use this method often. 54 respondents marked frequent use of storytelling in teaching Bible stories. The reading and analysis of Bible stories was also quite popular. In addition teachers mentioned creative activities, singing and drama. In most schools the use of audio-visual materials was restricted by the lack of equipment. In her conclusions Lilleoja maintained that the RE lessons of respondents appeared to be methodologically varied.

CONCLUSION AND DISCUSSION

There is a generally positive attitude towards RE among pupils, teachers and principals surveyed. Using the outcomes of additional research, one can argue for a similar attitude in society as a whole.

Previous analyses of the surveys among pupils, teachers and school principals enable one to draw three groups of conclusions:

1. Issues of educational policy and the legal framework
    1.1. Taking into consideration the notably high range of positive attitudes towards the need for RE, its status in the framework of education needs to be improved.
    1.2. The proposal to transform some parts of the RE curriculum from optional to compulsory status requires that a position be taken. The idea concerns first of all the courses Ethics, World Religions and Religion and Culture as the most evaluated RE topics among teachers and principals.
    1.3. Making space for RE in the national curriculum is a problem that needs to be solved by educational policy decisions. In the current situation it might be complicated to leave these decisions only to the schools.
    1.4. Some problems of RE point to the insufficiency of the legal framework. The obligations of schools and the procedure in organising RE classes must be regulated more clearly.
    1.5. RE should not be taken as 'a branch of the Church' in school. Non-confessional RE is not aimed at bringing up Church members. Its aims are primarily educational. Several possibilities for positive co-operation between schools and churches are not, however, excluded.

2. Issues of **RE Curriculum Development.**
    To become an integral part of the whole educational process in schools and to be targeted, the RE Curriculum has to find a 'common ground' for all participants. It has to take into consideration the general educational aims of the national curriculum, the attitudes and views of colleagues and interests and expectations of pupils.
    2.1. Among the aims of RE, attention paid to moral education should be a pervasive aspect.
    2.2. Among others topics, World Religions and Religion and Culture should deserve more attention.
    2.3. The lower evaluation given to topics pertaining to Christianity raises didactical questions that need to be taken seriously. Teaching about Christianity after a long period of atheistic propaganda could be quite a challenging task. Such teaching has to address people's prejudges and provide knowledge that could lead to reasoned attitudes.
    2.4. The emphasis on 'imparting knowledge' among the aims of RE, as teachers saw it, seems to point also to the fact that a fear of 'conversion' and evangelisation needs a special sensibility.
    2.5. The RE curriculum needs some space to include topics raised by pupils themselves. Such an approach can guarantee that pupils' interests and expectations are met and thus learning motivation increases.

3. Issues of **RE teacher training.**
   3.1. The deficit of RE teachers requires special attention. To make sure that all Estonian schools will be able to offer RE classes in the near future, the number of RE teacher training students must be increased. Complementary in-service training courses must be offered to prepare more teachers for RE.
   3.2. RE teacher training programs have to devote attention to the development of the personal qualities of future RE teachers. There is a need for mature open-minded personalities who know the context of their work and who are motivated and able to overcome objective and subjective obstacles in their work.
   3.3. RE teachers have to be prepared to use a wide range of active teaching methods pupils expect. Also readiness for dialogue, sensitivity and respect towards pupils and their questions are needed. The ability to build bridges between the content of RE and pupils' everyday life and present problems is a necessary skill.
   3.4. Special attention has to be paid to developing teachers' creativity. Often they have to manage in a situation in which the lack of good study materials is a serious problem. Thus they have to be able to prepare by themselves.

REFERENCES

- Au, I. & Ringvee, R. 2000. **Kirikud ja kogudused Eestis**. Tallinn, Ilo. Pp. 139 – 141.
- Bryan, A. & Cramer, D. 1992. **Quantitative data analyses for Social scientists**. Routlege.
- Hansen. H. 2000. **Religioonisotsioloogilise küsitluse 'Elust, usust ja usuelust' II pressikonverentsi abimaterjal**. Tallinn, Eesti Kirikute Nõukogu, Eesti Piibliselts, Eesti Evangeelne Allianss.
- Hansen, H. 2001. **Uuringust 'Elust, usust ja usuelust'**. – Ühiskond, kirik ja religioonisotsioloogilised uuringud. Rahvusvahelise konverentsi materjale. Tartu. Eesti Kirikute Nõukogu, Tartu Ülikooli usuteaduskond, Siseministeeriumi Usuasjade osakond, Eesti Evangeelne Allianss, Eesti Piibliselts.
- Lilleoja, L. 1998. **Usuõpetus Eesti üldhariduskoolide 1989 – 1997**. Magistritöö. Tartu Ülikooli filosoofiateaduskonna pedagoogika oskond. Tartu.
- Lilleoja, L. 2001. **Usuõpetajate kaader: saavutused ja kitsaskohad**. – Ühiskond, kirik ja religioonisotsioloogilised uuringud. Rahvusvahelise konverentsi materjaid. Tartu. Pp. 67 – 69.
- Lilleoja, L. 2002. **Mida pakub usuõpetus?** - Ettekanne Eesti Usuõpetajate Liidu aastakonverentsil 25.01.2002, Pärnus.
- **Põhikooli ja gümnaasiumi riiklik õppekava**. 2001. http:/www.hm.ee.
- Riigi Teataja I 1999, 24,358. **Põhikooli- ja gümnaasiumiseaduse muutmise ja täiendamise seadus**. Vastu võetud Riigikogus 10.02.1999.

- Raunio- Hannula, O. 2001. **Uskonnonopetus Virossa lukiolaisen näkokulmasta**. Yleisen käytannölisen teologian *pro gradu*-tutkielma. Helsinkin Yliopisto.
- Seppälä, J. 1998. **Oppimiskäsitys ja uskonnonopetus**. – Pyysiäinen, M. & Seppälä, J. (Ed.-s). Uskonnonopetuksen käsikirja. Juva, WSOY. Pp. 103 – 136.
- Tooding, L. –M. 2001. **Andmeanalüüs sotsiaalteadustes**. Tartu. Tartu Ülikooli kirjastus.
- Valk, P. 1999. **About Some Attitudes Towards the Church and Religion in Present-day Estonia**. – Religionen in der sich anderten Welt. Gesellschaft für Anthropologie und Religionswissenschaft. Münster, 1999, pp.147-156.
- Valk, P. 2000. **From the Soviet Atheism to the National Identity – a Specific Background for the Religious Education in Estonia**. – PANORAMA. International Journal of Comparative Religious Education and Values. Vol. 12/ No. 1, 2000, pp. 78 – 93.

Indizes

1. Sachen

Abhidharma 103
Achämeniden 78
Adulthood, young 155
Āgama 138
Al-Aksa-Moschee 210
Al-Kuds 209
Anerkennung 30
animate/inanimate objects 50
Anomie 135
Anthropology, theological 122
Anti-Soviet agitation 21
-- image 22
-- opposition 20
Aristotelianism. 50
Aryans 139
astrology 9, 49
Auge, böses 222
Augsburger Religionsfriede 77
Authentic existence 164
authors 140
Avataṣakasūtra 99
awīlūtu 28
bad karma 7
Baptisten 202
Bar Kochba-Aufstand 206
base text 138
-- humanistic 137
Bekenntnis 187, 201
belief system 160
Benandanten (italienischer Fruchtbarkeitskult) 231
benevolent friends 100, 114, 115
Bewährung 67
Bewährungsgedanke 68
Bhagavadgītā 138
Bibelübersetzung 171
bible history 248
biblical people 165
Bistum, Estnisches 171
-- Livisches 171
Bodhisattva 100, 105, 109

bodhisattvahood 99
brahmanism, monotheistic 139
buddha-consciousness 118
buddha-field(s) 100, 109
buddhadharma 103
Buddha's teaching 100
Buddhismus 61, 62
buddhology 107
Byzantine theology 122
Calvinismus 67
caste-system 139
certitudo salutis 68
channeller 3
Christentum 86, 190, 205
christian ethics 163
-- festivals 248
-- world-view 47
-- worship 248
christianity 16
christology 119, 121, 122, 124
-- Eastern Orthodox 124
church wedding 131
civil religion 134
co-existence: church and state 15
collaboration 15
compassion 110, 111
concept of heavens 50
conception of time 49
consciousness 100, 104, 105, 107, 110, 115
coping 1
creation 49
creator of culture 145
crisis 5
-- of faith 160
critical thought 160
cross 131
cultural context 138
-- environment 139, 142
-- man 148
culturalization 148

culture 137
curse 7, 8
cynic 168
Dämonologie 222, 223
decline of religion 131, 136
Denken 57, 60
— ästhetisches und künstlerisches 65
— mythologisches 60
— philosophisches 58
— religiöses und mythologisches 65
— vorlogisches 57
Denkens, Entwicklung des 57
— reflexives 61
deputyship 128
Deus absconditus 70
dharma 103
Dharmadhātu 99, 115
disease 10
dogma of Chalcedon 121
dogmatics 247
Donatisten 195
dream 157, 158, 162
Dreifaltigkeit, heilige 224
Dschihads 79
Duldsamkeit, religiöse 77
Early Christianity 166
Eastern Orthodox Theology 119
education, moral 245
— religious 239
empiricism 132
emptyness 102
enlightenment 120
erdichtetes Gewissen 193
Erra-Epos 42
esoteric 3
— magazine 7
Essenes 140
Estnisches Bistum 171
ethics 247
Eucharistie 56
— mittelalterliche 77
— multikulturelle 75
European enlightenment 149
Eurozentrismus 65
Evangelium 193
existentialism 164
Experiment 48
Fanatismus 189
Fatalismus 67

Felsendom 210
Fluch 32
Folklore 222
Folklorist 226
freedom 156
— religious 246
friendship, mutual 159
Fundamentalismus, islamischer 75
Gaṇḍavyūhasūtra 99
Gebetsrichtung 209
Gegensatzpaar 57
Gelbsucht 36
Gemeinschaft 27
Generation Y 156
Gerechtigkeit 38
Geschichte, heilige 205
Gesellschaft 27
Gesundheit 30
Gewissensfreiheit 187, 192, 200
Glaubenszweiheit 200
Glück 30, 38
Gnadenstand 68, 69
gnomic will 123
Gospels (Matthew, Mark, Luke) 138
Gottesdogma 69
Gottesferne 31
Gotteskonzept 75
Grundgesetz 187
guilt 120
— inherited 120, 121
Haram al-Scharif 208
Häresie 189, 222
healing 10
— in New Age 10
heavens 50
Hebammen 220
Heidentum 222
Heiliges Land 205
help-seekers 6
Hexenfolklore 231
Hexenglaube 215, 218
Hexenhammer 223
Hexenkultur, schamanistische 220
Hexenprotokolle 225
Hexenprozesse 215, 218
Hexensabbat 221, 230, 231
Hexentheorie 220
Hiob-Texte 34
Historiosophie 205

histrionic reactions 135
Holy Communion 126
honour-shame inclusio 166
Huayan school 106
Huayan-Buddhism 106
human 139
human nature 121, 123
—— Christ 124
—— person 50
humane 139
Humanismus 191
humanistic 138
—— base texts 137
humanization 148
identity 159
Ideology, Marxist 15
illness 10
Imagination 160
Imputatio 120
Independenten 202
individual piety 134
individualism 120, 128, 156
Individualklage 39
Inkas 89
inner authority 161
Inquisition 215, 222
Interpretatio Romana 85
Intifada 205
Intoleranz 189
Islam 75, 79, 86, 190, 205
Islamismus 75
isolation 135
Jahve-Tempel 206, 208
Jātaka literature 112
Jebusiter 206
Jesus-Seminar 166
jeta grove 100
jewishness of Jesus 168
Judentum 190, 205
Kaiserkult 77
Kalyāamitra 113
karma 7
—— bad 7
kausaler Zusammenhang 32
Kingdom of God foundation of Jesus 145
Klagelied 36
Klagemauer 208
Knesset 211

knowledge, unprejudiced 110
Konsensus-Toleranz 190
Koran 209
Kultgemeinde 43
Kultur 26
—— altindische 61
—— polysysteme 66
Leninist-Maoist communism 149
levels of secularization 134
Lex naturae 68
Livisches Bistum 171
Lokadhātu 116
love relationship 158
Lunyu 137
lutheran Theology 119
Lutheraner 202
lysiology 102, 111, 112
Mādyamika-Schule 58
magic 9
Magie, schädigende 222
Mahābhārata 140
Mahāyāna 115
—— philosophy 100
—— sūtras 99, 106, 108, 112
Mahāyāna-Buddhismus 57, 58
makarisms 166
Manichäer 195
Marduk-Hymnus 36
Marduk-Ideologie 41
Marduk-Kult 41
Martyrium 201
Marxism 16, 149
Mathematik 63
meaning to life 135
mechanistic view of nature 48
mediation 3
Medieval Thinkers 51
Meditationssymbole 60
Medium 1
Mennoniten 201
Menschenopfer 95
Menschenrechte 79
Mentalität des Werwolflaufens 228
mentoring 161
Metaphysics 48, 56
Middle Ages 125
miracle 6
mission 248
Modern Science 47, 48

modernization 134
Monosystemik 61
Monotheism, Christian 119
mysticism 125
Mythenschaffung 61
Mythologie 60
Mythology 132
Nabû / Nanaja-Kult 84
Nabû / Tašmētu-Kult 84
Nabû-Kult 83
natural sciences 47
Naturgesetzte 43
Nebeneinander von Kirchen 200
Neubabylonisches Reich 41
Neues Testament, estnischsprachig 171
Neutralität 188
Neuzeit, frühe 188
New Age 1, 248
New man 148
New Religions 247
New Testament 163
non-confessional education 245
Nonnenstand 96
occupation 158
Ökonomie 74
Omar-Moschee 210
ontological sphere 117
oracle 6
Ordnung 38
original sin 120
Palästina 211
Palästinenser 205
Persischer Golf 39
persönlicher Gott 85
pharisees 139
Philosophie, vergleichende 59
physico-theology 55, 56
Pluralism 133
policy, educational 240, 250
Polysystemik 65
Polytheismus 80, 85
posttraumatic stress 135
powerlessness 135
powers of darkness 7
Prädestinationslehre 67
Prasangika (rhetorische Technik) 58
predestination, astrological 9
Propheten-Brief 33
Prophetie 28

Protestant theology 120
Protestantism 133
Protestantismus 67
Protestantismus-These Max Webers 67
Pythagoräer 57, 64
Pythagoräismus 63
Rassismus 65
Red Army 17
Reformation 188
Reformationszeit 187
Religion 25
religion and culture 247
Religionsfreiheit 187
Religionsfriede, Augsburger 77
religious communities 162
Renaissance 120
renewal, man's 144
resistance 15
Säkularisierung 74
Sanskrit 99, 101
Śāstra (treatise) 106
Schamanismus 220
Schlechtes Gewissen 36
school 101
Schweiz 196
science 132
scientific investigation 50
— revolution 48
Scriptures 138
Sechstagekrieg 206
secularization 131
seer 6
Sekte der Hexen 223
self-estrangement 135
self-sufficiency 164
semiosphere 104, 105, 108, 112, 116
semiotics 103
— modern 138
Sermon of the Field 166
— of the Mount 163
Shāstras 107
Shengren 144
social-scientific methods 165
society 120
— industrialized 131
Sonnenjungfrauen (Inkas) 89
sorcerer 4
Soviet Estonia 15
Soviet regime 16

sozialer Friede 38
Speyerer Mandat 196, 199
—— Reichstag 188, 195
spiritual development 112
Spruchliteratur 38
Staat Israel 205
Staatsgewalt 74
Staatszwangskirchentum 191
Stadtklage 39
stages of secularization 133
state campaigns 17
—— holidays 17
—— security agencies 19
Stereometrie 63
Stoa 77
Streitgespräche 61
substitution 127
sunday 131
Sūtrapiṭaka 138 // Suttapiṭaka 138
symbols, religious 131
symptoms of secularization 135
Tang era 106
Täufer 187
teacher training 251
teacher-disciple relationship 146
teaching 140, 142
timeless 164
teaching of Jesus 163
technology 132
Teufelsgeschichten, kannibalistische 230
Teufelsglaube 228
theologians 164
Theologiereform 193
theologies, systematic 132
theology, Bonhoeffer's 127
—— Byzantine 122
—— Christian 15, 119
—— Eastern Orthodox 123
—— Protestant 120
Thron Allahs 210
Tiermetamorphose 224
Todesarten der Täufer 196
Todesstrafe 198, 199
Toleranz 187
—— politische 74
—— religiöse 73, 74, 77, 95 (Inkas)
Toleranzedikt von Mailand 77
Totengeist 31

transcendence 163
Transzendente Norm 26-28, 30, 34, 38, 43
Trauma 6
treatise 106
Trinity 119
underground resistance 20
understanding of Humanity, Christological 119
Unglück 31, 38
unity of humanity 128
universe 50
Upaniṣad 139
Ur-Klage 39
urban settings 133
Uus Testament 171
Vajrayāna 60
values, religious 132
Vedas 139
vision of the future 155
Völkerrecht 212
Volkes, jüdisches 208
Wahrheitsanspruch 189
Wasserprobe 233
Wastne Testament 171
Weltbild, klerikales 65
Weltreligion 79
Werbär 222
Werwolf 222, 223
Werwolfglaube 215
Werwolfprozesse 232
Werwolfsagen 220
western thought 47
Wiedertäufermandat 195, 197
Wissenschaft, experimentelle 65
Wolfsmoral 228
world religions 247
worldview 135
—— christian 47
—— general 132
Wormser Edikt 197, 199
xiaoren 144
Y-generation 156, 159
Zahl 63
Zauberei 222
zerology 102
Zionismus 205
Zwei-Reiche-Lehre 192, 194, 199
Zyklus, demographischer 94

2. Namen

a) Götter

Anūna-Ištar 34
Erra 43
Inti 95
Ištar-Anūna 34
Išum 43
Jahwe 70, 205
Jehova 70
Marduk 36, 41
Mullil 40

Nabû 33, 83
Nanaja 84
Nanna 39
Nannar-Sîn 41
Ninurta 81
Pachacamak 95
Satan 223
Tašmētu 84
Wiracocha 95

b) Geographische

Ägypten 205
Alt-Livland 225
Central Asia 99
Chalcedon 121
China 99
Cuzco 90
Europa, antikes 77
India 139
Jerusalem 205

Livland 172, 225
-- Alt- 216
Mesopotamien 25
Nepal 99
Palästina 211
Tahuantinsuyu 90
Tibet 99, 114
Ur 39

c) Personen

Adam 120
Antiochus IV. Epiphanes 206
Aquinas, Thomas 53
Aristotle 48
Assurbanipal 33
Bacon, Roger 51
Blume, Christoph 171
Bonhoeffer 127
Bruno, Giordano 47
Bruiningk, Hermann von 225
Buddha (, Gautama) 60, 101, 105
Buridan, Jean 52
Calvin 67
Čandrakîrti 60
Copernicus 48
David 206
Epiktet 77
Eve 120

Fischer, Johann 172
Galilei (, Galileo) 47, 48, 52
Gezelius, Johannes 217
Göseken, Heinrich 171
Grebel, Konrad 195
Gutslaff, Johannes 171
Hardung, Nicolaus von 172
Hellwig, Jacob 171
Helwys, Thomas 202
Herodes der Große 206
Hubmaier, Balthasar 201
Ḥammurapi 78
Jesus 166, 248
Jhering, Joachim 171
Johannes Paul II. (Papst) 209
Joris, David 202
Junzi 144
Kepler 48

Krämer, Heinrich Institoris 223
Kyros II. 78, 206
Luther, M. 124, 125
Magnus, Olaus 225
Mahatma Gandhi 148, 150
Mañjushrī 101, 111, 113
Masson-Oursel, Paul 59
Maximus the Confessor 122
Melanchthon, Philipp 198
Muhammad 209
Münster, Sebastian 225
Müntzer, Thomas 198, 201
Nabonid 41
Nāgārjuna 59, 60
Neubaud, Heinrich 172
Newton, Isaac 48, 54
Ockham, William 52
Paul, Toomas 171
Penn, William 203
Peucerius, Caspar 225

Philolaos 63
Pythagoras 63
Salomo 206
Samantabhadra 113, 117
Samuel Clarke 55
Schütz, Marcus 172
Simons, Menno 201
Smyth, John 202
Sprenger, Jacob 223
Stalin, J. 16
Sudhana 101, 111, 113, 114
Torquemada (Grossinquisitor) 232
Virginius, Adrian 172
Virginius, Andreas 172
Weber, Max 67
Weizmann, Chaim 205
Wilcken, Johann Georg 172
Williams, Roger 203
Zwingli, Huldrych 196

3. Stellen

a) Neues Testament

Matthew 4,21-22 143
Matthew 5,17 142
Matthew 6,25-33 163
Matthew 7,13-14 143
Matthew 10,28 146
Matthew 10,34-37 146
Matthew 12,49-50 147
Matthew 16,24 146
Matthew 23,13-36 166
Mark 2,6-12 143
Luke 6,20-26 166
Luke 12,22-31 163
Luke 13,18-19 145
1Petr 1,4 174
1Petr 1,4-5 174
1Petr 1,6 178

1Petr 1,11 176
1Petr 1,12 176
1Petr 2,7-8 173
1Petr 2,11 177
1Petr 2,12 178
1Petr 2,17 178
1Petr 2,21 175
1Petr 2,24 182
1Petr 3,6 182
1Petr 3,10 180
1Petr 3,15-16 173
1Petr 3,18 183
1Petr 3,20 183
1Petr 4,7-8 174, 180
1Petr 4,14 181
1Petr 5,4 181

b) Mesopotamische Literatur

Akk. Spruchsammlung 143-147 31
Anūna-Hymnus 55-88. 121-132 34
ARM 10,4:28-34 33
ARM 10,50 28
BWL, Babylonian Theodicy I 49 82
BWL, Babylonian Theodicy XXII 239 83
BWL, Ludlul bēl nēmeqi I 43-50. 82-92 36
BWL, Ludlul bēl nēmeqi II 1-5.23-30 36
BWL, Ludlul bēl nēmeqi II 34-35 81
BWL, Ludlul bēl nēmeqi II 36 80
BWL, Ludlul bēl nēmeqi II 36 74
BWL, Ludlul bēl nēmeqi IV 48-49 36
CH XLVIII 20-24 75
CH XLIX 53-80 32

Erra-Epos II C 11. 12-17. 32-34 42
Kyros-Zylinder 22-26 78
Or. 36, S. 105-132, Z. 196 83
RA 22, S. 169-177, Z. 14 73
SAA 3, S. 35: Nr. 14, Z. 1 73
SAHG, S. 225: Nr. 45 80
šimâ milka, S. 184 82
šimâ milka, S. 216 81
šimâ milka, S. 220 82
Sum. Spruchsammlung 14.39 32
Sum. Spruchsammlung 26 A 12 31, 34
Sum. Spruchsammlung 28.9 31
Sum. Spruchsammlung UET 6/2 252 32
Sum. Spruchsammlung UET 6/2 299 31
Zwiegespräch Asb.-Nabû 1-12. Rs. 6-8 33

c) Qoran

Sure 2, 256 76

Sure 17,1 209

d) Indische Literatur

Bhagavadgītā IV, 1-3 142
Bhagavadgītā VII, 15, 24-25 141
Bhagavadgītā XI, 12 141
Dhammapada 294 147
Gaṇḍavyūhasūtra 3 117
Gaṇḍavyūhasūtra 12 116, 117
Gaṇḍavyūhasūtra 34 110
Gaṇḍavyūhasūtra 35 110
Gaṇḍavyūhasūtra 40-41 111

Gaṇḍavyūhasūtra 46 113
Gaṇḍavyūhasūtra47 113
Gaṇḍavyūhasūtra 100 112
Gaṇḍavyūhasūtra 271 110
Gaṇḍavyūhasūtra 272 111
Gaṇḍavyūhasūtra 428 115
Gaṇḍavyūhasūtra 431 118
Gaṇḍavyūhasūtra 432 109

e) Chinesische Literatur

Lunyu I, 14 146
Lunyu II, 4 144
Lunyu VII, 1 142
Lunyu VII, 20 143
Lunyu IX, 32 144
Lunyu XII, 22 147

Lunyu XII, 5 147
Lunyu XV, 28 143
Lunyu XV, 38 144
Lunyu XVI, 13 147
Lunyu XIX, 25 141

4. Wörter

a) Akkadisch

kattû(m) 83

latāku(m) 82

b) Indisch

bodhi- 100
buddhadharma 145
budh 100

dhamma 145
dharma 145

c) Chinesisch

wen 145

zhi 148

d) Inka

aclla 89, 90
aclla huasi 95
coya pasca 90

mama cuna 91
Sapa Inca 95